The Many Meanings of Play

The Many Meanings of Play

A Psychoanalytic Perspective

Edited by

Albert J. Solnit, M.D.

Donald J. Cohen, M.D.

Peter B. Neubauer, M.D.

Yale University Press

New Haven and London

Designed by Sonia Scanlon.
Set in Janson type by DEKR Corporation,
Woburn, Massachusetts.
Printed in the United States of America by
Vail-Ballou Press, Binghamton, New York.

**Library of Congress Cataloging-in-Publication
Data**

The Many meanings of play : a psychoanalytic
    perspective / edited by Albert J. Solnit,
    Donald J. Cohen, Peter B. Neubauer.
        p.   cm.
    Includes bibliographical references and index.
    ISBN 0-300-05438-6 (alk. paper)
    1. Play therapy. 2. Child analysis.
I. Solnit, Albert J.   II. Cohen, Donald J.
III. Neubauer, Peter B.
    [DNLM: 1. Child Psychology. 2. Play and
Playthings. 3. Psychoanalytic Therapy—in
infancy & childhood.   WS 105.5P5   M295]
RJ505.P6M36   1993
618.92'8917—dc20   *1663938*   *11-16-93*
DNLM/DLC
    for Library of Congress   92-48988
                                CIP

A catalogue record for this book is
available from the British Library.

The paper in this book meets the guidelines
for permanence and durability of the
Committee on Production Guidelines for
Book Longevity of the Council on Library
Resources.

10 9 8 7 6 5 4 3 2 1

Special Dedication

The participants in the study group on the Many Meanings of Play in Child Psychoanalysis wish to use the occasion of the publication of this volume to signal the richly creative contributions of Peter Neubauer to the entire field of child psychoanalysis. He has been the exemplary child psychoanalyst: wise, committed to the development of the young, and playful.

Contents

Part III Developmental Dimensions

The Many Meanings of Play

Introduction

Albert J. Solnit, M.D.

Donald J. Cohen, M.D.

Peter B. Neubauer, M.D.

From its origins, psychoanalysis has been fascinated by the special meanings of play in childhood. Many of the pioneers and founding child psychoanalysts—Anna Freud, Melanie Klein, Berta Bornstein, Marianne and Ernst Kris, Erik Erikson—were gifted in their observations and understanding of children's play. They were also good players, in the consulting room and in life.

For more than six decades, child psychoanalysts have observed children from the first years of life through adolescence at play in their homes, in nursery schools, on the playground, and, most intensively, in the therapeutic consulting room. They have studied children's play in pediatric hospitals, in residential care, and in psychiatric wards. They have seen children playing after all types of trauma—surgery, separation, kidnapping, war—and at every phase of development. In clinical assessments they have used their observations of how children play and how they engage the psychoanalyst as observer and participant. During clinical treatment, children and psychoanalysts have spent months and years playing together as the psychoanalyst learns about the child and conveys the insights gained to the child through interpretation and in the process of playing.

From this vast domain of observation and experience, child psychoanalysis has developed a sense, or multiple senses, of the inner mental processes that underlie children's play. The psychoanalytic theory of play is not a formal, deductive set of hypotheses but an orientation to the complexity of the child's inner world. Within that inner life, play is a mental process that builds upon and integrates many other processes in the developing child's mind—thinking, imagining, pretending, planning, wondering, doubting, remembering, guessing, hoping, experimenting, redoing, and working through. The child at play, using these varied mental processes, integrates past experiences and current feelings and desires. In the repetitions of play the child masters what he or she has experienced; through the creativity of play, through internal playfulness and external play, the child reviews, advances, and conquers old and new territories.

The Many Meanings of Play

By "the many meanings of play" we wish to convey the multiple roles that play has for children and for psychoanalysts who work with them. Among them are:

The ways in which *play expresses and represents the child's experiences* and then *communicates* them to others

The functions of play in *weaving together* the child's past and present, as well as his or her future potentials

The *therapeutic use of play*—its role as a window into the child's difficulties as well as its mobilization in therapeutic interventions

The *affective qualities of play*—the pleasures in play as well as the special seriousness with which children may play

The ways in which children may use play to *learn about and cope with unhappiness, conflict, and trauma*

Thus, play takes on special meaning as a *window into the operations of the child's mental functioning and self representations*. Among the most interesting aspects of play are the ways in which it reflects inner life, tensions, and the child's response to internal and external challenges; the therapeutic mediation of play; and its *potential power to help move development forward* by allowing the child to review his or her current situation, explore new possibilities, experiment with new solutions, and find new integrations. There are other meanings of play as well, which are discussed throughout the volume.

For child psychoanalysts, the oedipal phase, from ages three or four to five or six, probably stands as the "gold standard," or archetype of children's pretend play. At this phase, children seem especially able to suspend disbelief and to engage in the highly demanding enterprise of pretending. They are able to make use of their emergent capacities for imagination to represent and transform their internal experiences. They can bracket the world of play from that of reality as they invite us "to pretend," along with them, that they are mommy or daddy at one moment and a little baby the next. Children in the oedipal phase have the richness of language and the imagination to script narratives, as well as a belief in their own ability to return to earth; these allow them to move far away from reality for excursions into imaginary worlds, including the longed-for and dangerous ones. In the process of acquiring a mature understanding of the ways in which other people think, feel, and act—an intuitive folk theory about the minds of others—children in the oedipal phase are especially interested in taking the roles of others in play and thus exploring their minds and intentions from within. Older children tend to become more realistic.

The complexities of playing can be formulated through the many different metapsychological perspectives that emphasize the structures of the mind (id, ego, superego); the instinctual, sexual, and aggressive energies that are channeled and sublimated; the interplay among levels of representation (unconscious, preconscious, conscious); the ontogenetic roots of different forms and themes; and the developmental lines reflected in play. The child's play can also be studied from the perspective of the central role of human relations, of the object world, in the themes and organization of play. In important ways, these theoretical points of view enrich the meanings of play and suggest new hypotheses and avenues for clinical and research exploration. But they do not replace the dense, phenomenological description of a unique play process. Just as there is no one reading of a poem or interpretation of a Shakespearian tragedy, there is no single formulation that captures the many dimensions of a good child psychoanalytic hour when the child and analyst are truly into the play.

Play in the oedipal phase does not suddenly appear de novo, nor does the play of children after the oedipal phase completely lose its sparkle. The earliest manifestations of what might be called the instinct for play—for creativity, playfulness, and pleasure in action—continue to be available, more or less, at each phase of development. The themes of oedipal love and hurts continue to make themselves felt in adolescence and adulthood; in turn, life is made more pleasant and bearable by the ability to make-believe. Play continues to develop, changing its outward forms and dominant motifs along with all the other facets of the individual's psychological, biological, and social life. Developmental pathways thus can be charted between the play of preschool and oedipal-phase children to the different modes and experiences of play in adolescence and playfulness in adulthood.

The capacity for play provides both the child and the adult with a powerful instrument for figuring out and coming to grips with realities, with mysteries and hardships. In war-torn countries as well as in the inner city, one can see children using meager physical resources to play, to assert that they are still alive, to try to understand and to transcend their experiences. The play of children who have been traumatized, like the play of children with severe emotional disorders, may lose its vitality and openness, becoming routinized and repetitive. When life is too bleak or a child is too ill, physically or emotionally, play may cease. This can be an ominous prognostic sign.

Origins and Plan of This Book

In 1984, under the auspices of the Psychoanalytic Research and Development Fund, seventeen child psychoanalysts and two adult psychoanalysts from the New York, New Haven, and Boston areas began to meet to study the many meanings of play in child psychoanalysis.* Two of the editors of this book comoderated the meetings, and the third was an ongoing consultant to the planning and implementation process. We met for three hours a month for more than five years.

A conference held in Jerusalem in 1986 brought together a series of reports from this U.S. study group and colleagues from London, England, and Israel (see *Psychoanalytic Study of the Child* [New Haven: Yale University Press, 1987], 42:3–219). In this international colloquium we became more aware of how the study process worked and how much more could be mined from the rich ore of psychoanalytic clinical empirical data, especially child psychoanalysis.

From the beginning we did not aim at consensus but favored the exploration of the many meanings of play that emerged from the diverse theoretical and clinical approaches of individual members of the group. Some preferred to understand play as *also* having a motor aspect, whereas others widened the concept to include thinking as a later substitute for action, thus having a significant psychic function in adult life. This is an example of the different views the following chapters reflect.

We decided not to organize the study of play by following it from preplay explorations through adult life. We could have chosen to focus on the line of development from body ego to play to games to work, positioning play between the pleasure principle and the reality principle. There was agreement that play serves to resolve problems and conflicts and that it furthers development, but that this function can be derailed or inhibited.

*More than half of the child psychoanalysts also practice adult psychoanalysis. The group consisted of Steven L. Ablon, Samuel Abrams, Delia Battin, Martin Bergmann, Donald J. Cohen, Phyllis M. Cohen, Alice B. Colonna, E. Kirsten Dahl, Alice Frankel, James M. Herzog, Robert A. King, Laurie Levinson, Eugene J. Mahon, Steven Marans, Linda C. Mayes, Peter B. Neubauer, Mortimer Ostow, Samuel Ritvo, and Albert J. Solnit.

Several of our chapters address the role of play: in normal development throughout life; as it reflects normal conflicts; and as it has become pathological. For example, there may be a compulsive repetition of play that has lost its power to find solutions, or play may be reduced by inhibitions and restrictions of the ego. Thus, play in child analysis is in the service of therapeutic action or developmental experience. Such play also reflects developmental capacities and tolerances.

We discarded the possibility of preparing a book systematically surveying the "many meanings of play in child psychoanalysis," with topics preselected according to an overall blueprint, and instead asked each participant to prepare a chapter based on his or her curiosity, imagination, and psychoanalytic experience. Perhaps in the spirit of our subject, we wanted to encourage in each member the intrinsic playfulness that characterizes sound adult analysis. We then took on the responsibility for seaming the chapters together into a cohesive volume. (We also assumed that a group that had met monthly for several years would intuitively be following an intrinsically coherent agenda in preparing the chapters.)

We make no effort to be comprehensive. As the table of contents suggests, theory, technique, and practice overlap in complex, subtle, and illuminating ways. Data from clinical psychoanalysis organized by psychoanalytic theory and viewed through psychoanalytic technique and the applications of such theory become related as they are anchored in each of the chapters.

At a time when so many children are at risk from environmental threats and when there may be a tendency to overlook the inner experiences of vulnerable children, the psychoanalytic study of play contributes to the broader field of knowledge about the emotional development and inner resources of children.

Part I
Historical and Theoretical Frame of Reference

1

Psychoanalytic Views of Children's Play

Steven Marans, M.S.W.

Linda C. Mayes, M.D.

Alice B. Colonna, M.A.

Psychoanalytic theories about the developing functions, structure, and content of the inner lives of young children derive in large part from observations of play activities in the consulting room. Child analysts seek to understand what the child is expressing through the language of play about his or her innermost fantasies and emerging relationships with others.

Even though it is difficult to develop a unified definition of it, "we all think we know what we mean when we speak of or hear about play, [and] in fact play is better described by its functions than by a formal definition" (Solnit, 1987, p. 205). The intent of this chapter is to present central psychoanalytic propositions regarding developmental characteristics and functions of coordinated activities that child analysts recognize and designate as "play." With these ideas in mind, we will address and review three broad questions about play in child psychoanalysis and trace the evolution of various conceptualizations relevant to each question. (1) Why do children play? (2) What are the various characteristics seen in children's play? (3) What happens to play in later childhood and adulthood; that is, are there direct derivatives of the very young child's play activity, or is work truly the heir to play in later life? Each of these questions has to do with the narrative function of play activities—the ways in which play scenarios and activities form coherent representations of what is uppermost in children's minds and most available in their repertoire of modes of expression. Although we focus on the play activities of children, the fate of their modes of expression over time will be discussed in relation to the creativity of adults as well.

Several caveats are important about our intent. First, though every child-analytic case report informs our understanding of play behavior, this chapter reviews selected works that focus on play *conceptually*. Second, though our broad questions are relevant to play between child and analyst, we will not focus on or systematically review the broad literature on the therapeutic uses of play in the analytic setting.

Functions of Play

During the earliest phases of the development of psychoanalytic theory, Freud used the phenomena of children's play to illustrate and identify the origins of various features of psychic functioning in adult life. Many of Freud's descriptions and formulations about play phenomena remain central to child psychoanalytic theory about the function of play. Examples are the nature of the child's orientation to reality; the genesis and use of fantasy; the tendency to achieve active mastery over experiences of passivity; the compulsion to repeat as a means of reworking trauma; and superego formation. The direct observation of the play of children in analysis has further informed analytic theories not only about the function of play but also about the importance of early childhood experiences in psychic development. These direct observations have changed our emphasis on the relative importance of certain functions of play.

Freud (1905) first referred to children's play when he suggested that play appears as the child is learning to use words and organize thoughts. Pleasure for the young child is derived from the repetition or rediscovery of the familiar. Play is not bound by the "meaning of words or the coherence of sentences" (1905, p. 128). Indeed, for Freud, this pleasure in the meaningless or absurd is both a characteristic and a function of play. Children's play comes to an end with the institution of the as yet unnamed "critical faculty" that rejects pleasure in the form of the meaningless or the absurd. Stated another way, children's play reflects the broader range of tolerance for the drives that can occur as long as the superego is not yet fully in place. Freud, however, did not allow the "critical faculty" absolute censorship over such playfulness in adults. As heirs to play, jokes fulfill the adult requirement for order and "reasonableness," re-creating the pleasure of play in their use of thoughts and words that, though they seem absurd, are always in the service of conveying specific meaning, often emphasizing incongruity and paradox.

Central to Freud's conceptualization of play in older children was his observation that it serves as an acceptable mode for discharge and satisfaction of instinctual drives and for mastery of experiences that make "a great impression" (1920, p. 17) upon the child. In contrast to his description of the play of young children, he pointed out that the older child at play does not disavow reality but rather suspends it in the service of reworking unpleasurable experiences. Such reworking is achieved through play by the child's reversing his or her original role of frightened, passive victim into an active, masterful role. Similarly, Freud suggested that play serves a reparative function as seen among the sequelae of traumatic experiences. This function of children's play was an example of a natural inclination toward a "revolt against passivity and a preference for the active role" in the service of practicing and assuming greater self-sufficiency (1931, p. 236).

Moreover, Freud emphasized that the compulsion to repeat is another driving force behind children's play, recapturing feelings associated with pleasurable experiences. The reexperience of pleasure and attempts at mastery of an unpleasant situation are not mutually exclusive (1920). For example, Freud's observation that the child's play is dominated by the wish to be grown up and to be able to do what the adults do speaks both to the child's oedipal longings and reverses the specific role of victim to father's expected retaliation. The child's mastery through a reversal of roles yields pleasure as he passes on the "disagreeable experience and . . . revenges himself on a substitute" (1920, p. 17).

Theorists after Freud continued to view play as having a discharge or modulating function for the child. Melanie Klein (1929) emphasized that play serves the function of discharge for infantile masturbation fantasies. According to Klein, these fantasies give expression to the infant's sadistic wishes toward the mother, which are projected and then provoke retaliation from the persecutory object. Play affords a relatively safe activity in which the infant may displace these wishes and avoid the anxiety associated with expected annihilation. Although Klein shared Freud's views about the role of the repetition compulsion and the child's use of play as a central means of achieving mastery of internal conflicts, other aspects of her ideas on play were her own contributions. Her developmental timetable, assumptions about the specific content of infantile fantasies, and the relative inattention paid to daily experiences as material for play represented a significant departure from the views of many of her contemporaries and of later contributors.

In keeping with the increased focus on the developing ego, Waelder (1932) elaborated on Freud's notions of the repetition compulsion as a way of facilitating the assimilative function of play in the child's attempts to master the environment. Through play, the child can turn passive into active, thereby gradually reworking originally painful or overpowering events through a sense of mastery of them. "Play may now be characterized as a method of constantly working over and, as it were, assimilating piecemeal an experience which was too large to be assimilated instantly at one swoop. The pain in an experience must be overcome before the experience can be repeated and enjoyed in play" (pp. 217–218). Asserting that the pleasure principle alone cannot explain the nature of children's play, Waelder highlighted the distinction between "functional and gratification pleasure." Drawing on the ideas of Karl Bühler, he pointed out that in addition to the pleasure sought in the gratification of wishes, children's play may be motivated by the pleasure "derived from pure performance" (p. 211).

The thrust of Waelder's contribution, however, was to examine the relationships among the strength of the developing ego, the child's vulnerability to trauma, and the use of play as a means of abreacting and assimilating overwhelming stimulation. He proposed that "difficult experiences of the past function as preparations for future tolerance" (p. 217) and that with age, both vulnerability to trauma and the flexibility of response diminish. The younger child's relative inexperience in the world makes her more vulnerable to "excessive stimulation" but, at the same time, less rigid in her responses. In this sense, play serves a psychic metabolic function and provides a means of breaking down and repeating overwhelming experiences until they are mastered and assimilated. The intent of play is "not so much the preparation for future activities in adult life as it is the assimilation of the mass of excitations from the outer world" (p. 218), which in turn strengthens the ego's capacity to tolerate and endure difficulties. The plasticity of the immature ego both necessitates and facilitates the abreactive function of play that occurs only in children.

Anna Freud (1965) proposed that the child's earliest play with his and mother's body promotes the child's capacity for differentiation between self and others and between fantasy and reality. Later play with toys, solitary role play, and group play give expression to displaced and sublimated drive energies and pave the way for pleasure in task completion, problem solving, and the ability to work. Although Anna Freud never devoted a monograph to the specific topic of play, her writings focused on the child's developing capacities for defense activities and ego adaptation that form the constituent properties of play (1965). She viewed play activities as one source of information about the child's developmental status and as a window onto the child's attempts to gain mastery over conflicts generated from within and those resulting from the demands of external reality (A. Freud, 1965, 1979). From Anna Freud's perspective, the importance of play lay in its role of moving the child toward an increased capacity for autonomy and self-confidence, socialization, and work.

Erikson outlined his studies of children's play according to libidinal zones and phase-specific conflicts. In 1937, Erikson focused on the developmental trend toward displacement of bodily experiences and associated aims and conflicts to the "manifestation of an experience in actual space" (p. 139). He pointed out that rather than displacing from "one section of their own body to another" most children "find objects in the toy world for their extrabodily displacements . . . externalizing the entire dynamic relationship between the zone and its object" (p. 161). The goal or central function of play is that it affords the child the "opportunity to experiment with organ-modes in extrabodily arrangements which are physiologically safe, socially permissible, physically workable and psychologically satisfying" (p. 185).

In later papers, Erikson outlined the function of play as preparatory for adult roles and for the expectations of society. Play allows children to try on adult functions and to alter these roles as they become more aware of "society's version of reality" (1972, p. 127). Through play, children elaborate their own identity based on the roles available for their observation and the external demands of their social world. Because of the vicissitudes of development, these external factors seem different to children at different periods of development and thus the roles are constantly being revised. "No wonder . . . that man's play takes place on the border of dangerous alternatives and is always beset both with burdening conflicts and with liberating choices" (1972, p. 127).

Like Erikson, Peller's conceptualizations reflect the influence of Anna Freud, Hartmann, Kris, and Loewenstein, and the shift in emphasis within psychoanalysis from drive theory to ego psychology. Peller (1954) viewed play as deriving from the ego's attempts to deal with the anxiety associated with "blows or deprivations exerted by reality as well as with pressures originating in the id or the superego" (p. 179). Her work, however, also went well beyond earlier ideas that play is primarily instigated by the repetition compulsion and attempts to rework trauma. According to Peller, play is a centrally organizing activity that illustrates the *interdependence* of libidinal—if not aggressive—urges and ego development. Play is a fantasy accompanied by action and is possible when the level of anxiety to be mastered is not overwhelming. The activity of play is gratifying in its own right but compatible with reality and superego requirements. Play, according to Peller, reflects the child's attempts "to compensate for anxieties and deficiencies, to obtain pleasure at a minimum risk of danger and/or irreversible consequences" (p. 180). Instinctual drives are not directly discharged in play but are able to enter into it with increasing degrees of sublimation as the child develops.

For Peller, the primary function of play is to deny, decrease, or work through the anxieties that are specific to each phase of development. Compensatory fantasies are the backbone of all play, whether they occur in response to the limitations of the toddler's body, control of the preoedipal mother, exclusion from adult relationships, or the dangers of the superego. In addition, Peller pointed to the nonconflictual spheres of functioning that are utilized and facilitated in children's play—for example, bodily competence, information processing, and cognitive structures (Hartmann, 1939; Piaget, 1945). Peller described different functions and features of play according to the developmental phase in which it appears. She referred to four basic types of play characterized as (1) play originating in relation to one's own body, (2) play rooted in the relationship to the preoedipal mother, (3) play instigated by conflicts at the oedipal level, and (4) postoedipal play or games with rules.

In his broad views of human functioning, Alexander (1958) posited three dynamic processes that govern life: the principles of stability, economy, and surplus energy. According to Alexander, play is "the exercise of surplus libidinal energy not required for the grim task of survival" (p. 178). Although agreeing with earlier psychoanalytic theories that play serves the function of repeating, abreacting, and mastering trauma, he argued that playing is an aim in itself: "Erotic play for the sake of pleasure is the first phase, and the utilization of the functions acquired during erotic play is the second" (p. 182). Although play may incidentally serve the resolution of conflicts and provide opportunities for ego mastery and development, "the solution of a problem is not imperative" (p. 186). In emphasizing this erotic or nonutilitarian discharge of surplus energies as the primary motivation for children's play, Alexander did not take into account the symbolic nature of play or its specific features as they relate to the development of the child's inner sense of self and others. In focusing on his own version of the instinctual sources and economy of play, Alexander departed from the mainstream of psychoanalytic theory, which emphasized the functions and characteristics of play in terms of the developing ego.

Greenacre (1959) elaborated on the function of play as it serves the development of reality testing in young children. She suggested that children's repetition of themes in play represents their attempt to verify the difference between fantasy and reality until familiarity with that difference has been adequately established for each of these significant themes. She saw play as a central activity employed for testing reality. She agreed with Freud's observation that imitating adult roles and functions is a prominent feature of children's play and highlighted the maturational sources of new capacities and their expression in the child's wish to be "grown up." Greenacre disagreed with Waelder's formulation that relief from trauma derives from the fusion of fantasy and reality that occurs in play. In the first instance, she suggested that mastery of trauma is never complete and that part of the excitement and fun of play derives from the persisting affects and tensions associated with the original traumatic experiences. Second, she argued that the greatest relief from the effects of trauma is afforded by a combination of the child's ability to *separate* fantasy and reality through play and, through that separation, to deal with the traumatic situation successfully. Greenacre also pointed out that with the establishment of secondary thought processes—particularly the introduction of a sense of time—the child is able to project memories forward as events to anticipate in the future, a capacity that broadens the functional repertoire of play. The possibility of now "anticipating" what was once unexpected and overwhelming and directing and controlling the remembered scenarios in play yields a greater potential for mastery.

Unlike previous psychoanalytic writers who emphasized mastery of the drives and traumatic experiences of the past, Winnicott (1968) focused on playing as it reflects and facilitates the development of the self in relation to others. As an extension of transitional phenomena, Winnicott viewed play as a "basic form of living" (p. 597) that serves the child's development of an autonomous sense of self in relation to others. He argued that the excitement of play is not primarily associated with displaced drive expression but rather with the child's pleasure in the "precariousness that belongs to the interplay" between personal psychic reality and the experience of control of actual objects (p. 598). The interplay derives from the infant's earliest experiences of magical control of the responsive mother and facilitates his trust in her availability and love *and* in his own magical potential. The internalization of these features establishes a template for later play—both alone and with others—in which the child can create, or re-create, a world that hovers between psychic and objective reality.

Winnicott did not explicitly address the function play serves in problem solving, negotiating tasks of development, or resolving conflicts. He referred to the special role of the body, observing, "The pleasurable element in playing carries with it the implication that the instinctual arousal is not excessive" (p. 598); he adds that when direct bodily excitement is too great, play will be disrupted. For Winnicott, however, instinctual discharge does not figure so prominently as a source of pleasure and motivation for play. Instead, play is a reflection of the child's capacity to occupy a space between psychic and external reality in which the child uses elements from both domains.

The various functions of play serve the child's attempts to establish a sense of self in a constant interaction between the inner world of fantasy and the external world of real experience. Mastery of instinctual life, adaptation to current and internalized demands and expectations of others, the resolution of conflicts, and practicing and extending motoric, linguistic, and cognitive skills acquired in the course of maturation are viewed as some of the essential functions of play as it promotes growth and assists the child's preparation for future roles and challenges of each new developmental phase.

It would seem that play, above all other forms of activity and expression in childhood, facilitates the appearance, organization, and consolidation of a number of fundamental developmental tasks in early childhood. Play provides a window on the elaboration of other mental structures. Play is central in early development because it simultaneously advances development and reflects the particular capacities available to children at any given time in their development. The types of play—autoerotic or dramatic, solo, parallel, or interactional—always reflect the developmental status of and interplay between the capacities for (1) balance of id, ego, and superego requirements, (2) reality testing and fantasying, (3) object relationships, (4) language, symbolization, and communication, and (5) mechanisms of defense and adaptation. That play reflects developments in each of these areas makes this childhood activity a central focus of clinical and theoretical investigation.

Status of Id, Ego, and Superego

To discuss the characteristics of play vis-à-vis emerging mental structures necessarily involves a consideration of what constitutes play. This is particularly true in considering play as a reflection of id, ego, and superego differentiation. Although it can be said that play, in part, serves as a transition from action to thought as trial action, a discussion of what constitutes play proper and when it begins has many facets and no single answer. Typologies (Erikson, 1937; Peller, 1954; Plaut, 1979) that distinguish the phenomena of play according to different stages of development reflect the fact that the term *play* does not signify one set of unified characteristics and functions that persist throughout the course of life. The prevailing psychoanalytic interest, however, has been on a particular kind of play that involves pretending. Pretend, or imaginative, play is usually initiated in the second year of life by the coordination of ego achievements, including the acquisition of language, the capacity to distinguish internal and external reality, the achievement of object constancy, nascent internalization of parental demands and expectations, and the defenses of displacement, externalization, the turning of passive into active, and identification. It is no coincidence that psychoanalytic writings have focused on the characteristics of play that begin to emerge during a period of development in which secondary thought processes gain ascendancy and ego-id and ego-superego conflicts obtain greater structuralization. With the addition of verbalizations to their actions in play, children can clearly mark out for themselves and the observer what is play and what is not. Pretend, or imaginative, play serves as a domain in which fantasies and conflicts can move from the internal to the external realm, at once owned and disowned on a stage set in suspended reality.

Anna Freud (1936, 1965) viewed children's play activities as promoting and reflecting the changing status of the ego's capacity to mediate among the demands of the drives, superego, and external world. Elaborating the developmental line "From the Body to Toy and from Play to Work," she took as a starting point the infant's primary narcissism and the pleasures of playing with her own and her mother's body. Such early autoerotic play promotes differentiation of ego boundaries. The pleasures and properties associated with the child's and the mother's body are invested in the first extrabodily plaything or transitional object (Winnicott, 1953). The developing ego capacity for symbolization expands the soothing transitional function of the cuddly toy, a bridge between self and mother, to the role of safe substitute for the child's ambivalent feelings toward the mother. The move to play material which does not "possess object status but . . . serves ego activities and the fantasies underlying them" (A. Freud, 1965, p. 80) is accompanied by the child's use of adaptive and defensive ego functions such as imitation and identification, displacement, condensation, sublimation, and the turning of passive into active. Along with the functional pleasure involved in mastery of bodily skills, task completion, and problem solving, the coordination of these ego capacities is facilitated by play activities reflecting phase-specific interests and conflicts.

Implicit in these formulations of the development of play are two notions: (1) the subject of the child's play is determined by the status of drive organization and object relationships, and (2) the modalities of play are determined by corresponding development of ego functions—memory, reality testing, symbolization, language, and motor skills. The form and complexity of play reflect the stability and integration of these capacities; the content represents the challenges and conflicts that arise from each phase of development. Accordingly, those who view the infant as endowed with the ego capacity for fantasy, conflicts, and some rudimentary reality testing (Klein, 1923, 1927; Searl, 1933; Winnicott, 1968, 1971) freely designate the infant's earliest manipulations of his and his mother's body as "play." For others (Erikson, 1937, 1972; Peller, 1954; A. Freud, 1965), these infantile activities yield functional pleasure while serving the beginning ego orientation to the world. Peller (1954) points out, "Earliest play emerges almost imperceptibly with non-play" and might best be characterized as a prestage of play that will later serve the child's attempts and ego capacity to achieve a "compromise between the demands of the drives and the dictates of reality" (p. 185).

Suspension of Reality: Reality Testing and Fantasying

As previously outlined, from Freud's earliest descriptions, play has been viewed by psychoanalysts as a bridge between fantasy and reality. He pointed out, "The opposite of play is not what is serious but what is real." He added that the child "likes to link his imagined objects and situations to the tangible and visible things of the real world. This linking is all that differentiates the child's 'play' from 'phantasying'" (Freud, 1908, p. 144).

Later, Freud (1924) compared the use of symbolization in children's play to that of the adult neurotic as a "substitute for reality" (p. 187) to be distinguished from the loss of reality that occurs in psychosis. Implicit in these descriptions is the characteristic that others have variously referred to as unreality or withdrawal from reality (Klein, 1929), a leave of absence from reality (Waelder, 1932), pretending (Peller, 1954), or suspending reality (Solnit, 1987; Cohen et al., 1987). The critical difference between fantasy and play is that in play the suspension of reality sets the stage for and is most often accompanied by action (Waelder, 1932; Peller, 1954; Alexander, 1958; Winnicott, 1971; Neubauer, 1987; Solnit, 1987). In addition, the suspension of reality presupposes (1) that the child is able to distinguish between reality and play, and (2) that the activities of play have no consequences in reality (Freud, 1908; Waelder, 1932; Alexander, 1958; Erikson, 1977; Plaut, 1979; Neubauer, 1987; Solnit, 1987; Cohen et al., 1987).

With the capacity to suspend reality, play reflects a significant way station between fantasy and direct action—if fantasy is thought of as preparation for action, then play is fantasy in trial action in which the child can simultaneously concretize the expression of a wish by proxy and control the action according to any contingencies that may heighten or diminish the yield of pleasure. Essential to the child's degree of directorial control of the narrative action is the confidence that however closely the action approximates real events or however intense it becomes, the action of the characters in play is not and does not need to be "real." With the suspension of reality the child is able to enact a preferred, active role in the re-creation of an experience of passivity or enact derivatives of instinctual wishes that would otherwise be repudiated by the superego or invite potentially dangerous consequences from the real world. If drive and superego pressure are too strong for ego regulatory responses and the child is unable to "trust the strength of his ego" (A. Freud, 1965) to mediate successfully between internal and external demands, then the suspension of reality cannot be sustained and the play will be disrupted (Freud, 1908; Waelder, 1932; Plaut, 1979; Neubauer, 1987). In the case of the psychotic or obsessional child, limitations of the ego or the severity of the superego will preclude the child's capacity to enter into imaginative play.

Object Relationships: Parental Attitudes toward Play

One of the most direct statements about play and object relationships is contained in Winnicott's notion that playing reflects a recapitulation of children's earliest experiences of omnipotence in their relationship with their mother. Because play establishes and draws on the infantile, magical control, it serves as a template for developing a sense of self and organizing a sense of me/not me.

Part of the child's early playfulness in the realm of self-differentiation involves the capacity to distinguish between me/not me while retaining through play the potential for assuming either role. If parents are unable to support this domain of pretend and creativity or if their own conflicts actively discourage or disrupt the child's pleasure in playful activities and imaginative play, then a significant avenue for expanding object relationships may be closed to the child.

Indeed, another aspect of play and object relationships is how parents' activities support and elaborate their children's play. Child analysts have been particularly interested in the role and influence of parents in the child's ability to utilize play in the service of intrapsychic adaptation (Kennedy et al., 1985; Winnicott, 1971; Plaut, 1979). In a study at the Anna Freud Centre, parental attitudes were examined in a group of ten five-year-old children for whom play was associated with anxiety, disapproval, and shame rather than pleasure and mastery. The children and their families were followed from birth through the course of well-baby clinic visits. Observations were made of the mother-infant interactions in the home and in a mother-toddler group and of the child in nursery school and in subsequent child analyses, and of the parent in guidance sessions.

In some cases, the absence of pleasurable interaction was apparent from early on in the parent-child relationship. In a second category, parents with serious concerns about their own fantasies and an intolerance for id derivatives tended to control their child's play by emphasizing reality in exaggerated ways. Alternatively, parents in a third group were unable to support or sustain the child's reality testing either through overemphasizing their own distorted, fantastic, and frightening versions of reality or by conveying to the child their own anxious responses to reality. The demanding, hypercritical, or sadistically teasing attitudes of other parents led to the child's defensive avoidance of and vigilance toward anything in the realm of pretend. In each case parental attitudes were seen to interfere with the child's capacity to use play and fantasy to help mitigate anxiety and to leaven the demands of the external world as well as soften internal expectations (Moran, 1987).

Similarly, Plaut (1979) emphasized the significance of the parents' ability to play with their children. He suggested that the "parent who was not able to play, freely and pleasurably, in earlier stages of his own life will have difficulty enjoying play with his or her children" (p. 227). As a result of this inability fully to participate in the child's life, the child will feel that she is not valued in her own right but only in the ways that she is learning to become an adult.

Relation of Play to Other Areas of Functioning in Children and Adults

That so many theorists and clinicians have speculated about the relations between adults' play or work and the imaginative play of young children may reflect in part a wish that the child's capacity to play would live on in the adult. They apparently expect play to serve some preparatory and facilitative purpose in other domains. Surely all that imaginative effort will in the end be evidently functional and positively productive.

At least two major themes characterize the work of the last century on the relation between imaginative play and other areas of functioning: (1) the relation between characteristics of children's play and adaptive functioning (problem-solving skills and social competency), and (2) the relation between children's play and creativity in adults. That such themes predominate in views of the concurrent and predictive relations of play to other functional areas also reflects the view that play along with other forms of imaginative activity is secondary to other forms of thought characterized by science, logic, and philosophy and that play serves primarily as the imitative testing ground for more rational, ordered thought and work (Sutton-Smith, 1984).

Play and Social Adaptation

It is an implicit assumption of child analysis that through the use of play, certainly the play between child and analyst, children learn more adaptive approaches to situations in their day-to-day lives. By imitation and practice, children in effect try on solutions and adaptations to potentially conflictual situations. Analytic views of play as an adaptive function are confirmed and supported by other theories of play that also have addressed the relations between imaginative activity and adaptive capacities (Fein, 1981). Sutton-Smith (1984) and Bruner (1972) both stress the importance of fantasy play for generating interest in the novel, more flexible approaches to unexpected or ambiguous solutions and overall a greater range of adaptive behaviors. According to their views, because children use the safe confines of play to test a variety of situations and solutions, they develop a series of strategies and associations that they apply to situations in their external lives. Such theories do not address the concomitant effects of practice within play on inner conflict resolution, nor do they suggest that it is such conflict resolution that allows the child a broader adaptive repertoire rather than the behaviors learned in play. They do emphasize, however, that play serves an adaptive and organizing function that is evident in other areas not directly involved in imaginative play.

Several studies outside of the field of child psychoanalysis support the socially and adaptively organizing functions of play. Studies of children's behavior in free-play settings indicate that children who participate more in dramatic play in which reality can be suspended also tend to be involved more actively in social contact with adults and peers (Marshall and Doshi, 1965; Singer, 1979) and to be more oriented overall to social interaction with others (Jennings, 1975). There is also evidence to support the notion that dramatic play is related to the children's capacity for flexibility in social and nonsocial situations and their ability to adapt to alternative solutions in a number of settings. For example, children who play imaginatively with objects, that is, use objects in the service of creating imagined scenarios, do better when asked to solve problems involving these objects (Moore et al., 1974). It has also been suggested that the capacity to use pretend or dramatic play enhances impulse control (Saltz et al., 1977) and serves an arousal-maintaining and modulating function (Fein, 1981)—that is, children who are able to engage in pretend play show a greater capacity for regulating states of anxiety and tension, a finding that complements and supports analytic views of the function of play.

Play and Creativity

From a phenomenological standpoint, it seems reasonable to consider play a creative activity and to posit its longitudinal connection with the artistic (and perhaps scientific) creativity of adults. At the very least, both play and artistic creativity involve imagination, originality, and invention. Freud (1908) proposed that "every child at play behaves like a creative writer, in that he creates a world of his own, or rather, rearranges the things of his world in a new way which pleases him" (pp. 143–144).

In addition, like the creative artist, children are intent about their play, invest a great deal of emotional involvement in the process, and use their play in part to present a carefully constructed demarcation between the fantasied and the real worlds. Freud (1908) also emphasized that play, like creative writing, can serve to present situations that, if real, would cause little pleasure but through imaginative activity can be both exciting and enjoyable. Thus, the child plays out separation and loss just as the poet writes of unfulfilled love.

Freud (1908) carried the relation between play and creativity deeper than these phenomenological similarities when he suggested that adults exchange the pleasure they once obtained through play for the pleasure obtained through daydreams. As with children, adults dream out their unfulfilled wishes and experiment in their fantasy life with a variety of solutions that often hark back to earlier times when such wishes seemed satisfied. In play and daydreams, the individual experiences the gratification of the wish that all will turn out well, the pleasure of limitless capacities, and the comfort of having control over the amount of psychic stimulation. The creative writer converts inner fantasies into works of art, and as Freud suggests, artists use their creativity as the adult substitute for the imaginative play of children. The motivation to play, to daydream, and to do creative work is gratification and wish fulfillment.

Other theorists since Freud have also proposed a relation between children's play and later creative activity in adulthood. Greenacre (1959) made two critical distinctions. First, she suggested that play in the service of creative imagination functions differently from play in the service of the neurosis or in the service of the conflict. Second, she distinguished creativity from productivity and defined creativity as "the capacity for or activity of making something new, original or inventive" (p. 62). It is the quality of originality, not the product, that defines the creative act and imaginative play.

For Greenacre (1959), the link between early imaginative play and later artistic creativity is based on the child's and the adult's tendency to repeat experiences. She suggests that throughout life, one source of repetitive activity is the need to establish or reestablish a sense of reality or familiarity in the perceived or remembered experience. Through play or creative activity, the individual gradually establishes an experience as familiar and then feels the pleasure and relief of familiarity. Such repetition is different from the repetition of a previously traumatic experience in an effort gradually to master such an experience. At the very least, repetition of traumatic experiences in the classic sense of the repetition compulsion limits the individual's freedom to experience reality through a variety of internal mental viewpoints inasmuch as the traumatic experience exerts an unconscious, constricting influence on perception. This, in part, could be the basis of the distinction between imaginative play and play in the service of conflict.

The artist, like the child at play, uses his artistic efforts to test the relation between the inner world of unconscious and preconscious fantasies and the outer world of reality experiences. The more creative work brings these two worlds into a relationship of connectedness and synthesis, the more it is experienced as satisfying and stimulating to the artist and aesthetic to observers. Such a notion of creativity and play as uniting inner and outer worlds is similar to Winnicott's concept of the transitional space. He proposes that play gradually communicates a relationship between inner psychic reality and external experience, and that the very "precariousness" of play is due to its always reflecting the boundary "between the subjective and that which is objectively perceived" (1968, p. 597).

Greenacre (1957) also emphasizes that though creative power is sometimes enhanced by a loosening of individual conflicts, artists rarely use their work to resolve conflictual situations. Indeed, a particularly restless quality characteristic of creative adults that brings them to the novel and unfamiliar is similar to the energetic explorations of playing children. Creative work brings the individual to the edge of unfamiliar stimulation and then to the comforting solace of connectedness and familiarity. It is this rhythmic ebb and flow that modulates anxiety in the service of imaginative play and adult creativity. As Greenacre noted, many creative artists do not wish to be relieved of their anxiety for they fear that with such relief they will lose their creative urge. Several theorists have considered modulation of states of discomfort or level of stimulation as the essential motivation for and purpose of play and creative work (Berlyne, 1960; Fein, 1981; Shultz, 1979). Although such theories do not take into account the possible inner fantasy configurations that lead to discomfort or heightened arousal, they do underscore the affective regulatory functions of play. Moreover, the rhythmic fluctuation in states of arousal has been proposed as a feature shared by adult work activity and children's play (Csikszentmihalyi and Bennett, 1971).

Theoretical considerations from both psychoanalytic and developmental psychology perspectives suggest that artistic creativity and daydreaming serve similar psychic functions for adults as imaginative play serves for children. Several investigators have studied the concurrent validity of a functional relation between play and creativity. For example, Dansky (1980) divided a group of preschool children (ages three and four) into players and nonplayers according to the amount of time the children were engaged in imaginative play during a free-play period. The nonplayer group was involved in imaginative play less than 5 percent of the observation time; the player group showed imaginative play at least 28 percent of the time. In a more structured, one-on-one play setting, children using more imaginative play were more likely to use objects in unusual or nonliteral ways and were able, when asked, to suggest more alternative uses for a given set of play objects. Similarly, Hutt and Bhavnani (1976) presented preschool children (ages three and four) with a novel toy and divided the group into those who did not explore the toy, those who explored but did not play with it, and those who explored and then used the toy in an imaginative play sequence. When the children were compared on a test of divergent thinking or problem-solving strategies, those using the toy imaginatively scored higher.

Predictive relations between imaginative play and later creativity in adulthood have been suggested by several analytic writers. Greenacre (1957) believes that the basic characteristics of creative talent involve a sensitivity to sensory stimulation and a greater than usual awareness of relations between various stimuli coupled with a "predisposition to . . . empathy" (p. 53) and sufficient sensorimotor equipment to allow for symbolization. These capacities, though subject to great individual variability, are aspects of imaginative play as well, and Greenacre posits that such characteristics were especially heightened in the childhood experiences of creative artists. Finally, such relations may not be limited to creative activity for, as mentioned earlier, Freud suggested a functional relation between the relief provided adults by jokes and the child's use of play. Jokes allow thoughts and fantasies to "escape" the censoring activities of the superego and provide an avenue for the release of instinctual tension and the expression of instinctual derivatives. In this form, humor and jokes are a direct heir of the child's play.

Conclusion

Psychoanalytic theories of play emerged from Freud's earliest formulations about children's activities as they demonstrated origins of central characteristics in the psychic life of adulthood. Whereas Freud used his observations of children's play in the service of building a theory concerning adult mental functioning, the work of Klein, Waelder, A. Freud, Erikson, and others focused on aspects of play as a part of attempts at understanding the development of children in their own right.

The simultaneous growth and mutual influences of child analysis as a subspecialty of psychoanalysis and of interest in ego development were reflected in the increased focus on examining specific functions and characteristics of play activities. Conceptualizations about the reasons children play and about the characteristics of those activities began to emphasize ideas about shifting internal and external demands in the child's life and the increasing array of functions available for adapting to them. These ideas added to previous ones held about the role of trauma and repetition compulsion in play. Greater attention paid to phase-specific characteristics in the child's ego development and object relationships helped to sharpen views about differentiating types of play and functions served according to periods of development.

As child analysis and ego psychological theories evolved, types of play were described according to various developmentally determined criteria. These include different sites and props employed in play activities; the various ways of using and representing others in play; autoerotic, solitary, or group dramatic play; games with rules; the use of differing amounts of narrative and action; and the like. Play may be viewed as both reflecting and advancing the child's growing capacities and negotiations of shifting developmental tasks. Differing types and characteristics of play could be seen as one view of the child's developmental status.

In addition, children's play may be seen as representing the earliest form of verbal narrative and expression of unconscious fantasies and wishes. The thematic content of the narrative provides a view of those fantasies that are most active for the child at that moment of play. The process of developing the narrative—that is, the shifts in play and the interaction between the different narratives—reveals the interplay between wish and conflict and the workings of defense. Further, creating a play narrative may actively facilitate the emergence and maturation of psychic structures such as more elaborate and adaptive defenses and more mature affective regulatory capacities. In each of these ways, children's play narratives provide a means for understanding the changes in mental functioning and structure.

In summary, a selective critical review of the psychoanalytic literature reveals evolving perspectives on children's play that reflect the dominant trends in, as well as departures from, the mainstream of analytic theory. Where Freud was initially concerned about what children's play could tell us about adult psychic functions, subsequent contributors first emphasized the equivalence of children's play and adult activities (free association, for example) and then focused on the importance of children's play as a set of phenomena worthy of consideration in their own right. Elaboration of notions about play has moved in both directions of the developmental spectrum—from the playful activities of infancy to the role of play and playfulness in adulthood and in the creative process.

In addition to current attempts to deepen existing conceptualizations, psychoanalytic investigators hope to expand the range of questions involving the role and fate of play in children who are, for example, confronted with acute trauma, chronic overstimulation, and deprivation. What are the differences in the form and content of play in the face of various forms of impingement on development? To what extent can psychoanalytic observations of children's play increase our understanding of the flexibility of developmental capacities and the range of adaptations available to the child in the face of internal and external limitations? Continued efforts to expand psychoanalytic views of plays will likely yield some answers to these and other issues and will most certainly help to raise, clarify, and elaborate on the questions that have not yet been asked.

References

Alexander, F. (1958). A contribution to the theory of play. *Psychoanal. Q.*, 27:175–193.

Arlow, J. A. (1987). Trauma, play and perversion. *Psychoanal. Study Child*, 42:31–44.

Berlyne, D. E. (1960). *Conflict, Arousal, and Curiosity*. New York: McGraw-Hill.

Bruner, J. (1972). The nature and uses of immaturity. *Amer. Psychologist*, 27:687–708.

Cohen, D. J., et al. (1987). Analytic discussions with oedipal children. *Psychoanal. Study Child*, 42:59–84.

Csikszentmihalyi, M., and Bennett, S. (1971). An exploratory model of play. *Amer. Anthropologist*, 73:45–58.

Dansky, J. L. (1980). Make believe: A mediator of the relationship between play and associative fluency. *Child Develpm.*, 51:576–579.

Eifermann, R. (1987). Children's games, observed and experienced. *Psychoanal. Study Child*, 42:127–144.

Erikson, E. H. (1937). Configurations in play. *Psychoanal. Q.*, 6:139–214.

——. (1972). *Play and Development*. New York: Norton.

——. (1977). *Toys and Reasons*. New York: Norton.

Fein, G. G. (1981). Pretend play: An integrative view. *Child Develpm.*, 52:1095–1118.

Freud, A. (1936). *The Ego and the Mechanisms of Defense.* New York: Int. Univ. Press, 1966.

———. (1965). *Normality and Pathology in Childhood.* New York: Int. Univ. Press.

———. (1979). Child analysis as the study of mental growth, normal and abnormal. *The Writings of Anna Freud*, 8:119–136. New York: Int. Univ. Press.

Freud, S. (1905). Jokes and their relation to the unconscious. *S.E.*, 8.

———. (1908). Creative writers and day-dreaming. *S.E.*, 9:141–153.

———. (1920). Beyond the pleasure principle. *S.E.*, 18:7–64.

———. (1924). Neurosis and psychosis. *S.E.*, 19:149–158.

———. (1931). Female sexuality. *S.E.*, 21:225–243.

Greenacre, P. (1957). The childhood of the artist. *Psychoanal. Study Child*, 12:47–72.

———. (1959). Play in relation to creative imagination. *Psychoanal. Study Child*, 14:61–80.

Hartmann, H. (1939). *Ego Psychology and the Problem of Adaptation.* New York: Int. Univ. Press, 1958.

Hutt, C., and Bhavnani, R. (1976). Predictions from play. In *Play*, ed. J. S. Bruner, A. Jolly, and K. Sylva. New York: Penguin, pp. 216–219.

Jennings, K. D. (1975). People versus object orientation, social behavior, and intellectual abilities in preschool children. *Develpm. Psychol.*, 11:511–519.

Kennedy, H., et al. (1985). Both sides of the barrier. *Psychoanal. Study Child*, 40:275–283.

Klein, M. (1923). The development of a child. *Int. J. Psychoanal.*, 4:419–474.

———. (1927). The psychological principles of infant analysis. *Int. J. Psychoanal.*, 8:25–37.

———. (1929). Personification in the play of children. *Int. J. Psychoanal.*, 10:193–204.

Loewald, E. L. (1987). Therapeutic play in space and time. *Psychoanal. Study Child*, 42:173–192.

Marshall, H. R., and Doshi, R. (1965). Aspects of experience revealed through doll play of preschool children. *J. Psychol.*, 61:47–57.

Moore, N. V., Evertson, C. M., and Brophy, J. E. (1974). Solitary play: Some functional considerations. *Develpm. Psychol.*, 10:830–834.

Moran, G. S. (1987). Some functions of play and playfulness. *Psychoanal. Study Child*, 42:11–30.

Neubauer, P. B. (1987). The many meanings of play. *Psychoanal. Study Child*, 42:3–10.

Ostow, M. (1987). Play and reality. *Psychoanal. Study Child*, 42:193–204.

Peller, L. E. (1954). Libidinal phases, ego development, and play. *Psychoanal. Study Child*, 9:178–198.

Piaget, J. (1945). *Play, Dreams, and Imitation in Childhood.* New York: Norton.

Plaut, E. A. (1979). Play and adaptation. *Psychoanal. Study Child*, 34:217–232.

Saltz, E., Dixon, D., and Johnson, J. (1977). Training disadvantaged preschoolers on various fantasy activities: Effects on cognitive functioning and impulse control. *Child Develpm.*, 48:367–380.

Searl, M. N. (1933). Play, reality and aggression. *Int. J. Psychoanal.*, 14:310–320.

Shultz, T. R. (1979). Play as arousal modulation. In *Play and Learning*, ed. B. Sutton-Smith. New York: Gardner Press, pp. 7–22.

Singer, J. L. (1979). Affect and imagination in play and fantasy. In *Emotions in Personality and Psychopathology*, ed. C. Izard. New York: Plenum, pp. 13–34.

Solnit, A. J. (1987). A psychoanalytic view of play. *Psychoanal. Study Child*, 42:205–219.

Sutton-Smith, B. (1984). Text and context in imaginative play and the social sciences. In *Analyzing Children's Play Dialogues*, ed. F. Kessel and A. Goncu. San Francisco: Jossey-Bass, pp. 53–70.

Waelder, R. (1932). The psychoanalytic theory of play. *Psychoanal. Q.*, 2:208–224.

Winnicott, D. W. (1953). Transitional objects and transitional phenomena. *Int. J. Psychoanal.*, 34:89–97.

———. (1968). Playing: Its theoretical status in the clinical situation. *Int. J. Psychoanal.*, 49:591–599.

———. (1971). *Playing and Reality*. New York: Basic Books.

2

From Play to Playfulness
in Children and Adults

Albert J. Solnit, M.D.

In 1987 a young Israeli actor, director, and scholar of drama, Shai Bar-Ya'acov, explained his view of theater to a journalist by saying, "the urge to do theatre is a very natural thing. It stems from the urge to play that exists in all of us. As we grow we have to funnel this urge into other forms. And that's what theatre is all about" (p. 205).

In this chapter, I follow the developmental continuity of play in childhood to playfulness in adulthood as it can be observed in the psychoanalyst's playroom and office. From illustrative observations of a child and an adult in psychoanalytic treatment, I outline this continuity as an abiding one worthy of clinical and theoretical study.

My focus on the continuity of play to playfulness, developmentally and clinically, is guided by certain theoretical assumptions and technical considerations:

1. Play begins toward the end of the first year of life, encouraged and fostered by playful attitudes of the care-giving adults.
2. Play in childhood, with rare exceptions, includes physical and mental activity.
3. Just as thought is trial action from the latency period onward, so play is trial thought in the younger child, especially in the oedipal period.
4. Play in childhood can be traced into adulthood as playfulness. Adults usually give up play, partly because they become self-critical of its regressive aspects and also because playfulness, especially playing with thoughts, fantasies, and imaginings, is more grown-up—that is, efficient, socially useful, and private.
5. Drama, dance, and music playing (as well as other artistic performances) are special forms of play that continue into adulthood with all the mental and physical combinations referred to above, and with the additional gratifications of aesthetic, rhythmic experiences being

expressed and appreciated by a socially approving audience, especially when gifted performers are involved.* In an advertisement, an anonymous copywriter said, "If music didn't exist, we'd never know the joy of tapping our feet" (*New York Times*, August 30, 1987).

6. Play and playfulness are inviting because they review the past, reflect on the present, and provide a constructive expression of curiosity that enables "players" to prepare for future challenges and opportunities.

Psychoanalytic Data and Concepts

The psychoanalytic observations that follow are mainly derived from selected psychoanalytic treatments and biographical data of a father (thirty-five to thirty-nine years of age) and an unrelated girl (three and a half to seven years of age). Both were involved in the longitudinal studies initiated by Ernst Kris and Milton J. E. Senn in 1948. The father also was involved in the study of simultaneous psychoanalytic treatment of all members of one family, which was reported at a Freud Lecture by Marianne Kris.

Psychoanalytic treatment of a child, an adolescent, or an adult benefits and to a certain extent requires playfulness for adult analysand and analyst, and playfulness enacted in play with a child. The adolescent is closer to playfulness in his or her psychoanalytic treatment.

If you ask a child analysand about the treatment, he or she may let you in on the pleasure, the relief, or the decrease in unpleasure that the child experiences, especially in the play component of the treatment. If you ask an adult analysand, he or she may realistically report that it is painful. The essential question is: does the adult analysand find relief through the psychoanalytic treatment by moving toward "playful"-ness through increasing use at all levels of thought as trial action? In an important sense analysands will not succeed if they cannot allow the speculative, pretending qualities of free association to be expressed. Free associations are closely related to playfulness. In Freud's terms (1905), if one's ability to jest, to joke, and to express incongruities is not available, the approximations that we call free association will be most difficult to achieve, if not impossible. Similarly, if the freedom to use figures of speech such as metaphors and similes is seriously constricted or inhibited, the capacity to free-associate will be

*See Reichardt (1985, p. 100): "One of the ways by which music can influence mental health and have therapeutic effect is perhaps its capacity to create transitional experiences, and a world of imagination and play."

difficult to achieve.* In an important sense, the process of freely associating in the clinical psychoanalytic situation is as dependent on the suspension of reality as are play and playfulness.

In the case of the father, Harry, it was not until his psychoanalytic treatment put him in better touch with himself that he could clarify his current perceptions and free himself from the burdensome aspects of his past memories. This process enabled him to gain a better understanding of his present dilemmas and to prepare differently (more adaptively and less defensively) for the future he was shaping as he moved ahead in his development.

Harry

Harry, thirty-five years old, accepted the recommendation of psychoanalytic treatment because of his repeated, unnecessary destructive disputes with his boss in a middle-sized manufacturing firm (Solnit, 1989). Psychoanalytic treatment revealed that he also suffered from chronic marital difficulties. He felt his wife did not respect him. There were frequent outbursts in which he sulked, felt put down, and withdrew into spiteful, stony silences, to the detriment of the marital relationship and with negative effects on his daughters, who felt rejected by him.

In the psychoanalytic treatment, two lines of memory were opened up which he had been living out neurotically but did not remember. The first was the recollection of having been sick and confined to bed for six months at the age of eleven. As he reconstructed the illness in his psychoanalytic treatment, he had been diagnosed as having a streptococcus infection, and the family doctor explained that he could damage his heart if he did not remain in bed quietly for six months. He then brought up a clear memory of his father sternly warning him not to move or he would damage himself. As we examined the clarity of this new screening memory, the patient gradually recalled that his mother and father had been very worried that he was too restless in his sleep and had tied his hands and feet to the bed frame to keep him from moving. In the transference, he felt "tied down" by the analysis. He recalled his anger at his parents and his fear of damaging himself. Later in the analysis we were able to reconstruct his deep conviction that he had made himself sick through masturbation associated with exciting fantasies of being overwhelmed by a strong woman—that is, being forced to have sex with a woman.

---

*The use of speech to express one's thoughts and feelings in language requires symbolizing, the major human vehicle for organizing and implementing the human experience.

Although this first line of recall was far from precise, it made sense to him and explained why he had been out of school for six months, a memory gap that had always puzzled him. It also led to his understanding why he was always trying to trap his boss into errors that led to anxious confrontations in which the patient felt put down and then became compliant and depressed.

In the next two years the patient's relationship with his boss gradually changed. He was promoted several times, until he reached a managerial level that was highly satisfying and in which he now was the boss of a large number of employees. He felt he was especially skilled in helping young "hell-raisers" when they entered the firm under his tutelage.

As the psychoanalytic treatment proceeded, there was an improvement in his working capacities and satisfaction, and he filled in further gaps in his memory. For the first time since adolescence, he recalled that when he returned to school after his six months of illness, he would play basketball after school despite his father's threatening prohibition. The father had indicated that since he had had the infection, which might have weakened his heart, he should not engage in vigorous competitive sports. He remembered that he had to play not only because he enjoyed it (he dearly loved and was highly skilled in such sports) but also because he was so anxious about falling ill again that in a counterphobic way he had to face the danger of competitive sports to find out if he was all right. Furthermore, he could not resist the pleasure it gave him once he allowed himself to think of playing the game.

In the analysis it was clear that playing basketball was also equated with masturbation. As he would begin each game, he experienced a mounting irresistible pleasure and tension with anxiety after which he felt relief that he had not died or fallen ill again. Once more he had passed through a dangerous situation. Subsequently, after graduating from high school and looking for work, he gave up sports and took what he knew would be a safe job that would not be too competitive. It was clear that he arranged for and accepted limits in his education and work that unconsciously he believed would offer safety and would avoid the danger of competition and greater satisfaction. In the analytic treatment it became clear that he felt that he had "damaged" himself and might damage himself further if he was too ambitious or competitive.

The second line of remembering was the painful feeling that his father had preferred his older sister and that his mother, though more even in her affections, never took his side when the father and older sister seemed to gang up on him. This was reconstructed both in the transference (he was certain that I preferred the woman patient who preceded him) and in clarifying his ongoing distortions of his relationship with his wife, when he would perceive his criticism and anger at her as her lack of respect for him. His sulkiness and stony silence were updated replicas of how he had acted when he felt let down by his father's preference for the sister and especially because his mother did not seem to take his side. At those times he believed that no one really admired and cared for him.

In the third year of his psychoanalytic treatment, Harry began to build a playroom and workshop in the basement cellar for his family and himself. It could clearly be seen in the psychoanalytic treatment that this was not an acting out against his treatment, though it was transiently in the service of resistance. It was a game whose rules he made. He thought of it as a second job, after hours, almost clandestine, but it was clearly his own game plan. He also set a symbolically significant deadline for finishing it, manifestly by Thanksgiving, but unwittingly wanting it to be his rebirth—his birthday was a few days after Thanksgiving. After this birthday, his fantasies suggested that he hoped his manliness at home and at work could be asserted and enjoyed. The play/workroom was a well-planned and executed drama, written, directed, and acted in by the analysand. During this time of building a better family room and a workroom for himself, the patient's psychoanalytic treatment provided a window into his inner world, while the outer world was relatively calm and unperturbed. Structures were being altered, revised, and improved, gaining additional resources inside and outside for the analysand and his family.

Throughout the renovation and construction, he came regularly to his psychoanalytic sessions while refusing any assistance with his carpentry, plumbing, electrical work, insulating, painting, and refinishing. He became increasingly anxious about what might happen when he finished it, wondering if the city inspector would approve his electrical and plumbing work, if the fire marshal would pass on the safety standards, and if I would get fed up with this preoccupation. His wife and children were supportive. In the psychoanalytic treatment, the multiple symbolic meanings of the room were reviewed and worked through, clarifying his neurotic core in its many manifestations. As he could see his success crystallizing, he became transiently hypochondriacal, and as his anxiety was worked through in the analysis, he began to assert himself tactfully with his boss. He believed he was as good a parent and perhaps a better "homemaker" than his wife. Until this period of his life, he had felt socially inferior, incomplete in his education (he neurotically decided not to go to college) and not as good as his father or as his wife. Gradually, his self-assessment became more realistic. He began to advance at work; he was a steady, much less sullen adult at home; and he viewed himself with approval as self-educated.

The room project, successfully completed on time, was a developmental achievement. It dramatized the analytic working through and freeing up of inhibitions of play, playfulness, and risk-taking (in the sense of the meaning of the Old English word for *play—plegan*). These neurotic inhibitions and obsessional developments had set in during the oedipal period when Harry felt displaced by his younger sister as the favorite of mother and father. He had felt inferior and unfairly treated. These traits were further elaborated and fixated by the trauma of his illness and its treatment when he was eleven years old.

In the transference, as he planned and began to build the room initially, he was resistant to the analytic treatment, feeling it interfered because of the time and energy it took. As this was interpreted and worked through, his pleasure in building his room increased. He became less anxious about the riskiness he experienced at the beginning that he might fail, that he might never complete it, or, the greatest danger, that he might succeed. Playfully, he allowed himself to know what "screwy ideas" psychoanalysts have.

A few days after he completed the room and felt satisfied by his accomplishment, he said, "In the past it was all right to know I was superior, but not to feel it, because then I couldn't think clearly." Playfully, teasingly, he added, "I guess it's okay in here since it's against the free association rule to think clearly."

In summary, as Harry recovered these memories and replaced unconsciously motivated destructive behavior at work and at home with the conscious memories of traumas and a sense of deprivation, his recollections were worked through. He came to understand how he arranged to have his difficulties at work and at home—he had been making choices about his way of shaping his personal relationships that served unconscious motives. These motives represented a neurotic residue of past burdens of trauma and deprivation. In his psychoanalytic treatment and in his life experiences, Harry learned that he could make other choices about his relationships once he was more aware of himself and how he behaved. Remembering liberated him. It enabled him to know the story of his life more coherently, although it did not provide him with a historically complete and accurate narrative about himself. Then he was able to gain relief from his persistently destructive behavior pattern at home and at work—especially at work.

Thus, in using the psychoanalytic treatment process, Harry uncovered the gaps in his memory and gained a more coherent view of himself in his current situation and as a preparation for future life experiences. As Freud (1914) had intimated, the patient said, "As a matter of fact I've always known it; only I've never thought of it" (p. 148).

In Harry's case, Loewald (1978) would say, "The movement from unconscious to conscious experience, from the instinctual life of the id to the reflective, purposeful life of the ego, means taking responsibility for one's own history, the history that has been lived and the history in the making" (p. 11).

We can add, Harry's recovery of the capacity for playfulness, of pretending, and of going from "pretend" to the play of constructing his "dream" playroom and workshop were dramatic expressions of the working through that facilitated his translation of his psychoanalytic treatment into a "real life's work."

Margaret

Close to her fortieth birthday, Margaret, who had been in psychoanalytic treatment as a child and who had kept in touch with her analyst over the years, spoke of the harmony and satisfaction of her ten-year marriage to Charlie, of her clear and conflict-free decision to leave the corporate world after ten years of great success and the permanent financial security it gave her, and of how much she enjoyed playing since her liberating retirement at the age of thirty-seven and a half.

Margaret had entered psychoanalytic treatment when she was three and a half years old because of transient phobic symptoms and because her anxiety had led to a significant constriction of her social interactions and to a sustained play inhibition. This was triggered by a traumatic separation experience in which she had felt abandoned. The psychoanalytic treatment lasted three and a half years, preparing her for a successful latency experience and enabling her to resume a progressive and normal development.

In playing as an adult, she always enjoyed dancing, music, hiking, and traveling. She developed a warm comradeship with her husband's twenty-three-year-old son and twenty-one-year-old daughter, his children by a previous marriage. Her newest hobby was making costume jewelry by hand. Fashioning the handmade jewelry was characterized by her as playful, colorful, fun, and "not very expensive." She explained that she displayed her work at jewelry fairs and that frequently it was children who brought their parents to see the "catchy" jewelry. She resisted the idea of making this into a business, although she had been successful commercially and artistically.

Spontaneously, she said to me, "You know, this interest began when I was in treatment with you." She then described a memory of her play in treatment that was factually accurate and had screen-memory characteristics of being sharp, clear, and emphatic. She continued, "I so enjoyed playing and pretending that I was a wealthy Texas oil well owner and that you, as my husband, gave me whatever I wanted. You made jewelry for me of paper, marbles, and Scotch tape. You were very clever and made me a necklace, a bracelet, a wand (I still have one with one of my dress-up costumes), and a crown (a tiara). We had a Cadillac and a Rolls-Royce." Then she laughed and said, "It all seems like a good story, a bit of a joke, but there it is."

As indicated above, Margaret's acute trauma had occurred after she began her psychoanalytic treatment as she was being driven home from nursery school by her mother. In the backseat, three-and-a-half-year-old Margaret was pretending to be a wild animal, making animal noises as she had learned with classmates at nursery school. The teachers and her analyst had been encouraged in the beginning of the treatment by Margaret's increasing spontaneity, since she had been so frozen and inhibited in play and social-izing when she started nursery school. Margaret's behavior in the backseat of the car was experienced by her mother as disobedient and nasty. She abruptly stopped the car in a marshland and told the little girl to get out, threatening to abandon her in this wilderness area. Following this, Margaret again became frozen and inhibited socially and in play at school. That trauma, as well as many other sources of Margaret's neurotic development, strengthened the analyst's conviction that she would benefit from psycho-analytic treatment, which was ongoing until after her seventh birthday.

Later, in this same follow-up interview, Margaret explained seriously that she might or might not have a child with her husband. Since he had two children by a previous marriage and the children were close to him and to Margaret, he was pleased to support whatever decision she made. Margaret was not yet ready—she might never be ready—to take on the long-term commitment to the care and raising of a child. She had no fear of pregnancy or of childbirth. She liked to be with children of all ages, loved to play with them, and was not too sensitive when their parents wondered if she was not too permissive in what she allowed children to do when they played with her. She explained to them that children need to feel free to play as an important, healthy way of growing up. On questioning, she remembered initially how apprehensive and constrained she had felt at nursery school and in her play sessions with me; but by the time she went off to kinder-garten and finished her treatment, she knew it was all right to play at school but not at home. Because of her mother's discomfort, she had to take her cues from her about how playful she could be. Her father was much more relaxed. Both she and her father liked to have projects, to be busy, to use their hands, whereas mother and sister preferred to collect and to classify things. Margaret's financial security was based on hard work that required a capacity for risk-taking that involved trusting personal relationships and a playful sense of humor.

Of course, there was much more to Margaret's psychoanalytic treatment and her development. This vignette simply illustrates how a play inhibition was overcome and became a nodal point—a marker for future progressive development that elaborated in sublimated forms what had been a paralyzing identification with her mother. The unresolved positive transference was also apparent when Margaret said to me, "You've always been a second father to me, even though we don't see each other very often."

Discussion

In *The American Heritage Dictionary of the English Language* (1981), the reader is referred to the Old English word of *plegan* as the basis for the modern word *play*. *Plegan* is defined as signifying "to exercise oneself." Other early meanings of *plegan* include "to pledge for, to stake, to risk, to sport."

In the same dictionary, the word *playful* is defined with an emphasis on fun, good spirits, and humor. It includes the following synonyms: *mischievous, impish, waggish, frivolous, jocular, good humor, silly, sportive,* and *frolicsome.* I would add to these: *humorous, incongruous, jesting,* and *teasing.* Though *playful* implies fun and pleasure, it also can refer to unintentional or lightly conveyed criticism, mockery, and humiliation.

Freud said:

Before there is such a thing as a joke, there is something that we may describe as "play" or as a "jest".

"Play"—let us keep to that name—appears in children while they are learning to make use of words and to put thoughts together. . . . *Play* with words and thoughts, motivated by certain pleasurable effects of economy, would thus be the first stage of jokes.

This play is brought to an end [in adulthood] by the strengthening of a factor that deserves to be described as the critical faculty of reasonableness. (1905, p. 128)

Individuals, because of self-criticism, commonly judge play in late latency and thereafter as absurd. Anna Freud (1965) referred to this when she pointed out that play requires the tolerance of regression, as in child analysis where "the child's play and his verbal expression gradually lose the characteristics of secondary process thinking such as logic, coherence, rationality, and display instead characteristics of primary process functions such as generalizations, displacements, repetitiveness, distortions, and exaggerations" (p. 100). Anna Freud is clear, however, in indicating that play in childhood is not the equivalent of adult work (p. 123), and that it is no substitute for free association—it is not the same as, nor is it equivalent to, free association (p. 29).

As indicated by Freud (1909), the direct observation of children "in all the freshness of life" (p. 150) supports the conviction that play is at its richest and most adaptive during the oedipal phase. Whether we observe children in a group setting where play is spontaneous (not directly involved with or directed by adults) or in the psychoanalytic situation where it is our task to understand the meaning, as well as to assess the readiness of the child to enter into dialogue about the play with the analyst, we continue to use observation of play for our own knowledge and not as a substitute for free association, dreams, or language. Waelder (1933) put it this way: "Play is . . . a leave of absence from reality, as well as from the super-ego" (p. 222).

Eric Plaut (1979) took issue with Freud's view that play is given up in adulthood and has its place mainly in childhood. He reviewed psychoanalytic theories and deduced that there was a lack of clarity and emphasis on what he calls "generation play," that is, the "parents' ability to enjoy playing with their children" (p. 227). In summary, Plaut asserted: "In psychoanalytic theory, play has been assumed to have a subordinate role, with the exception of early childhood play. In the past 70 years much evidence has accumulated that play is of central importance throughout life" (p. 230).

Developmental Considerations

Freud (1908) established developmental foundations for his study of play when he stated:

> Might we not say that every child at play behaves like a creative writer, in that he creates a world of his own, or, rather, re-arranges the things of his world in a new way which pleases him? It would be wrong to think he does not take that world seriously; on the contrary, he takes his play very seriously and he expends large amounts of emotion on it. The opposite of play is not what is serious but what is real. In spite of all the emotion with which he cathects his world of play, the child distinguishes it quite well from reality; and he likes to link his imagined objects and situations to the tangible and visible things of the real

world. This linking is all that differentiates the child's "play" from "phantasying." (pp. 143–144)

It is useful to find the limits of our definitions, the boundaries covered by our concepts of play and playfulness, if we are to maintain reasonable scientific rigor and to ensure that these concepts of play can be useful and avoid the diffusion of being overextended and overgeneralized. Just as "thinking is an experimental action" (Freud, 1933, p. 89), so, conversely, are the actions of play and the effects of playfulness efforts to engage in experimental thinking. Simply, action can be a trial of thought, especially when, as in play and playfulness, the action is based on the suspension of reality—that is, the use and practice of pretending or of making believe and of trying on. In an important sense, play can be the dramatic expression of what later becomes metaphor in language.

In outlining the boundaries of play as a concept, I begin with the analytic thinking of an infant expert. In a personal communication (1984) Sally Provence wrote:

It seems to me that what we describe as play in infants we do primarily because whatever the activity it is accompanied by signs of pleasurable affect. In the beginning one doesn't have to assume any specific mental content. As the relationship with the mother (and others) develops, and as cognition matures, those behaviors that we refer to as play in infancy go more and more toward a specific content of either ideas or fantasies.

I elect not to call the earliest infant behaviors play or playful if the affect doesn't indicate satisfaction or pleasure. If there is displeasure or uncomfortable tension, I do not call it play.

Two qualifiers may be useful in the light of this study:

1. If the activity is not pleasurable but is tension-relieving, we can still consider it play, accompanied by a sense of relief—the avoidance of unpleasure.
2. If the activity (such as masturbation) and its mental content become primary, replacing the trial action by an action that is realistically meaningful, primarily sought for its own gratifications, and in which the "pretend function" is replaced by direct pleasurable gratification, it no longer is play; the gratification overshadows the mental content. In these instances, play—that is, pretending—has been replaced by direct gratification; and the requirement that play represent a vicarious approach to thinking and doing has been replaced by the activity becoming a primary route to gratification, important in its own right,

rather than an activity that represents an indirect or trial approach to conflict, defense, memory, preparing for the future, or differentiating past, present, and future. Play by definition is not orgasmic, though it may lead to orgasm, at which point it ceases to be play. One might say that when metaphor becomes declarative rather than comparative, play loses its metaphoric richness.

Theoretical Considerations

In conceptualizing play on the basis of psychoanalytic observations and theoretical constructs, we bring theory closer to observation. In this context: play is between acting (behavior) and thinking, between behavior and emotions (acting and emoting).

Sally Provence indicated that much of what is called play in the first weeks and months of life comes under the heading of perceiving and exploring.* Infants explore, at first visually and then tactually; finally, with the emerging of motor skills, they have the capacities to seek out their own novel situations and persons.

As Oliver Sacks (1990) has put it:

The infant, the human infant at least, is born into chaos, at least so far as complex perceptions and cognitions go. The infant immediately starts exploring the world, looking, feeling, touching, smelling, as all higher animals do, from the moment of birth. Sensation alone is not enough; it must be combined with movement, with emotion, with action. Movement and sensation together become integrated to form a "category," a coherent brain response. (p. 47)

I would add that as these skills emerge, infants also can seek out repeatedly what gave them pleasure and relief from unpleasure. "With the advent of language, the child then has a way to communicate his findings to others and a tool for symbolization, abstraction, and communication of meaning" (Sacks, p. 47). The same developmental markers have a similar significance for when "play" begins.

Mayes (1991) also points out that, as in exploration when there is gross maternal deprivation (Spitz, 1945), children do not play because play is related to persons who are significant to them (have a primary psychological relationship and attachment to them). There are other striking similarities in developmental aspects of play and curiosity (exploration):

*For many of these observations and formulations, I am grateful to Linda Mayes (1991).

1. Both are pleasurable and self-sustaining.
2. Both enable psychoanalytic treatment to begin when they are related to the analysand's inner life and workings of the unconscious mind. Once the individual is curious about his or her inner life, or can play or be playful to the degree required for access to the inner life, then the psychoanalytic treatment can proceed.
3. Both emerge out of the affective matrix of early mother-infant interaction and are responsive to social stimulation.
4. Both depend on significant access between primary and secondary process thinking.
5. Both emerge during the second year of life, although forerunners are apparent earlier.

Thus, we seek to establish a view of play as a reflection of ego functioning, that is, between action (behavior) and mental activity (thinking and feeling). This capacity appears in an early immature form as soon as a capacity for object constancy and object permanency is available, enabling the child to expect the pretend world and the reality to be different—as in, for example, the game of peek-a-boo and the capacity to acquire and exploit transitional objects, which also assumes the difference between pretend and reality.

Similarly, the ability to recollect is dependent on this line of development; to remember a person or an event when they are not concretely present is a capacity that requires that the person imagine (pretend) that the person or event is available in the "mind's eye." Remembering, however, is only a first step toward pretending the person is there. Metaphorically, one can run off that movie (or videotape) inside one's head. This ability is also expressed by the capacity to feel alone—to have private thoughts and feelings in the presence of others (Winnicott, 1958).

Again, in the use of games as a channel for play, we see the same principles, but the beginning of the game, the rules to be followed, the aim of the game, and how it facilitates winning and losing tend to allow the underlying fantasies to be more private, discreet, and less observable—and often all the more comfortable to have. Thus, many games remain playful, and others become nonplayful, increasingly approaching a pathway to direct gratification and no longer mainly a pretend world. Gambling games may be the best example of this perversion of play into nonplay activities.

The limits of our knowledge do not allow us to spell out conceptually the differences and similarities of play and playfulness in boys and girls. One example of this is the observation that in nursery school girls are more likely to hum as they play, whereas boys are more likely to be boisterous.

This has not, as far as I know, been systematically studied, however. Nor have the developmental differences in the play of boys and girls been systematically investigated, though one can be certain that there is a large overlap or perhaps as much in common as there are differences.

Although there are exceptions, it is assumed that healthy development is associated with play in childhood and playfulness in adulthood; and conversely the incapacity of children to play and of adults to be playful is often a symptom of inadequate or deviant development that may be associated with symptoms, symptomatic behavior, and constricted (inhibited) or deviant development, cognitively and affectively.

And finally it becomes clear, as theory, technique, and practice are brought together, that free association, the fundamental rule of how the psychoanalytic method is applied, requires an ability to pretend, to suspend judgment, and to imagine much as we do in play and playfulness. It is expected that as a psychoanalytic treatment proceeds, the analysand, with the help of hearing himself or herself in the presence of the analyst, with the assistance provided by interpretations and working through, will become increasingly able to approximate the optimal free association capacity and expression—increasingly able to be "playful" as an adult or to play freely as a child.

In conclusion, through play and playfulness, uncertainty can become the stimulus for more pleasurable and productive approximations of reality and for more assured continuities between the past and the present, as a reassuring preparation for the future.

References

Freud, A. (1965). *Normality and Pathology in Childhood*. New York: Int. Univ. Press.

Freud, S. (1905). Jokes and their relation to the unconscious. *S.E.*, 8.

———. (1908). Creative writers and day-dreaming. *S.E.*, 9:141–153.

———. (1909). Analysis of a phobia in a five-year-old boy. *Collected Papers*, 3:149–289.

———. (1914). Remembering, repeating and working through. *S.E.*, 12:145–156.

———. (1933). New introductory lectures on psycho-analysis. *S.E.*, 22:3–182.

Loewald, H. W. (1978). *Psychoanalysis and the History of the Individual*. New Haven: Yale Univ. Press.

Mayes, L. C. (1991). Exploring internal and external worlds. *Psychoanal. Study Child*, 46:3–36.

Plaut, E. A. (1979). Play and adaptation. *Psychoanal. Study Child*, 34:217–232.

Reichardt, E. (1985). On music: Cognition and archaeological meaning-schemata. *Scand. Psychoanal. Rev.*, 8:100.

Sacks, O. (1990). Neurology and the soul. *N.Y. Rev. Books*, Nov. 22.

Solnit, A. J. (1987). A psychoanalytic view of play. *Psychoanal. Study Child*, 42:205–319.

————. (1989). Memory as preparation. In *Dimensions of Psychoanalysis*, ed. J. Sandler. London: Karnac Books, pp. 193–217.

Solnit, A. J., and Kris, M. (1967). Trauma and infantile experiences. In *Psychic Trauma*, ed. S. S. Furst. New York: Basic Books, pp. 175–220.

Spitz, R. A. (1945). Hospitalism. *Psychoanal. Study Child*, 1:53–74.

Waelder, R. (1933). The psychoanalytic theory of play. *Psychoanal. Q.*, 2:208–224.

Winnicott, D. W. (1958). The capacity to be alone. In *The Maturational Processes and the Facilitating Environment*. New York: Int. Univ. Press, 1965, pp. 29–36.

3

Playing: Technical Implications

Peter B. Neubauer, M.D.

It is not unexpected that the exploration of the many meanings of play leads to technical considerations. The understanding of the function of the mind affects the psychoanalytic process of intervention. As we know, any outline of psychoanalytic technique is hazardous not only because it could be mechanically applied but also because there are so many individual variations and constellations that interventions that may be useful at one time may be inappropriate at another.

Keeping this in mind, I shall discuss technical considerations under four headings: (1) the role of displacement in play, (2) the participatory role of the analyst in the play, (3) play as a preparation for the next step in development, and (4) play and playfulness in adult analysis.

The Role of Displacement in Play

Freud understood very early that the play of children transforms passivity into activity and provides a change from the experience of being a victim to that of being the aggressor. Furthermore, this change can be a replay of the original situation, or it can employ the mechanism of displacement. This serves the purpose of achieving distance from the unpleasant affect of the primary situation to allow the ego to find solutions. The first model of play is exemplified by the child who returns home from the dentist and now plays dentist. The second refers to Little Hans, in whom the fear of the father is displaced by the fear of horses. Another alternative is shown by the child playing that he is a knight or a soldier with weapons that give him the power to defeat his enemies.

If we consider the role of play to be an attempt at finding new solutions to conflicts, it is important that we permit the child to complete the play in order to observe what the acceptable solution is, or to see whether mounting anxiety will terminate the play prematurely. We can find here a parallel to the dream and dreaming that leads to a nightmare.

Many children resent vehemently the analyst's attempt to interrupt their play in order to elicit more associations or to undo displacement, just as the daydreamer resents any interference before the wish fulfillment has been achieved. In play we can observe the powerful need for gratification of the drive components and the need of the ego to master the play. Thus we have to follow its course to its preferred solution, as we follow the dreams before we expect associations. We know of the repetitive play in which the child, over a long period of time, is unable to find a solution. The repetition can be modified only when the analyst interprets defense and finds access by other means to the unconscious fantasies. But we have to keep in mind Waelder's suggestion (1932) that the repetition of play may allow a piece-meal, slow modification of the earlier conflicts over a long period of time, thereby leading to significant psychic rearrangements.

In Winnicott's sense (1971), play is located in the mind where unconscious and preconscious wishes meet reality and where in this transitional space new formulations, new combinations, and new integrations can occur. The child playing superman or superwoman suspends reality enough to follow the wish for unnatural power, but side by side the maintenance of reality prevents the wish to go so far that he or she will fly out the window. Sometimes, when observing a child's intense and dramatic play, we find it surprising that enough reality is retained that there is no harm to the child or others.

Winnicott has shown that the inanimate world can be part of the transitional world where the "blanket" is endowed with human characteristics. Thus, to reduce play in the psychoanalytic situation to only the historically determined conditions and employ it just to reconstruct earlier experiences is to strip play of its creative element. The child who plays dentist after she has received dental treatment guides us to her original fear of being the passive victim, but she also alerts us to her capacity to use play to undo this passivity. One would surely give both experiences due recognition and appreciate the mind's ability to use play as a repair. A one-sided approach that leans on the technical aim to link the displaced content of play to the primary experience neglects those elements of play that search for solutions in an arena in which it can succeed. This raises the question of whether children can achieve solutions using the defense of displacement. The term *defense* is used here in full recognition of the psychic use of defense as a normal function. Or the question may be posed: which conflicts, or aspects of conflicts, at which time in development can be worked through in displacement? We also have to recognize the nonconflictual strivings of the ego, the maturational and developmental pull toward reorganization.

This is an area that needs much investigation. In each individual case the analytic process will reveal the points of fixation, the relentless power of the unconscious fantasies, and the degree of flexibility available for trying out new solutions when there is distance from the original painful experience.

I do not question the value of our theoretical model of conflicts, but rather stress the *weight* we assign to the mind's search for relief and sustenance, new choices, and new integrations, while I recognize the weight of the repetition of old conflicts. One can also consider the connection between the content of a child's dream and the content of a specific wish fulfillment in play and assess the power of the censors, while we are aware of the obvious difference of the levels of consciousness in dream and in play. Play of children is bound to action; and enactment of the past and present will therefore involve the action of the analyst. Side by side our verbal responses assist in building a bridge between the present and the past in the life of the child, leading to the transformation of the act to the thought, to put into words that which the child still needs to enact.

We have again to differentiate those conditions in which the repetition does not lead to a new solution and those acts that provide discharge patterns that permit new forms of psychic constellations. It is understood that the child needs to be able to symbolize in order to fulfill the role of play and to employ the mechanism of displacement.

The following vignette illustrates this point. A four-and-a-half-year-old boy is at the beginning of his psychoanalysis. He enters and immediately announces that he is a ghostbuster. He has three cars; he declares that the analyst is his partner in busting the ghosts and assigns three other cars to him, though they are smaller than his. He proceeds to slay a ghost, demanding that the analyst participate. But he changes his aim and is satisfied to jail them. He says, "Now we are both leaders; you are on my side."

This vignette documents the displacement of the struggle from the original objects to the ghosts. The analyst is invited to participate in the play. That the boy asks the analyst to be an ally in his fight informs the analyst about his patient's ability to establish a treatment alliance. With this alliance the child wishes to take on the fight with the ghost, and he also wishes to be the more powerful of the partners. His change from slaying the enemies to jailing them deserves notice, as we are still too early in the analysis to know whether this expresses his fear of total destruction of love objects or is a beginning compromise solution of his phallic or oedipal strivings, or whether both aims coexist. He can accompany the play-act with verbal comments, which will also allow the therapist to take part in the play on an active and a verbal level. The boy is a fighter at home, primarily with his mother; he is afraid of his father but tries heroically to have him as a friend, which only leads to further disappointments. We do not yet know the meaning of the ghost, who he is or they are, and on which developmental level the child experiences the fear and carries out his fight.

This play, in many variations, was repeated over one year, and he continued to need the help of the new ally to become more courageous in winning the fight. The question arose of how long this alliance should go on to give the patient the assistance he asked for: how far could it go to support the developmental progression? What would have happened if the analyst had instead interpreted his fears of doing it alone, his castration fears, or those that may have been prephallic? Often the analyst chooses a middle ground, chooses to open doors to unconscious fantasies while participating in the alliance. The child will guide us in the balancing act, and often enough he will insist that he has to experience the partnership "in deeds, in action," since at that age the words alone do not have reparative power. This need for the concrete experience has many roots and varies greatly from child to child. The dependency on the adult demands expression of the adult's availability to protect. This need emerges with increased significance when there is deprivation in the object relations of the child, or when there has been a disruption of them. Thus, the rule of abstinence, the wish for the analyst to be a real person as well, and the transference projections have to be understood in the context of the object relations, and they will color the analytic interventions.

These explorations demand an additional consideration. Is the wish to make the analyst an ally a transference expression, a repetition of the relationship with the father, or is the analyst a new object that permits new experiences where others failed? When we have evidence that there has been deprivation or developmental deviation, our model of treatment based on conflicts will have to become complemented by additional interventions. Even when there are sufficient neurotic conflicts to select analysis as the treatment of choice, there are often other pathological conditions that will influence the scope, the when and how, of our interventions.

I referred to the role of deprivation and its effect on the technical implications. Other influences that may have to be taken into account include physical illness, maturational or developmental delays, precocity, or the unevenness of the ego apparatus.

The Participation of the Analyst in the Play

At the appropriate time the analyst may suggest that he or she wishes to help fight these threatening ghosts and, in order to help, would like to know what these ghosts want and why they are after the patient. The importance here is that during this time, these explorations are offered *within* the context of the play's aim and *within* the arena of the displacement. After this step, the analyst may become active in the assigned role, furthering new solutions or at least offering the patient's ego new choices.

Still, such approaches appear to lean too strongly on the ego's faculty to consider suggestions; we seem to be paying insufficient attention to the power of unconscious fantasies and to the defenses against them. As the playing continues and changes occur through the realignment of drive, ego, and superego influences, the analyst's participation in the reenactment and verbal expression can stress either one or the other factor, dependent on his or her understanding of the underlying conflict and defenses.

It would lead us too far away from our topic to include here all the other components of child analysis as they intersect with playing during and as part of treatment. There is the significant extra-play relationship to the analyst, which allows us to observe the difference between this relationship and the role given the analyst in the play. There are often drawings and paintings, the expression of motor action outside of the playing, the demand for direct gratification.

What I am stressing is that our understanding that play is an attempt to resolve conflicts should be employed in reaching these new solutions. We have to keep in mind that children play in order to dissolve not only old conflicts but also those normal and abnormal conflicts appropriate to the phase in which they happen to be during the period of analysis. Maturational and developmental processes may transform conflicts during phase progression. Their appearance in the play demands a careful differentiation in order to intervene appropriately and not to confuse normal conflicts with pathological ones, new conflicts with those that are repeated. Playing gives the opportunity to make these decisions and to choose the mode of intervention.

Play as Preparation for the Future

The aim of adult analysis has at times been defined as the elimination of past influences that interfere with the appropriate ego functions, and the aim of child analysis is the undoing of those past factors that arrest or deviate development. Thus, reconstruction and construction of the past, the lifting of the repressed, and regression to points of fixation guide our interventions. The genetic point of view becomes a pivotal orientation of the analyst's work with children; after the elimination of early conflicts, development will then be able to correct itself. The increased interest in development and maturation toward new phase organizations and new integrations of psychic forces lends a new dimension to child analysis. Anna Freud's work, especially her propositions of lines of development (1965), adds this dimension to the understanding of the child's health and abnormality.

When we examine the playing of the child, we observe drive influences, ego and superego functions as they contribute to the manifestations of symptoms and the derailment of the developmental progression. I want to emphasize that the play reveals not only points of fixation but also the steps that lead the child into the future. When he turns passive into active, he accepts a role "as he wishes to be or wishes to become." He wants to be a hero, to resolve preoedipal and oedipal strivings, but he also ascribes to the hero certain faculties: how to maneuver an army, how to fence with his sword, how to pilot the airplane or drive the car, how to build bridges and jails. The latency child will spend much time improving those skills that served to solve past problems and to prepare himself for future function. What he wishes to become may be an escape from the conflicts, a denial of past failures, or a reaction formation that attempts to compensate for inadequacies. The play may reveal the influence of the ego ideal and the work of the ego to master.

Thus we attempt to understand play in the context of the child's psychic structure and where the child locates himself in the developmental process—that is, within an orderly developmental sequence. Is the child primarily past-oriented, or is he bound to the reality and concreteness of the present, or do his strivings emphasize future attainments?

When a child's developmental and maturational pull is powerful, or when a new phase orients her toward new directions, she may resist looking at and reexperiencing the past. She wishes instead to change insight into foresight. It will influence our play participation—how the past has to be reorganized under the auspices of future goals. It will affect the tolerance for postponement of gratification while she is impatient with the present. This is different from children with strong regressive swings, who have the wish to experience now what they had wished to experience in the past; they need to repeat past pleasures to fulfill now what they had wished for in the past.

A seven-year-old boy plays that one of the Ninja turtle dolls is an attractive, very fat, "blown-up lady"; she is getting married. All the other doll turtles are present, and the turtle Michaelangelo snuggles up behind her, sniffing her "tushy." The patient gets more and more excited and anxious.

Then the husband comes, and he knows if he kisses her once, they will be separated for at least ten years.

Here we see the preoedipal excitation and the banishment as punishment. The regressive pull is evident; the forward movement blocked. Here the analytic intervention will address itself to undue fixation and regression; the anal component and the separation fears intervene in the appropriate developmental task. In other children the forward pull into latency or adolescence may avoid the solution of preoedipal or oedipal conflicts or rely on the new maturation and extrafamiliar expansion to overcome older conflicts.

Another form of play shows the complexity of psychic functions. It is the conscious use of play to gratify conscious interests. I refer to the doctor play of children. Under the guise of playing doctor and patient, they satisfy the sexual curiosity that cannot be pursued directly. Whether this is done as a cover should outsiders observe them or as a cover for their own guilt or shame is not always clear.

As the displacement is not unconscious, the children use an acceptable disguise that is distant from the original intent, using the appearance of sublimation to appease the superego demand. This disguise is not uncommon; one can observe it in the play of siblings when the older one initiates "play" with the younger one to satisfy his rivalrous hostility. This often ends up in fights or in the victim crying. The older behaves "innocently" for it was only meant to be play.

There are many examples in adult life of playfulness being used as a disguise to dim the sense of guilt. Here play is an attempt not to resolve problems, to search for new creative solutions, but to retreat from reality to avoid the consequences of self-serving intentions. The "as-if" behavior or personality disorder may be based on this use of playing with the suspension of reality without psychotic disorganization. This technique of intervention requires us to know whether play is still play.

The technical implications are clear and the intervention within the play quite different from the fantasies of a child who experiences a pull into latency, avoiding the resolution of preoedipal or oedipal conflicts by building latency structures or by relying on the new organization to modify earlier conflicts.

Play and Playfulness in Adult Analysis

How can we apply our knowledge of the role of play in child analysis to the analytic process for adults? If we hold the position that play is an attribute of children only, or when our definition of play refers to action as an essential characteristic, then its application to adult analysis will be limited to the "playfulness" of the adult. If, on the other hand, we consider play to be an attempt at a solution of conflicts, of the establishment of ego mastery, whether this is done in action, words, or fantasy, then we find a more common ground that links child and adult analysis.

Freud (1905), in his earliest reference to play as a joke, regarded play as compelling children to practice their capacities, and he viewed play with words and thoughts as motivated by pleasurable affects and economy.

When play is understood as an expression of pleasurable strivings, and by the suspension of the demands of the reality principle, without losing the capacity for reality testing, play is a mental faculty that demands new mental combinations. Thus play and creativity are close associates, and the role of imagination must be added to the role of fantasy and wish fulfillment.

It is not surprising therefore that Winnicott (1971) referred to psychoanalysis as play in which the conscious suspension of the demands of reality without losing the sense of reality is important to free preconscious and unconscious fantasies and wishes and is a necessary condition for the therapeutic endeavor.

Many of the considerations that I have outlined as having technical implications for the analysis of children can therefore be examined as to their applicability to the analysis of adults. I have stated that displacement is a significant mechanism that allows a distancing from the primary unacceptable experiences, and I have raised the question of whether and under what circumstances and to what degree one can work through and resolve conflicts in displacement. I assume that this question is of equal interest to the analysts of adults. Beyond transference as displacement, our adult patients often re-"play" primary conflicts with their siblings in their friendships and later in their rivalry with their colleagues or their mates; and thus we can observe in adult analysis the powerful mechanism of displacement. Therefore, what I have said about the child analyst's stance and technical considerations may also be applicable in adult analysis.

This would caution us not to overemphasize or reduce the psychoanalytic process to the genetic search without supporting the opening of new vistas that span the past, the present, and the future. The freeing of association is therefore expanded from the narrower view that it is a path only to early conflicts and, by modifying the influence of the censors, enables imagination and playfulness to facilitate the psychoanalytic process. Surely, such expansion will be supported by the "playfulness" of the analyst, when we understand this to imply a collaborative search and when it is not misunderstood to be a deviation from the serious stance of the analyst or his or her neutral position. This reminds us of Freud's formulation (1905) that the opposite of play is not what is serious but what is real.

One obvious difference between the play of adult patients and the play of the child is the collaboration of the analyst who accepts an assigned role. The analyst of adults will expose and explore the patient's wishes, what and who he wishes the analyst to be, whether it is a repetition of primary object choices or represents the patient's present unfulfilled needs. I have described different models of pathology and of interventions; this is not specific for children. The same widening scope, the understanding that neurotic conflict may coexist with deficiencies or developmental and maturational deviation, is to be recognized in the treatment of adults. Transference as repetition, or the analyst as a new object based on structural and extra-neurotic pathology, demands widening of our intervention strategies. As the action part of the play of children is transformed to the verbal and thought arena, the participating actions of the analyst are modified as well.

Preparation for the Future

We often encounter the assumption that the developmental and maturational pull is an exclusive characteristic of childhood and adolescence. The adult organization and reorganization are different from those that occur in childhood, when phase organizations with the establishment of new primacies and discontinuities reveal qualities quite different from the changes that occur in adult life.

In old age there is even a regressive pull in which the preparation for the future is overshadowed by the reliving of the past. Still, we must keep in mind where individuals see themselves in the context of their life span, the self within the dimension of the individual sense of time. From the study of children, we are alerted to the great variations in which some wish to be as they have been and continue to seek fulfillments of past wishes, whereas others live in the present and emphasize whom they wish to become; for them, gratification lies in future achievements. This can also be observed in adult patients whose insight may lie more heavily on hindsight, present view, or foresight. The playfulness of the adult will reveal whether the conflict is located in the past, in the present, or in expectations of the future, as it is revealed in dream fantasies and how the conflict is resolved.

It is clinically self-evident that we do not consider either of these positions to be exclusive, that there will always be a mixture of or interplay among past, present, and future. I am concerned here with the relative emphasis the individual patient gives to one or the other. It points to the openness of the analyst to the whole life process and his or her inclination not to reduce the analytic work to the resolution of past conflicts and leave the rest to the ego of the patient as it searches for new solutions.

Solnit (1984) explored how to anticipate specific events such as illness, surgery, divorce, other separations, or any potentially traumatic event. I have addressed myself to how to prepare for a new step in development. Solnit writes about the knowledge of the past as a preparation for both the present and the future and therefore emphasizes the continuity in the change of developmental and psychic structure. He cites case material that demonstrates that "when the present obliterates the past [we have to help the] ongoing construction of the past as preparation for the present and future" (p. 618); and he stresses the importance of making an effort to revise the past in preparing for the future, emphasizing the search for solutions of old conflicts to safeguard the future. In his examination of the role of memory, he states that the past "can be revised in memory . . . to achieve the coherency that results when traumatic or potentially traumatic experience is worked through and integrated into the fabric of a coherent personality of the developing child, adolescent, or adult" (pp. 631–632). When we include in this formulation the function of play, the revision in memory, then it confirms the need to see both in the context of the time sequences as the past is reshaped in order to adapt to the present and to prepare for the future.

References

Freud, A. (1965). *Normality and Pathology in Childhood*. New York: Int. Univ. Press.

Freud, S. (1905). Jokes and their relation to the unconscious. *S.E.*, 8.

Solnit, A. J. (1984). Preparing. *Psychoanal. Study Child*, 39:613–632.

Waelder, R. (1932). The psychoanalytic theory of play. *Psychoanal. Q.*, 2:208–224, 1933.

Winnicott, D. W. (1971). *Playing and Reality*. London: Tavistock.

Part II
Clinical Dimensions

4

To Play or Not to Play

Delia Battin, M.S.W.

To play or not to play—that is the question that must confront every child at one developmental moment or another, even when childish spontaneity seems to suggest a total absence of conflict. Play, for all its frivolity, is very serious business indeed, as Montaigne remarked hundreds of years ago.

The factors that impede or promote play are difficult to grasp. When all goes well constitutionally and developmentally, play seems so natural that the expression "as easy as child's play" seems to grow out of universal experience. When things go awry, play gets impeded or destroyed by etiologies that may be subtle or gross and yet difficult to pinpoint. The psychoanalytic study of one case in depth, though it lacks statistical consensual validation, does offer a glimpse of the subtle cogwheels of play as they are set in motion and gather momentum. This microanalysis of a subtle process in statu nascendi or in statu morendi* should yield not only diagnostic information but therapeutic strategies. By studying the gestation or demise of play, I hope to be able to discover ways of preserving it.

Case Presentation

I will present the case of an intelligent, precocious neurotic child and attempt to show how endowment, precocity, and trauma disturbed her playfulness and at times made her unable to play at all. I wish to show how the therapeutic process released her play from neurotic conflict.

Background

Stephanie began treatment at age seven. She sat on a grown-up chair and said she had asked her parents to see a therapist because she wanted to

I would like to thank Eugene J. Mahon and Peter B. Neubauer for their insightful critiques of previous versions of this chapter.

*I wish to find a contrapuntal phrase to capture play not only as it is born but as it may prematurely die.

try to understand what it was like for her sister, Lisa, two and a half years her junior, to be handicapped (Lisa was severely retarded, a source of tragic attention for the whole family). This representation of her own needs through identification with another, even more needy than herself, was typical of Stephanie's defensive character, largely expressed as her style of reaction formation and self-effacement.

Stephanie informed me she knew all about treatment from her parents who were both currently undergoing psychotherapy. "You talk and find out what's inside," she said. She was not sure how that worked. When I suggested that playing and talking might help figure out what she was worried about, Stephanie made it clear that play was not one of her interests: she felt much more comfortable with language than with play.

Stephanie proceeded to describe three dreams, explaining she knew of the importance of dreams. In one, Lisa was hanging from a refrigerator door, swinging in midair over a cliff. Stephanie tried to reach for her. Lisa fell into a lake. Stephanie felt so thirsty that she drank all the water in the lake. Lisa was lying at the bottom and got up. In the second dream, Stephanie was standing in front of a wall in her room with her mother and Lisa, as if waiting for an elevator. The wall opened up and an enormous spoon appeared. Stephanie got terribly frightened and woke up. In the third dream, Stephanie was walking with her father in a forest. Her father told her to go up a tree. She did. Magnificent scenery opened up in front of her eyes, a beautiful lake with big white swans.

These dreams obviously revealed much of the child's interior landscape. In the first dream, one could see her struggle between her wish to do away with Lisa and her reaction formation that dictated that she save her; in the second one, it seemed that Stephanie felt needy, scared of her needs, and experienced anger at not being spoon-fed perhaps; the third appeared to be a reflection of the child's turning to the father exclusively because of mother's preoccupation with Lisa. I made no interpretations, very much aware that Stephanie's pseudoadult behavior, including the narration of dreams, represented compliance and defense. As a matter of fact, this was confirmed months later when Stephanie said she had first come into treatment thinking I would be like a person with a crystal ball ready to see all her secrets, something quite frightening to her.

If dreams, not to mention all revelations in analysis, can be compared to crystal balls, it is crucial for a young analysand to know that only dreamers can discover the secrets they have hidden in crystal—with a little help, to be sure, from the analyst as experienced guide and interpreter.

I explained to Stephanie that it was understandable that she had many feelings about her troubled family; some of them she knew about, but others were unknown to her. The task would be to figure them all out in order to find ways to be less unhappy. I suggested again that we could play and talk. It seemed that Stephanie did not know about the pleasure or the healing powers of play. Each time she came, Stephanie walked straight to the grown-up chair, reiterating that she liked to converse with me, surely thinking she was an ideal patient.

Before proceeding any further with the analysis proper, let me give you some more background information. It was not surprising to hear her well-meaning parents describe Stephanie as an "ideal" child: sensitive, responsible, very communicative, and attentive to everybody's needs. They thought she did well in school. The only negative comment they had repeatedly heard had to do with Stephanie's extreme shyness and tendency to withdraw in peer situations. Her mother had been concerned about Stephanie's potential aggression toward Lisa and had stopped Stephanie's "game," when she was about four, of lying down on top of Lisa. It was Stephanie who had called this a game.

Stephanie was a "wanted baby" after four years of marriage. As an infant, she was all smiles, very responsive, ate and slept well. Motor development followed normal or somewhat precocious lines. She sat at five months, crawled soon thereafter, and walked at twelve months. A brief period of stranger anxiety was present at seven months.

Stephanie was breast-fed. At ten months, upon finding the cup, she weaned herself promptly. Her first word at eleven months was "cookie." The beginning of the second year reflected a typical love affair with the world as Stephanie went through her practicing phase. The rapprochement process was unremarkable except for a meaningful detail: around eighteen months Stephanie tried and succeeded in changing her own Pampers, which was much applauded by her parents. At two, Stephanie spoke in full sentences. Toilet training presented no problems. At about two and a half, she one day asked her mother to hold her on the toilet; her mother did and from that day on Stephanie went to the toilet on her own.

Very soon after Stephanie had toilet-trained herself, Lisa was born. Her parents remembered very little about Stephanie after that, so preoccupied were they with their feelings about having a very retarded daughter and with their marital relationship, which ended in divorce when Stephanie was five and a half. After the divorce, Stephanie showed some intermittent clinging and dependent behavior.

Stephanie apparently was not exposed to children her age until she was three and a half, when she entered a play group. She showed no separation anxiety, perhaps helped along by her transitional object, a lilac-colored blanket that had been her constant companion since birth. In the play group, Stephanie was extremely shy and sensitive, her feelings easily hurt.

Stephanie entered school at four. She was much liked by her teachers, who were concerned about her excessive sensitivity and her tendency to befriend children with problems. Her teachers did not communicate any concern about Stephanie's problems in the area of play. It was to be Stephanie herself who described to me how uninterested she was in playing games, especially kickball.

Course of Analysis

During the first eighteen months of treatment Stephanie studiously avoided toys that most children take to readily. There was no play in evidence during this first phase of the analysis. In fact, instead of playing, Stephanie sat on a chair like a grown-up, her pseudoadult presentation of herself quite revealing in one way and quite resistant in another. I had to be acutely sensitive to this technical dilemma in which defense, fantasy, character resistance, and transference seemed to be stifling her playfulness. Let me be more specific. Stephanie talked about Lisa's disease, on the one hand, and her pet gerbil Anemone's death, on the other. Anemone had been crushed by a rock in his cage. Stephanie bemoaned the fate of little helpless creatures who can be crushed by big forces, an obvious reference to her early fears in the relationship with me. Anemone's replacement killed her own offspring, which provided Stephanie a peg on which she could hang similar and even deeper transference fears. She said this new gerbil had killed its baby because it was only a "practice baby" and therefore dispensable. The obvious connections between the "practice baby" and her retarded sister were easier for Stephanie to see than the less obvious connection in the relationship with me. In other words, she was able to remark that the damaged "practice baby" gerbil was like Lisa. But she was not able to say, "Maybe I'm just an analytic 'practice baby' of yours who could easily be gotten rid of."

This worry that the strong, the big, the adult, could easily dispense with the weak, the small, the infantile, was revealed once again when she mentioned an idea she had had when her mother was pregnant with Lisa. At first she thought that her mother's belly would blow up if she touched it (an obvious reference to her own aggression); but then she also commented about herself being in the womb and how her growing bigger may have caused a boy, who was with her in the womb, to shrivel up. This multiple determined fantasy, or "idea," as Stephanie called it, could be understood from many angles, but at that point Stephanie seemed to be wondering and worrying about her status in the new relationship with me. Was it safe to be a child with me? Would I crush her like a helpless gerbil? Would she be dispensable as a retarded "practice child?" Was she safe? Would I be able to accept her if, instead of being the victim, she was an aggressor who made boys shrivel up?

The interpretive stance during the early months was a typical defense analysis posture well suited to help Stephanie feel understood. I sympathized with the plight of helpless small gerbils and told her one could understand a small gerbil wanting to be bigger and more adult so that the stone could never crush him. Through the interpretation of such displacements, Stephanie gradually became more comfortable with direct expression of affect in the relationship with me, though she still was unable to play. This became obvious toward the middle of the first year when Stephanie elaborated on the fantasy about Lisa in her mother's belly. This time the fantasy had a new wrinkle: the baby was punching the mother in the face. This fantasy was a response to Stephanie letting herself become aware that I saw other patients, like a little boy she noticed leaving my office. She was angry with me for spending time with the boy. In fact, she was able to say that seeing that boy made her feel like number 2 in my affections. When I interpreted the displaced aggression, saying "That will fix me!" Stephanie laughed and seemed pleased that I could tolerate the attack; in fact, she revealed even more of her aggressive wishes—mainly that Lisa should go back into her mommy's belly and "shrivel up" till she became sperm again and could go back into her father's penis.

This direct expression of anger toward her mother, toward Lisa, toward her father, and toward me led to a castration dream. In the dream, her father was a slave sawing wood and cut his penis in half.* Stephanie's associations made it clear that earlier she had thought she was a slave in the analysis: she had the idea I would be wearing a green Indian robe and would hypnotize her with a watch, learn her secrets, and divulge them. One meaning of this dream became clear when Stephanie mentioned an association that dealt with her wish to go to a Halloween party as a bag lady, even though her mother wanted her to disguise her gender and go as

---

*This castration fantasy, or "half castration fantasy" to be more precise (Neubauer, 1989), probably had multiple determinants, but the most obvious and cogent one is that Stephanie's conflict with aggression might have led to her wish that only half of her fantasy would come true. It is as if she were saying that half of the Oedipus complex would be enough for her to handle.

a bum. She obviously rejected her mother's projected penis envy; yet in the next breath she said she would not mind having something special, as a bum had. I completed her thought, saying, "You mean a penis?" And Stephanie laughed. She went on to say that girls have something special, too: they make babies; but they need the man's seeds. If boys could pee standing up and play with their penis, she could play with herself, too.

This sexual aspect of playing is not without significance; in conjunction with the problems of aggression, it may well have contributed much to Stephanie's inhibitions. When asked what she thought as she played with herself, she described the following fantasy: she dropped money on subway tracks; the money kept growing in quantity; she tried to get it, fighting a monster who also wanted it. In fact, Stephanie admitted that the masturbation occurred after her fantasy as a way of calming the anxieties that the fantasy evoked. All this material emerged in response to my interpretation of Stephanie's direct expression of anger in the analytic situation. Stephanie was asserting herself with me, but at the same time she worried that maybe she was being too phallic and in danger of "monstrous" retaliation and castration.

Toward the middle of the second year of treatment, there was even more graphic evidence of Stephanie's increasing spontaneity. She was more the child now and less the adult; she let me catch a glimpse of her greed as she said she wanted more time with me. But even more significant, she complained one day that she had missed a rhythm class in school to come for her analytic session.* She immediately wanted to undo her aggression by saying, "But I have you." I interpreted her defensiveness, telling her I knew how important rhythm was for her; I could understand her mixed feelings when she was presented with a conflict between rhythm class and analysis. Stephanie turned to the Plasticine in the office for the first time. This was a very significant moment: my tolerance of Stephanie's conflict allowed her to feel more comfortable with very personal, even negative feelings toward a significant object. Her turning to play as a response to this intervention confirms the therapeutic power of interpretation.

Stephanie made a "duck with no brain" out of the Plasticine, describing at the same time her fantasy of being a butterfly able to fly to other planets, still checking on Lisa from time to time, the "duck with no brain." The "duck with no brain," which at first would seem to represent her anger at me or retaliatory anger at herself, had become displaced onto Lisa in a

*Rhythm class referred to a combination of gymnastics and dance that Stephanie was beginning to like very much.

manner that was quite characteristic of her. (I will return to this analytic moment later in my discussion.) Stephanie could fly away from the anger, but not from its imagined consequences. As she struggled with her affects, she found a sublimated expression of them in creating a poisonous mushroom out of Plasticine, a gift that I accepted nondefensively as an important direct communication to me. This was a pivotal metaphoric moment: it allowed Stephanie to go on and review genetic material that shed new light on her current defensiveness. She described how left out she felt after Lisa was born, how her mother played with Lisa, making passageways with sheets and pillows, and she, Stephanie, made her own bigger ones, repressing anger and feelings of rejection in an orgy of industry. Stephanie also remembered other defensive precocious industriousness on her part: at eighteen months she would diaper herself—not because she was wet but to invoke the good feelings of her mother diapering her.

In this very important session, a meaningful piece of her past had been connected with her current defensiveness. Stephanie was beginning to develop insight into the precocious pseudoadult self-reliance and how it clearly screened a child self, full of need, longing, envy, and anger. Stephanie was aware of this new way of looking at and understanding things. For the first time she commented on the difference between me and other adults. Stephanie felt that I was able to help her with certain worries that other grownups could not.

Stephanie's ability to tell me she missed the latency activity in school (rhythm class) and her newfound ability to use play materials in the analysis were important indicators that she was beginning to settle into a more age-appropriate sense of herself. This became clearer in her relationship with her peers and also found significant expression in the analysis. The child who used to sit stiffly and talk now turned to drawing and playing with Plasticine with all the industry so characteristic of this stage of development. The analysis from this point on became a mixture of playing and words.

Stephanie's newfound comfort and playfulness were not free of intrapsychic turmoil. She wondered if people moved in their dreams like Lisa, an obvious reference to her sister's condition and to her worries that wishes would not confine themselves safely to the world of dreams but might require acting out for their fullest expression. I told her that getting in touch with all her feelings would obviously frighten her if she thought she would lose control of them. She immediately turned to the Plasticine and fashioned pellets of various colors, which she placed in a container that she had made. She said the blue pellets were sad feelings, the red the mad ones, the green her mean feelings—and then there were gray pellets that were so-

so feelings, the ones that were not clear to her. I commented, "These are all the feelings we are trying to understand together."

The fear that people might move in their dreams was another example of one of Stephanie's basic dilemmas: unconscious instinctual desires could become conscious expressive activity if one was not careful. For Stephanie, being careful had meant not playing at all, thereby robbing herself of one of childhood's time-honored means of seeking solutions to dilemmas such as she was facing.

A little later, Stephanie told me how comfortable she felt with me. Yet it was not long before her new comfort aroused fear in her, expressed in the recovery of an early childhood memory or fantasy in which a piece of her transitional lilac-colored blanket was given to Lisa. It felt like a friend of hers was being cut rather than a piece of cloth. The transferential implication was clear: her newfound trust in me must inevitably lead to loss or something being cut off.

During the next few months—indeed, right up to the summer vacation— the analysis moved on two levels: Stephanie's deepening relationship with me and the history of her relationship with other objects. Her new ability to play with me had brought her closer to me than ever, not as a pseudoadult, but as an affective, playful, intimate child. She wanted to possess me unconditionally. She drew my bedroom with a single bed in it. She insisted that all the paintings she saw in the waiting room and in the office were done by me. While she examined this preoccupation with me, Stephanie also began to yearn for her "mother and father of old," as she put it. She longed for the relationship she had had with her mother before Lisa was born, and she envied Lisa's relationship with her father.

Stephanie's wish to recover her lost babyhood fascinated and frightened her. She noticed and tried the "baby" chairs in the playroom for the first time but retreated from her fantasy promptly by saying, "They are too hard." At that point she talked of an idea she used to have when she was little—that the baby's head would tear up the mother in the act of birth. It was clear that she was worried that her babyish regression in the analytic situation might destroy me. When this was interpreted to her, she expressed a wish that she and I might have a baby together.

As summer approached, Stephanie concocted a clever scheme that might undo some of her anticipated sadness in my absence. She would dictate her dreams to me before she left and would go on writing them down in my absence. While this material was under scrutiny, Stephanie brought a story she had written about her pet rabbit, which for the first time made me aware of what a bad speller and reader she was at nine and a half years old.

Her next association led to a genetic reconstruction: she used to dictate stories to her mother and read them to herself when she was missing her mother. She then remembered her lilac-colored blanket and how soothing it was and how the blanket was as old as herself. While she was re-creating these transitional, dyadic, blissful states in her current relationship with me, an unconscious fear emerged. She noticed two doors in my office. Maybe I had a husband. She repaired this narcissistic injury by suggesting that I marry her father. Later she said she wanted to marry me and remembered how she used to say that to her father when she was about three years old.

This wooing of me led to a dream in which she was on the balcony of a building like mine. A black-scaled monster went to her, asking for a kiss. She kissed him, but he threw her over the edge. While she spoke, she drew the dream, the act of drawing giving her some additional control when language seemed unable to carry the total affective load of the dream. The dream was an obvious punishment for her desire for me. Her plight at this point in the analysis could best be expressed in a poignant question she asked her father at that time: "How could a big penis fit into a little vagina?" Her father told her that when the vagina is lubricated the penis fits in easily. This physiologically correct answer did not address the psychological import of the child's question. But in all fairness, it was a difficult question to answer. I understood her question to reflect the transference love she held for me and whether her childish "anatomy" was good enough for me. The issue here was not anatomy alone but self-esteem and all the other components of her personality. I chose not to address this from an id vantage point but to be supportive to the ego that was daring to express very genuine affect to a grown-up. I told her that her love was important, the fact that she was small did not make her love small, and that in time she would be as big as I was; love is not measured by size or by weight but by how much you feel. Stephanie was able to say for the first time that she felt she had enough time with me. She added that when Lisa was home she was able to play "avalanche" with her and enjoy it.* Stephanie also mentioned she was worried about her reading and spelling difficulties in school. She thought her mother might help her with them.

The significance of the avalanche play can hardly be emphasized too

---

*"Avalanche" was a game Stephanie had recently made up. It involved a pillow and falling down; it had multiple determinants. One can see its origin in the "game" Stephanie had devised when Lisa was a baby and her mother had interrupted for fear of Stephanie's aggression.

much. When one considers that Stephanie had banished almost all expressions of rivalry and aggression from her behavior with Lisa after her mother had admonished her for the "lying-on-Lisa" game, this newfound ability to be aggressively playful with Lisa in the avalanche game was a developmental advance of the highest order. She played this game for months, as if to say she had finally found a way to topple the rival without harming or killing her. In this context, Stephanie's ability to discuss her reading and spelling difficulties without shame was an equally significant developmental achievement. Stephanie's reality testing had expanded considerably. Transference and play had to be given equal credit.

The post-avalanche phase of the analysis was very productive. Stephanie was less cautious in play and in transference elaborations as well. If the avalanche metaphor allowed her to revisit the lying-on-Lisa game and reclaim the imploded aggression for more adaptive expressiveness, the analysis from that point on was an attempt to claim or perhaps reclaim her lost phallic and phallic-oedipal enthusiasm.

Stephanie became interested again in the two doors in my office. She wondered if my husband used "the other door," as she called it. She wished I had no husband. She had an immediate castration dream. "She is going to the bathroom panting and making red stuff. Two teachers tell her it is her period." Stephanie's associations revealed that her period was indeed on her mind. In fact, she had seen her mother taking out a tampon, and Stephanie wondered what her own vagina was like. She did not dare to put her finger in there; it was scary—or maybe not. It was clear that Stephanie was worried about being punished for her wish to get rid of my husband, not to mention her father and mother in the positive and negative oedipal struggles. This was confirmed by Stephanie in an insight that contributed to her understanding of her oedipal conflicts and also to understanding her reading and writing difficulties. Stephanie said she had wished to undo the separation of her parents, undo her own oedipal triumph by writing letters from each parent to the other. But she had not been able to write at age five, and she had felt that she would never learn to read and write. It became clear that her inability to write the letters of reconciliation had led to the so-called learning disability.

Stephanie's self-image and body image were consolidating. She was beginning to think of her vagina not merely as castrated anatomy but as a fun feminine organ that made her the same as her mother and me. While she was becoming more comfortable with her vagina, her play repertoire expanded a little further: she became more comfortable at playing kickball with her peers.

Stephanie turned ten proudly, telling me she was now a two-digit citizen. It was not only in the schoolyard that Stephanie's freedom with playing became obvious. Play now became an ally of her associations to dreams as the next analytic hours demonstrated. She dreamed that her mother's boyfriend, Michael, and a Chinese lady were making love in a room on top of a football arena. Then, back in the apartment, Stephanie saw Michael and her mother fighting. First her mother was packing and stopped. Then Michael was leaving. As Stephanie described this dream, she made long blue nails for herself out of Plasticine. She said, "Chinese have very long nails." Then she rolled the nails into blue balls and said, "Disgusting." Then she asked me where I was from. I humorously said, "I'm not Chinese," implying that it was not within my power to grant her wish to remove the analytic situation to a faraway land where the incestuous implications of the material could be examined from a distance. Stephanie got the point: she was able to continue to unravel the meaning of her dream. She did want to make out with Michael and send her mother away. She also wanted me to be the Chinese lady and she the man. Both sides of her bisexuality could be examined. She played the recorder for the first time in my office. She remembered that when she was little she wanted to have both a penis and breasts.

Stephanie got furious about seeing a package with my name on it as "Mrs. Battin." She said now she knew for sure I was married. A few sessions later, she "nosed" the envelopes on my desk, looking for my husband's name. At the same time she pulled a hair out of her head, explaining that she had seen a movie in which a woman gave a lock of her hair to her lover as a token of love. She wanted to do the same with me. She also made reference to Rapunzel, who used her hair to acquire a prince and a baby. In that session she showed me she was losing a tooth and was excited about getting a new kitten. She also remembered that when she was little, she would roll toilet paper around her finger to make a tube, which she would then pee through to find out what it was like to have a penis, an example of early phallic play that must have succumbed rather quickly to conflict. In fact, Stephanie's phallic conflicts were not resolved until her analysis.

Both sides of the Oedipus complex, both sides of her bisexuality, found expression in this hour. She wanted to be nosy and phallic, on the one hand, and wanted to be castrated with no hair, on the other. If she could not have a penis, she certainly could get her prince and her baby, not to mention her kitten. She talked about getting married, having a boy and a girl, and becoming a second Cézanne, a woman Cézanne. As she looked at my degrees on the wall, she pulled out another strand of hair. This time she also said that girls have twelve holes while boys only have nine, another example of her struggle to have more than boys—concealing the obvious worry that perhaps she had less. At that point she said my husband had to be a nice man and she would live happily ever after with him. She immediately repudiated the wish, saying she was only joking.

This frankly oedipal behavior in the hour led to a dream that allowed us to reconstruct a primal scene fantasy. In the dream, Stephanie was exploring the school together with a boy, a schoolmate. She went by a door that looked like a saloon door: you could see under it. As she passed by, she first saw a naked woman. As she went back, she saw a couple making love in public. She felt it was disgusting to make love in public. I wondered if she had seen her parents making love when she was little. When little children see their parents making love, they often think they are fighting. Stephanie lit up: she had left out a piece of the dream. In the end she thought the couple was fighting, stuck together. She probably did see her parents making love. She remembered that at the time she had drawn a blind man and his woman fighting in a sleeping bag. She drew that scene as she talked.

That was also the time when she would dream of black-scaled monsters fighting. These monsters were like the one she had had to kiss before she was thrown over the balcony. She mentioned a dream from early on in the analysis, in which the monsters were punching babies. She also spoke of the faces of a man and a woman on a record cover: those faces had frightened her when she was little; they looked unreal, distorted. Now she remembered that at the time she had wished a picture of herself as a child would be included on the cover. I told Stephanie that the faces of her parents making love might have seemed distorted, given how angry she was for being excluded. Stephanie remembered that she had felt bad about her curiosity being aroused by the parental bedroom and the sexuality of her mother and father.

The analytic work on the primal scene was most productive. It allowed us to unravel several condensed developmental images. It would seem that the forbidden lying-on-Lisa game, her drawing of the blind man and woman fighting in the sleeping bag, the memory of the man and woman on the record cover and the excluded child, and her curiosity about the sexuality in the parental bedroom and again the excluded child all blended together in a neurotic knot that made it impossible for her to play with these ideas any further. At such developmental moments, repression and inhibition seem safer than curiosity and exploration until analysis can grease the wheels of development again.

Immediately after the primal scene reconstruction, Stephanie began to play with identification, a most important kind of playing that is, of course, mainly invisible. Let me explain. Stephanie went home, found a recipe, and began to cook before her mother came home from work. This to me did not seem like Stephanie being the adult, but rather Stephanie identifying with her mother, embracing a maternal sense of herself and enjoying herself. Stephanie's new attitude appeared in the analytic situation as well: for the first time she plopped down on the rug in the playroom, threw a tennis ball at me, and said, "Catch." She was indeed more playful, more like a typical latency ten-and-a-half-year-old. At the next session when she found a deck of cards, for the first time she invited me to play. Indeed, she seemed to be acting her age with more conviction than ever. She had discovered that play was fine and an ideal way to work out childhood conflicts. This remained true throughout the rest of the analysis.

Discussion

My discussion will focus initially on play and *regression* and on play and *aggression*. In play we see a complex compromise between forces of progression and forces of regression, not unlike an artist's creativity in which regression in the service of the ego is really regression in the service of progression. Ironically, it takes a healthy ego to regress adaptively and flexibly rather than utterly and irrevocably. Stephanie's analysis makes it clear that two images of regression may have given her pause and interrupted her playfulness: (1) the image of the baby destroying the mother's body in the act of birth and its counterpart, the image of the analyst destroying the practice baby analysand in the regressive forces of analysis; and (2) the chronic experience of her sister's permanent regression, a retardation that seemed to defy all therapeutic attempts to undo it. It was as if her sister was playing dead and could not stop. If Stephanie was conflicted about the concept of regression and its consequences, the nature of aggression and its outcomes also raised many confusing questions in her mind.

It seems very probable that Stephanie's first playful (or not so playful) activities with her sister (lying on Lisa at four) were inhibited either by Stephanie's own fear of instinctual expression or by her mother's critique of this play or most likely by both. I do not mean to suggest that Stephanie's problem with aggression began with the lying-on-Lisa game; rather, the game, a product of the conflict, also reflected the conflict that must have begun before the game and certainly persisted after the disappearance of this game. If one were to draw a developmental line from the lying-on-Lisa game, to the avalanche game, to kickball, to the catch-a-ball play with me, one would have a sense of the vicissitudes her aggressive and libidinal instincts passed through from age two and a half to ten and a half.

To leave the transference out of this picture would distort the progression fundamentally, of course. In fact, the first year of Stephanie's treatment highlights the transference resistance that so inhibited her play. Each interpretation of this transference resistance seemed to grant Stephanie permission to lean on the transference as much as she wished. Stephanie's expectation was that I, the analyst, would forbid displays of aggression in transference play, just as the mother had forbidden aggression against the sibling. In this context, Stephanie's achievement in the avalanche game was most significant. It signaled her retrieval of her aggressive instincts from neurotic inhibition and their rechanneling into age-appropriate expressions in childhood activity.

It is interesting to compare the concept of transference and the concept of play. Both concepts rely on displacement to set them in motion. In transference, unconscious attitudes toward significant early objects are displaced onto current objects, particularly so in the regressive climate of the analytic situation. In play, a child displaces intrapsychic concerns with animate objects such as parents, siblings, and peers onto the smaller, more controllable, inanimate world of toys and playthings. We know from experience with children in institutions who cannot play at all that children can invest love in playthings only after the primary care givers have invested love in them first. In libidinal as in financial economics, you cannot withdraw what has not been deposited! An analyst dealing with transference or play is basically studying displacements, sometimes promoting them, sometimes dismantling them, depending on a host of technical factors from diagnosis to stages of treatment (early or late phases of transference neurosis, and so on). The details of the technical considerations need not concern us here. The point being stressed is that transference and play are measures of psychic development. Their absence or presence is not without psychological implications. In Stephanie's case, it seems clear that the transference fears of an analytic practice baby being crushed by a powerful adult analyst need to be addressed before the analysand can feel safe enough in the analytic situation to take a chance on the displacements of play.

Stephanie's libidinal development could be outlined in a manner similar to that outlined for the aggressive instinct earlier. She believed that a child's needs were too much for a parent to handle and that children should find their own narcissistic ways of weaning themselves, diapering themselves, toilet-training themselves, amusing themselves on their own terms. Stephanie's play with sheets is a graphic example of how her dependency needs, object-related at first, began to turn toward narcissistic solutions: when Stephanie found Lisa and her mother playing with sheets, Stephanie's attempts to play with larger sheets on her own was a narcissistic strategy that could hardly be expected to bring the child any significant relief from her conflicts. The giant spoon in one of the first dreams she reported was surely a representation of the underlying deprivation that narcissistic maneuvers could never satisfy. The great needs that the spoon symbolized did in fact find preoedipal and oedipal expression in dramatic imagery, which the brief report of her analysis has outlined.

Stephanie's ability to "play" therapeutically with primal scene material and oedipal fantasy in the later stages of her analysis stands in striking contrast to the inhibition that characterized the beginning of her analysis. Her first drawing of the blind man in the sleeping bag seems to have been a furtive depiction of sexuality and its consequences (a blind man and his girlfriend in makeshift sleeping quarters) when compared to her later drawings of the analyst's imagined sexual life. Her dreams and drawings of monsters display a similar progression from preoedipal panic (a monster that punches babies) to oedipal anxieties and attempted mastery (she dares to kiss even when the monster may retaliate).

It is interesting to ponder the relationship between play in general and drawing in particular. A child's aesthetic life has many components: music, dance, drawing, coloring, sculpting with Plasticine, and so on. If sublimation is passion transformed, as Loewald (1988) put it, children have several modes of transformation at their fingertips, it would seem. Although the precise interlocking of all these aesthetic components is beyond the scope of this chapter, the relationship between Stephanie's drawings and her other play activities deserves a few comments. Her mother was an architect who forbade some of Stephanie's aggressive games. The act of drawing may have received maternal sanction in Stephanie's unconscious, whereas the act of playing may have aroused maternal disapproval. Drawing, which confines activity to a relatively small area of paper with relatively limited hand motion, may have seemed safer than play and its more far-reaching implications, geographically and psychologically. If a picture is worth a thousand words, surely it is because of its compression of a thousand affects into the narrow framework of a page of paper. In other words, drawing may seem safer than playing to certain children, depending on the nature of their conflicts and their strategies for dealing with them.

Stephanie's play with Plasticine was perhaps the most pivotal moment in the entire analysis. But the point I am stressing is that her ability to be angry with me, her analyst who interfered with her rhythm class, seemed to unlock the doors of play for her. It was with Plasticine that she was able to sculpt the affects and conflicts that had been so unspeakable up to that point. With Plasticine she could represent the duck with no brain, the poisoned mushroom, and the minipellets that were meant to signify affects of all kinds. In other words, Plasticine helped her analyze murderous wishes and guilt in relation to her sibling (the duck with no brain), and Plasticine helped her represent murderous and loving feelings toward me (the mushroom was an aesthetic gift even though poisonous). The discovery of Plasticine represented a victory over precocity and reaction formation (diapering herself, toilet-training herself). She had rediscovered her anality in a new aesthetic creative transformation. And it was not just anality that the Plasticine allowed her to revisit but oedipal sexuality as well. When the analysis turned to oedipal issues (Stephanie becoming more and more "nosy" about my sexuality), Plasticine helped her represent her long phallic Chinese nails that could lead to oedipal triumph or humiliation.

Let us return for a little further microanalysis to what I am calling the pivotal moment. Stephanie, confronted with her own anger in the transference, reaches for a reaction formation at first. When this defense is interpreted, she reaches for Plasticine and makes a duck with no brain. If this were to happen in an adult analysis, the analyst would surely be startled by the sight of Plasticine and such concrete representation of psychic conflict. The startled analyst would reach undoubtedly for a theory such as "acting in" to get out of a clinical dilemma. By contrast, the child analyst welcomes the "acting in" which is not conceptualized in that manner, giving the phenomenon the simple designation "play." Why is this so? This difference between adult analytic technique and child analytic technique is surely at the heart of this discussion about play. Why is play welcomed by the child analyst? From a Freudian point of view, one would argue that infantile sexuality that cannot be denied, yet cannot be expressed fully or maturely until adolescence (at least), needs active expression in the displacements of play throughout childhood. From a Piagetian point of view, one could argue that until the formal intrapsychic thought of adolescence makes hypothetical-deductive reasoning the hallmark of the teenager, the earlier preoperational and operational thought processes of the young go hand in hand with a much more action-oriented "being in the world," which is the hallmark of childhood and its playgrounds.

When Stephanie makes the duck with no brain out of Plasticine, the analyst continues to pursue the unconscious threads of instinct and defense in the associative material. The duck with no brain may reflect an analyst with no brain, an analysand with no brain, or a sibling with no brain, depending on the conflict between direct expression and defense at any given clinical moment. But the form is different when Plasticine is available. The Plasticine with its olfactory and tactile components is a little closer to the body and its zones, a little further from the psyche and its reaction formations, thereby giving the analysand an opportunity to wean herself from precociously chosen defense mechanisms and experiment with less fixated, more adaptive ones.

It is tempting to compare her freedom with Plasticine and her newfound freedom with contact sports (kickball). In fact, it is probably not too wild to suggest that all prelatency play with Plasticine lends some freedom to the organized games of latency, a connection that can be only inferred rather than perceived, given the disjunction the infantile amnesia wedges between prelatency and latency. When Stephanie finally felt comfortable kicking a ball in the schoolyard in competition with her peers, she was totally unaware of the role that Plasticine had played in this achievement. When I say Plasticine, I mean Plasticine in the therapeutic context of play, transference, and interpretation.

Without play, without Plasticine, would Stephanie have accomplished her developmental goals? This is, of course, an unanswerable question, but it does invite speculation about how play helps children overcome conflict and enhance their own development. Although play can help resolve conflict, conflict itself can inhibit play. When neurotic conflict is born of fear of instinctual expression, play would seem to be the ideal context in which conflict can be broken into its components and rearranged in the most adaptive manner. Play, an action by definition—not impulsive action but rather organized action—is more suited than even language for bending impulses toward its purpose. This is not meant to minimize the role of verbalization in taming instincts (Katan, 1961); I merely stress that play is a unique language that combines mastery of action and symbolic expression in unique age-appropriate titrations. When conflict overwhelms play, making it impossible for the child's natural endowment to heal her or him, a therapeutic climate has to be established in which interpretation of resistance and transference can lead the mind back to its own resources.

Toward the end of her analysis, Stephanie's skills as an artist were considerable. For instance, her drawing of a square dance was full of verve and action and had an expressive spontaneity of line that went beyond the usual naive vigor of children's drawings and stamped her as a particularly talented artist in the making. It is not easy to trace the connections between the presence or absence of early play and this later achievement of aesthetic mastery. Yet one is convinced that there is some aesthetics in the play and some play in the aesthetics. Similarly, one senses that a drawing of a monster punching a baby, though not a work of art of the highest order, does clear the way for later, less conflictual aesthetic products by removing what Kubie (1958) called neurotic distortions of the creative process. In a sense, creative art does not spring from Zeus's head like Athena but may rely on the anxiety-reducing sketch works of early drawings and early childhood play-things. The sublime is connected with the infantile even when those connecting tracks are covered with years of repression. The aesthetic may seem to be divine, but it is a human product of the zones of the body and the conflicted and nonconflicted skills of the mind.

As a final thought, is it not interesting to speculate about the acquisition of one semiotic skill (language) as opposed to another (play)? Why would Stephanie find language so easy to acquire and maintain, and play so difficult? In this particular case one is tempted to suggest that play's closer affinity to action makes the aggressive component more difficult to disguise. One cannot generalize about this insight since language itself can succumb to aggressive conflict—for example, elective mutism or stuttering. In fact, one senses that language and play may go hand in hand, one semiotic avenue joining another in complex intersections that are as yet poorly understood. Is adult language after all not at its free associative best when informed by a playfulness of the human spirit stripped of all neurotic undermining and compromising? If play is the great experimental laboratory in which developmental scripts are refined and rehearsed before completion, then the conflict captured in the title "To Play or Not to Play" may have consequences tragic in scope, Elizabethan in intensity, Shakespearean in depth, if not addressed promptly and analytically as soon as the curtain of development is raised.

References

Freud, S. (1916–17). Introductory lectures on psycho-analysis. *S.E.*, 15 and 16.

Katan, A. (1961). Some thoughts about the role of verbalization in early childhood. *Psychoanal. Study Child*, 16:184–188.

Kubie, L. S. (1958). *Neurotic Distortions of the Creative Process*. Lawrence: Univ. of Kansas Press.

Loewald, H. W. (1988). *Sublimation: Inquiries into Theoretical Psychoanalysis*. New Haven: Yale Univ. Press.

Neubauer, P. B. (1989). Personal communication.

Solnit, A. J., and Stark, M. H. (1961). Mourning and the birth of a defective child. *Psychoanal. Study Child*, 16:523–537.

5

Conceptual Worlds: Play and Theater in Child Psychoanalysis

Phyllis M. Cohen, Ed.D.

Matthew Cohen, M.Phil.

The role of elaborate imaginary play in the therapeutic process of child psychoanalysis has been described by many authors. In this chapter, we develop a descriptive model that can serve as a way to understand one aspect of the therapeutic process and how it relates to the symbolic life of the child and the child's life as he or she actually lives it.

In child analysis using dramatic play with oedipal and prelatency children, we sometimes see a three-part process—the construction, the exploration, and the integration of a *conceptual world*. This process tends to unfold over a number of months (or even years) and usually begins only some time after the initial phase of an analysis. These conceptual worlds are an example of Winnicott's (1971) "third area" of cultural experience—contained neither within the world of inner reality nor in the actual world in which the child lives. If there is a developmental line that leads from the type of solitary imaginary play with dollhouses and small figures to fully fleshed-out enactments of adult theater (Freud, 1908), the transitional phenomenon of "cosmogonic play" lies closer to the theater than to the solitary-play end of the spectrum.

Cosmogonic play can be conceived of as a type or mode of playing that occurs in child psychoanalysis. In cosmogonic play there is continuity across sessions and a narrative of sorts, implying a world of meanings, values, and experiences that are shared by the child and the analyst. It usually involves the assumption of roles by both the analyst and the analysand. As an activity that engages two people, it uses the communi-

We appreciate the encouragement and contributions of Samuel Ritvo, T. Wayne Downey, Barbara Nordhaus, Sally Provence, and Donald J. Cohen. We are especially appreciative of the collaboration and guidance of Albert J. Solnit, whose ideas and mentorship are reflected throughout this chapter.

cative style and ways of presentation and representation of a constructed, shared reality that can be characterized as histrionic. For these reasons, cosmogonic play can be said to be a type of *dramatic* play. The metaphor of dramatic play and the language of the theater more generally are highly compatible with psychoanalysis. The theater provides the analyst with a range of concepts used to understand the transference and countertransference. In the interpretation of the transference we speak of the assumption of different roles; the theater also provides metaphors of masking and disguise. The processes underlying dramatic play in analysis (including cosmogonic play) appear to be developmental precursors to the processes underlying the creation of theater. It is thus convenient to apply terms and ideas from the adult theater to children's dramatic play, even if the relation has not been adequately explored. This is supported by the long tradition in psychoanalysis of using ideas, terms, and metaphors derived from the theater, such as the unfolding of process and plot, foreshadowing, text and subtext, dialogue, and character.

Yet dramatic play as it is used in child analysis is the cocreation of the analyst and the analysand, only one of whom has reached a level of symbolic functioning and has the intellectual capacity to understand "the idea of the theater." During the period of prelatency, the child lacks a conceptual appreciation of the theater, even as the line between reality and fantasy is often blurred. Although one of the key formulations of psychoanalysis, the Oedipus complex, is based on theater, Freud himself did not look to see if the child's understanding of the drama was the same as the adult's—he did not see children in analysis. Although the adult analyst may have a sophisticated understanding of the structures underlying play and the features it shares with theater, it is not clear what the child's own understanding of the dramaturgy of dramatic play is. A careful examination of a certain type of dramatic play, what we call cosmogonic play, the exploration of a conceptual world, can provide some clues. It will also help answer some questions of how this dramatic play can be therapeutic in effect and why it seems to be particularly effective for children between the ages of four and nine.

Cosmogonic play takes place in a location, the analyst's office, that exists as both an objective and an experiential space. A photograph would show that a child analyst's office is often cluttered with material and physical things. Yet, from the child's point of view, the office has the potentiality to be an empty space, like a theatrical stage (Brook, 1968). Despite its limitations in size—the analyst's office was about eight by ten feet—it can allow for any type of imaginary activity to be created, for the conceptual worlds that are created in the analysis of children exist in a potential space (Winnicott, 1971) that, like the theater, is only partially bounded or affected by the constraints of normal space and time (Loewald, 1987).

The construction of a conceptual world within a potential space involves the type of activity that Freud (1908) referred to as building castles in the air (p. 145). Cosmogonic play begins with laying out the groundwork—establishing a rapport between the child analyst and the child, and letting the child express his thoughts and desires in literal and metaphorical speech and action. As the analyst watches the child at play and as they play together, the analyst is learning or developing a type of symbolic language in which she can communicate with the child. For a child who possesses a rich fantasy life, this symbolic language might already exist in a fully developed form. The analyst will then have to learn how to translate her own ideas into types of expressions that are already familiar to the child. For a child whose symbolic life is more impoverished, the groundwork to the construction of a conceptual world might involve the development of forms and structures that can be used as building blocks for the architectonics of the world.

The analyst recognizes important, vital, and recurrent themes that emerge in this part of the process. If she acts upon them and encourages their coalescence into a single, conceptual space, a coherent world can eventually be constructed out of this material, which has consistency and meaning for the child. The creation of a conceptual world does not occur in a single session. It can come in fits and starts and may take months before it is fully realized.

The analyst must be sensitive to what the child has to say and what he does. She must be particularly aware of the repeated themes and motifs that come up across sessions. It is important that the analyst not try to impose her own point of view on the child at this time. Her task is to be observant and to lead the activity and discussion into territory that is not inimicable to the child. The world that is constructed must be a familiar place, and although not always comfortable, it must always be recognized as the child's own creation. As Winnicott (1971) states, "Analysts need to beware lest they create a feeling of confidence and an intermediate area in which play can take place and then inject into this area or inflate it with interpretations which in effect are from their own creative imagination" (p. 120).

One of the challenges for the analyst is not to be guided too heavily by experience acquired through past analytic cases. A conceptual world, no matter how similar it might appear to another child's, in order to be effective is constructed in a way that is unique to a particular child. It is a product of his imagination. The analyst must allow for this particularity, indeed encourage it, for only through the child's full and total involvement will the therapy have positive results. The three-part process we describe here is thus not prescriptive; it is descriptive of what emerges for certain children when standard psychoanalytic technique is patiently and tactfully employed.

The second part of the therapeutic process involves the exploration of this constructed imaginary world. The motifs that emerge in the first phase of the therapeutic process form the conceptual skeleton that holds together the imaginary world. In the construction of the conceptual world, the analyst acts largely as a tactful facilitator—helping the child express relevant concerns. Her role differs little from that of an adult's analyst. Once inside the conceptual world, however, the analyst is no longer simply a silent observer—she becomes an actor. She must be actively complicit in maintaining the world and also focus her attentions on trying to change it. Within the field of play that exists between analyst and analysand, the analyst is not a neutral object—she has a charge. That charge involves her in the process of trying both to observe and to liberate the way the child feels and acts; it also entails an analytically guided facilitation of the child's interests and affects as the child elaborates and modifies the nature of the conceptual world he and the analyst are constructing. Thus, even while the analyst and the child are exploring the conceptual world they have created, its topography and geography are changing around them.

If the world that was constructed in the first part of the process is in fact consistent and meaningful to the child, it will prove to be resilient and have great continuity as well. Both the child and the analyst will be able to enter into it without hesitancy from the very beginning of the analytic hour, if they so desire. The use of props is helpful in maintaining this consistency and continuity.

As in the work of Melanie Klein and later Anna Freud at the Hampstead Clinic, each child in analysis in the cases described below had his own drawer, a small container where many of the important properties used in the child's play were stored. The material objects stored in such drawers can have many functions, but there seem to be three that are particularly relevant to cosmogonic play. First, the props, although not always necessary, can help activate the world. Like props and scenery in the theater, they serve to provide a graphic description of the place of action (Bogatyrev, 1938). Second, the props are used and take part in the action of the play. They serve to support dramatic action as well as open up possible avenues for play. Third, these particular objects are a way of making the world more particular and meaningful for the child. While the world is undergoing change, the objects anchor the conceptual world and give it stability and continuity.

We will later return to a fuller discussion of the theory that may help account for the therapeutic action of cosmogonic play, exemplified by observations during the analyses of four children. As we present these descriptions, it is important to remember that we are abstracting only one mode of play from among the many that were used by each child in analysis.

Clinical Material

The four cases described below have some common features. All were children of academic or professional families of at least moderate means. The first three children were diagnosed as having learning disabilities. The fourth child, although quite bright, was also described by his teachers as learning-disabled because of his extreme behavioral problems.

The four children entered analysis between the ages of four and six and terminated between the ages of seven and nine, having been seen for two to four years. In the course of each of the analyses, a conceptual world was constructed, explored, changed, and then either destroyed or divested. The nature and valence of the transference changed, but it changed within the overall construct of the world.

Finally, all four cases could be called successful—the children seem to have benefited from the analyses. They were at greater ease with themselves and others, showed improvement in their academic performances, and found more pleasure and satisfaction in their experiences of both the world of inner reality and the actual world in which they lived.

Case 1: Tommy

Tommy, a glassy-eyed, seemingly emotionally detached six-year-old, was in first grade when he entered treatment. He was recommended for therapy because of the emotional distance he showed as much as for his difficulties in learning. Tommy was a second-born child. His parents, both academics with advanced degrees, were very attached and close to his older brother, Michael, who was outgoing and successful. But they were perplexed by Tommy and saddened by his lack of academic success. They observed that he was not learning and was not outgoing like Michael, but they could not understand why.

It became evident in the first phase of treatment that Tommy was a profoundly sad and troubled child. His parents had no sense of what he was experiencing. To the best of their knowledge, they thought that Tommy was well cared for, and they truly believed that they were doing as much as they could for him. Tommy had been in day care since he was a small child. He never showed any separation anxiety in parting from his parents; neither was he ever aggressive in his manner. He was quiet and showed no expression of affect whatsoever when he was left by his parents at day care early in the morning and when he was picked up in the evening. Yet the experience was very stressful for Tommy. What was hardest was the disorientation in his sense of time. He could not understand how long he would be left alone at day care, when his parents would return, and so on. The days seemed to go on and on endlessly. He was adrift in an ocean of time, helpless, with no safe harbor within sight.

Tommy's dramatic play developed around this very metaphor. In the conceptual world they created, Tommy and the analyst were two sailors on a ship at sea. It was a stormy sea with many dangers—hidden rocks, sea monsters, pirates. He was a crewman, and she was "Matey," his buddy. In their dramatic play, Tommy spoke to Matey in an (assumed) British accent—and she answered him in turn with the best imitation of a British accent she could muster. Sometimes he assigned to the analyst the role of captain; at other times he treated her as an equal. Occasionally, Tommy himself became the ship's commanding officer.

In the early sessions of the exploration of this conceptual world, shipwrecks were common. The sea was tempestuous, and it seemed impossible to control where the ship would go. The maps and charts that Tommy constructed, with the encouragement and aid of Matey, were of great importance. He depicted the sea's geography, the position of dangerous rocks, monsters, and pirates, and the whereabouts of safe harbors and ports of call. These charts were quickly drawn with crayon, pen, or marker on plain white paper and were carefully stored in his private drawer from session to session. They did not seem to be objects prized in and of themselves, but rather seemed to be useful for the exploration of Tommy's conceptual world. He frequently revised them or even redrew them from scratch. The topography of the sea was always changing, and one needed to have an accurate representation of it.

The other important device was a single-lensed telescope, which in the dramatic play was represented by putting one's two hands together and holding them up to one's eye. In their play, the child and Matey would stand on the deck of the ship or on top of cliffs (chairs and couches) and try to focus the lens to see what lay about them. This imaginary device was elevated by the analyst, with the consent and complicity of Tommy, to a level of critical importance in the development of the conceptual world. It was used as a way of assessing one's current situation and to understand what lay ahead. With the careful, assiduous employment of this powerful instrument for observation, one could safely navigate the treacherous seas and reach a safe harbor.

Often, when the sea became stormy and there was danger of a shipwreck, the telescope had a sense of urgency associated with it. The waves washed over the side of the ship. The wind howled. "I can't see anything! The telescope won't focus for me!" cried Matey. "Here, you take it!" she shouted. Tommy "took the telescope," put it up to his eye, and started to focus it. "What can you see? Do you know where we are?" Matey shouted, barely able to make herself heard above the fury of the storm. Fortunately, this time, Tommy saw where they were and was able to guide the ship to safe harbor.

The telescope was interpreted by the analyst within the frame of the conceptual world. Tommy discovered that he had the capacity to see around him. He learned that one of the ways of overcoming the anxiety of being abandoned and having to be alone was to look around him—not to close his eyes and see the world through a glassy-eyed stare, but to see where he was and act upon that knowledge. It is significant that the telescope was represented by a part of the body, specifically the hands. The hands exist close to the border of potential space and the inner world. This allowed for the "telescope" to be internalized with greater ease than if it was represented by a more external, physical object. As Winnicott (1971) has described it, the hand, as it is used to stimulate the oral erotogenic zone and "in quiet union" (p. 1) in infancy, is the first object of the intermediate area.

With time, both Tommy and his Matey became old sea hands. Through their use of charts and especially the employment of the telescope, they eventually memorized the sea lanes. As the world became a more peaceful, friendlier place and the theme of "man against the sea" became less interesting for Tommy, another theme emerged inside of the same conceptual world. Up until this point, the analyst had at the back of her mind the theoretical assumption that the storms, the shipwrecks, the pirates, and so on were an expression of aggression and (denied) hatred, perhaps toward Tommy's older brother, who had his parents' admiration and love. But the material that emerged at this point of the analysis suggested other interpretations.

As the transference deepened, the dramatic play increasingly revolved around the idea of Tommy being marooned on a desert island with Matey.

Here the word *Matey* was used by Tommy primarily not as a way of expressing friendliness and the state of being buddies with the analyst. In the context of the transference at this point of the analysis, it meant something more akin to the word *mate*, as *lover*. This suggested that the earlier torrential storms were a representation of the fearful side of the primal scene, and the scenes on the deserted island were a way to express its more affectionate, intimate side. Where previously Tommy metaphorically had to fight off his fears and anxieties, now he was able to express unchallenged affection and closeness, without the rivalry of his older brother or father. As Erikson (1963) states, in his description of the efficacy of play therapy, "The most obvious condition is that the child has the toys and the adult for himself, and that sibling rivalry, parental nagging, or any kind of sudden interruption does not disturb the unfolding of his play intentions, whatever they may be" (p. 222). Tommy now had his Matey (mate-mother-analyst) alone in the privacy of a secret island.

In this phase of Tommy's fantasy world, being marooned on a desert island also was associated with the earlier experience of being alone, isolated, and abandoned. Now, however, even though marooned on a desert island, he no longer experienced the fear of abandonment, for he had his Matey with him. He could never be abandoned again because he had integrated his mother into his own self; he had his claim on her, which had become internalized in his enhanced self-esteem. Tommy would never have to feel completely alone on a metaphorical island in the middle of nowhere; he would always carry around inside of him a representation of his mother as a newfound or rediscovered selfobject (Kohut, 1971). Tommy was at this point ready to divest himself from the potential space he had occupied with the analyst. The analysis was ready to terminate.

By this time, at age eight and a half, Tommy had shown considerable improvement in school. His glassy-eyed stare had become more focused, and he was showing signs of vitality and interest in life. He also was more outgoing and more readily expressed his emotions. The emotional stress and anxieties he had experienced lifted; he no longer felt disturbed or helpless in being alone. From current communications with Tommy's parents, we have learned that he has met with academic success in high school and now shows promise as a playwright. Tommy has been able to use his rich and creative imagination, which we saw in his conceptual world, and relate his fantasies to a public audience. This supports Freud's (1908) hypothesis that imaginative activity is a continuation of and substitute for the play of childhood.

Case 2: Rob

Rob was also six years old and in first grade when he entered analysis. Like Tommy, Rob was the second-born child of an academic family. His older brother, Peter, was a very successful student and much admired and praised by his parents. But like Tommy, Rob did not meet with academic success and was having troubles in school. Perhaps more serious than his academic problems was his encopresis. Although he was six, he constantly defecated in his pants in the most visible, public situations. Rob was a physically abusive, aggressive child. It was difficult for anyone (teacher, parent, sibling, analyst) to be in the same room with him. But Rob was not only frightening; he was also frightened inside.

Rob was engaged in a love-hate relationship with his mother, who was visited by frequent bouts of depression. His mother was attached to him but was incapacitated in her attempts to care for her son in a consistent way because of her own affective disorder. Rob's father was a kind and well-meaning person, but he did not have an appropriate model from his own upbringing for how to be a father. Despite his best intentions, he was unable to provide the necessary support for Rob. He simply lacked the necessary parenting skills.

Rob was two years old and had not yet been toilet-trained when his parents decided to go on a vacation. They departed very abruptly, without preparing their children in advance. Rob was left in the care of a female friend of the family who was going through a breakup of her marriage at the time and was in a very emotional state. She attempted to toilet-train Rob in a most aggressive, almost sadistic, manner. The traumatic experience of being abandoned by his parents and its association with feces and bowel control had a profound effect on Rob's development. The giving and with-holding of feces became directly related to the way Rob interacted with his mother. Central were issues of control over his body and over the bodies of others. Through the act of defecation, Rob expressed power; he was able to control other people and make them do certain things, such as keeping distant from him because of the smell, cleaning up after him, and so on. Although Rob's encopresis repelled people, at the same time he brought them closer to himself. The feces were a love object, a present for his mother. He would try to hold them in, hold this representation of his mother inside of himself. Even the toilet became invested. When he saw his feces in the bowl, he did not want to flush them down; he wanted to save them.

In the conceptual world that Rob constructed, he and the analyst were on a basketball team. Rob was a player and the analyst was his "Coach." In a very controlled way, over and over again, Rob threw a ball into the wastepaper basket in the office, which the analyst thought was only a minor displacement from the major symptom that had brought him to treatment. Rob would consume entire sessions shooting baskets from all sides of this small room. He would try every possible approach, every possible set, every possible style of throwing. It was the Coach's job to provide him with support ("I'm right here with you!") as well as to describe the way he performed. Sometimes the Coach might be assigned the role of teammate; at other times, the Coach would play a competitive game against Rob, and the two would keep up an enthusiastic dialogue about the game.

In no instance, however, did Rob ever openly discuss his encopretic behavior. Frequently, he defecated in his pants during the analytic hour or just before it. But whenever the analyst (or anyone else) asked him if he had just defecated, Rob always denied it. Thus, during the entire analysis, the topic of his encopresis was rarely discussed openly at the literal level.

While in analysis, Rob became interested in swimming—another physical activity. The activity of swimming and the swimming pool in particular became, however, just another way for Rob to articulate his encopresis. By defecating in the swimming pool, the physical act became even more public and more repellent to the people around him.

Preceding his analytic sessions, he tended to defecate on top of a radiator. This too had the effect of making a normally (semi)concealed act more public. The fumes from his feces would carry through the halls and up and down one or more flights of stairs. The analyst began to understand the association of defecation with swimming and sitting on top of a radiator: both were linked with his mother, symbolized by the pool's water and the radiator's warmth. Thus she received Rob's feces, even as he drove people away from him and re-created the trauma of being abandoned.

In her role as Coach, the analyst more and more came to shape the way Rob behaved. It was the responsibility of Coach to know all the vital statistics. She was always counting, keeping score. Even the statistics from Rob's swimming were part of Coach's business: "9.3 seconds . . . 2 for 5 on the free-throw line." Coach, who was expected to keep close track of Rob's physical behavior, became obsessive about it, and Rob himself encouraged this. When she forgot something or made a mistake in her counting, Rob became upset: "The score is 52 to 28! . . . My time was 7.8 seconds."

As he made the identification with Coach, Rob himself became aware of his behavior and all of his physical "statistics." He gradually lost interest in swimming and playing basketball with Coach. His great concern with his physical prowess became less pressing. Ultimately, the statistics became Rob's own concern, and he took pride in being his own manager.

After three years of analysis, Rob's encopresis became more and more infrequent. It reached the point where he no longer defecated in his pants at school, but he occasionally continued this symptom at the analyst's office, a persistent marker of the crystallization of the encopresis within the transference. In the analytic situation and through the fullness of the transference neurosis, Rob was actively aware of the conflicts in trying to control his behavior. Finally, over time, the symptom disappeared from the analyst's office as well. Rob met with more success in school. In recent communications with Rob and his parents, we learned that as an adolescent, Rob again became interested in sports—in a positive, healthy manner, without the obsessive concern for statistics and the control of his body.

Case 3: Benjamin

The conceptual world that Benjamin created was drier and more sterile than those of Tommy and Rob, largely a reflection of his personality and more limited capability for imaginative activity. Benjamin was also younger than Tommy and Rob when he began his analysis. Although only age four, he was already showing signs of having a severe learning disability. His language was impaired, and he had yet to learn his colors. He also had minor motoric problems and was somewhat awkward and clumsy. Benjamin had been seen by a neurologist, who recommended special school placement on the basis of what he felt was an organic impairment in cognitive and motor functions. The exact nature of the disorder was never clearly diagnosed.

Benjamin's father, a professor of education, wondered if Benjamin was perhaps autistic, as he seemed very impaired and lacked basic social skills as well. Yet he also identified with the boy. He himself had been both socially and motorically awkward while growing up. At the time of Benjamin's entering analysis, his mother had recently given birth to a second child. The jealousy aroused by his younger sibling complicated Benjamin's feelings related to his own perceived intellectual and physical deficiencies.

Early in Benjamin's analysis, it became clear to the analyst that his disabilities in learning were caused at least as much by emotional factors as by constitutional determinants. He was a very rigid, anxious boy, constantly feeling and then reliving the experience of stress evoked by the most trivial failures. The analyst thus recommended withdrawing Benjamin from the special school he was attending and asked his parents to consider having him placed in a regular classroom, with the support of an aide. The school seconded this recommendation and the parents agreed.

Compared to the dramatic play of both Tommy and Rob, most of Benjamin's play was on the whole unimaginative and uninteresting. He typically occupied himself by playing with blocks or coloring books. One theme seemed to capture his interest, though, exciting and involving him: the re-creation of Benjamin's school, and particularly the student-teacher relationship, in the analyst's office. This was the repeated motif that formed the skeleton of Benjamin's conceptual world.

When that world was first explored, Benjamin cast himself in the role of the stupid student and the analyst as his demanding, critical teacher. His dramatic play was thus very masochistic; he was constantly being punished for his inability to carry out certain tasks successfully. The difficulties in his learning seemed to be related to how he perceived his "damaged" body, for Benjamin's cognitive impairments and physical deficiencies had become intertwined in a complex web of causality. He could not do something because he was stupid. He was stupid because he was clumsy. And he was clumsy because he could not do something. Thus, his difficulties in the conceptual world of the school were due to more than just a disability in learning; they stemmed from and captured his damaged self.

Over time, the conceptual world began to change. Increasingly, Benjamin himself assumed the role of teacher, and the analyst became the stupid student. This change was encouraged by the analyst—she readily and enthusiastically took on the constructed persona. In the context of this transference, the most negative aspects of his own self were projected. "You're always too stupid. I'm giving you too much work. The work is too difficult for you at your age." Benjamin wished to be young again—to be infantilized. His feelings of disability and helplessness as a student brought him back to the world of the helpless, protected, cared-for infant. He wished he could be close to his mother like his little brother. Yet even as Benjamin took on the role of teacher, which allowed him to express the most painful aspects of his self-portrait, he assumed responsibility and command. From this new vantage point, he no longer felt as insecure about his learning disabilities. He was ready to divest himself from the conceptual world he had created.

Another factor that led to the termination of the analysis was Benjamin's involvement in sports. A pediatric neurologist suggested that a good way of building up self-esteem in children with minor motorical handicaps and disabilities was playing soccer. The children would run up and down the field, chasing after the ball, while the parents watched from the side. Minor motorical difficulties could hardly be noticed by the parents, the child's teammates, or the child himself. This proved to be the case when Benjamin joined a soccer team on the recommendation of the analyst. Benjamin's father, who had never played a sport, watched his child with pride. He, too, joined in the activity and became the coach for his son's team. As a result of their mutual involvement in the sport, Benjamin's father no longer identified with his son because of his clumsiness; neither did Benjamin's own identification with his father focus on this aspect of the self. Benjamin came to internalize the image of his father as coach. This idealized aspect of his parent helped form Benjamin's emerging ego ideal. This, along with the work in the analysis, allowed for the breaking of the complex web of causality that had given rise to his perception of his damaged self.

Case 4: Jason

Jason was five years old and in kindergarten when he started analysis. Although an early reader and able to do complex mathematical calculations in his head, Jason was having difficulties in school, and his teachers felt that he had a learning disability. Indeed, it could be said that Jason did have a learning disability, although he was quite intelligent. When asked to do something in school, Jason typically refused. When he was forced to do his work, very often he arrived at the correct answer, but used an unusual method. Jason's negativeness and aggression were causing major problems at school, both socially and academically. Nobody seemed able to figure him out. He was a very angry child, uncontrollably aggressive and not to be trusted—he could be, and often was, destructive of property and hostile toward the other children in his class as well as toward his teacher. He was simply not containable, and the school was ready to expel him.

Jason's parents were both hardworking, intelligent architects, but they claimed that they had "no idea" why Jason should be behaving so aggressively to everyone around him. This later seemed to be a case of denial, for much of Jason's difficulties were caused by their own marital difficulties.

The contributing factors underlying Jason's behavior were varied and complex. One of the major concerns was his feeling of abandonment. As a preschooler, Jason went to day care while his parents were at work. When he was two years old, shortly after the birth of his younger sister, his father left home unexpectedly, without prior warning. He disappeared for a number of months; no one knew where he was. Although eventually the father did return to the family, Jason's mother became depressed and was an inconsistent care-giver for a time. She later pulled out of her depression and became a devoted mother. But when Jason was six and had been in analysis for about a year, his mother contracted life-threatening myocarditis and was hospitalized for six months in another city, located several hours away (by air) from Jason's hometown.

The sudden, unexplained disappearance of his father, owing to marital problems and his desire to escape the responsibility and stress caused by the birth of his daughter, had made a permanent imprint upon Jason. It was interpreted by him from a depressive position. He felt that his own anger and aggression had caused his father to disappear. The hospitalization of Jason's mother was also interpreted from this position. Again, he was convinced that his own anger had caused his mother to go away to another city. At the same time, his parents made the projective identification of their own anxieties and insecurities upon Jason: "We don't know why Jason is behaving like this." Their denial of anxiety and its projection upon Jason allowed them to be calm, even while Jason himself was becoming more and more distraught.

In the conceptual world, the analyst and Jason were in business together. The analyst's office became a business office. The physical properties were quite extensive—stationery, documents, models for development and marketing. Sometimes the analyst and Jason were coworkers; at other times Jason assumed the role of boss and the analyst was his subordinate. He would tell his employee what to do, fantasize about all his "great ideas" for a "new product," and so on. At certain moments the analyst assumed the role of a high-ranking executive, while Jason was an employee of the company. As an executive, the analyst was expected to point out the important "issues" and could discuss Jason's past "business failures." The conceptual world did not have a playful quality to it—its tone was very serious. Jason would get angry if the analyst was slow to respond: "Come on! What are you doing there?"

The nature of the product changed over time. During the course of the analysis, a number of different products were discussed, modeled, and toyed with. Not many products panned out; few seemed to have any real commercial capabilities. One product in particular, however, seemed to have serious economic possibilities—a phone-watch. "It will become absolutely necessary for every executive to own one," Jason, the businessman, said. "With a phone-watch, you can know where the most important people are all the time." For Jason, that most important person whom he occasionally referred to, by way of example, was his mother.

Although he seemed tough and aggressive, Jason was actually very sensitive. He was constantly worrying about the possibility of his parents disappearing, how his own actions might cause this, and what he should do to prevent it from happening. In order to cope with this anxiety, he put some protective space between himself and his parents, the people closest to him and most linked to his anxiety concerning abandonment. Rather than passively accepting his parents' disappearances, Jason became defensively aggressive and angry. The rage he felt at his parents for his father's disappearance and his mother's depression and hospitalization was eventually generalized to include nearly everyone.

Similarly, Jason's early maturity (he appeared very adultlike both in and outside of the conceptual world he constructed) had a defensive function. In other ways, however, Jason remained very infantile. His bed was covered with stuffed animals and he could not sleep without a light on. His apparent maturity was thus part of Jason's false self (Winnicott, 1971), constructed to distance himself from the insecurities of being a child and dependent on adults.

The phone-watch Jason designed was a way to express his fear of abandonment and his desires and their underlying motives for wanting to be in touch with his parents. The internalization of the phone-watch and the process of identification that took place in the third part of the analytic process allowed Jason to cope with the insecurities aroused by his experience of being separated from his parents. This separation was both physical, as when his father left when he was two years old or when he was dropped off at day care, and emotional, as in the distance he experienced between himself and his mother when she was depressed. With the identification and internalization of his "product" and the conceptual world he created, Jason became less aggressive and troublesome; the school no longer was threatening to expel him.

Although the phone-watch was clearly the most interesting and relevant product for Jason, it was not the last "idea for a product" that he toyed with in his conceptual world. Just before termination, when Jason was eight years old, he was discussing the possibilities of a paper airplane mail-order business: "We could sell do-it-yourself kits, parts, paint. If a part broke, you could send away for it and it would arrive in two days."

The paper airplane mail-order business was a way of dealing with separation and the termination of the analysis. He showed some anxiety at the prospect of termination and the resultant separation from the analyst. The positive transference caused him to want to hold on to the analyst, not let her disappear. Jason offered all kinds of incentives to his business partner for not dissolving their partnership. He proposed promoting certain airline companies in their model business; then he and his business partner would "definitely" get free tickets on real airplanes—they could go any place they wanted together. The business showed an associative connection between Jason's memory of his mother's hospitalization and his fantasies concerning the analyst after the analysis terminated. Just as he had taken an airplane when he visited his mother while she was hospitalized, he could visit his analyst any time he wanted, even after the analysis ended, if he had free airplane tickets.

It was a difficult termination. The conceptual world had not been destroyed, although it had changed. Jason was no longer as aggressive; the collaboration was not as one-sided. In the end, Jason reluctantly agreed to make the analyst a "consultant," whom he could call upon in times of need. He agreed that he could manage the day-to-day affairs of the business on his own. Both Jason and the analyst were thus able to divest themselves from their business partnership and the conceptual world they had created between them.

Discussion

In psychoanalytic work with children, the conceptual world that is created by the child and the analyst has some continuity, reflecting the stability within the multiple determinants of the child's personality as well as his neurotic and developmental disturbances and defenses; yet, simultaneous with its exploration, the parameters of this potential space are also potentially and actually undergoing change. Changes within the conceptual world reflect and advance the therapeutic action of the psychoanalytic work and are due, in large part, to the charge of the analyst within the field of dramatic play. At the front of the analyst's mind, she is fully engaged in the conceptual world and partaking in the construction and exploration of this world in collaboration with the child. At the back of her mind, though, she is guided by a theory of therapeutic action—she has constructed or is in the process of constructing a theory concerning the child's instinctual life, self-esteem, ego functions, and so on, which guides her actions in a particular direction. Yet even if the analyst could possibly know what was best for the child and how the conceptual world "ought" to be changed, the process of change can happen only through discourse; both the analyst and the analysand must "agree" to the new condition before the conceptual world can actually be any different. Otherwise, the conceptual world of the analysis can be invaded by the same demands for acting as if or as a false self that might have led the child into difficulties in the first place.

Changes in the conceptual worlds must have some degree of continuity and consistency with the conditions and rules of the already constructed world. They build upon the symbols and structures that are in place. The changes cannot be too radically discontinuous with the past or they might result in their nonacceptance by, or resistance from, the child, or in the disruption or cessation of the play episode, or perhaps in compliance and further reinforcement with the child's compliant false self.

These changes may not be (and usually are not) literally discussed by the analyst and the child. They tend to happen at the preconscious or the implicit level. They involve a certain amount of trust between analyst and analysand and heavily depend upon the analyst's tact. If trust is absent, as when a negative transference holds sway, change may become a source of contention. For example, suppose the analyst wishes to introduce a new theme or area of activity. To explore the child's hatred for his brother, whom he coldly placed in a prison several weeks ago, she might say, "We've taken our rocket ship to the moon so many times before. What do you feel about going to the planet Mars and seeing if your little brother is still being held prisoner by the Martians?" If the child is trusting and the analyst is tuned in—that is, the transference is positive enough to sustain the anxiety aroused by the child's cruel fantasies concerning his brother—he will accept the introduction of this material, a change in the topography of the conceptual world he is cocreating: "Sure! Let's go to Mars! I'm not afraid of the Martians. Warp drive 72!" If the relationship lacks trust, if the transference has a more negative valence, or if the introduction of the theme is too frightening or discordant with the child's tolerance for such an exploration, then the child is likely to be resistant to any change, no matter how small. The child might say, "But we don't have enough fuel," or simply, "But this rocket ship doesn't go to Mars. It only goes to the moon," or even, "Shut up. You're talking too much." If the analyst then goes on to insist on the change, it might result in the cessation of the sequence. The valence and intensity of the transference are thus determinative factors in the ease of the give-and-take of change within a conceptual world.

One of the ways the analyst can change the nature of the conceptual world is through the use of interpretation. As Melanie Klein (1961) states, "It is important that the analyst should be able to convey to the child the meaning of his phantasies—whether they are deeply repressed or nearer consciousness—and to verbalize them" (p. 47). Interpretation can go on at a number of different levels with reference to the conceptual world. The analyst can make an interpretation within the parameters of the conceptual world itself, without disrupting its continuity. For example, an overly aggressive child and the analyst are playing with toy cars. The child moves her car quickly, without paying attention, running over blocks and other toys. The analyst might interpret this behavior in a way that allows for direct continuity with the play, within the frame of the conceptual world or play episode: "Wow! You're going so fast! I can't keep up with you!" Or the interpretation can take place outside of the frame of play: "I wonder why you're going so fast. You do it when you get excited." This type of interpretation, however, runs the risk of disrupting the play altogether (Ritvo, 1978). Or the analyst might remain within the general frame of play but step outside of the specific play episode or conceptual world to give her interpretation. One strategy that is often used here is including some sort of a linguistic sign or marker—for example, "I'll bet you in a million years that you never thought about . . ."

Eventually, if the analysis has proceeded reasonably well, the third part of the process will be reached—gaining a distance from the constructed world as the process of synthesis and reincorporation of the imaginary world takes place through the child's identification with the attitudes of the analyst. This world is no longer the same as it was when the explorations by the analyst and the analysand began. By her very presence, as much as by her actions and interpretations, the analyst fosters, facilitates, and enables the child to change the nature of this world in order to give adaptive strategies and bring a new psychological repertoire of defenses and ways of understanding and perceiving to the child. Through incorporating the now changed conceptual world and the process of identification with its contents, the child is able to move ahead in his development, unburdened by infantile shame and anxieties that interfere with autonomous ego functions. The therapeutic modification of the child's emerging conceptual world is thus similar to the interpretation of the transference in adult analysis, which results in the waning of the Oedipus complex and allows for the achievement of a new sense of self as an autonomous person and other internal, post-oedipal achievements.

The achievement of the phase of development that is latency may indicate that the child's development is enough on track that the analysis can terminate. These children may still have problems, like any other child, but with hard-won integration of the conceptual world and the termination of analysis, the way they think and feel and the way they understand and experience the world can be considered on course or comparable to their peers. They are able to participate more fully and adaptively in a shared world of experience with the people around them. The child's development beyond the conceptual world constructed in analysis is thus concurrent with the actual world becoming a more interesting and pleasurable place to live in.

The move toward latency and the abandonment of the created conceptual world are parallel to the putting aside of the transitional object. Just as the material symbol of the union of mother and child can eventually be discarded as the symbol is internalized and becomes integrated, so a conceptual world can outlive its function and no longer be necessary after a certain point. One may still return to a transitional object or a conceptual world with fond nostalgia, but if development is to move ahead, the child must divest himself from it at some point. The three phases of cosmogonic play—the construction, the exploration, and the integration of a therapeutically modified conceptual world in child analysis—are thus consistent with Freud's (1908) three-part model for the structure of fantasy, daydreaming, and creative writing. Freud proposed that activities of imaginative creation draw upon three periods of time: past, present, and future—the three periods of our ideation. So, too, with conceptual worlds. The world is constructed out of the memories of past experience and builds upon the particular styles of play the child has developed in the past. This activity is performed in the present and is related to the circumstances of the child's inner reality and the world in which he lives. It carries with it the idea of wish fulfillment (a frequent undercurrent in the many episodes of dramatic play), but more profoundly the integration of conceptual worlds effecting a new internalized sense of self for the future life of the child. This is similar to Solnit's (1987) formulation that play in the service of recollection can lead to mastery.

These varied aspects of the therapeutic process that is facilitated by the creation and integration of therapeutic worlds were seen, from differing perspectives, in the analytic processes of the four ego-impaired boys.

Jason's difficulty in termination was due in part to the nature of the space he created and its relation to the rest of his life. The conceptual world was not marginalized as "child's play." Jason was serious; what he was doing was in many ways real to him. In the conceptual world of business that Jason created, he was honing his skills as a businessman, rehearsing for his future occupation and engaging in activities that were important and real to him. With the absolutely serious determination that only a young child can have, he once actually requested "development funds" from his parents to support the "research" and "test-marketing" of the phone-watch. This request apparently caused a minor crisis in the family. His parents had no idea how they should respond. They did not know if Jason was "only playing" or whether his request for money was serious and real. They felt that they could not make the decision for themselves and came to the analyst for consultation. Jason's conceptual world was not far removed from the real world in which he lived.

This is among the primary reasons we feel that conceptual worlds are closer to adult theater than to children's solitary imaginary play. As Freud (1908) states, the opposite of children's play is reality; this hardly seems to be the case in a number of the conceptual worlds we have described. The child does not necessarily distinguish the conceptual world from reality. This, we believe, is a sign not of pathology but of the overflowing of creativity. Like theater, conceptual worlds exist in a potential space that is often precariously close to the borders of reality. Stanislavsky (1963) recognized the affinity between life and art; avant-garde theater since Pirandello has exploited this closeness, playing on the edge of reality and fantasy.

The space that a conceptual world occupies can be conceived of as a liminal space, betwixt and between (Turner, 1967, 1969), or as a transitional space—neither entirely within the inner world nor bounded by the constraints of reality and the external world (Winnicott, 1971). As a type of transitional space, it is not governed by the rules of reality or fantasy and is a part of neither of them and both of them at the same time. Some conceptual worlds, such as Jason's, seem to be very close to the border of reality. Others, such as Tommy's, are much more distal. Still others, such as Rob's and Benjamin's, seem to be approximately intermediate in distance between the child's inner reality and the world in which he or she lives. In any case, a conceptual world is not subject to reality testing, for that would involve resolving the paradox that is essential to the definition of any transitional phenomenon. A conceptual world, an intermediate area of experience, provides relief from the strain of relating inner and outer realities. To subject it to reality testing, to make clear the distinction between apperception and perception, would mean the loss of the value of this paradoxical space (Winnicott, 1971).

Freud (1908) expresses the dialectic between reality and fantasy in the intermediate area of experience in his discussion of play. "Might we not say that every child at play behaves like a creative writer, in that he creates a world of his own, or, rather, re-arranges the things of his world in a new way which pleases him?" (p. 143f.). That is the paradox of transitional phenomena: a potential space both is created by the child and is based on things (and objects) that are already present and waiting to be "rearranged," created, or to become the object of the child's cathexis (Winnicott, 1971).

It is clear that cosmogonic play, as an imaginative activity that borders on reality, has the potential to be of therapeutic value. We do not believe, however, that the simple construction of this world by the analyst and the child is in itself of real use. Although imaginary play may be useful in temporarily relieving stress, anxiety, and aggressive and sexual drives and impulses (Klein, 1976), the acting out of fantasies does not seem to be therapeutic in itself, as if it achieved a catharsis. What is critical in therapy using conceptual worlds (or any type of play) is the analyst's intervention, her charge within the field of the constructed world, and the direction in which she enables the child to be aware of choices leading to a conceptual world that better prepares the child for progressive development. The child identifies with this therapeutically modified world and the interpretations the analyst has made concerning the things that go on in it. These become internalized, leading to new modes of representation, symbolic processes, and other abilities. (See, for a related discussion of play, myth making, and therapy, Vandenberg, 1986.)

It is not accidental that the construction and integration of conceptual worlds seem to have so much therapeutic value for children at the particular age of Tommy, Rob, Benjamin, and Jason. As Moran (1987) notes, play can help facilitate emerging ego functions. Among these are increasing self-reflection, monitoring, and the ability to choose among alternatives. It is just these abilities that are practiced when a conceptual world is constructed and explored with the analyst. "The child's play is the infantile form of the human ability to deal with experience by creating model situations and to master reality by experiment and planning" (Erikson, 1963, p. 222).

Through identification with the contributions of the analyst to the conceptual world, the child is able to internalize skills that allow him to move forward in his symbolic and cognitive development. The child learns about secondary process thinking, including the orderliness of relations, coherence of plot lines, causality, abstraction, and the value of attention and concentration through the mutual activity of exploring a shared world. He also learns about the expression and modulation of strong positive and negative feelings. Thus, the therapeutic benefit of the dramatic play and its analysis lies in both the interpretation of defenses and in the mobilization of intellectual abilities. Here, again, cosmogonic play can be seen to be related to the creative, imaginative activities of adults as well as to children's play, as described by Anna Freud (1965). It is a form of mental activity that takes its roots in primary process modes of experiencing while moving the individual forward developmentally through the creative activity of bringing into existence higher levels of representation. This play modality thus exemplifies how the process of sublimation functions in the enhancement of development.

For example, in the case of Tommy, through the construction of the telescope in the conceptual world, he learned the value of paying attention and looking around him. The act of seeing was not only a mechanism of defense against his anxiety and fear of abandonment; it was a way for him to further his own values and ambitions. It opened up a world of experience to him, let him attain academic competence, and allowed for the blossoming of his developmental capacities. In the construction and exploration of the conceptual world, he also learned about sharing, mutuality, and trust.

For defensive, anxious children like Tommy, before a conceptual world can be constructed it is necessary to bridge the interpersonal gulf between the child's self and the object (the analyst). "Dependence is maximal. The potential space happens only *in relation to a feeling of confidence* on the part of the baby [or child], that is, confidence related to the dependability of the mother-figure or environmental elements, confidence being the evidence of dependability that is becoming introjected" (Winnicott, 1971, p. 118). Thus, by the time in the analysis that a conceptual world can be explored, the child is already on the road toward becoming well adapted and socially adept. As Winnicott describes it, "The potential space . . . depends on experience which leads to trust. It can be looked upon as sacred to the individual in that it is here that the individual experiences creative living" (p. 121). An analysis of an emotionally disturbed child that has progressed to the point where the exploration of a conceptual world is possible can have a successful termination. For the construction of a conceptual world necessarily involves breaking down the neurotic or infantile defenses that prevent the child from experiencing mutuality and establishing a transfer-ential relation based on trust.

It seems then that the construction of a conceptual world involves a genuine transferential relationship with the analyst. The transference and the countertransference in such play can be related to the assumption of a role by an actor in the theater. We see a complex dialectic in the relation of the self to the character portrayed. As Stanislavsky (1963) describes it, in order to play Romeo's love, "you recall your life, you transfer your emotions to your role. This passion, *"love,"* you analyze into its component moments of logical action. All of them together constitute *love*. . . . To all the stages in the unfolding of emotions there will be corresponding logical sequences. Along these stages you will step into your role, because you took from your own life everything that concerns love and you transfer it to your role. These are not merely *bits of Romeo*, they are *bits of yourself*" (p. 111). But theater is not a solitary activity; it takes place through different levels of collaboration—the director with the actors, actors with actors, the director with the designers, the actors with the audience, and so on. All these people are involved in the activity of the creation of an imaginary world, involving both the suspension and the heightening of reality, as in the constructed conceptual worlds.

Children who have created conceptual worlds during their analyses may retain a vivid memory and appreciation of these creations years after the termination of their treatment. After having been out of analysis for a number of years, the child might unexpectedly ask, "Do you remember when . . . ?" and then launch into a long description of her experience of this world at a level of understanding that shows surprising appreciation for its symbols and metaphors. Although much of the material is, of course, later repressed, it is obvious that through the building, exploration, and integration of therapeutically modified conceptual worlds the child is manipulating certain symbolic materials in a sophisticated way, materials that, like Rob's aversion to talking about his encopresis, could not be discussed at a literal level. Much of the analyst's own self, the way she thinks and feels, also becomes internalized by analytic patients. Her influence may still be apparent in the children ten years or longer after the termination of the analysis. In coconstructing a conceptual world, she has provided some of the basis for the individual's progressive ego development; she has shared a part of her own self.

Thus, we see that cosmogonic play facilitates emerging ego functions, provides a model for creative imagination and secondary process thinking, and is a way to effect therapeutic change. This type of dramatic play has a strong relation to reality and influences the development of symbolic functions used in the world that the child lives in. To the extent that a conceptual world is an intermediate area that is the coconstruction of the analyst and the child, both have a shared dramaturgy and engage in a process of genuine collaboration.

References

Bogatyrev, P. (1938). Semiotics in the folk theater. In *Semiotics of Art: Prague School Contributions*, ed. L. Matekja and I. R. Tuitunik. Cambridge, Mass.: MIT Press, 1976.

Brook, P. (1968). *The Empty Space*. New York: Avon, 1972.

Erikson, E. H. (1963). *Childhood and Society*. 2nd ed. New York: Norton.

Freud, A. (1965). Normality and pathology in childhood. In *The Writings of Anna Freud*, 6.

Freud, S. (1908). Creative writers and day-dreaming. *S.E.*, 9:141–153.

Klein, M. (1961). *Narrative of a Child Analysis*. New York: Delta, 1976.

Kohut, H. (1971). *The Analysis of the Self*. New York: Int. Univ. Press.

Loewald, E. L. (1987). Therapeutic play in space and time. *Psychoanal. Study Child*, 42:173–192.

Moran, G. S. (1987). Some functions of play and playfulness. *Psychoanal. Study Child*, 42:11–29.

Ritvo, S. (1978). The psychoanalytic process. *Psychoanal. Study Child*, 33:295–305.

Solnit, A. J. (1987). A psychoanalytic view of play. *Psychoanal. Study Child*, 42:205–219.

Stanislavsky, K. (1963). Creative work with the actor: A discussion on directing. In *Directors on Directing: A Source Book of the Modern Theater*, ed. T. Cole and H. Krich Chinoy. New York: Bobbs-Merrill.

Turner, V. W. (1967). *The Forest of Symbols*. Ithaca, N.Y.: Cornell Univ. Press.

———. (1969). *The Ritual Process: Structure and Anti-Structure*. Ithaca, N.Y.: Cornell Univ. Press.

Vandenberg, B. (1986). Play, myth, and hope. In *Play, Play Therapy, Play Research*, ed. R. van der Kooij and J. Hellendoorn. Berwyn, The Netherlands: Swets North America.

Winnicott, D. W. (1971). *Playing and Reality*. New York: Penguin, 1980.

6

Born Blind: Playing in a Sighted World

Alice B. Colonna, M.A.

Albert J. Solnit, M.D.

In a recent exchange of letters, Walt Stromer, a blind professor at a midwestern university, complains to Oliver Sacks (1991) that in his review of *Touching the Stone* Sacks has misunderstood how it is to become blind as an adult. Stromer (1991) writes, "I do know that the concept of darkness is not an appropriate metaphor for blindness. Those who are born blind have no first-hand experience as to light or dark. On the other hand, I don't know any person blinded later in life who would accept darkness as an accurate comparison."

In the exchange between Stromer and Sacks there are references to the inner eye, how it does or does not vanish with blindness. As Sacks puts it, "The particular point at issue is the extent to which loss of eyesight in adult life leads to a loss of visual imagery, visual conceptions of 'inner eye.' It is possible that this varies a good deal—as seems to be the case with auditory imagery, and auditory thinking, the 'inner ear' in those who have been deafened in adult life."

Keeping in mind auditory and visual factors, we are addressing the play activities of blind children—those born blind or who become blind soon after birth—in a sighted world. As sighted adults we try to traverse both the blind experience (much of which we have learned from adults who became blind after childhood) and the experience of childhood (much of which we have learned from sighted children).

With these disadvantages, we also keep in mind that as the child begins to speak at about twelve months of age, visual, auditory, olfactory, kinesthetic, and tactile perceptions are involved in the formation of language competence.

During the first year an internal map of the world is constructed from a mass of incoming sensory data. Once a certain degree of thought, based on this experience, is achieved, the child goes on to acquire a range of communication skills of which language is the most important.

Cognitive development therefore depends on the evolution of thought processes that are themselves dependent on normal brain function. It follows that either damage to the neuronal substrate underlying the evolution of thought or environmental deficiencies that limit sensory experience will lead to cognitive deficits that present clinically as disorders of communication.*

In a significant sense the blind child's approach to socializing and play in a sighted world is handicapped by the absence of part of the brain's capacity, the visual function. The eye is a vital elaboration of the brain's structure and function.

Psychoanalytic Theories of Play

Play as a means of better understanding the inner world of the young child was of great interest to Freud, who, in an important sense, mapped out for future theoreticians certain areas to be examined. He characterized children's play as essentially "serious." At the same time, he indicated that, in accord with the child's developing sense of reality, play was not "real." It seemed to have a quality midway between fantasy and reality and to represent the child's attempts to assimilate or integrate reality according to his or her own developmental stage with the cognitive awareness appropriate to it. Freud's perception of the importance of play seems to have represented a mixture of his imaginative creativity and his rigorous attempts to explore the meaning of this phenomenon of early life as he observed its manifestations in adult patients and as he learned about children, perhaps from his daughter Anna, who was in direct contact with children.

Freud's book on jokes contains important insights into the role of play in childhood, for in a sense he viewed play as a precursor to jokes. He stated:

Before there is such a thing as a joke, there is something that we may describe as play or as a jest.

Play—let us keep to that name—appears in children while they are learning to make use of words and to put thoughts together. This probably obeys one of the instincts which compel children to practise their capacities (Groos [1899]). In doing so they come across pleasurable effects, which arise from repetition of what is similar, a rediscovery of what is familiar, similarity of sound, etc., and which are to be explained as unsuspected economies in psychical expenditure. It is not to be

*From a commentary on the autistic child in *Lancet* (May 18, 1991), 332:1191–1192.

wondered at that these pleasurable effects encourage children in the pursuit of play and cause them to continue it without regard for the meaning of words or the coherence of sentences. *Play* with words and thoughts, motivated by certain pleasurable effects of economy, would thus be the first stage of jokes.

This play is brought to an end by the strengthening of a factor that deserves to be described as the critical faculty or reasonableness. The play is now rejected as being meaningless or actually absurd; as a result of criticism it becomes impossible. Now, too, there is no longer any question of deriving pleasure, except accidentally, from the sources of rediscovery of what is familiar, etc., unless it happens that the growing individual is overtaken by a pleasurable mood which, like the child's cheerfulness, lifts the critical inhibition. Only in such a case does the old game of getting pleasure become possible once more; but the individual does not want to wait for this to happen nor to renounce the pleasure that is familiar to him. He thus looks about for means of making himself independent of the pleasurable mood, and the further development towards jokes is governed by the two endeavours: to avoid criticism and to find a substitute for the mood.

And with this the second preliminary stage of jokes sets in—the *jest*. It is now a question of prolonging the yield of pleasure from play, but at the same time of silencing the objections raised by criticism which would not allow the pleasurable feeling to emerge. There is only one way of reaching this end: the meaningless combination of words or the absurd putting together of thoughts must nevertheless have a meaning. The whole ingenuity of the joke-work is summoned up in order to find words and aggregations of thoughts in which this condition is fulfilled. (1905, pp. 128–129)

Among child analysts there is a consensus that play is an important feature of childhood and that the lack of it represents an impoverishment of the personality. Child's play is therefore one feature taken into account in assessment. Anna Freud (1965) viewed play as one of several major sources of knowledge about the child and his or her inner life, along with information from parents and the child's verbalizations and drawings. Absence of play was not, in her view, a symptom in itself, for she considered the major criterion for health to be the child's capacity to maintain progressive development.

Play, in terms of "pretend" or "imagination," is probably at its peak during the oedipal period when it can be observed easily and demonstrates directly the way in which children view themselves, with some emerging sense of past and future. In this period they maintain an unselfconscious attitude to play that is no longer in evidence in the later periods. During latency, play is associated with games; that is, delay, practice, and objective rules take over. In the group setting or in analytic work oedipal children are open in showing the ambiguities, contradictions, and conflicts that they will soon criticize in themselves as their defenses develop and as they attempt repression, reaction formations, and putting down earlier, now ego-alien, wishes and longings.

Freud noted the interesting connection between play and humor, linking play to the capacity for symbolization and playing with words. Ambiguities and contradictions become the focus for jokes shared between mature individuals; and the shared pleasure in using such incongruities as inappropriate words or unexpected outcomes becomes the focus as "wit" develops.

Imaginative play involves the creation of mental images dramatized in behavior. To a considerable extent, children in their play reflect the way adults around them relate and use language. Much of what we learn from play is the way in which it relates to scenes and events taken out of context, often being concerned specifically with play roles—make-believe or pretend activities.

Psychoanalysts are concerned with how far play in childhood remains an important feature of life in adulthood as well as in what way and to what degree it is altered and incorporated into the capacity to work as the individual gradually moves from the pleasure to the reality principle.

The Relation between Vision and Play in Infancy

At the Anna Freud Centre, observations of blind infants and toddlers under the leadership of Dorothy Burlingham from 1958 into the 1970s led to a sustained interest in the role of vision in various areas of early development, including the early interaction and playful behavior between mother (or other care-giver) and child.* In these studies, looking seemed to stimulate the infant's curiosity and desire to reach out to the outside world. Along with touch and the feeling of comfort or discomfort, hunger or satiation, it played a role in the establishment of the differentiation between self and other. It was noted that blind infants could be outgoing, active, and in good

*Observers made home visits and also observed mother-infant and mother-toddler pairs in hospitals and during planned excursions.

contact with the outside world through stimulation of sound and touch in the context of and proportionate to the intensity of interactions with the care-giver. It was clear that with these early foundations the blind toddler and preschooler appeared much more like normal sighted children than those whose care-givers had, through their depression or withdrawal, been unable to relate closely to the sighted young child, to enjoy the infant and his or her progress. In some of the blind children we have known, the mother's pride in the child's achievements became an important element in the confidence and persistence of the children. What has been especially noted in the early observation of blind infants has been the way in which they are alerted to the tone of voice and the touch of the care-giver. (Olfactory experiences have been less well studied.) Tone of voice conveyed much of the pleasure or displeasure, praise or blame, that served as a main focus for the blind infant. This provided the baby with clues both to the mother's affect and to what she admired and encouraged—ways for the infant to please her. Thus, the child became sensitized and focused upon one person who was experienced as the source for all feelings of safety and well-being. Noted among the blind children in this group was their frequently asking, "Are you watching me?" This showed how important the adult's attention was, just as there were many examples of the insistence on being the only occupant of the lap of the care-giver (similar to the behavior of sighted toddlers).

In a sense when we considered play in the first year or two of life (before language), it was usually in the context of a care-giver–infant unit and much of the child's activity was in response to and interaction with the mother's interest, encouragement, and pleasure. In this respect the blind child seemed to focus in an intuitive fashion and "glued" himself to the care-giver with whatever perceptual tools were available to him.

We were able to note which of those children who became blind before or soon after birth and who underwent hospitalization in the presence of the mother could maintain this close bond (which has been described as the toddler's clinging to the mother like a rhesus monkey—in other words with a primitive grasp). This contrasted with those who were alone in the hospital with the confusion and fear of the unknown, the inability to be aware of pending interventions of feeding, bathing, and the routines and procedures that take place in the hospital. Since not all interaction is comfort-giving or pleasurable, the question of anticipation is important. Vision is especially important in this respect partly because it gives an early warning signal; there is time to perceive and react according to the distance involved. Visual experience transmits clues as to whether the intervention will be tension-reducing and pleasurable or unwelcome and painful.

In hospitalizations the mother serves as an auxiliary sighted ego, warning or comforting the child who awaits medical and other procedures. Many clues can help the sighted infant anticipate what might happen. The rhythm of day and night for preparation of bath or bedtime has an important visual component, whereas the blind child has to learn associated equivalents or needs to be supported by a familiar adult functioning as an auxiliary ego. For example, recently a blind child had to be hospitalized for dehydration. His mother was unable to be with him, and his therapist came in several times to help him, to explain procedures, and to permit him to verbalize his anger, expressed mainly in his trying to remove the IV, which he hated. Nurses at first were sympathetic but soon became impatient and told him if he pulled out the IV, it would only be stuck in again. He was also angry and confused over having to wear a mask and not being allowed to go near another child of the same age (five years) because of risk of infection. He needed the therapist to interpret what was happening and to help him deal with his anger. The therapist thought that her being with him at a crucial time when the mother could not was a turning point in her long-term work with him.

In the absence of sight, the mother provides direct physical contact as support and reassurance as well as verbal interaction with her infant. Later as the infant begins to crawl and walk, the mother elaborates her support with more specific physical and verbal guidelines. Warnings of danger along with encouragement and preparation of the environment become important in enabling the blind toddler to feel competent and to persist in expressing and pursuing what curiosity suggests. As independence develops, the mother serves as the child's eyes in development-promoting ways.

Those blind children who have been able to maintain an active stance have done so through an almost continual interaction with one or usually more than one consistent care-giver (such as a grandmother or aunt). The "others" in their lives have become known through voice, touch, smell, and the feel of the part of the body they come in contact with. The need for what might be called "visual interpretation" or "lending one's eyes" has an exclusive quality and does not easily generalize into the child feeling intensely involved with and yet separate from the family as a group. Direct individual attention is required, and the infant or toddler is alert to which person is interacting with her. There is more of a sense of being *in* or *out* of contact rather than feeling (socially and securely) satisfied in the presence of others. This would complicate the conditions necessary to achieve the capacity of being "alone in the presence of others" as described by Winnicott (1958).

The Anna Freud Centre was begun in 1947 for the purpose of training specialists in the study and practice of child psychoanalysis. In association with this center, community services were established where observations were made in a well-baby clinic and two nursery schools, one of which was for children blind from birth. This filled important clinical needs, since the United Kingdom was offering only residential settings for preschool blind children. One of the authors of this chapter functioned initially as a teacher and later as therapist for one of the children in this group.

In their preschool years when they were with other blind children either in their group environment at the nursery school for blind children or in analytic treatment at the Anna Freud Centre, it was noted that the children made a complete distinction between the present and the absent care-givers. The absent person was rarely mentioned, and it was difficult to know how far she was a psychological presence for the blind child as an extension of being a concrete physical presence. Our children were always attentive to the telephone, which served as a link to reach the important persons in their lives. The doorbell, signaling the arrival of a longed-for or unexpected person with the connotation of separation, was important. On other levels, to a significant degree, blind children appeared to have object-constancy capacities and to maintain a positive feeling about the therapist whether they were frustrated or gratified. If sight were miraculously restored, would the "all-or-none" quality described become replaced by a fuller, more subtle object-constancy capacity?

Object relationships have an important place in play, as does the complex aspect of vision and other perceptual experiences in terms of the child's sense of safety and knowledge of and orientation in space. Blindness not only interferes with ordinary play and sharing with others to reach a common goal but also appears to inhibit fantasy formation, since the visual props are missing. In the therapy, there was evidence that play did not reveal the child's concerns, conflicts, and fears in the way that usually takes place with sighted children. The blind child was very absorbed in finding areas of safety in which he could experience pleasure. This was very different from the way in which sighted children try out various alternatives and demonstrate their anxieties, defenses, and fantasies. (Systematic studies in this area are yet to be conducted.) For these reasons, it is useful to describe the way in which blind children learn to function both in the group and in the psychoanalytic setting. These observations will further highlight how the blind differ from sighted children of the same age.

Analytic Treatment of a Blind Preschool Child

The treatment of young blind children is in principle the same as that of sighted children, but several features of their treatment differ greatly from the treatment of sighted peers. In particular, the therapist must be aware of activities available for blind children to elicit the knowledge of their inner lives and help them cope with problems caused by struggles of the ego in dealing with inner and outer reality. One wonders how the transference develops. How does the blind child experience and use contact with the therapist as he or she is encouraged to play with and talk to this new adult? In the treatment, the analyst offers materials that will invite the child to verbalize and play out some of the concerns that give him difficulties. Where does the analyst begin when the child needs him as his "eyes"? What toys will stimulate his imagination and help him understand his fantasies? Since the blind child is very dependent upon the verbalizations of the sighted care-givers and must trust them to help him avoid dangers, how will he understand interpretations and to what extent will he accept them as useful? Will the child take interpretation literally and concretely? What is his perception of an adult who "plays" when the adult is perceived as a voice, an arm, a hand, or a lap?

Another important area relates to the parental perception of the therapy. The parents of the patient we are about to describe were rightly proud of their son and confident they could help him. They participated in and supported his verbal abilities and active attitudes. Having played a positive and successful role in his life, how did his mother feel about turning him over to a therapist who hoped to learn about his inner life and feelings? How would this be affected by the child's need to turn significantly from her to the therapist, a new "care-giver"?

Richard was the second of three children in an intact young family. The youngest was a girl twelve months old when Richard came to the nursery at age three about a year before beginning therapy. His blindness was not discovered until he was fourteen months of age, at which time, under examination urged by his grandmother, retinoblastoma was diagnosed. One eye was removed immediately, and the other received radium therapy necessitating several hospitalizations. Richard had had a little sight in the first months of life, and his parents denied any visual problem, though his grandmother commented frequently that the eye looked peculiar. He was treated as a sighted child for the first year and was thus stimulated and involved in active ways, which he experienced positively. After his sister's birth, he was encouraged to touch her, help in some of her care, and assist in her toilet-training by informing his mother when she was ready to leave the pot, needed a change, and so on.

Richard's father and an eight-year-old brother were very much involved in sports and spoke of them often. They tried to include Richard and played games with him. This promoted his identification with males and their activities. At times his brother took on the father role, especially in regard to sports. Richard had his own toy cars, which actively provided for play with his older brother.

Richard also had a teddy bear, which he took everywhere with him. He often played hospital, with the bear being Richard and he being the care-giving mother. Richard was afraid of the wind (a not uncommon fear among blind children) and disliked sand (which he was familiar with through seaside holidays). He was friendly and talkative with the home visitor, but his speech was often babyish and not easy to understand. Richard's mother seemed tense and standoffish. The parents had not visited much during the hospitalizations, saying that the hospitals were well set up and the personnel better trained to help him than they.

Although Richard compared well with other children in the nursery group for blind children in that he was active, curious, friendly, verbal, and competent, his language difficulty and his hesitations and anxieties seemed directly related to blindness (fear of loud noises, lack of pleasure in task competition), which, it was felt, could be better addressed if more were known and understood about his inner life. Although all the children had a "special time" with a therapist, Richard's parents initially found the notion of psychological intervention puzzling and felt threatened by it. But in time, and with the help of Richard's grandmother who was very positive and undertook to bring him every day, Richard's parents came to see our in-volvement as a positive feature and were supportive. The fact that, like the other children, Richard made such an all-or-none kind of relationship with whichever adult he was with complicated our efforts to maintain a sense of his affective life. Other adults seemed not to exist for Richard. This exis-tential kind of dependency relationship with its internal narcissistic satis-factions affected all those who worked with him. Adults helping Richard felt both stimulated and drained.

Richard used toys relatively well. He efficiently operated an electric car at home and built towers, garages, and railways in the nursery school, doing so very carefully, even standing on a chair to make them higher. He loved knocking them down and worried that the teacher or another child might do this.

From my first meeting with Richard I was aware of the impact of his need for an adult as continual translator of visual reality; it was powerful in making the sighted adult feel needed and narcissistically satisfied. This was accompanied by an awareness of the continual anxiety to which he was subjected and his tendency to underemphasize his inner difficulties because of the dangers from outside.

When I came to collect Richard from the nursery school for the first time, many questions arose in my mind as to how he would understand and respond to meeting with me—a new person. Since I was neither a familiar teacher nor a parent, I wondered how he would think of our work together. Prior to this time, I had been a group teacher and was familiar with many of the special needs of blind children. For a long time, each of two teachers had at times gone on excursions with one or another child since it was clear that each child enjoyed and benefited from the one-to-one contact (lending one's eyes). It was subsequent to this observation that the second part of Dorothy Burlingham and Anna Freud's program to learn more about the inner life of the blind child—namely, treatment—was added to the educational work of the nursery for blind children. Child analysts working with the children could bring to bear new views and understandings different from those that had been explored in the educational setting.

Richard, on my first visit, was polite, but seemed apprehensive, as though he would have preferred to dismiss my presence. He found it difficult to leave the teachers and the nursery, employing what seemed like delaying tactics. Later it emerged that this was probably his way of attempting to assess a new situation, revealing his method of making transitions and dealing with separations. He encountered a telephone as we left and lingered with it. Obviously, it was a tool he had used in talking to his parents, other relatives, and friends to cope with separation and enhance his ability to communicate with absent persons. (Thirty years later the telephone continues to provide the possibility of instant contact, under their control, for these children.) On the way out, Richard stopped to ring the doorbell, a way of gaining the attention of teachers and peers as well as signifying to them his departure and separation. As we walked out of the front gardens, Richard bumped his head on the gate, an immediate sign of his vulnerability and his need to be helped in striving for independence while feeling safe and protected. After the bump, he cried briefly, with some anger and indignation. We climbed the steps of the building across the road, and he commented as someone left, "While we are going up the stairs, somebody is coming down." Richard had unusually good hearing. Encountering the waiting room indoors, he examined it with his hands, at first asking repeatedly, "What is this?" He seemed pleased to try to answer his own questions by touch when the question was reflected back to him. He spoke in these terms as he spent the hour exploring the waiting room and hallway.

The next day he seemed more definite in his reluctance to leave the familiar surroundings of the nursery, showing me how he could build with blocks and how much pleasure he gained from knocking the building down. This was a little puzzling in that though he enjoyed the attention and praise given him and realized how much the teachers would have liked to preserve what he built for a time, he also enjoyed provoking a mildly negative reaction as he became restless and aggressively destructive and not nearly as pleasant for the other children in the nursery. When I insisted that we leave the group, his anger accelerated, and with a gesture of annoyance, he pushed bricks and toys from shelf to floor. Getting his coat, he threw the hanger on the floor, too, demanding that I put it back. I verbalized his sense of frustration at his lack of control of the situation and his anxiety about what going with me entailed.

Once outside the door, he ran along the way and across the street, pulling me by the hand. He felt a car parked on the street and asked where my car was, requesting that I take him to it, which I did. We spent the hour in my car, which intrigued him. Once helped inside, Richard took over, sitting in the driver's seat exploring the various switches and buttons. Fascination with mechanical devices is characteristic of the behavior of many children, blind and sighted. This behavior dramatizes how many children transform a passive longing and position into an active one as they take control of a situation. He wanted to start the engine and was elated when I did so; he demanded to use the horn, the windshield wipers, and the heater. Being in command of the sudden blast of the horn excited him. After a time, I decided the neighbors might object, so we moved a few blocks away. He was pleased and continued exploring. He wanted to master the hand brake and gears and asked about the headlights, commenting that they did not work. As I tried to think out a response, he continued his exploration of the dashboard, finding it difficult to leave when it was time to return to the nursery.

Richard was eager to come the third day and more exuberant in pulling me across the street. Although he asked to revisit the car, he seemed very willing to come to the "new" treatment room. It seemed that familiarity with surroundings and trust in me went together. The initial reluctance was apparently based on the fear of the unknown; for the blind child transitions are difficult and not as available to them as they are to sighted children. Often they are experienced as sudden, dangerous, and fraught with unknown hazards. Richard clung to my hand. In the clinic building he asked for a telephone and called the receptionist across the street. In the treatment room for the first time he instructed me to close the door (a clear-cut separation or to keep frightening thoughts out?) and began a systematic tour of the room. This slow, laborious tactile journey taught him what a sighted person learns with a glance upon entering an unfamiliar place.

One characteristic deficit of blind children in a sighted world is the incompleteness of their composite "radar system"—the component sensory capacities for responding in a coordinated manner to the multiple stimuli, challenges, and demands of the external world. At a glance, the sighted child sees the larger picture of the external reality and what may be expected. Within this gestalt, the sighted child orients and chooses how and where to take the next step or how to respond and adapt to both external environmental demands and the desire or task that motivates the child from inside. It is very different for the blind child, who is oriented in the world by smell, sound, and touch, but lacks the visual component, a capacity essential to the well-functioning sensory "radar" in a sighted world. One child, when asked what sight might mean, thought it was like having very long arms. As I noted in these early sessions with Richard, it was as though he had in mind what he came upon through touch and what he could do with it. By using touch to make a first contact in outlining place and contents and uses, he dealt with whatever came his way. It was accordingly whatever came his way first that directed what he would do or what fantasy would be evoked. In contrast, the sighted child sees, chooses, touches, and brings to bear his own fantasies to express his intentionality and to mold his inner ideas to the overall picture.

On encountering lockers, Richard asked about them. I informed him that other children kept their private belongings under lock and key. He chose a space for his things. Much later in the treatment, Richard liked to crawl into his locker and close the door, begging me to lock it. In crawling around outside the locker, he found a doll in a doll bed and picked it up and squeezed it. When the doll's head fell off, Richard showed some concern and spoke to the doll soothingly, showing that he had been acquainted with dolls and was perhaps reenacting a situation with his younger sister. He blew a kiss on the doll's leg and returned the doll to its bed. When questioned about his little sister at home, he acknowledged her existence but did not speak of her further. He asked me to help him play with a car and to show him how to play with some blocks, and then he was ready to leave. It seemed that he was accustomed to being "shown" how to play.

It again became clear how much blind children need to use the adult as a part of themselves in order to function adaptively in a sighted world. Richard demonstrated the need to replace vision in order to complete, in an essential way, the composite of perceptions so necessary to differentiate, clarify, organize, and focus on those aspects that provide efficient warnings of danger, conflict, and pleasure in the outer world. Without the visual component the blind individual needs to find a compensatory way of organizing multiple stimuli and demands in order to use the focusing, suppressing, and repressing ego functions in an adaptive and development-promoting manner. Richard demonstrated how he warded off a discussion of his sister in order to concentrate on the puzzling, demanding, and threatening "here and now."

There was also a frequently expressed fear that he might cause damage, breaking or destroying something or injuring someone. Richard eventually spoke of how worrisome his sister was for him, in the "messes" she made, and how disgusted he felt. When he was encouraged to elaborate these concerns, he often would say, "Be quiet. . . . I told you to be quiet." In moments of distress he expressed his anger by the desire to hurl objects. On occasion he said, "I don't want to talk about all kinds of things that are horrid." His modes of responding to anxiety were associated with all-or-none reactions, which were closer to what could be thought of as primary process thinking. For example, the meaning of *broken* and his fear of the omnipotence of his angry feelings were confusing and difficult to discuss as treatment progressed. He might say, "Shall we talk about broken windows?" or "Can I break one?" or "I'm going to break a window; it goes smash, smash, smash." He wanted to throw the ball out of the window and said, "What will it sound like? What if it is a hard ball?" Rolling a ball down the stairs and listening to it bounce, he might say, "I better hold the bannister. Otherwise I might roll down the stairs like a ball."

As a sighted person, I always found it difficult to understand his view of the world and to try to help him clarify it through words that might have meanings different from those in ordinary discourse. Blind children have to depend on the words of sighted adults to piece together their knowledge of reality. When I tried to explain that my lateness for a session was due to the fact that a car had been parked across my driveway and I had to find the owner in order to move it, he asked, "Why didn't you tell the car to go away?" Other confusions came up about the car. When I had dented a fender and had to take the car to the garage, he was anxious about it and too frightened to touch the dent. There were smells, such as tar on the road or paper paste, that he disliked and recoiled at touching or approaching.

Many words had frightening connotations, too. Years later I was puzzled when Richard as an adult told of a terrible nightmare he had had repeatedly, though only when he was sleeping alone. He dreamed of string. He conveyed his fear that string, perhaps like clay, might engulf and swallow the body altogether, like quicksand, so that one would be totally imprisoned by it.

In following Richard's curiosity and independent strivings, I offered him the opportunity to explore and use mechanical devices such as the typewriter, which he heard upon leaving or arriving. Trying it out, he would become frustrated and bang it angrily, disappointed that his efforts to imitate the sighted adults brought no satisfaction beyond the tactile-auditory experience.

Richard would "play at" using forbidden anal language, adding, "I am leaving you," and slamming the door as he went out to the hall. Once he sat sadly sucking his thumb, and when asked about it, he replied, "I 'spect it's 'cause I'm blind." This followed a weekend when his brother had been out with a sports group and Richard remained at home.

Richard was very frightened at any reference to the rag-and-bone man who went about with his horse and cart purchasing old items. Richard, talking about this, said he took old things such as shirts, shoes, and other articles. He volunteered that he was not frightened by the horse, but he did seem frightened by what he produced as the curious cry of the horse, imitating a somewhat unintelligible eerie noise. It never became entirely clear what had been so terrifying, but several times in this context the active Richard appeared to be totally paralyzed, needing to be picked up for reassurance.

Much of this emerged as the time for an impending hospitalization drew near. Many instances of fear and panic occurred in the context of his inability to anticipate and prepare for danger. The panic caused by the rag-and-bone man seemed associated with hospitalization and the sound of a gurney being wheeled into a ward to carry the patient to the surgical theater. On this occasion Richard demanded that I close the door to keep out flies that buzzed outside. He tried to barricade the door to keep the pediatrician out, fearing she would take him to the hospital. The anticipatory anxiety made orientation more difficult for him. Attempting to reassure himself about permanence, he asked the teacher to leave his sand castle for the next day. She agreed, while pointing out that if it rained it would wash away. He was worried about this and said if it rained, he would wave his shovel (like a wand) and make it stop.

Discussion

Much of the work with Richard focused on helping him verbalize inner and outer reality, sort it out, and integrate and comprehend his various perceptions and clarify his idiosyncratic interpretations of what he felt, heard, smelled, and sensed without the executive visual organizing capacity. At times Richard felt that his behavior caused great damage to others, to the world, and to himself. There were repeated efforts to ascertain how adults would react to his beliefs. Evidently a great deal that is communicated by the adult's facial and postural expression is profoundly reassuring to sighted children but not available to blind children. The lack of visual experience leaves the blind child in a state of uncertainty and apprehension. Safety is in the hands or eyes of the companion. The fear of regression looms as very threatening to blind children in treatment, just as in our group when the blind children stimulated each other's regressive wishes and loss of control as expressed in their shouting, throwing, and kicking. The notion they loved to share of "throwing the teacher into the dustbin" contained many exploratory speculations, including efforts taken for granted by sighted children in learning the differences in size and shape among people. They gain a sense of the whole physical person, whereas blind children depend on voice, touch, and smell to gain such comprehension.

It is very difficult for sighted adults to understand the world of the blind child. To provide "new" or learning tactile and auditory experiences for Richard provoked complex reactions and anxieties. At times they could be overcome, but at other times the fear and negative reactions were relatively resistant to reduction and mastery. This was the case with working with clay, which was offered and encouraged in the program. A blind adult recalled how intensely he had hated clay and the experience of the sticky material covering his hands, preventing him from using his hands in other ways. Conversely, this same man recalled many scenes vividly, often those when he apparently enjoyed the feeling of "naughtiness," as had Richard in playing with clay. He needed to know and try out what limits there were. At the same time he worried about consequent damage.

It would appear, therefore, that the experience of play is bound up with that aspect of ego functioning that differentiates the inner and outer worlds. It is difficult to know how far blind preschool children are able to develop imagination, to put themselves in the role of another, even though they often reverse roles in their play with care-givers in what appears to be a form of imitative behavior. Imagining, as sighted people conceptualize it, requires the capacity to form the visual aspect of mental representations as a primary component of such psychic functioning. This probably cannot take place without a relatively stable concept of spatial orientation, which is established much later and in a different fashion in the blind child. The route the blind child takes is difficult to follow, partly because our understanding has to depend largely on verbalizations, and these come to the blind through the sighted adult labeling and demonstrating. If we follow in the *Oxford English Dictionary*, some of the many definitions of the verb *look*, we find many meanings besides "use one's sight," namely, "to contemplate, examine, make mental search, inquire, aim one's attention, observe"—all of which suggest figuratively many mental functions that help take distance from, gain perspective on, and integrate the stimuli we refer to as the impact and demands of reality.

The move into latency generally implies a resolution of oedipal wishes and confidence in the child's ability to acquire skills and envision a future in which he or she will competently take the adult's place. In the observations and psychoanalytic treatment of blind children, it is clear that the broader psychological configurations of the blind oedipal child are fundamentally the same as for the sighted child. The differences have not been systematically studied, but it is not a theoretical leap to assume that the blind child's continuing needs for the auxiliary ego visual functions of sighted, closely related persons (especially parents, siblings, teachers) have a modifying impact on the formation and resolution of the oedipal conflicts and on the continuing residual expression of oedipal wishes.

Blind children use a variety of ways in which to adapt physically and mentally to a sighted world as they become aware of themselves. In this connection, Freud's formulation of the ego as a body ego is useful. Freud stated, "The ego is first and foremost a bodily ego; it is not merely a surface entity, but is itself the projection of a surface" (1923, p. 26). In a footnote that first appeared in the English translation in 1927, he added, "I.e., the ego is ultimately derived from bodily sensations, chiefly from those springing from the surface of the body. It may thus be regarded as a mental projection of the surface of the body, besides, as we have seen above, representing the superficies of the mental apparatus."

Human blindness reminds us that body and brain are intimately interwoven in the functions of the mind, as they are in the child's play. Thus we conclude:

1. Blind children have an ego deficit that requires that they have more care and guidance in order to be safe and oriented spatially and socially,

and to enable them to sort out and organize the many nonvisual stimuli that impinge upon them.

2. Blind children with the assistance of sighted persons gradually develop special physical and psychological mechanisms to compensate for their visual deficit. Systematic psychoanalytic and nonpsychoanalytic studies of blind children at play will enable us better to understand ego capacities and reparative potentials as well as bringing improved relief to blind children and adults.

3. Central to this line of thinking is our need to acquire a better understanding of why blind children have difficulty playing in a sighted world. It is all the more important for blind children to be enabled to play, to pretend, to explore, to express, and to practice physically and mentally those functions of play and playfulness so essential to their achieving the fullness of the human experience and the capacity to reflect upon the human condition.

References

Burlingham, D. (1972). *Psychoanalytic Studies of the Sighted and the Blind*. New York: Int. Univ. Press.

———. (1979). To be blind in a sighted world. *Psychoanal. Study Child*, 34:5–31.

Colonna, A. (1968). A blind child goes to the hospital. *Psychoanal. Study Child*, 23:391–422.

———. (1981). Success through their own efforts. *Psychoanal. Study Child*, 36.

Curson, A. (1979). The blind nursery school child. *Psychoanal. Study Child*, 34:51–85.

Fraiberg, S., and Freedman, D. (1964). Studies in the ego development of the congenitally blind child. *Psychoanal. Study Child*, 19:113–169.

Freud, A. (1965). *Normality and Pathology in Childhood*. New York: Int. Univ. Press.

Freud, S. (1905). Jokes and their relation to the unconscious. *S.E.*, 8.

———. (1923). The ego and the id. *S.E.*, 19:3–66.

Greenacre, P. (1959). Play and the creative process. *Psychoanal. Study Child*, 14:61–80.

Nagera, H., and Colonna, A. B. (1965). Aspects of the contribution of sight to ego and drive development. *Psychoanal. Study Child*, 20:267–278.

Peller, L. (1954). Libidinal phase, ego development, and play. *Psychoanal. Study Child*, 4:61–80.

Sacks, O. (1991). Letter to editor. *N.Y. Rev. Books*, April 11.

Sandler, A.-M. (1963). Aspects of passivity and ego development in the blind infant. *Psychoanal. Study Child*, 18:344–360.

Sandler, A.-M., and Wills, D. (1965). Some notes on play and mastery in the blind child. *J. Child Psychotherapy*, 1:7–19.

Stromer, W. (1991). Letter to editor. *N. Y. Rev. Books*, June 13.

Wills, D. M. (1965). Some observations on blind nursery school children's understanding of their world. *Psychoanal. Study Child*, 20:344–365.

Winnicott, D. W. (1958). The capacity to be alone. In *The Maturational Processes and the Facilitating Environment*. New York: Int. Univ. Press, 1965, pp. 29–36.

7

Play and the Construction of Gender in the Oedipal Child

E. Kirsten Dahl, Ph.D.

Popular opinion and child development research stress pervasive and significant differences in the pretend play of boys and girls. Nonpsychoanalytic studies demonstrate sex differences in activity level, thematic content, characters, and toy choice (see Rubin et al. [1983] for a thorough review of child development research concerning sex differences in children's play). Psychoanalytic theory has argued that manifest differences in the imaginative play of boys and girls result from latent substantive intrapsychic differences in the construction of gender. For example, Erikson (1950) believed that the differences he observed in the use of the play space by ten- to twelve-year-old children had been centrally influenced by the subjective experience of anatomy. Erikson's conviction that the child's sense of spatial organization is dominated by the biological genital schematization has frequently been used to argue that significant differences in the play of boys and girls reflect a bisexual construction of gender with the predominant emphasis closely tied to anatomical morphology.

In this chapter, I intend to show that though on its surface the play of oedipal-age children does appear to illustrate such a dichotomous, categorical expression of gender, when the manifest content is examined for latent fantasies the multidimensional nature of children's notions regarding gender emerges. I contend that it is the flourishing of imaginative, symbolizing play during the oedipal period that allows the child to construct a more complex, densely layered, and highly individual sense of gender. This oedipal psychological construction involves a retroactive transformation of an earlier, dichotomous, biologically rooted gender identity that is more closely linked to anatomy. One of the central story lines that engages the oedipal child involves the internal dilemma created when the

I thank Elizabeth Brett, Donald J. Cohen, Steven Marans, Stanley Possick, and Lynn Whisnant Reiser for their critical suggestions during the writing of this chapter.

child hates and wishes to destroy those objects who are also loved (see chapter 18 for a fuller discussion of such thematic content). This chapter explores the ways in which the vicissitudes of aggression both drive and are reflected in gender construction. Although I recognize the contribution of libidinal issues to the development of gender, it is not my intention to investigate that contribution here.

I begin by examining the play of six boys and four girls of oedipal age who participated in a study of normal children's play during a clinical interview. Differences in the thematic content between the sexes are explored to demonstrate that "gendered" fantasies are given surface presentation in the play of oedipal-age children. These surface presentations permit the observer to think of gender as a dichotomous, categorical variable.

I shall then consider the play from early in the psychoanalyses of a boy and a girl. The surface of the pretend play of these two analytic patients is quite similar to the play of the study boys and girls. But when the play of the two child patients is examined through the microscopic lens provided by their psychoanalytic treatment, we are able to see the ways in which both children entertain multiple possibilities across multiple "subvariables"; these eventually become organized into a complex gender fantasy structure that is personal, nondualistic, multileveled, and multidimensional.

The Play Study
Methodology

As described previously (Cohen et al., 1987), twenty children were recruited from a nursery school for a study of children's play during clinical interviews. Each child attended three forty-five-minute play sessions with a child analyst who knew nothing about the child's history, background, or developmental status. The sessions were videotaped from behind a one-way mirror and then transcribed. This report draws on the data generated during a study designed to test the validity and reliability of a scoring protocol developed to analyze the videotapes and transcripts. The videotapes of the second sessions of the first ten children to participate in the study were selected. Because data analysis focused on determining the validity and reliability of the coding protocol, no effort was made to divide the sample equally between boys and girls. The protocol specified the minute-by-minute coding of thirty predetermined imaginative play themes organized along six dimensions: the body; interpersonal relations; morality; aggressivity; secrets, birth, and babies; and techniques for structuring the play.

Data

The play themes of the boys and girls in this sample were more similar than dissimilar. Across all thematic dimensions, boys and girls were sharply differentiated along only two of the six dimensions. The boys were much higher than girls on all themes pertaining to aggressivity, and girls were much higher than boys on all themes having to do with birth and babies.

Within thematic dimensions, however, there were some notable differences. Of those themes pertaining to the body, the play of the boys tended to be organized around themes having to do with the power, size, and capacity of the body; their play reflected a concern with how big and powerful the body was and what the body could do. In contrast, when the girls' play presented themes having to do with the body, the content concerned bodily functions: eating, sleeping, and toileting. The girls made more references to their bodies and those of their characters and touched their own bodies more than did the boys.

In keeping with the girls' narrative emphasis on themes involving bodily functions, birth, and babies, their play was significantly different from the boys' in the use of family members as story characters; these were the predominant characters in the girls' narratives and virtually absent from the boys'. Along this same line, the girls' narratives reflected a concern with loss of the object, with comings and goings of significant others, and with the notion of two characters excluding a third. These themes were very weakly represented, if at all, in the boys' play.

Given the boys' narrative focus on aggressivity, it is not surprising that their stories were sharply differentiated from the girls' by the presence of themes having to do with destruction; the tearing down, crashing, bashing, and blowing up of inanimate objects and property were frequent story lines in the boys' play and virtually absent from the girls'.

A characteristic story narrated by one of the girls began with an elaborate, detailed setting up of a dollhouse and then a placement of the family dolls in the interior of the house. The family dolls would be described in terms of their family relationships: mommy, daddy, big sister, little sister, baby, and so on. Much of the play might consist of moving the characters around the interior of the house in precise, quiet domestic play. Gradually this domestic scene would give way to a more dramatic scenario.

Linda, age five, began her second interview by engaging the analyst in conversation about family life. She spoke regretfully of not having enough time with her daddy and about her anxiety concerning attending kindergarten in the fall. She then narrated a long story about kite flying with her parents, describing animatedly how big her kite was and how high it flew. With some excitement Linda described telling her daddy to run as fast as he could so the kite would not fall down. As she chatted, she began to play with the toy kitchen utensils, ending her kite narrative to explain that her mom did not let her help in the kitchen because of "things that are sharp and cutting."

Linda then began to pretend she was preparing soup, cutting up vegetables and garlic; four times she "cut" her finger, exclaiming "Ouch!" dramatically each time. Repeatedly utensils and cans became stuck, and Linda pretended to fix them. As she struggled to fix various "complicated machines," Linda chatted about ethnic differences between her mom and dad. As she talked, she moved from her cooking play to the dollhouse, examining toy furniture. Looking at a dollhouse toilet, Linda commented forcefully, "Things are all scattered around," and she then began to tidy up the dollhouse. As she continued setting the scene, she periodically spoke with mock irritation of how messy the house was as she reflected with pleasure how well she was "organizing" it.

As she arranged the dollhouse, Linda placed the small family figures in the various rooms, beginning with the mother in the kitchen, whom she described as not wanting anyone "bugging her." She put the father in the bathroom taking a shower, while the two sisters took a bath in the same room. She placed the baby in "his walking thing." A little later she stated that the mommy and daddy had their own private bathroom. Having arranged all the rooms and all the family figures (a mommy, a daddy, two sisters, a brother, and two babies), Linda began to speak for her characters. The story she narrated concerned one of the sisters, who was eight years old and was told by the mommy to watch the baby. Linda had the sister carry the baby upstairs and wash "his" hands. As if to suggest how hard the sister worked to take care of the baby, Linda described her as too little to reach the sink, and at another point she spoke for the sister, "I'm tired." Abandoning the apparently too difficult work of caring for the baby, Linda had the sister go off to play hide-and-seek with the other sister.

The remainder of the session, fourteen minutes, was occupied with dramatized variations on the theme of hide-and-seek. The longest play sequence, lasting four minutes, was at this point as Linda concentrated on an elaborate game of hide-and-seek between the two sisters, Karen and Lucy. Although Linda described Karen as becoming tired from the game, Lucy continued to hide; Linda then made the father yell at Lucy not to hide. Lucy disobeyed her father and hid herself excitedly as the father and brother searched. For three minutes, Linda had the father search in and out of the house for Lucy, who finally shouted, "Daddy!" and came home. Immediately following Lucy's return, Linda dramatized the family's discovery that their baby "is lost!" In this sequence, Linda focused on the dad's actions; the house was very dark as the dad searched and yelled for the lost baby, now referred to as a girl, Ann. Although the father was depicted as joyfully finding Ann, he then turned angrily on Karen whom he blamed for losing the baby. Linda dramatized Karen "being snotty" to the dad. Linda said in an excited whisper, "She's in trouble," adding with a giggle, "That must be fun for Karen!" Linda drew her story to a close as the session ended by having the daddy spank Karen; Karen cried and the dad, sending Karen to her room, said affectionately, "That was just a spanking, honey." Throughout this fourteen-minute narrative sequence, Linda sustained an intense, animated involvement with her imaginative play, speaking dramatically for each character and conveying a broad range of imagined affects. During the final sequence as first Lucy hid from the dad and then Karen teased and was spanked by him, Linda's affect was one of excited and amused pleasure. Through language, affective communication, and eye contact, Linda made sure that the female analyst understood her narrative.

The theme of family members hiding from, teasing, and excluding other family members was a common one for the study girls. Susan, age five, told a story in which the kid, a little boy, was sent up on the roof by his parents. Giggling, Susan excitedly described the boy as wearing "a summer dress in the ice-cold snow." Susan told a later version of this story in which the kids were throwing out the mommy and daddy "because they don't like them."

A typical story told by the study boys was quite different. Themes of bodily integrity and bodily damage, transformations of the body, and issues of good and bad were prominent. The characters were primarily nonfamily figures, frequently robots, robotic vehicles, policemen, or robbers. With mounting excitement, a study boy would describe how big and powerful the characters were; demonstrations of the characters' power involving crashing or attacking behaviors followed such enactments. The narrative sequences reflected a concern with the possibility of bodily injury or damage and wishes for bodily transformations in the service of increased potency or repair of damage. Issues of morality were also explored, particularly with reference to the goodness or badness of wielding destructive power over others. The wish for power was presented as a wish for absolute power over another's body, and this power was inevitably experienced as hostile and destructive. The expressed wish was to attack, damage, or destroy the body of another in the service of exercising total power.

There was nothing comparable in the play of the girls. When the body was given representations in the girls' play, they were often fleeting, hidden in stories presenting complicated, sometimes obscure, relationships between people, usually family members. Sometimes these ephemeral references to the body took the form of questions about what could be seen and not seen, as in Linda's and Susan's stories about hiding. Linda's brief, playful references to cutting herself were also typical.

Although none of the narratives told by either boys or girls involved direct presentations of or statements about gender, the surface differences in thematic content can be understood as being partially shaped by underlying fantasies having to do with gender. The boys' stories appeared to reflect an almost directly expressed concern with the integrity of the body and the wish to be big and powerful; this wish seemed to be driven both by the wish to ensure bodily integrity and by the wish to exercise absolute power over other bodies. The fantasies generated by the wish for a potent, big, intact, invulnerable body were experienced by the boy as both exciting and frightening. Relationships with other people were presented in their narratives in terms of access to power over others, as if people were defined in terms of whether or not they were powerful. People were described as embodying dichotomous characteristics: big or little, intact or damaged, powerful or vulnerable, good or bad. Aggression was directly expressed in the boys' narratives and was experienced as hostile and destructive, in the service of winning and sustaining power over another's body.

In marked contrast, the girls' narratives were concerned with complex, emotionally laden relationships between family members. Their narratives seemed to be driven by questions having to do with the nature of ambivalent attachments, separations and reunions, and triadic relationships in which one of the three was potentially excluded. Much like the boys, although in a very different context, the girls attributed dichotomous qualities to their story characters; people were presented as big or little, loving or angry, loved or ambivalently cared for, included or excluded. Aggression in the girls' narratives was masked; although the hiding or throwing out of characters in the story was often accompanied by excited laughter suggestive of mild sadism on the part of the playing girl, within the play the actions were presented as "teasing."

It is tempting to read the differences in the play of these boys and girls as reflective of a sharply differentiated sense of gender identity. The boys' stories seemed to reflect fantasies organized around fears of bodily damage and wishes for potency and power; the girls' narratives might be understood in terms of fear of the loss of the object and wishes for an exclusive loving relationship. Perhaps one could even argue, as Erikson (1937) did, that a gendered sense of body is represented in this play: the study boys' play reflecting presentations of phallic power, castration anxiety, and various compensatory strategies, and the study girls' play suggesting a sense of interiority, hidden passages, and a concern with what can be seen and not seen. On the surface the presentations of aggressivity seem to be absolutely differentiated by sex, with the boys illustrating the vicissitudes of destructive aggression quite directly and, in stark contrast, the girls alluding to the possibility of hostile aggression only in the episodes of teasing.

Although the stories presented by the children in this study were richly detailed, the nature of these data is not of the same order as that generated during a therapeutic psychoanalysis. The study child's relation to the analyst, although friendly and relaxed, did not have the communicative depth of a child in the middle of an analysis, nor could the research analyst understand the study child's inner world with the microscopic precision available during analytic treatment. These research narratives suggest that, not surprisingly, the oedipal-age child is certainly preoccupied with thoughts about his or her body and the bodies of others, his or her objects and the drives; they also reflect the stamp of a genitally schematized body ego. The nature of the data, however, does not tell us how the manifest play has been shaped by underlying fantasies and does not answer whether the stories about gender told by oedipal-age children are as simple as they seem.

Analytic Material

I turn now to the play of an oedipal-age boy and girl during their psychoanalyses. Neither child had been brought for treatment because of concern about their gender identity; both had been referred because of parental concern about specific symptoms exhibited by the child. Evaluation revealed both children to be struggling with conflicts primarily oedipal in nature. In exploring the play presented by these two children in their initial treatment hours, narrative structures and themes similar to those presented by the study children can be seen. But the data generated in the course of the entire analytic treatment allow us to examine the play under a more powerful lens in the service of exploring what latent fantasy configurations may find representation in the manifest play.

Clarissa

Four-and-a-half-year-old Clarissa was brought for psychoanalytic treatment by her parents because of her shyness, inhibition of activity, elective mutism at nursery school, and her anxious preoccupation with death.* Clarissa was described by her parents as an intelligent, articulate child who enjoyed playing imaginatively.

Although Clarissa did not speak during the beginning sessions, she turned to play readily as a mode of communication with me. During the first sessions Clarissa introduced a series of characters: a sad little girl who was always thrown away because her mother did not like her; exhibitionistic twin boys who could do "fancy" tricks; a hungry and angry dolphin and wolf who ate me while cuddling with me.

In her third session Clarissa sorted all the small figures into two piles: male and female. She made the nurse and the sad girl figures stand up. One of the twin boys grabbed the girl and then angrily threw her away. Then Clarissa threw all the girl characters away. The sad girl cried, but no one paid any attention. The boys stood high above all the other characters and did special tricks and everyone clapped enthusiastically. Looking cross, Clarissa knocked over all the special boys. Using gestures, she connected the sad, thrown-away girl character to the story of Gretel (of Hansel and Gretel) being sent away by her father and eaten by the witch.

Three sessions later Clarissa presented a similar, but slightly altered story. This time when the twin boys began to do their characteristic exhibitionistic tricks, they were suddenly surrounded by wild, angry animals. Clarissa then introduced the hungry wolf and dolphin who, she emphasized, had *big* mouths and *big* teeth; she demonstrated how the wolf and dolphin were always hungry and never felt "filled up." The wolf and the dolphin wanted to eat me up and at the same time be cuddled by me. In the next hour, Clarissa played the following story. The sad, thrown-away girl was really very special. Her name was "First Class" and she was "fancy," just like Clarissa's therapist and unlike Clarissa herself. Clarissa loved the sad girl very much because she was so fancy and special. First Class was friends with the wolf and dolphin who obeyed her command to eat up all the people she did not like. Everyone except First Class was afraid of the wolf and the dolphin. The only *person* First Class liked was Papa. Papa loved First Class back and kissed and cuddled her. Papa and First Class ran away together, but Mama angrily dragged them home. Then First Class furiously ordered wolf and dolphin to eat up all of Mama's babies.

As Clarissa played out this story, she looked increasingly anxious, pointing out various broken places on the dolls. She was especially disturbed by

*One theme found in this case material has been reported elsewhere (Dahl, 1983).

the policeman doll, who, she noticed, had a small hole in his neck. She insisted that this doll be put away before she continued the story.

At the end of this hour, Clarissa was very animated and became quite adventurous in her explorations of the office and hall.

On the surface of this play taken from early in Clarissa's analysis, she appears to insist on a dichotomy between boys and girls: boys have penises, can be active, and are admired; girls have "nothing," are passive, despised, and discarded. There are elements in this play, however, that do not fit such neat categorization, suggesting instead alternative fantasies of female activity and power: the angry, hungry, affectionate wolf and dolphin are presented as friends of the sad girl, under her active control; the sad girl is transformed as First Class—beloved by Papa and capable of excited activity. Certainly we can understand this play as representing unacceptable wishes significantly transformed by secondary processes and defensive activity, but only the data from Clarissa's full analysis can help us untangle the strands of this apparently seamless construction in play.

The unfolding story of First Class occupied much of Clarissa's three-year analysis. Clarissa used this character to represent complex fantasies about herself as a girl. First Class was active and powerful; she could be angry and punishing, as well as sexy and affectionate. Although First Class did not have a penis like the fancy twin boys, her body was intact, not defective or castrated. First Class was presented as enjoying being admired, playfully exhibitionistic, and proud of her body. If she was not grown-up like Mama, she was not little either. Although Clarissa frequently presented First Class as losing the oedipal battle for Papa's exclusive love and as the target of Mama's jealous rage, First Class often won Papa's admiration and affection. In time, Clarissa invented a second female character, "Little Nothing-at-All," who was employed in the representation of primarily negative features—little, angry, hungry, discarded, and passive; and then a third female character, "Sexy," who represented pleasure in the female body and the capacity to contain genital excitement. As Clarissa developed her play stories over time, aggression not only was represented by the fancy boys but was expressed directly by the female characters as well. This aggression was in the service of display and exhibitionism, and, in a fashion similar to the play of the study boys, it was employed by female characters to crash, bash, and destroy other characters who threatened to check their power.

Through her play involving such characters as First Class, Nothing-at-All, Sexy, Mama, and Papa, Clarissa was able to engage in extended discussions with herself concerning such questions as: What is the nature of the female body? What does it mean to have one's genitals hidden from sight or to have "outside" genitals? Is there a position between being grown-up and big or a baby and little? How does one experience sexual excitement while sustaining a sense of bodily integrity? How can one be both active and receptive? What is the meaning of the anatomical difference; is it good or bad? Can you have a penetrating mind and a penetrated body? As the analysis drew to a close and Clarissa became established in latency, it was possible to see via the window provided by her play how she organized her answers to these questions into a highly personal, complex, bisexually gendered fantasy construction through which she was able to keep in an integrated suspension multiple possibilities concerning her body and the drives: active, receptive, whole, admired, and admiring; loving and hating as well as loved and hated; neither grown-up nor too little; aggressive without destroying or being destroyed. For Clarissa, this unconscious complex fantasy configuration was what informed her notion of what it meant for *her*, as an individual, to be female as well as her ideas about what it meant to her to be male. Her play made clear that her sense of "femininity" involved associated notions of "masculinity," not simply externalized to the real world, but held via fantasy as aspects of herself.

Max

Max began psychoanalysis at the age of four years ten months, because of the increasing restriction of his daily life as a result of his two phobic preoccupations, lightning storms and leaky pipes. His parents described their only child as an intelligent, verbally precocious, but imperious little boy who was afraid to be out of their sight at home and who played by himself in a very inhibited manner at nursery school. Max had no friends, and his parents felt that he was anxious and depressed much of the time.

During his first analytic hour, Max looked solemn and anxious, walking stiffly to my office, talking continually in a high-pitched voice about his concern that there might be unseen leaky pipes in the ceiling. Max's verbal capacities seemed those of an older child; although sometimes his statements seemed defensively intellectualized, frequently his language was surprisingly apt and emotionally vivid. Once in my office, he quickly set to work arranging a fire station with elaborate hoses, many fire engines "ready to go," and lots of busy little firemen.

At first the firemen seemed eager to go put out a fire "someplace else." They scurried around getting their equipment ready, lining up their trucks. With sirens blaring, the firemen in their trucks raced off across the room searching for the dangerous fire. Each time they thought they had discovered it and prepared to put it out with their hoses, they would find, "It wasn't so big after all." Suddenly one of the men shouted, "Our firehouse is on fire!" In a panic, they all rushed back to the fire station. The fire grew bigger and bigger. The firemen seemed helpless to put it out. Max himself looked more and more anxious. The more water the firemen squirted on the fire station, the more leaks began to appear in the roof. Max repeatedly "interrupted" his play to Scotch-tape over the leaks. When I commented that the firemen seemed to be squirting out an awful lot of water, Max went white, stopped playing, and began to dismantle the scene. Having put everything away, he turned to me and said, "Now that I've told you all about my worries, what will you do about them?"

Over the next sessions, Max elaborated this story. In some versions, the fire would break out immediately at the fire station, threatening to engulf the firemen themselves. He spent more and more time trying to repair the leaky roof caused by the firemen's unsuccessful attempts to put out the fire. Frequently Max would turn from this play to pretending to repair other objects in my office; he was acutely aware of seemingly minor damage of office equipment. He also developed a second story presented in play. There was a land of Little People. The Little People lived in constant fear of the Big People. The Little People wanted to steal the Big People's land, but they were too little. If the Big People found out about this wish, they would come and kill the Little People, so the Little People were always trying to shrink down and be even littler so the Big People would not see them and would not know what they wanted. It was especially hard for the Little People to stay hidden because the Big People were always stringing up bright lights all over the place. Sometimes the lights would go out, and then the Little People would sneak out, creeping into Big People Land, and try to destroy buildings and people. The Big People inevitably spotted these destructive Little People and would pursue them in a fury, turning on huge, powerful spotlights so that they could not get away.

During these sessions, Max, apparently unable to conclude the story in play, would begin to behave in an imperious manner toward me, ordering me to get him more supplies or assist him in some specific activity of construction. Often he would turn from the battles between the Little People and their enemies to making elaborate drawings of the lighting systems employed by the Big People; these were notable for the immense poles from which the ovoid lights projected and the elaborate wires connecting the poles and lights.

The themes represented in play during these hours early in Max's two-and-a-half-year analysis were reminiscent of some of the study boys' narratives. Max appeared to be quite anxious about bodily integrity; expressions of aggression were direct and appeared as a wish for absolute power; and themes of retaliation for phallic wishes were prominent, as were apparently compensatory fantasies of superpower and superstrength. Like some of the study boys, Max turned to technological inventions to enhance the power and invulnerability of the body. In play he created a phallic world in which males battled for ultimate superiority; at times his castration anxiety appeared virtually undisguised.

As the analysis proceeded, the two play stories of the firemen and the Little and Big People were superseded by more complex play about a little boy named Pretty Kitty and his mother and father. Through the displacement afforded by this play, Max was able to detail his oedipal wishes and fears and give representation to the various defensive strategies he characteristically employed. At the same time, this play became an avenue for Max's discussions with himself about what it meant to him to be a boy. Initially Pretty Kitty's feminine name seemed to represent a defensively employed disguise through which his erotic longings for the oedipal mother could be expressed safely. As the play unfolded over many hours, however, it was possible to observe how Max struggled to integrate his wishes to be creative and nurturing, wishes he identified as being like his mother, with his longings for phallic power; he asked poignantly in one session, "How can one be a *boy* and love Vivaldi, too?" Many of Max's "discussions via play" focused on exploring what it meant to be little or big and whether an acceptable "big enough" could be achieved. Questions concerning the meaning of size were associatively linked to his concerns about power; aggression could be used not only to ensure continued bodily integrity but to protect his creative, nurturing capacities as well. If he could not give birth to real babies, could he create music, pictures, or ideas? If he did not have an "inside like girls," how could he contain or hide his fiery, aggressive, and sexual feelings?

Max's capacity for play allowed him to try out many different narrative solutions as he explored these questions; play allowed him to hold in suspension contradictory answers as he searched for still other alternatives. Via play he could be simultaneously the "pretty" but phallic boy, the actively seductive mother, and the terrifying but forgiving father. These characters could be destroyed, resurrected, transformed, and transmuted, and it all could be played over again. Although these characters were composed in part from identifications with his mother and father, their creation drew in equal measure on fantasies generated by Max himself as he explored what it meant to him to be a "boy who loved Vivaldi."

Discussion

Freud believed that the child's development of a sense of "masculinity" or "femininity" is a crucial precipitate of the Oedipus complex and is driven by the child's discovery of the genital difference (Freud, 1905, 1925, 1931, 1933). Deutsch (1930, 1932) and Brunswick (1940), elaborating Freud's formulations, emphasized that central to the construction of "femininity" is the transformation of active strivings to a relatively more receptive mode; a crucial dilemma for the girl was thought to lie in relinquishing activity without succumbing to the dangers of masochism. In this classical formulation of gender construction, the acquisition of "femininity" is complicated by the linked questions of how and why the girl relinquishes the early tie to the active, preoedipal mother, how the girl achieves a relatively more "passive" orientation toward the oedipal love object, and how the girl achieves a sense of bodily intactness constructed from a perception of lack or absence. More recent psychoanalytic scholarship (Panel, 1989; Stoller, 1985; Tyson, 1982, 1989) has emphasized the preoedipal roots of gender construction beginning as early as the second year of life. This view posits the atraumatic development of a core gender identity through identifications with the parents. In this formulation the acquisition of "masculinity" is complicated by arguing that initially both the boy and the girl, via identification with the preoedipal mother, construct a sense of themselves as "feminine"; the central question then becomes how and why the boy relinquishes this preoedipal "feminine" identification with the mother in favor of a "masculine" identification with the father. Tyson (1982, 1989) proposes a developmental progression from the acquisition of the early core gender identity through the later, oedipally driven construction of gender. Critical to both the classical and the more recent psychoanalytic formulations regarding the construction of gender is the assumption that gender is a dichotomous, categorical variable: "masculine"/"feminine."

The data presented in this chapter show that during the oedipal period the child begins to elaborate a psychological gender identity that is multidimensional rather than a simple dualism. It is during this period that the child begins to "fill in" the earlier core gender identity, generating meaning as the child repeatedly imagines, intuitively and in exploratory or pretend behavior, what it is to be "masculine" or "feminine." This process of filling in results in the establishment of a psychological identity that is no longer categorical but a dynamic fantasy configuration that is an oscillating, shifting, albeit by the close of the oedipal period relatively stable, fantasy organization of gender for the particular child. Gender as constructed by the oedipal child usually is a complex variable composed of several super-ficially dichotomous but actually continuous terms such as big-little; pow-erful-weak; intact-damaged; something-nothing; active-passive; masculine-feminine. This highly personal construction involves fantasies concerning the body, objects, the drives, and the interrelationships between mind and body and inner and outer reality. These fantasies not only draw upon identifications with the parents but originate as well in the matrix of bi-sexuality, thereby preserving the capacity to resonate with fantasies of being the other sex (Dahl, 1988).

As we have seen in the play of the study children as well as that of Clarissa and Max, the vicissitudes of aggression and activity play a crucial role in the construction of gender. The play of the study boys presents the clearest form of one of the central questions the oedipal child entertains: what will happen to me and to my body if I succeed in my wish to be big and have power over people? In the play of the study girls, this question is posed in a slightly different version: who is "big enough" or has sufficient power to ensure an exclusive tie to the loved object? The study boys present in play their fantasies of what appears to be an almost exclusively phallic world—wild, untamed aggression, hate, absolute power, destruction, and bodily mutilation. This phallic world appears to be one in which tenderness and love are unknown; the body is either in danger of being damaged or already mutilated; one is either tyrannically powerful or weak and humili-ated. The play of the study girls presents a sharp contrast, almost an obverse of the boys' phallic world—as long as one remains safely "inside," all is tenderness; aggression is concealed behind domestic care; the body is already crippled or damaged; activity is dangerous. Although the study girls' con-cern with themes having to do with achieving an exclusive tie to the loved object might be understood as deriving from the central oedipal conflict, their muted presentations of aggression, hate, and interpersonal conflict suggest a preoedipal valence: anxiety about object loss. When the play of the study boys and girls involves themes associated with aggression, it is as if the imaginative world becomes starkly phallic; and in this imaginative phallic world gender is construed as dichotomous and biologically rooted.

When, however, we examine themes pertaining to aggression and activity in the light of Clarissa's and Max's analytic material, we can see how defensive maneuvers have shaped the play of the study boys and girls. The study boys appear to mute or disguise both the aim of absolute power and its object; in contrast, the study girls emphasize aim and object but conceal the destructive intensity of the aggressive wish behind a façade of teasing. The play of the study children suggests that the phallic world, with its insistence on a dichotomous gender identity rooted in castration fantasies, may be employed defensively during the oedipal period.

In contrast to the study girls, Clarissa's play gives direct expression to destructive, hostile, aggressive wishes through the wolf and dolphin characters, and Max, in contrast to the study boys, through the Pretty Kitty narrative gives creative shape to both the aim of destructive power and its objects. Both Clarissa and Max struggle with the questions of whether activity and aggression must always be employed destructively and whether all activity must be relinquished as a defense against destructive wishes. As each explores possible answers to these questions in play, further questions arise. What if *I* am big and my parents are little? What if I am good and they are bad? What is it to be little; does little necessarily imply broken, weak, passive, anatomically female? What is it to be big; does it necessarily imply intact, destructive, anatomically male? Each of these questions then leads via associative pathways to further questions.

The capacity to entertain such complex, associatively linked dilemmas and to hold in suspension multiple potential answers is made possible by crucial developmentally elaborated capacities of the oedipal period, most especially the capacity to play imaginatively. Imaginative play permits the child to engage in conversations with different aspects of herself or himself; play allows the child to hold in mind many different possibilities simultaneously as well as to try out differing combinations of and balances between and among various fantasies. Play gives the child a method for representing the continually shifting dimensions in a way that permits the construction of, and a tolerance for, a multidimensional notion of gender. Through the integrative function of play, new organizations of fantasies occur. Some of this internal dialogue is generated by the tension between the developmentally older, "categorical" core gender identity and the more recently elaborated explorations of a multidimensional gendered self that is ushered in with the capacity to play imaginatively. Clarissa's play presents destructive aggression under First Class's control; wolf and dolphin destroy those who attempt to abridge First Class's power. Clarissa wondered via play whether such a wish for destructive power meant that a girl must have a penis, and if she does not, must the girl be "nothing at all," passive, and isolated? Max entertained the question of whether a creative boy could also be destructive. Was his creativity "feminine"? Did his wish to create render him weak or vulnerable? How could a boy contain his creative longings if he had no "inner space"? As the oedipal period wanes, these multidimensional fantasies gradually become consolidated into an apparently integrated, unique whole.

We can understand aspects of the play narratives presented by the study boys and girls as reflecting, much as Erikson (1950) proposed, the stamp of the body ego; to the degree the body ego involves schematization of the actual genital morphology, we can expect the play of oedipal boys and girls to carry a biologically grounded dualism: male/female. But as gender refers primarily to psychological experiences and attitudes, rooted in the archaic matrix of bisexuality, the play of oedipal children entertains multiple possibilities across a number of dimensions.

The contrasts between the play of the study children and that of Clarissa and Max appear sharp as if the play of the former was more forcefully shaped by a dualistic conception of gender. The narrative lines of both the study boys and the study girls are distinguishable along a number of dimensions: direct expression of aggression; representations of the body and its capacities; nature of the relationships between characters; use of toys to set the stage. The stories of the study boys revealed undisguised aggression in the service of representing fantasies of powerful or vulnerable bodies, absolute control over other bodies, and the explosive power of sexual excitement. Their story characters' relationships centered on the uses and abuses of power; the fact that their characters were generally unrelated by family ties, were instead depicted as mythical, supernatural, or inanimate objects, may have enabled the boys' direct expressions of destructive aggression. In contrast, the study girls located their narratives within the home and within family relationships; destructive aggression was disguised, emerging as an exclusion or rejection of one character by another. It may be that the girls' creations of family-centered narratives served to control and defend against more aggressive fantasies; certainly the frequent story theme of people hiding or being lost suggests a wish to keep some story elements hidden. If taken at face value, these play narratives of the study children lend plausibility to the notion that gender identity is rooted in body morphology and constructed from identifications with the same-sex parent.

If, however, we turn to the play Clarissa and Max presented early in their analyses and examine it in the light of the play that unfolded as their analyses progressed, we see that the surface clarity of the play of the study children is illusory, concealing highly condensed, dynamically complicated narratives shaped by multiple forces: the body ego, the drives, object relations, and defenses. The play of Clarissa and Max illustrates how personal, subjective, and idiosyncratic is the construction of gender. The development of a sense of what it means to be a boy or girl does not occur along a linear, normative path but involves for both boys and girls engagement with a series of intrapsychic dilemmas in which various possibilities are enter-tained. The question for the observer is not only how the terrain was traversed but also which solutions were entertained; what has been gained and what has been lost in the final construction (Grossman and Kaplan, 1988)? Imaginative play not only *reflects* how a given child is traversing the dilemmas inherent to gender construction; the capacity to play imaginatively *enables* the child to explore what may be gained and at what cost in the traversal of a particular dilemma. It is through the creative possibilities inherent in play that the oedipal child can entertain and keep in suspension multiple, potential solutions to the problem of gender, only gradually weav-ing these potentialities into a unique, apparently seamless, whole.

References

Brunswick, R. M. (1940). The preoedipal phase of the libido in development. In Fliess (1948), pp. 261–284.

Cohen, D. J.; Marans, S.; Dahl, E. K.; Marans, W.; and Lewis, M. (1987). Analytic discussions with oedipal children. *Psychoanal. Study Child*, 42:59–83.

Dahl, E. K. (1983). First class or nothing at all? *Psychoanal. Study Child*, 38:405–428.

———. (1988). Fantasies of gender. *Psychoanal. Study Child*, 43:351–365.

Deutsch, H. (1930). The significance of masochism in the mental life of women. In Fliess (1948), pp. 223–236.

———. (1932). On female homosexuality. In Fliess (1948), pp. 237–260.

Erikson, E. H. (1937). Configurations in play. *Psychoanal. Q.*, 6:139–214.

———. (1950). *Childhood and Society*. New York: Norton.

Fliess, R., ed. (1948). *The Psychoanalytic Reader*. New York: Int. Univ. Press.

Freud, S. (1905). Three essays on the theory of sexuality. *S.E.*, 7:123–247.

———. (1925). Some psychical consequences of the anatomical distinction be-tween the sexes. *S.E.*, 19:241–258.

———. (1931). Female sexuality. *S.E.*, 21:223–243.

———. (1933). Femininity. *S.E.*, 22:112–135.

Grossman, W. I., and Kaplan, D. M. (1988). Three commentaries on gender in Freud's thought. In *Fantasy, Myth and Reality*, ed. H. P. Blum et al. Madison, Conn.: Int. Univ. Press, pp. 339–371.

Marans, S.; Mayes, L. C.; Cicchetti, D.; Dahl, E. K.; Marans, W., and Cohen, D. J. (In press). The child psychoanalytic interview. *J. Amer. Psychoanal. Assn.*

Panel (1989). Current concepts of the development of sexuality, reported by M. A. Scharfman and S. A. Vogel. *J. Amer. Psychoanal. Assn.*, 37:787–802.

Rubin, K., Fein, G., and Vandenberg, B. (1983). Play. In *Handbook of Child Psychology*, vol. 4, ed. P. H. Mussen. New York: John Wiley, pp. 693–774.

Stoller, R. J. (1985). *Presentations of Gender.* New Haven: Yale Univ. Press.

Tyson, P. (1982). A developmental line of gender identity, gender role and choice of love object. *J. Amer. Psychoanal. Assn.*, 30:61–86.

———. (1989). Infantile sexuality, gender identity and obstacles to oedipal progression. *J. Amer. Psychoanal. Assn.*, 37:1051–1069.

8

Cookies for the Emperor: The Multiple Functions of Play in the Analysis of an Early Adolescent Boy

Robert A. King, M.D.

Art is at once our greatest refuge from the world and our surest connection with it.
—Goethe, *Elective Affinities*

In common with all the other gods, Proteus enjoyed the gift of prophecy, and had the power to assume any shape he pleased. The former he was wont to exercise very reluctantly; and when mortals wished to consult him, he would change his form with bewildering rapidity, and, unless they clung to him through all his changes, they could obtain no answer to their questions.
—H. A. Guerber, *The Myths of Greece and Rome*

In late childhood, overt imaginative play usually goes underground, transformed into and enriching the inner world of fantasy, daydream, and reverie. In adolescence, this inner world serves many functions: as a safe arena for catharsis, as a realm of rehearsal and "trial action," and as a source of those visions of mastery and accomplishment that give substance to the still nascent ego ideal.

This inner world of fantasy, as brought alive in the transference relationship, is the subject matter of psychoanalysis. In child analysis, imaginative play is often the "royal road" that permits the analyst (and analysand) to scrutinize the configuration of the child's inner object relations, drives, and defenses. In the psychoanalysis of adolescents, however, the regressive temptations of imaginative play are rejected as "childish" by most teenagers, who prefer instead the medium of talk or structured games.

This chapter presents material from the uncompleted analysis of Guido, a young adolescent boy who related to the analyst almost exclusively

This chapter reflects the many valuable comments and suggestions of the members of the Study Group on the Many Meanings of Play in Child Analysis.

through the medium of imaginative play. The analysis took place during a two-year hospitalization. Because the dynamics of Guido's symptoms remained obscure within the setting of the hospital, it was only through Guido's use of play in the analytic setting that it became possible to obtain a fuller clinical understanding of his inner life. The material illustrates the multiple functions that such play served in this analysis and raises important developmental, metapsychological, and technical questions that transcend the specific case.

Case Presentation
History

Guido entered the hospital as an inpatient at twelve years of age after outpatient therapy had failed to alleviate his long-standing depression, withdrawal, school failure, and minor delinquencies. Guido's history was rife with disruptions and losses. After several years of marital strife and intermittent separations, Guido's parents finally divorced when he was four. Over the years Guido was in the custody of first one and then the other parent.

Given his parents' preoccupation with their own concerns throughout much of his childhood, it was difficult to discover from them how Guido experienced these many disruptions. As early as age seven, however, he had begun to show signs of depression and regression, which were exacerbated by a brief period at a military boarding school. From age nine on he resided with his father, stepmother, and stepsister, where his labile moods, passive-aggressive behavior, and poor school performance kept him the focus of many arguments. He maintained intermittent contact with his remarried mother.

At the hospital, Guido lived in a residential cottage with a house parent and six other children and attended the hospital's therapeutic school. He saw me, his analyst, four times weekly in my office on the hospital grounds. In keeping with the customary therapist/administrator split, all practical administrative decisions regarding Guido, such as passes, privileges, and restrictions, were made by the administrative psychiatrist who directed the adolescent division. Although the administrator and I maintained regular collaborative contact, I had no role in these administrative decisions.

The Opening Phase

Seen for the first session at his cottage, Guido spoke openly and directly about his problems; he was rarely to do so again during the first year of treatment. He said that he had trouble with school, trouble getting along with people, trouble with his moods. "I can be friends with animals more than with people. If I see a dead cow, it makes me cry. My goal is to stop people from slaughtering animals, to make the world safe for dolphins."

Despite this initial frankness, Guido subsequently had great difficulty speaking directly about himself and rarely talked about the events of his life, past or present, or about friends, activities, or school. Instead, from the first hour in my office, he played. He began by having the toy animals and soldiers he found on the desk fight a vicious battle. The animals were fighting for their freedom, and the bloody battles often ended with the animals devouring the people. Although the animals' insurrection was justified in terms of the humans' predations, it soon became clear that the animals were as cruel and sadistic as their oppressors.

Guido's initial honeymoon with the hospital quickly disappeared. At the therapeutic school and in his residential cottage, he was withdrawn, apathetic, and moody. With both peers and staff, he was mistrustful, uncommunicative, and easily aggrieved. Despite bitter complaints about being kept from his home, he did little to maintain contact with his family or to work toward passes home. He spent several analytic hours theatrically mock-planning various escapes, detailing how he would kill the clinical administrator, the teachers, or me and escape through the window. There were periodic outbursts of "I hate everyone, including myself; I'm ugly and weird, and never should have been born. The world is full of problems. I'm mad at everybody." Although he provocatively wrapped a sash cord around his neck in class, he denied feeling suicidal. But his wish to take flight from a painful internal and external reality found expression in a drawing showing him and his cat taking off in a rocket ship and waving, "Good-bye, cruel world."

Attempts to engage Guido in direct discussion of his feelings and concerns, however, were unproductive. If pressed, Guido responded with histrionic imitations of someone being crazy, rolling his eyes, breathing heavily, writhing and grimacing terribly. He similarly rejected any interpretive attempts or efforts to refer the play themes back to the events of his life, past or present. For the most part, such interventions were ignored, mocked, or met with a resentful, "Shut up and play."

Although Guido rebuffed direct interventions or comments, he continued to play prolifically, utilizing a variety of modalities: puppets, toys, dramatic enactment, and cartooning. Using toy figures, hand puppets, and props that he fashioned out of Styrofoam cups and the like, Guido would spend most of each hour playing, sometimes acting all the parts himself, sometimes assigning various personae to me.

In the course of this play, one boy puppet, Chuck, soon became Guido's proxy in various scenarios (such as Sir Chucksalot; Chuck Funghi, boy detective). Chuck was kidnapped, taunted, and tormented by various supervillains, such as Dr. Ook, who carried him off to the planet Ook to lock him up forever.

At times I was directed to play Chuck, but my attempts to find out why these terrible punishments were being inflicted on me were in vain. "Because you were born, because you're dumb" was the reply, and the evil villains would continue to taunt and threaten me. Occasionally, putatively helpful figures would come along and offer themselves as allies. It soon developed, however, that either they too were powerless and were destroyed or they were villains in disguise—a theme of constantly dashed hopes and betrayal by people who offered to help. Although on one level, Chuck's recurrent battles against his would-be tormenters were initially intended in part as angry, sarcastic commentary on the hospital and its staff, they also expressed the sadomasochistic fantasies that colored Guido's perception of all relationships.

These predominantly anal-sadistic and retaliatory themes heavily colored other libidinal concerns (oral or genital, for example) that gradually made their appearance. During most of the first year of the analysis, women figures rarely made an appearance, save for occasional female puppet "fun units" (robot prostitute-slaves) or gorily dispatched villainous women warriors. (Outside the analytic setting, Guido was especially mistrustful of women teachers, nurses, or child care workers.) Although Guido hinted at pubertal sexual interests, these were presented as fraught with aggression and danger. For example, in one cartoon sequence he portrayed his family going to the movies. The movie was X-rated, and his stepmother stalked him with a knife. Nonetheless, he came into the theater loaded with candy, popcorn, and other oral supplies. The image of a naked lady on the screen gave way momentarily to a threatening male face and a gigantic fist that reached out from the screen to punch Guido in the face. ("Pow, right in the kisser!") In the last frame, Guido was still sitting there, contused and beaten, watching the naked lady. ("That's all folks! Ha-ha-ha!") The moral appeared to be that this is what happens when you try to enjoy yourself.

In another early play sequence, Guido giggled as he wielded the puppets. Chuck visited the doctor, who ominously informed him, "You are going to get a dick operation, because you only have the dick of a one-year-old. . . . There's doodoo in your underpants." The doctor and nurse puppet taunted him that they would chop off his penis so that a new king-sized one would grow. Chuck was then given medicine that made him grow a huge Pinocchio-like penis, which extended across the room knocking everyone about. The doctor's true name was then revealed as Dr. King.

During this initial period, Guido's play was highly fluid and prone to regressions and disorganization. This fluidity was apparent in the play's kaleidoscopic *content*, which usually concerned aggressively charged, polymorphous perverse libidinal themes, and in the play's *variable ability to contain* his emotional turmoil. Thus, during the first few weeks, the play itself would often break down into agitation and halfhearted assaults on me, my office, or Guido's own person. (However, although he provocatively brandished pillows or other objects, Guido seemed more intent on trying to discomfort me than to hurt me.)

Seen from the perspective of the drives, Guido's play served a clearly *cathartic* function in giving relatively direct vent to aggressive and polymorphous libidinal impulses. Traditional, conventional forms, such as cartoons, superheroes, archvillains, were used to clothe and elaborate perverse, sadomasochistic fantasies, which included voyeuristic and exhibitionistic components. These fantasies, in turn, were complexly influenced by Guido's unstable relationship with his capricious mother, an intermittently nurturant relationship with his unreliable and self-absorbed father, and the stimulating influence of a new stepmother and stepsister.

Thus, sadistic, aggressive themes, tinged with narcissistic rage, predominated. Their expression in play served more than cathartic purposes, however. They also represented *defensive* attempts to cope with lifelong hurt, vulnerability, and disappointment by means of converting passive into active, compensatory, grandiose self-sufficiency or a manic defense against depression. Attempts to manage paranoid and depressive anxieties were apparent in Guido's repetitive creation of various split-off good objects or aspects of the self (the "good animals" or "good guys"); these, however, were in constant jeopardy of becoming contaminated by Guido's rage or deteriorating into hated and hateful persecutors.

Although these instinctual concerns threatened at times to overwhelm the patient (and analyst), Guido also showed a well-developed capacity for narrative or artistic representation that simultaneously served *adaptive* and *interpersonal* purposes, as well as cathartic and defensive ones. Guido's play not only served a defensive function by displacing and disguising the true objects of the painful affects in his life; it also created what Neubauer (1987) has termed an "arena of displacement" or *Spielraum* in which these painful affects could be permitted representation via what might be termed, by way of analogy, the "dream works."

Characteristically morose, withdrawn, and guarded in his daily life at school and in his residential cottage, Guido was able, in his analytic hours, to mobilize and reveal in play to the analyst (and to himself) the angry, hurt affects that dominated his inner life. Thus, in addition to serving as a compromise between drive discharge and defense, Guido's strong push toward representation through play served other preservative, reparative, and interpersonal motives. On the one hand, play was compelling to Guido as an escape from a painful and intolerable world of reality. On the other hand, seen from the perspective of the synthetic function of the ego, the play attempted to give narrative form and meaning to his own inarticulately chaotic inner life, a form and meaning that was shared with me, albeit in a carefully controlled fashion. By simultaneously revealing and disguising himself, engaging and fending me off, Guido used play as a means of making and regulating contact. My intermittent sense of being sadistically controlled indicated the stringency of Guido's "conditions for contact," a phrase Ekstein (1966) used to describe certain borderline children, with a deliberate echo of Freud's (1910) "preconditions for loving."

Each of these many perspectives on the function of Guido's play carried important, but at times divergent, implications for the analyst's role and activity. When did the analyst serve as a new real object, a transference figure, an audience, or a collaborator and coauthor in the patient's play? Correspondingly, which activities or interventions of the analyst were likely to be experienced as helpful, empathic, or deepening the therapeutic relationship and which were experienced as disruptive or intrusive? In the first few months, comments, questions, or interpretations were either ignored or rebuffed as intrusions. As a result, during this initial period, the sole viable approach seemed to be to accept the only overture for relating that Guido offered—that of play—and to confine interpretation to within the metaphor of play (Ekstein, 1966).

Consultations with the Inspector

After the first few months, Guido's play became better organized and disruptions less frequent. The analytic hours continued to be peopled with various superheroes and villains, pieces of whose regalia Guido would often bring to the office. These included Big Caesar, who wanted to restore the Roman Empire, pitted against Animal Master, who, disguised as a mild-mannered veterinarian, redressed wrongs and protected animals throughout the world. A talented cartoonist, Guido drew pictures of the Big G. and his gang, a rather seedy-looking crew of mobsters. At times, Guido himself played the Big G., who together with his henchmen, Dr. Laser-finger, Dr. Heat-wave, and Captain Boomerang, comprised a gang who could not shoot straight. The Big G. and his gang would start out by trying to terrorize me, threatening to shoot up the office or zap me with their exotic weapons; however, they most often ended up hitting themselves by mistake.

Despite the frequently humorous and pleasurable aspects of the play, work with Guido could also be frustrating. Large parts of hours would be taken up with seemingly sterile, repetitious play in which opposing warriors and armies endlessly annihilated one another. In addition to this stereotypic, perseverative play, Guido's strenuous resistance took other forms. He sometimes deliberately pretended not to understand even simple statements on my part. On other occasions, he tried to confuse me by denying or misrepresenting some otherwise trivial fact; indeed, at times he succeeded in leaving me feeling bewildered or uncertain. At still other times, he acted extravagantly goofy or histrionically crazy. Commenting directly on either the defensive or projective identificatory aspects of this behavior ("You would like me to know what it feels like to be jerked around and confused") seemed largely unproductive.

Consequently, when one of Guido's characters, Inspector H2O, the world's greatest detective, made an appearance (played by Guido himself), I decided to seek his assistance. I explained to the Inspector that I was up against a very tough case, the case of Guido, and described the fiendishly clever weapons that had been deployed against me, neutralizing and immobilizing anything I tried to do to help: the repulsion field, the stupidity-ray, the goofy-ray, the confusion-ray, and so on. Any advice Inspector H2O could give would be greatly appreciated.

The Inspector's advice proved very useful. In the guise of Inspector H2O, Guido listened very seriously and said, "Well, this is a very interesting case. It's clear he didn't get enough attention and affection growing up. He's having trouble getting started. He needs your help. He needs for you to kind of give him a little push to help him get started. Show him you're friendly and he'll open up. I think he's just scared. He is scared that his father will be cheated, or maybe that he will be cheated. I think you should just kind of let him know you like him and give him a chance. Make him comfortable, tell him to relax, and he'll come along."

Taking this advice to heart, I lessened my interpretive zeal. As I did so, the themes of loneliness and abandonment that underlay many of Guido's fantasies of compensatory grandiosity emerged more clearly in the play. As we traced the myth of the birth of the hero, one of Guido's superheroes explained that he had been given his powers by a dying predecessor who had made him a superhero "so he wouldn't have to feel lonely," commanding, "The only friends you may have in the world are animals." On one of the rare occasions that Guido spoke about himself directly, he said he was "interested in power—to have an army and a castle, to rule people, to save the animals, to stop criminals; the power to save all the ones who do good." Asked what sort of powers Guido felt was available to him, he helplessly turned his thumbs down and said, "None at all."

In an extended series of hours before my first vacation, Chuck and several characters took shelter against catastrophes that threatened to destroy the world. With his mother dead and his father away in the army, Chuck tried to find a safe place for himself. In the course of this, General Ook, who fluctuated between being Chuck's partner and one of his adversaries, revealed that he was really Chuck's father. Chuck denounced him as a "Benedict Arnold," but then relented, saying, "You really did love me all those years." Soon thereafter, in some parlous adventure, General Ook altruistically let go of the life raft, saying, "I'll let go; I've been a rotten father to you." Then the play returned in a more stereotyped way to old themes of mutual annihilation. I observed to Guido that with my impending vacation, Chuck again felt abandoned, and evil geniuses again took over the world. Guido's response was, "Stop whining to me."

The sessions following my vacation were filled with resentment and complaints. I was arraigned and indicted by Count Inferno on charges of "general weirdness and bad psychiatry." Mephistopheles presided over the imaginary trial at which numerous other patients and characters denounced me. Guido himself testified that he liked me, but only after having sworn to tell "the lie, the whole lie, and nothing but the lie." I was sentenced to be "shot in the balls and in the eyes." In fact, the hour ended with Guido becoming overwrought and actually shooting me with a rubber band.

At the beginning of the next hour, Guido announced he could not stay. He hurried out, and a second later, there was a knock at the door, a signal that usually heralded the arrival of one of his characters. It was Inspector H2O. I confided to my erstwhile consultant that Guido and I had been having a rough time, that Guido had felt very upset and abandoned during my vacation, but it was hard to talk about.

The Inspector again listened carefully and said, "Well, listen, let me get this straight now. He's a smart kid, imaginative, looks nice, right?" I concurred. "Well," the Inspector continued, "he's got a lot on his mind. He doesn't know how to use therapy; you've got to help him learn how to use it."

A few minutes later, however, the Inspector irascibly said, "Listen, why don't you just dump this kid? This kid is obviously ignoring you. Why don't you just get rid of him?" I replied that I thought Guido was perhaps worried about this; he might have felt I was dumping him by going on vacation. At this point, the Inspector quickly retorted that he had better things to worry about; he had spent the whole night chasing the cat burglar. He imperiously ordered me to get him a beer, stretched out on the couch with a blanket, and turned his back to me, pretending to sleep. I said I was always glad to have the Inspector pay a visit and to make himself comfortable, but I was not sure whether the Inspector was going to sleep because he was comfortable or in order to give me the cold shoulder. The Inspector flashed a big grin and said, "You're crazy." In his sleep, however, the Inspector sang a medley of Beatles hits: "You can't always get what you want," "Help me if you can," and "Take a sad song and make it better."

On other occasions, however, the Inspector was less helpful—for example, when he came in, looked around at the various props Guido had made, and asked, "What is this stuff?" I explained it was the stuff Guido and I used to work together; it was hard for Guido to talk about some things directly, so sometimes we had to play about them. The Inspector shook his head incredulously and said, "Boy, that sounds pretty childish to me." (Guido was always very furtive as he opened the office door, lest anyone should see we had been playing with the toys.)

The Nature of the Therapeutic Alliance

Guido's fluidity and ability to operate on several levels at any given moment and over time were striking. These fluctuations occurred along several dimensions: libidinal phase, relative balance of drive versus defense, affective tone, closeness to reality, preferred play mode, and relatedness to the analyst. Glaring discrepancies existed between these levels of functioning. For example, his seemingly near total inability to speak directly about himself during the first year of the analysis could coexist with his ability to create a proxy, Inspector H_2O, who could articulately and insightfully describe his situation.

As the first year's work progressed, these shifts and seeming anomalies continued to raise important developmental and diagnostic issues. On the one hand, many aspects of Guido's functioning—his intense concerns over aggression, his propensity toward splitting, his fantasy attempts to relieve a pervasive sense of powerlessness through compensatory grandiosity and pseudo-self-sufficiency—seemed to reflect not only the impact of external trauma but also significant depressive, narcissistic, and perhaps even bor-

derline character pathology (Kernberg, 1984). On the other hand, his fluidity, his desperate struggle with the drives, his difficulty in articulating
feelings, and his wariness toward adults could also be seen, from a developmental perspective, as typically early adolescent features of a repeatedly
traumatized boy.

The tenacity with which Guido continued to cling to the play mode was
also puzzling and challenging. Interpersonal relations appeared to Guido so
fraught with dangers of abandonment, attack, and disappointment that the
buffer of play seemed necessary to create an arena of safety. (Of course,
these threats reflected not only Guido's subjective experience of his chaotic
past but also the dangers of his own projected aggression and narcissistic
rage.) Interpretation outside the play and other analytic interventions threatened to disrupt this safe haven by challenging the "suspension of disbelief"
essential to Guido's illusion of control and robbing him of a vehicle for
expression. Implicitly echoing Winnicott's (1970) aphorism, "The reality
principle is an insult," Guido experienced most explicit analytic interventions as at best unempathic interruptions and at worst thinly veiled attacks.
(As one of John Barth's fictional heroes put it, "All self-knowledge is bad
news.")

Another related conceptual and technical challenge was the difficulty of
defining what islands of therapeutic alliance might exist in the stormy
transferential sea of Guido's relationship to me. Guido initially acknowledged that he had come into the hospital to get help, but this tenuous
explicit alliance soon evaporated as he brought his characterological ambiv-
alences to bear on the new objects that the hospital provided. Nonetheless,
in the implicit "play contract" that Guido offered and through proxies such
as the Inspector, he tacitly acknowledged a wish for communication and
cure. His use of play to communicate, however, seemed predicated on his
concurrent ability to use the play mode to control and titrate the degree of
intimacy and dangers attendant in relating to me. Thus, through the play,
Guido both revealed and disguised, acknowledged and disavowed, his feelings. While fending me off, Guido also used the play to keep alive my
interest and hope, as though saying, "Don't get too close, don't expect too
much, but don't give up on me!" In this respect, Guido's play was an
elaborate Scheherazade scheme, an extended attempt to seduce, control,
charm, and disarm me. Indeed, as the play unfolded, the Scheherazade
theme became explicit in a sequence in which I was required to entertain
and assuage Guido's drowsy, testy Emperor with nightly tales.

Guido's morose withdrawal and passive aloofness left teachers, child care
workers, and peers feeling thwarted in their efforts to engage him. Indeed,

even after several months in the hospital, he remained, as one teacher put it, "the boy nobody knows." The dynamic meaning of his external behavior thus remained frustratingly opaque to the usual kinds of scrutiny that an intensive therapeutic milieu permits. Within the analytic context, however, Guido's ongoing dramatic play revealed many of his most important concerns, including his ambivalence and wariness about most relationships, his despair over finding reliably gratifying attachments, and his fantasies of compensatory narcissistic grandiosity.

"Emperor or Nothing"

In the school and hospital setting, Guido rebuffed the staff's attempts to encourage activities or gratifying relationships. In his play, however, Guido's motives in refusing to risk the vulnerability implicit in acknowledging needs or aspirations became clearer. For Guido, grandiose omnipotence seemed the only safe way to secure his needs. Thus, in one hour he came in with a new belt buckle to which he had attached various devices. Rearranging the couch cushions, he devised a drill ship in which to drill to the center of the earth. Back at base headquarters, I tried to maintain radio contact with the ship as it drilled its way through the earth. Guido hit the kingdom of the Mole people and cast me in the role of their leader. He then proceeded to kill me off and crown himself the Emperor of the Mole people, to whom he proclaimed imperiously, "My rules are simple: obey or die!" Queried on his dictatorial style, he insisted that he just *had* to be Emperor. "It's life or death being Emperor; I am going to be Emperor or nothing." He agreed when I remarked that he felt if he couldn't be Emperor, it was like being nobody at all. Appropriating the blanket from the foot of the couch as his imperial toga, Guido announced that he was going to lead an expedition back to the surface to steal food; he would conquer the earth, kill all the policemen, and clean out all the restaurants. When I remarked that the Emperor was feeling pretty desperate and certain that no one up there would want to help him get food, he replied, "I know the earth better than you. It's savage up there. Now that I am the King, it's going to be different; no one will push us around again."

Although Guido rarely spoke openly of his relationship with his family, his play occasionally permitted glimpses of his discontents. For example, in family meetings with his social worker, Guido began to reproach his father for his perceived unreliability and emotional unavailability. The father had difficulty in hearing these grievances without launching defensively into counterattacks that usually led to Guido's withdrawing. During this period, Guido spent one analytic hour stacking the couch cushions into a very high but tippy throne. He sat on it as the imperious Mummy God, demanding of all who came by, "You must praise me." Even a moment's hesitation in singing the appropriate hosannas was met with instant punishment in the form of terrible lightning bolts. I remarked that some people became terribly upset and mad unless they could feel constantly and totally admired. Guido replied, "You mean my dad?" He spent the rest of the hour angrily hurling thunderbolts, but he made it clear that this was a god with feet of clay, whose excesses inevitably led to his toppling off his shaky pedestal of cushions. Guido's identification with the aggressor was also apparent in the vicissitudes of his puppet protagonist Chuck who would become as ruthless and as nasty as the villains from whom he tried to save the world. When I remarked on this, Guido interrupted, "I know just what you're going to say: that I've become just like my dad. He yells at me, I yell at him."

Guido's play in the analytic setting also provided a fuller picture of the dilemmas that intimate relationships posed for him. These complexities of Guido's internal object relations became apparent in his diverse uses of the analyst, explicit and implicit. In the overt dramatic *content* of his play, Guido starkly portrayed the conflict between his hopeful wishes for contact, help, and support on the one hand, and, on the other, the feared reemergence of bad objects, hurt vulnerability, and his own primitive sadism, which continually threatened to undermine his play characters' relationship with one another and with me. For example, over several weeks, Guido, in his role as Rex Pacino, ace test pilot, frequently enlisted me as his partner for various dangerous missions—sailing the high seas or sledding across the frozen tundra to search for Big Caesar's hideout. Partnership with Rex, however, was precarious. At best, Rex was imperious, high-handed, or contemptuous. During our campaigns against Big Caesar, Rex often abused or deceived me. Pretending to step outside our imaginary tent for a quick smoke, Rex left me behind to be blown up by a hand grenade he had planted in the tent. Inquiry or protest on my part drew only a string of invective: I was "a faggot," "a chicken," "a traitor." On several occasions when we were stranded on a life raft in the mid-Atlantic, Rex announced we were running low on food. He then eyed me hungrily and instructed me to say feebly, "I guess I'm not going to make it." Where Rex's next meal was coming from seemed all too clear. Thus, as Rex's comrade, one never knew from moment to moment whether one was going to be a partner, a mentor, a nurturer, an enemy, or a degraded object to be controlled, tortured, deceived, abandoned, or eaten.

Guido was aware of this inconstancy and devised a play metaphor to represent it. In an hour that followed Guido's having seen me walking on the hospital grounds with another patient, Rex enlisted me in yet another mission against Big Caesar, one with a Götterdämmerung-like climax. I was unfortunately wounded, and, ostensibly more in sorrow than in anger, Rex had to give me the coup de grace. Next, after finishing off Big Caesar, Rex proceeded to shoot all of his own men and finally himself.

In an attempt to find out what happened I called on Inspector H20, one of the few times that I actively attempted to evoke one of Guido's personae. I asked the Inspector what was going on and wondered if it related to my encounter with Guido earlier in the day. The Inspector informed me that Rex was suffering from *korika*, a "disease like Dr. Jekyll and Mr. Hyde. There's a good guy and a bad guy in the same body, fighting and not knowing which way to treat people." The theme of Rex's korika and its possible treatment recurred periodically throughout the analysis.

"A Good Interpretation Is a Feed" (Winnicott)

Guido's wants and aspirations remained enigmatic in the hospital setting. In the play, despite their frequent greed and grandiosity, Guido's various characters were for the most part able to repudiate the painful aspects of their longings for care or admiration; instead they could simply command or omnipotently seize whatever they wanted. Within the safe context of ongoing play, however, Guido gradually began to represent and acknowledge his thwarted longings more clearly and to tolerate the vulnerability this entailed.

Over the next several weeks, the plot shifted. Big Caesar had escaped to the moon where we finally defeated him, preventing his dastardly plot to destroy the earth. As before, however, Rex himself now took on many aspects of Big Caesar. Now Rex himself destroyed the earth, being careful to save two of every living creature as well as a few mercenaries and a large number of "good-looking women" whom he took along on his spaceship. As we wandered about the universe looking for a place for Emperor Rex to establish a colony, Rex held gala shipboard suppers. Rex's guests at these gourmet candlelight extravaganzas of steak and pizza were the good-looking women and me, who had now been promoted to Captain of the Guard. (Interestingly, one of the "good-looking ladies" bore the name of Guido's mother.) Over a series of several analytic hours, these bacchanals were followed by the Emperor ordering me, the Captain of the Guard, to tuck him in, to serve him imaginary cookies, and to tell him bedtime stories that I was ordered to make up. I used the opportunity to regale the drowsy Emperor with several interpretive tales. One of Rex's favorites, which he demanded to be retold on several occasions, concerned a boy, also named

Rex, who had had a hard time of it growing up and who felt he could not count on people loving him or caring for him the way he wanted. As a result he worried that people would not like him just for being himself. He vowed that when he grew up, he would become Emperor of the World and could then order people to give him the sort of love, care, and admiration that he wanted. Whenever he felt slighted or jealous, he became so hurt and angry that he just wanted to blow up the whole world and everyone in it.

This sequence of sessions had a genuinely cozy feel that was unique in the overall context of the analysis. Although Guido and I shared other moments of empathic contact or mutual enjoyment in play that was especially exciting, creative, or communicative, these "bedtimes for the Emperor" were among the very few times that Guido permitted himself to represent himself as receiving and enjoying care and nurturance. Brief though they were, they retained a memorable significance as a hopeful sign that islands of nonthreatening, pleasurable human contact might be possible for Guido.

The Evolution of Play during the Middle Phase and the Emergence of Direct Discourse

As the hospitalization entered its second and final year, Guido began to hazard a few tentative attachments with his housefather and one or two peers. In the analytic work, Guido's tenacious insistence on play posed a continuing technical and diagnostic dilemma. From one perspective, it could be regarded as a defensive fixation—a rigid avoidance of external reality in favor of a perseverative transference reenactment of primitive sadomasochistic fantasies. From this perspective, too extensive collaboration (or collusion) by the analyst in play ran the risk of countenancing, or even encouraging, an untherapeutic regression that served no progressive purpose. This view seemed to mandate more strenuous efforts on my part to interpret the play in relation to external reality and to confront more vigorously the play's defensive function. As before, however, such attempts were usually unproductive and experienced by Guido as a breach in empathy. For example, even within the play, when as Captain of the Guard I remarked how it always seemed to be a matter of kill or be killed, Guido replied, "Stop giving me all this complicated stuff. Why don't you just shut up and let me have a good time. Bring in the dancing girls!"

In contradiction to the view of Guido's play as primarily regressive and defensive, his play also seemed to serve important communicative and organizing functions. As noted, the play provided the context in which moments of empathic contact with Guido were possible. Furthermore, as the material of the second year illustrated, Guido was able to use the play as a means of organizing, and subsequently articulating, his own perceptions of internal experiences that earlier in the analysis could only be compulsively reenacted. These developments in turn gave hope that the analyst's collaboration in the play served a therapeutic and progressive function, rather than being simply a surrender to Guido's defensive attempts at omnipotent control or a collusion in a sterile transference reenactment.

The progressive developments during the second year of analysis took several forms. Guido's play became more highly nuanced and expressive of his concerns about himself and his increasingly unsettled family life. Perhaps most significant, however, was Guido's ability to find his own voice and to speak directly at times without the mediation of play about his feelings and perceptions.

While still remaining in displacement, Guido's play began to deal in greater detail with the events in his life. Among the most important of these was the impending divorce of his father and stepmother, a development that was to unleash forces that ultimately disrupted both the hospitalization and the analysis.

One recurrent play theme concerned the failure of compensatory grandiosity and the beginning of tentative explorations of other means of survival. As the second year began, Guido was scheduled to go home over Christmas for his first extended pass. In his Christmas Eve hour, Rex set off on an expedition to the planet Zagar to see if there was any chance of its sustaining life. Although Guido's home visit was disastrous, all I learned on his return was that Rex's mission had not gone well. The natives had what we needed, but we were going to have to fight against overwhelming odds to wrest it from them. Rex's various stratagems failed, and he began to despair of being Emperor. He blew up his ship or rampaged around the universe picking bigger and bigger fights with our few remaining allies. When I remarked that being Emperor did not seem like so much fun or get Rex what he needed, he replied, "Well, let's just blow up ourselves, the universe, and everything with us."

During one analytic hour, Emperor Rex ordered me to change places with him and instructed me how to act. I was to order him imperiously about, while he parodied my usual style by asking dumb questions and shuffling his feet. Next, as Emperor, I was to demand admiration, asking him, "Do you love me?" to which he responded with fulsome paeans of praise: "I love you most. Even your feet smell wonderful. I give you Christmas presents instead of my wife and kids. You are perfect." Nonetheless, as Emperor, I too got bored with the endless battles. Rex glibly gave me his advice: "Listen, Emperor, I think what you should do is settle down, be friendly, share your life with someone." When I worried about finding someone reliable, Rex said, "If they leave you, just find someone else."

Chuck, his puppet alter ego, also despaired. Laying down his blood-soaked sword, Chuck tried to give up being King, complaining, "It's no fun; it's a disappointment; I resign." He decided to take time off to be a farmer or to go camping, lamenting sadly, "I never really had a father or a mother. All I had was the old swordmaster, and when I got to like him, something happened to him too. I've got to find out what I want. I'm a terrible person. Here I've killed helpless people; I should be locked up." Bucolic tranquillity did not make for exciting play, however, and Chuck soon found himself embroiled in battles again. "It shows, even if we change our way of life, deep down we're still warriors. There's nothing we can do to change it."

In a new series of adventures, Condor Flint, secret agent, embarked on various dangerous missions, accompanied by his much abused sidekick, Corporal King. Condor Flint used these missions to demonstrate how tough he was—for example, crushing soda cans with his bare hands. As Condor showed me the trick, however, he warned, "You can't let people know your soft spot; you have to have them think you're tough." His soft spot, he confided, was animals.

As his father embroiled Guido in the escalating marital difficulties, Condor found himself caught in a conflict of loyalties between two warring factions. Finally, he blew them both up, announcing, "I know whose side *I'm* on: mine!" He proceeded to plunder the universe, singing his pirate anthem to the tune of "The Yellow Submarine": "We rob from the rich and shit on the poor."

For the first time, Guido began to talk about himself directly. The experience was uncanny because although I had spent four days a week with him for a year, I felt as though I had never heard the sound of his own voice. In response to his upset look at the beginning of one hour, I asked if there was something troubling him. He responded by telling me directly about the possibility of his father's divorce and described the complicated dynamics of his reconstituted family. He wondered who would get what possessions; he would insist on the cat. He went on to say, "It's funny, I never thought I'd ever find anybody to get along with me, that I'd have to find someone just like me, interested in just the same things, like drawing and dolphins. Now if somebody says something, instead of just saying,

'You're crazy,' I think, 'Maybe it makes sense in some other way.'" He wondered how he was doing. In assessing himself, he said, "The fog is clearing. Before, I didn't understand anything about myself; I was just running around doing things." He went on to ask, "Do you believe in fantasies? Do they ever come true?" He related his own fantasy that when he grew up, he would have a desert island to which he would go with his animals. He wondered, "Do you believe in Freud? All that stuff about penis envy, like if a boy sits where his father was when the father is away, does that mean he wants his father's penis?" He didn't believe in all that stuff about sex.

These moments of direct talk were for the most part isolated. Attempts in subsequent hours to take up where we had left off were ignored, rebuffed, or met with a retreat into stereotyped play. Only rarely was it possible to penetrate this insulation. For example, after a prolonged period of repetitive sadistic play, I suggested that he wanted me to know what it was like to feel helpless and upset, sitting on the sidelines while people bashed away at each other, much as I imagined he might have felt watching his parents fight it out. This led to a striking few minutes in which Guido told me in his own voice, "You know, my life is lousy; I'm hassled at the house, upset and confused. I never had a decent day in my life." He wondered why it had happened; was it somehow his fault? He said, "If you were religious, you might think that. Do you believe in Adam and Eve or evolution?" He felt as though the only good thing in his life was his lost dog. I sympathized with how upsetting things had been for him and said I was glad he had been able to tell me how upset he was, because I knew how difficult it was at times for him to trust anyone. He said he wished he had never been born and wondered what he should do. I suggested that it sometimes might help to talk as we were talking. It was very hard for him to leave at the end of the hour.

Guido now began to speak directly about dilemmas and defenses that had previously been accessible only through play. For example, he came in and announced he was ready to talk, but insisted he really wanted help around only one thing. Biting off a plug of chewing tobacco, he announced that he had decided he wanted to be a mercenary. It would be a crummy life, living in crummy tents and eating crummy food, perhaps getting killed, but it would be *his* crummy life, of his own choosing. His father and I would just have to accept the fact that he was going to be a mercenary and that he was going to smoke cigars and chew tobacco. Looking very queasy, however, he went on to say that he wanted me to help him get rid of his sensitive feelings; he couldn't be a really good mercenary until he got over his qualms about killing people. He felt he needed a shell to be less sensitive. For example, if his roommate was bossy, Guido felt that he did not know how to handle his mixed feelings of hurt, helplessness, and retaliatory rage. If he took the chance of starting to like somebody and to trust him, he began to worry that the person might disappear.

Thus, despite the upsets and threats to the treatment posed by external family events, Guido was able to expand the bridgeheads of relatedness established through the medium of play in order to share his feelings more directly and explicitly.

A final story from the last weeks of the analysis illustrates the increased sense of hopefulness Guido was able to draw from this contact. Entering the office and miming pulling a mask over his head, Guido transformed himself into Tiajuana Snake, space adventurer, who regaled me with his latest adventure. While exploring the solar system, he encountered a space-ship piloted by Guido, a boy who was upset by his parents' divorce and who had decided to commit suicide by plunging his spaceship into the sun. Pulling alongside, Tiajuana tried unsuccessfully to talk him out of it as their two ships plummeted side by side toward the flaming surface of the sun. At the last possible moment, when Tiajuana was about to break off and turn back in order to save himself, there was a knock on Tiajuana's airlock. It was Guido, who had decided to live. Boasting of his prowess as a rescuer, Tiajuana went on to tell me that Guido had gone on to prosper and had become an architect and builder of cities.

Discussion

Guido's case illustrates the difficulty of discerning what elements of the analytic situation are mutative for a seriously disturbed, but maturing adolescent. As the analysis continued, Guido's play became more organized, more nuanced, and more communicative. Guido also developed a greater tolerance for his ambivalence and had fewer bouts of disorganization, rage, and despair.

This progressive evolution, of course, also reflected multiple factors external to, but impinging on, the analytic process. For example, the two years of analytic work extended over a substantial portion of Guido's early adolescence, a time of intrinsically rapid physical maturation and psychic reorganization. Furthermore, the analysis took place in the context of a dynamically oriented residential treatment setting, which provided its own rich array of mutative ingredients, including reliable and empathic adults, firm but caring structure, highly individualized psychoeducation, and an enhanced opportunity for social growth and engagement with peers. All of these factors no doubt exerted important ameliorative influences in their own right and provided a context for the analysis proper.

Despite these caveats, Guido's use of play in the analysis served a crucial therapeutic role, beyond providing the setting for my interpretive activity. Of course, while specific interpretations often had no apparent positive effect, it is possible that, taken collectively, my ongoing interpretive activity within the metaphor of play formed an important part of the analytic situation's matrix of empathic containment. But moments of excessive interpretive or therapeutic zeal were clearly experienced by Guido as disruptive intrusions or attacks. This reaction may have reflected technical deficiencies, such as poor timing or wording, or a more fundamental threat to the suspension of disbelief essential for play. More likely, however, at this stage of Guido's development, he perceived reality as a source of inevitable pain rather than potential gratification. The analyst's attention to both inner and outer reality thus often seemed to Guido to be aversive, even punitive. Winnicott remarked in his typically aphoristic style: "Contrasted with this [creative apperception] is a relationship to external reality which is one of compliance, the world and its details being recognized but only as something to be fitted in with or demanding adaptation. Compliance carries with it a sense of futility for the individual and is associated with the idea that nothing matters and that life is not worth living" (1971, p. 76). (Or, as one of Zola's critics complained, "Why is it when you talk about reality, you invariably mean something unpleasant?")

The contention that the play itself served a crucial therapeutic function raises important questions about the uses of play in analysis. If play potentially serves an intrinsic developmental function, under what conditions can its progressive potential be realized? Guido had been a prolific cartoonist for some time before entering treatment, although the contents were largely the same mix of sadomasochistic, polymorphous perverse fantasies as first appeared in the analysis. What was different about his play in the analysis?

Although play offered Guido a means of representing his painful inner world, his interpersonal dilemmas, and his carefully guarded hopes and longings, it was the *shared* aspects of this representational activity that gave it mutative potential. Play permitted Guido to establish and maintain his relationship with the analyst and served as his principal means of communication for much of the analysis. In the analysis, Guido was able to use the vehicle of play to buffer his intense wariness and to create a "transitional space" (Winnicott, 1971) in which he could meet and use me, provided I tacitly agreed to accept his terms for engagement. Guido thus permitted me to provide an implicit holding function, albeit one conditioned on a developmentally early mode of relating in which I was tacitly asked to enjoy, admire, and join Guido, while permitting him to use me. Guido's progress seemed to reflect in part his use of play in the analytic situation to create a secure setting in which he could experience pleasure and a sense of empathic containment and contact under conditions he could control. Winnicott believed that clinical work is intrinsically linked to communication within the transitional or "potential space," which he linked to play and other creative phenomena: *"Psychotherapy is done in the overlap of the two play areas, that of the patient and that of the therapist.* If the therapist cannot play, then he is not suitable for the work. If the patient cannot play, then something needs to be done to enable the patient to become able to play, after which psychotherapy may begin" (Winnicott, 1971, p. 63).

References

Ekstein, R. (1966). *Children of Space and Time, of Action and Impulse.* New York: Appleton-Century-Crofts.

Freud, S. (1910). A special type of choice of object made by men. *S.E.*, 11:163–175.

Havens, L. (1986). *Making Contact.* Cambridge, Mass.: Harvard Univ. Press.

Kernberg, O. F. (1984). *Severe Personality Disorder.* New Haven: Yale Univ. Press.

Neubauer, P. B. (1987). Personal communication.

Winnicott, D. W. (1970). Definition of creativity. Unpublished paper, quoted in M. Davis and D. Wallbridge, *Boundary and Space.* New York: Brunner/Mazel.

———. (1971). *Playing and Reality.* New York: Penguin.

9

Verbalization and Play in the Treatment of a Five-Year-Old Boy

Laurie Levinson, Ph.D.

Andrew's recollections of his psychoanalytic treatment from five to nine years of age were written nine years after the completion of his analysis, when he was eighteen.

Patient's Introduction

I remember myself as a very different little boy before my analysis. I kept all my feelings inside, and I didn't know at all what I was feeling. I remember that it took me years and years to really let myself be angry at anyone. I was sure that only a good boy would be liked, and I desperately needed that approval. A good boy, I thought, did not cause problems. The normal kid made demands and made life hard for adults, but I, on the other hand, strove to act just like an adult, to be someone to admire and call mature. I was very quiet, and whenever a question was asked me, my answer was, "I don't care." Whether it was what flavor ice cream I wanted or what I wanted to do with someone, I never wanted anything myself and always accommodated others.

My analytic sessions with Dr. Levinson, whom I called Laurie because I was only five, were where I could begin to find and accept my reactions to the world. The analysis made me want to take the risks of feeling, so I could enjoy the pleasures of being a human and not a robot. I slowly started to understand that I *did* crave and want, and that fulfilling my wishes could make me happy.

Mostly, I talked in my sessions, creating stories. That seemed to be the adult thing, the *right* thing to do. Only through the stories I created could I let Laurie in on my feelings. As I told them, Laurie never forced me to realize that I was talking about myself. Had I realized that the adventures were peepholes to my life, I would have plugged them up.

I imagined good guys battling bad guys, and usually these bad guys represented the thoughts and feelings I thought were "worst." Bad guys had to be punished by the supercharacter, the big, conscious, censoring me.

I developed routines that I returned to regularly, each story developing a structure and characters with which I could create new adventures. My play was based on imagining situations in which I created one world after another, capturing aspects of my own life, as if writing them down to be able to look at them from the outside.

My stories allowed me to have Laurie on my side. Together we would find criminals and punish them. Each story let me play out a fantasy, chastise myself for it, and also test to see what Laurie's reaction to it would be. I began to see that though she knew what the bad guy had done, she was not so intent on punishing. She didn't say, "Oh what a terrible man!" and so I started to wonder whether my angry feelings were really so dangerous. I could see a glint of fun in her face, when I dared to say things like, "I think fires are exciting." The criminals were people like me, with whom I could eventually laugh, and say, "I love you, because you're normal, and you're me, and you will help me get pleasure from and love life." Laurie's warm, forgiving heart, which taught me to accept my feelings, was crucial, but so was her sense of humor, and willingness to play along, because she became a kid with me, a friend of mine, with whom, if I wanted, I could share my troubles through my characters' exploits.

I had to hide my feelings in real life, but in the stories that I made up, I knew I would not be punished. Everything was "just a story," which I could pretend was not really about me, anyway. Telling an adventure was easy because it was just like talking about someone else. The characters were exciting and real and important to me.

It was a wonderful feeling being completely free in my stories. I was suddenly given the creative power to make whatever I wanted to happen, and so usually my character had power that I, a little boy, didn't have. Whether I had machines that could punish people or move me places or make me know everything, or whether I had a strong, magical body that would make people belong to or care for me, my stories gave me a chance to rule. Whatever pains were impossible for me to heal in real life, I could cure in my sessions with just a thought, just a snap of the fingers.

My stories helped me to associate fantasies and wishes with the feelings inspired by life. I began to notice that when something bad had happened to me, a character in my story would want to kill or punish someone. Like this, I learned what was happening within me. If a friend in school hurt my feelings, then I'd want some bad guy to get hurt. I'd be angry. I actually had to *find* my angry thoughts in messages my stories were giving us, because those "awful" feelings were so hidden from me. But slowly, as I felt safer to experience more, I felt freer and happier in life. Now eighteen, I look back on my analysis, grateful for how it helped me to grow.

In the pages that follow, you will find examples of how we discovered my reactions, and how Laurie helped make me more accepting of my feelings. You will see how I used the props of the office (chairs, a Boy-Girl doll, and a Sherlock Holmes puppet) and the two real characters available to us, to create stories that mirrored my outside life, and whispered to Laurie the stories of my heart, stories that she taught me to tell louder and louder.

Introduction

In Andrew's introduction, he directed his memories of his analysis to the stories he created with me. These stories, always accompanied by elaborate and quite theatrical enactments, represented Andrew's unique form of playing. Traditionally, we think of adults in analysis communicating through words, and children, through less verbal and often nonverbal playing. The subject of this chapter is the role of Andrew's precocious use of language in his play and the manner in which he used verbalization more as one might expect of an adult. One question that may be posed is: to what extent is such a verbal precocity a hindrance to development, leading to such maladaptive defenses as isolation of affect, intellectualization, and denial? One might just as well wonder whether such an unusual verbal capacity represents a gift that can lead to the enhancement of creative potential, in that more access exists to unconscious thoughts and fantasies.

Because of Andrew's talent with words, his analysis differed in a technical sense from the analyses of many young children. With the majority of early latency children, we tend to devote a large part of the treatment to observing and labeling play activity. Once understood by the analyst, the action of the play is translated into words for the child. In Andrew's case, what he was feeling was found in the stories he told rather than in nonverbal play. Therefore the task at hand was to connect Andrew with the feelings embodied by his fictional characters, whose conflicts were of course his own, and to undo his excessive use of maladaptive mechanisms of defense.

Another aim of the treatment was to encourage and support his capacity for play, both a therapeutic and a development-promoting activity. This process was interwoven with the therapeutic action necessary for Andrew's recovery from neurotic inhibitions and for the resumption of progressive development.

Case Presentation

Background

Andrew entered analysis at the age of five with a joyless and purposeful air that expressed a determined attempt to ward off eruptions of feelings and thoughts too uncomfortable for him to tolerate. Of particular interest in the initial months was the entrenched and ubiquitous gender identity focus of his play, with rapid reversals and quick shifts between active and passive modes of relating. One could see the tyranny that these preoccupations had assumed over his external and internal worlds. As his play developed in the course of treatment, other elements made their way into its alterations. The gender identity character of their vicissitudes was consistent in conflictual and defensive expressions.

Andrew was referred to me by his father's therapist, who felt the boy needed analysis because of anxiety dreams, enuresis, asthma attacks, and general apprehensiveness. In addition, Andrew was an only child who was being deeply affected by the stormy nature of his parents' relationship, one that was marked not so much by open battles as by a constant sniping at each other over their mutual grievances. Any story told by one parent would invariably be disparaged and contradicted by the other.

Both parents were born and raised abroad, having come from families who set a high premium on learning. Having met at the university during tumultuous political events, they may have been rebelling against their families, and it is possible that the relationship was based on their being accomplices in this rebellion. From the time I met them, the marriage was openly unhappy. The father's professional activities took up a great deal of his time and were used to justify his frequent absences. The mother saw his career as a rival for his love and interest. Andrew was the sole focus of the unambivalent love of each parent, and they stated that they were making attempts to work things out for his sake. Essentially, however, the parents led quite separate existences, coming together only when an activity involved their son. The burden for Andrew of his centrality in this relationship was evident and manifested itself in many ways—both in and out of the treatment.

Andrew was born in this country. The mother had a normal pregnancy and delivery; Andrew's developmental milestones were all precocious, save for his nighttime enuresis, which persisted until he was six. It was typical of this child that he asked his father, "*Why* do I wet my bed?" He spoke early, first in his parents' native language. By the age of two and a half he was able to understand English but refused to speak it. When he entered nursery school at three, his teachers remarked that they were unable to discern that his first language was not English. Quietly and vigilantly listening to babysitters and to television, he had speedily acquired a meticulous command of the language, and from the beginning of our relationship he took great pride and pleasure in the use of *words*. His English was a rather formal one, punctuated occasionally with certain foreign constructions. Andrew's intellectual endowment and the ease with which he acquired language skills facilitated a precocious use of languages for defensive purposes. In his play during sessions he devised complicated fantasy games, rich in subtlety and complexity for such a young child. His strong need for step-by-step verbalization and explanation of his play afforded him the reassurance of retaining the interest and attention of the object. Words conferred upon Andrew magical powers to regulate his affects and his instinctual strivings, both libidinal and aggressive, and, most important, to control his anxiety regarding overwhelming feelings of helplessness. Games for this boy tended to consist of lengthy narratives with varied and elaborate subplots, digressions, and subtexts—but always with Andrew retaining his fantasied, dramatized position as master of the universe.

Treatment

When we were introduced in my waiting room, I saw a rather shy and delicate-looking little boy with a serious and gentlemanly demeanor. Andrew was clearly a child of exceptional manners, which I came to see as a reflection of his basic character. In general he related to most people in a considerate and genuinely polite way. Our first session proper got underway with drawings of designs that reminded him of an octopus, and then a monster, which in turn reminded him of his frightening dreams of monsters, in which Andrew's father would phone the police, who would put the monsters safely in jail. Andrew informed me that he knew, of course, that there were no such things as monsters in real life—only in scary dreams. I agreed, adding that even dream monsters could be very frightening and that the work we would do together would be to understand the hidden worries that caused such problems. Andrew's response to this introduction to treatment was to nod knowingly: "I knew that already." The material that followed the monster discussion was his announcement that he wanted to draw his family. He drew a huge father and laughed merrily, telling me how very big his father was. He then drew himself, examined the drawing carefully, and blurted out, "It's a girl! I don't know how to draw boys." He told me that it was the long hair that made it a girl, or that "It could be a boy pretending to be a girl." Andrew put no arms on this picture of the "boy-girl" drawing. In his picture of his mother one could see a definite resemblance to his self-drawing. He referred to his mother as "he." This ambiguity was also evident in his lack of "boyishness" at the start of the analysis. He was not actually girlish, but rather overly gentle and quite nonassertive.

Referring back to the subject of hair, he spontaneously remarked that he used to have blond hair, but that for some unknown reason it had changed to its current light brown, which he did not like as much. His best friend, Johnny, had very blond hair, which Andrew thought was much "prettier." I later came to know that Johnny was an extremely effeminate little boy who openly expressed his wish to be a girl. At the end of this session Andrew observed the drawing of himself, saying, "I wonder why I chose the brown crayon. I wasn't thinking of my eyes, but they *are* brown." I started to say, "You are a boy—," but before I could add "who is curious," he interrupted me to ask with incredulity, "How do you *know*?" I responded that he certainly had many questions and perhaps even doubts about himself and that together we could explore the sources of and reasons for his perplexities.

It was not long into the treatment before Andrew introduced a fantasy game, the focus of which was a baby doll. This doll possessed the unique ability to be both a boy and a girl; when the eyes were open, it was a girl; when they were closed, it was a boy. He referred to this doll as the "Him-Her" or "Boy-Girl" doll, a conflictual aggressive wish, often associated with separations. In one story Andrew had the baby crying, declaring how unfair it was that the parents could leave the baby out of their grown-up activities, like staying up late or going out for the evening. He made the baby cry "so loud that the parents will have to come to her." Andrew told me to be the mother and he played the father; we were to be extremely angry at this pest of a baby who was either keeping us awake or preventing us from being alone with each other. At this point Andrew called the doll "He-She." I described the doll as feeling quite fortunate to be able to switch from boy to girl and back again. Andrew added, "But really it's best to be both." He continued, telling me that to be both a boy and a girl gave a person a great deal of power. He agreed with a resigned expression to my comment that real children often were completely without power to control the world of the grown-ups. One could see in this material how Andrew's feelings of helplessness and rage, coming from all levels of development, converged in this particular solution to his fears of separation and loss; he could maintain the illusion of being in control by never staying with one gender for too long. Only he knew whether he was a boy or a girl, and this was part of his secret power.

Soon Andrew was taken up with many games of good guys fighting bad guys, or good animals fighting bad ones. His anxiety was manifest in his repeatedly asking me, "What? What?" He wanted to know what I was thinking. Could I read his mind? He wanted to know and at the same time was afraid of it. I told him I thought he wanted my help in mastering his fears, but also was frightened that I might not think well of a boy with all this fighting on his mind. Would I think him a good guy or a bad guy? He drew a good guy crocodile and had him bite off the tail of a bad crocodile. Andrew declared, "Now he can't hurt anybody." The theme of castration as a solution to anxiety and retaliation as punishment for exciting aggressive impulses was to prove a prominent one in this treatment. This example of rendering himself impotent by projecting onto the bad crocodile his own incestuous and aggressive strivings and impulses represented a retreat to safety, consonant with earlier fantasy play with the Boy-Girl doll, and found reinforcement in what had been instituted against his fears of separation and loss.

I drew a picture of a person who had a terrible fight going on in his mind: good thoughts versus angry bad thoughts. Andrew became quite involved. "This is Mr. Muddle," he said. "He is so confused and does everything wrong. He has so many questions he's afraid to ask and so many bad feelings." I volunteered to help Mr. Muddle with this confused state of affairs. Andrew was adamant: "*No!* You *can't* help him. He is *too* bad, and he thinks you think he is bad. You won't ever like him." This session took place prior to a weekend and Andrew was morose. He said that while we were apart Mr. Muddle would do everything wrong. I asked if Mr. Muddle got especially confused when he was angry—just as he (Andrew) was always so angry with me for being unavailable on weekends. He replied, "I will put my shoes on my nose and my hat on my ears and make everything topsy-turvy." I told him that I supposed he was mad at me for my neglect and letting me know he would neglect himself to try to make me feel as bad as he felt. To criticize me, a grown-up, was experienced by Andrew as a terrible crime, deserving punishment.

Andrew's reaction to the idea of being angry with me for not being with him was to turn the baby doll into its female persona. She screamed and cried and demanded so much of her parents that they (we in the play) eventually became so fed up that they went off and abandoned her altogether. Suddenly the baby turned into a monster baby who tried to kill me, her mother, for the crime of leaving her. I pointed out to Andrew that he wished he could sometimes be like that monster baby and thereby intimidate the grown-ups into doing his bidding. Then he became frightened that if he were to be found out—if his parents were to discover that he was not the perfectly good boy he so wanted to be—they really would flee from him, if not physically then emotionally. Andrew reassured me that this was all just a bad dream the two of us were sharing; it was all right though, because the dream had a good ending in which the monster baby usurped all the power and bossed around the grown-ups. This scenario, in which the baby doll went from being a boy to a girl to a monster-girl-baby, often came into the play when Andrew was unable to contain his wishes to hurt the objects of his disappointments. We later understood his need to "play the girl" as a protective device. If he was already castrated, then no one could punish him in that way; if boys were not permitted to be angry, then perhaps girls were allowed this luxury; if his parents stayed up arguing over him and spoke of separating, then maybe they would stop fighting and stay together for a girl—or at least for a boy who could pretend to be a girl. Like a magician, Andrew tried to divert the attention of his parents from the issue of their unhappiness and possible separation by playing gender-switching games in fantasy.

The ability of the baby doll to change sexes at will was strongly linked to Andrew's wish for magical powers. For months we played many fantasy games in which Andrew was a great magician, or investigator with special powers, capable of the most magnificent feats. His strength lay in what he termed his "magic fingers." All he had to do was to touch or point at people or objects and they would conform to his wishes.

The ability of the baby doll to change sexes at will was but one manifestation of Andrew's longing for magical powers. For the first few years of treatment he played various games in which magic and omnipotence figured prominently. The purposes of his play were many and were certainly overdetermined in relation to his developmental sequence; but here I shall focus specifically on his use of language as one crucial aspect of his intellectual precocity, which skewed his defenses toward an obsessional constellation characterized by isolation of affect and the pressing need to "explain away" the deeper meanings of his play.

Andrew informed me with great conviction at the beginning of treatment that he definitely believed in magic. To my inquiry, he said, "Well, maybe there isn't *really* magic, but there is make-believe!" He added, "I have magic fingers. If I want, I can touch you and turn you into ice cream or candy. To get rid of my worries all I have to do is snap my fingers and they disappear." Andrew's introductory remarks about the magic residing in his fingers, in his thoughts, and in his actions reflected the major themes of his play.

One afternoon Andrew arrived for his session and went immediately to his drawer, from which he extracted some magic markers, a tin pencil box, and a sheet of paper; he told me that he would draw a map of the world. This was the introduction of an ongoing activity that alternated with the Boy-Girl doll and that he referred to as "World." The play (which he insisted was real, not a game) consisted of the Mind, which he pretended resided in a tin box in the playroom and knew more than anyone; the Examinizor, a particular black pen, the function of which was to determine the precise location of the trouble spot of the moment; and the Ray-Gun Shooter, a wooden block used as a gunlike weapon possessing a plethora of magical destructive powers. Andrew informed me that it was his intention to record our adventures in the World and ultimately send them to a newspaper, where they would be printed for all to read. As one would expect with the play of a child moving into latency, Andrew's World changed over time in both form and content, with all sorts of elaborations, additions, and subtractions.

In a session when Andrew bitterly related that his best friend, Johnny, had told him that he had a new best friend, Andrew began our first adventures featuring the two of us as ace detectives who had been called in by the police. They wanted our help with a particularly difficult case involving a burning and exploding volcano located in a remote mountainous region of the world. Andrew, as always, was chief detective, and he cast me in the role of his assistant. Our initial task was to consult the Mind, who informed us that the explosion had been caused intentionally by a criminal who enjoyed setting fires. The Mind suggested that the directions to this place could be found in a special toilet, the whereabouts of which were well known to the Examinizor. We easily found the toilet, only to discover that it was inhabited by a school of vicious sharks. Andrew was undaunted. The sharks were there to protect the Mind and to help us. Our directions were to head to Peru, where we would be given further instructions. Off we flew on a private jet to the Peru airport, where we were met by a representative of the Mind, a Mr. Magooshy, who led us at once to the site of the burning volcano. Andrew used his Ray-Gun Shooter to put out the fire and then turned his interest to the criminal. Where was he hiding? As luck had it, the criminal was crouching behind a large boulder, laughing with glee at his exciting and destructive fire. Andrew sneaked up behind the man and dusted him with a special fainting powder. This adventure ended with Andrew's triumphant exclamation: "And now I will jail this bad criminal forever at the bottom of the volcano!"

During the action, Andrew's speech was pressured and tense as he ordered me to obey his commands. He literally dashed from corner to corner of the consulting room, enacting the stages of our journey. As he described the burning volcano, his eyes were bright with excitement: "It's yellow and orange and green and has a giant cloud of smoke coming out. I don't know if I have the power to put it out—I *do* have the power! I *do* have the magic dust!" After he had relegated the criminal to the bottom of the volcano, Andrew turned to me with a shy grin and whispered conspiratorially, "I think fires are exciting, too." Within this context it was quite clear to both of us that Andrew had used the World as his designated locale for revenge upon Johnny and punishment for his own pleasure in that very revenge. When the adventure had finished, Andrew, then aged six, suddenly became very affectionate, sitting close to me and putting his head on my shoulder. He said he felt sleepy and asked if I would read him a book called *Mr. Grumpy*. He nodded silently when I commented that killing criminals was a pretty tiring job.

Johnny's rejection of Andrew continued to be a worrying preoccupation. A few days after the session described above, Andrew came in looking pale, wheezing, and complaining of fatigue and weakness. He reported that he had bumped his head at school while racing with Johnny. Johnny had won the race, and Andrew had run into the wall. He was obviously feeling hurt by and angry with Johnny, but on this occasion was unable to turn to his usually available source of words—either for defensive purposes or to vent his feelings. In passing, Andrew mentioned that he had been to the circus on Saturday and had seen some clowns splashing water on a burning house. He laughed merrily as he recounted this incident, but quickly stopped himself when I wondered what about the scene had been funny to him. He looked me square in the eye and said, "That is a secret I can't tell you."

There followed a pause of perhaps a minute, while the two of us sat in silence. Andrew then jumped up, apparently having regained his lost energy, and said, "Let's do World. Today we are going to visit the real Mind. He lives downtown and only I know where. You can come with me, but you are not allowed to see him—that is only for me." We set off in a special high-speed car (two chairs in my office), but were quickly smashed broadside by a "crazy driver." Andrew was enraged. "Now our plans are spoiled. I'll never get to the real Mind." He summoned the police using a special button on his Ray-Gun Shooter and a policeman instantly appeared. Andrew addressed the policeman in haughty and imperious tones: "You *will* fix our car for free, right? . . . No?! Then who are you anyway? The police always obey me. You must be a bad-guy criminal in disguise." Just at that point, a real police officer came along. Andrew was now having a mild temper tantrum and yelled that the real policeman must arrest the impostor at once. "Take him to jail and lock him up! He is going around tricking people to make them think he is nice, but he's just a bad guy." Andrew then turned to me and said in a stage whisper, "That guy with the disguise deserves to get punished." With a note of resignation Andrew spoke of being mad that we missed visiting the real Mind, who could have helped us out of this World problem. When I asked how, he said, "Well, he would never have let us get hit by that car." Andrew, as usual in such circumstances, was thus reproaching *me* for not sparing him the painful experiences of abandonment, disappointments in love, and betrayal by adults. He asked me what I was thinking, and I replied, "If only I had been in the school yard with you, then maybe I could have helped you win the race and not bump your head into the wall." Andrew looked surprised: "I wish you had magic to make Johnny like me again."

Andrew's World continued to provide him opportunities to express in play his conflicts, their derivatives, and all kinds of solutions. One day he happened to notice a Sherlock Holmes puppet that had, in fact, been in the consulting room for months. He exclaimed with pleasure at Sherlock's cape and hat, telling me that his father had read him stories about this famous detective. Andrew knew that Holmes had had an assistant, but wanted to know when and where Holmes had lived. What was the name of the assistant? He knew the stories were make-believe, but pressed me for the details, which I provided. Andrew decided that we should invite Sherlock Holmes to join our adventures in the World. I asked what he planned to do about the assistant, and Andrew invented the following adventure.

We phoned the home of Dr. Watson, who, according to Andrew, was not only Holmes's assistant but also his best friend. To Andrew's dismay, Watson was nowhere to be found. The housekeeper answered the phone and told us that Watson was in Vermont, but then he wasn't there either. Andrew opened his eyes wide, and with high drama proclaimed: "How *silly* of us! Dr. Watson has no housekeeper; this is a trick." We rushed to our private plane, arriving in London with amazing speed, and hurried over to Baker Street, looking first for Holmes. After an exhaustive search, we concluded that no one was home. Andrew had one last idea. With a great flourish, he flung open the door to the closet and there was the wretched Dr. Watson, trapped and surrounded by snapping alligators.

Suddenly Andrew assumed the role of Sherlock, who had changed his mind. Rather than wanting to find Watson to save him and keep him on as an assistant, he decided that Watson had to be killed. Here Andrew had the puppet whisper to him that the assistant had to die because if he stayed alive, he would want to usurp Holmes's power. Andrew's solution was to train the alligators to bite a stick. He then moved the alligators closer to Dr. Watson and, pointing to the doctor's arms, called out, "Bite the sticks! Bite them!" The alligators obliged and Andrew finished him off by shooting Watson in the eye. "Dead! Great! Now there is only me, Sherlock, and I can take over. I've killed my best friend because he wanted to be number one detective and I know that there's only room for *me* to be number one." At this moment, Andrew had me take over the Sherlock role, but provided me with specific directions regarding what to do and say. I, as Sherlock, had to become full of remorse: "I did want to be the only one, but now I feel bad and selfish and greedy." Andrew was most understanding: "Well, you know we could make Watson come alive again with the special gun; but I think he should stay dead because if he would live, then he would try to kill *you* and take your power."

I went back to my analytic role, saying that I could see how hard it was when two best friends both wanted to be number one. They seemed to believe that the only solution to the sharing problem was for one of them to be killed. But having then lost his closest and dearest (as well as most envied and hated) friend, the survivor appeared to be feeling very lonely, regretting what he had done. Andrew broke into an atypical huge grin: "I *know* what this is about! It's about me and Johnny." I added that I thought that the problems between him and Johnny were rather like those between him and his father, with Andrew always wanting to come first with his mother, but convinced that he stood no chance unless his father was completely out of the picture. Andrew listened carefully and began to laugh, telling me he was glad he had discovered Sherlock Holmes and brought him into the "World." As he left the session, he turned to call back to me, "Please make sure that puppet is here tomorrow."

Andrew's relationship with Johnny was complex in that contained within it were important displacements of his oedipal conflicts, namely, his fears that the consequences of his competitive strivings would redound to him in the form of either direct retaliation or a more insidious withdrawal of love— whether from his father for Andrew's wishing to triumph over him in brute strength or intellectual prowess; from his mother for his desire to have her all to himself and fear of being spurned or mocked by her; or from me in the transference as I came to represent the unbeatable rival, the unattainable mother, the doctor with no magic powers, and the analyst who made him share me with others.

Seeing another child emerge from my office on a Friday afternoon was a distressing blow to Andrew's tendency to deny that he ever felt jealous of my other patients. On the one hand, there was almost a denial in fantasy that he was my *only* patient, as he was the only child of his parents. On the other hand, he was all too aware of the constraints of our relationship, evidenced by his frequently lying down on the floor at the end of sessions and informing me that he was staying and I should get rid of the next person. Once his magic took hold, Andrew was able to find new solutions to the Friday and sharing obstacle. He informed me that he would change me into chocolate (his favorite food) and eat me; I would be in his stomach where he would have me all to himself. Andrew was able to see clearly in this context how his magical powers protected him from his anger at having to share me with others. Bypassing the aggression and jealousy, he simply became Boy Wonder, who could never be disappointed by anyone.

I once asked him just exactly how he was so successful at getting rid of the thoughts and feelings that bothered him so. He smiled broadly: "I only have to snap my fingers; if I do, then *you* won't even mention worries either." I told him that I had no intention of pushing him to talk about anything until he was ready. Andrew looked somewhat taken aback: "But sometimes I want you to ask me—to *make* me talk." I asked whether there was anything in particular he wanted me to make him talk about. "Today I want to know about that Boy-Girl doll and why I sometimes think it's better to pretend to be a boy who would rather be a girl." I wondered what his ideas were, and he replied with great thoughtfulness, "Sometimes I get very scared that my parents will stop living together and that it will be my fault—or at least that I can't stop them. Then I will have to decide who to live with and I don't know and the whole thing makes me very mad!" I commented that it was at such times that he believed being a pretend girl could save him; girls had more power than boys.

Andrew associated to an event of the day. He had fallen at school and had hit his head. With conviction he said, "When that happened I wanted to be a girl, because girls don't hit their heads." Andrew went on to describe how because girls were weaker, people took better care of them, so they did not get hurt as often as boys. We could see his belief that girls' power lay in their vulnerability, an idea that Andrew found more acceptable than his notion of boys' dangerous aggression, which was capable of driving away the objects of his desires. When I linked his angry wishes to hurt his parents with his thought that the fall had been a punishment for these wishes, Andrew agreed. Was this not similar to the day he had bumped his head trying to beat Johnny in a race? Here I was able to show him how he used the girl-boy confusion as one way of avoiding the consequences of his rage—consequences in terms of his own overly strict superego as well as the fear of real abandonment. It was as if Andrew were saying, "Now you see me; now you don't. Now I'm a boy, but I can easily pretend to be a girl." In a somewhat different manner, his World provided him with a way of controlling what he felt to be bad wishes but also allowed him safely to express them and to play them out. It should be noted that Andrew never evinced any real effeminate behavior, nor indeed any wish really to *be* a girl. Rather, he was always pretending, adopting a disguise in his attempts to hide his real, helpless, angry, little boy self from the eyes of his own vigilant superego. Thus he alternated between magical omnipotence and feelings of utter helplessness and danger.

The theme of Andrew's need to be safe and all-powerful was continued in a fantasy game in which he lived alone in a house between his two parents, who each had a house of his or her own. Andrew did not need them for anything because he had a special computer with magic buttons that were capable of supplying all his needs. In fact, his parents had to come to him whenever they needed something. Andrew was most gracious and offered to provide anything, from special foods to clothing to fixing things in their respective houses. He was absolutely clear about his own self-sufficiency and his pleasure at living alone; he also spoke openly of preferring that his parents live separately, for that way he would never have to share and never have to choose which he loved best. He could see how turning the tables on reality was his way of ensuring that even if the catastrophe of separation did occur, he would be prepared. He would not feel lonely or bereft—they would need him and he would therefore be indispensable.

Andrew reported a dream that again demonstrated how effective were his reversals in keeping at bay his fears of deprivation and loss. He dreamed that he was alone on a plane going to visit his grandmother across the ocean, when he suddenly realized that the plane did not have enough fuel to reach its destination safely. A "nice man" on the plane phoned his parents, who came to join him. All four of them, Andrew, the parents, and the "nice man, floated down to earth together."

By the end of the second year of treatment the gender identity and "World" preoccupations abated and gave way to a greater awareness and more open discussion of Andrew's feelings of disappointment and sadness.

Now aged seven and a half, he composed a poem relating to his treatment and entitled it "My Analysis." Its opening stanzas are as follows:

You'll never believe
How grown-ups deceive
Their children in so many ways.
All their days are filled with plays . . .
But NOTHING to do with children!

Feeling left out can make children shout;
But nobody dares to do it.
They keep bad feelings inside
Where they think they should hide
In order not to have a fit.

Discussion

This was a long analysis of an intelligent and imaginative boy with exceptional strengths and a rich and supple adaptability. He had recourse and easy access to a large verbal store and fluidity in his gender-ambiguity fantasy play, affording ample avenues for the expression of his fears—all of which provided me with the opportunity of seeing the interaction of instinctual arousal and the defensive work in regulating his anxiety.

Andrew's play was obsessionally repetitive, and in the repetition there entered ever new extensions and nuances, closing every chink in the defenses. This richness in imaginative play allowed scope for his feelings, but seemed at the same time to embolden him to overcome his apprehensions against revealing what he had been so intent on keeping secret. From an early point in the treatment there were unmistakable signs that Andrew considered the consulting room a "safe place." In treatment, for instance, he could indulge in playing with dolls, unusual in itself, for nowhere else did he play with dolls or other "girlish" things. It was evident that regardless of the nature and manifest content of what Andrew was preoccupied with at any given moment, he was always intensely engaged, to a greater or lesser degree, sometimes under greater pressure than others, in undoing the ferocity of the "wild" and the "bad" in his created World. He idealized the strong, the fearless, and the good; he invoked and identified with an omniscient and omnipotent moral authority who could observe evil being done anywhere in the world and was swift to punish and exact retribution. He wavered in imposing punishment between destroying the perpetrators of bad deeds or immobilizing the dangerous and evildoer in prison in perpetuity.

Andrew expressed fantasies of possessing magical powers by which he could, at "the blink of an eye" or "the snap of his fingers," change gender; or he might, if he so chose, revert through regression to absolute baby-hood—but a baby so special and talented and, above all, so driven to do *good*, that he could right all the world's wrongs. This innocent and powerful baby was, on inquiry, totally self-sufficient. It could satisfy the needs and wishes of all others, but itself was independent of needs and desires, untouched by cravings and longings. This was a feature of Andrew's personality; he rarely, if ever, asked for anything, whether for Christmas or birthdays; he often went without lunch, saying he wasn't hungry and that food "meant nothing" to him.

Upon being confronted with anxiety, Andrew would avoid thinking about his great fear, very quickly plunging into fantasies in which he was no longer helpless. One day on seeing a homeless man in the street, Andrew asked his father where he would go if his parents separated. When he reported this in treatment, he said that his father had turned the question back to him. Andrew had answered that first he would live with Mommy and later, when he was older, with Daddy. His father had reassured him that no separation would take place—but that if it did, then Andrew was correct about where he would live. Andrew responded to this episode with an exacerbation of anxiety that was manifest in the session by withdrawal and silence and crawling under a small table. Moroseness, however, soon gave way to a fantasy expressed in play: he now had his own house (under the table), equidistant from that of each parent, and with his magic computer his parents were completely dependent upon *him* for their basic needs. He elaborated this fantasy, explaining to me that in truth he was really a brilliant robot who needed nothing because he could do everything. He added as an aside that of course robots had no feelings—just electrical connections and cleverly conceived wiring.

As the analysis proceeded, his concept of defending against hostile impulses changed from that of the boy-girl to the boy-girl baby to the ruler of his World to an affectless and perfectly constructed robot. The robot represented yet another attempt at trying through disguise to divest himself of the dangerous instinctual pressures by being something or someone else in which he could find refuge from his unacceptable desires. Andrew had pretended to be a girl in fantasy not because he ever truly wanted to be a girl but rather because there were only two choices. If being a boy had such dire consequences, then being a girl or living in his own magical World might solve the problem. When these defenses were analyzed, and he became more aware of what he struggled with, Andrew mounted another attack on his "bad wishes." As a robot, he would be perfect and safe and in a position to approach competition well armed. Yet he was able to see the high price he paid for giving up his humanness. The idea of being a mechanical robot left him feeling empty and ultimately aware of his very human longings.

The fantasy play during the treatment of this boy, aged five to nine, illustrates special forms of defense. Andrew's frequent recourse to switching gender, both with the doll and with himself in fantasy, served as a defense not against secret feminine wishes and longings to be a girl but rather as a function of grandiosity and omnipotence—a magical solution to the anxieties aroused by his feelings of helplessness. He was able to observe his creation of a World totally under his control and to see that even that had been a protective, if not completely adaptive, choice. The time had come to face the idea that the real world was far from perfect but had many potential gratifications. Entering this new world involved the relinquishing of much-loved and long-cherished dreams of glory. At the age of nine, when the treatment ended, Andrew completed his poem, characteristically wanting everything to be put into words.

> Now I can think of new ways to link
> The past and the present in me.
>
> I'm neither a robot
> Nor am I perfect.
> I'm not a magician—
> More like a physician.
> In fact, it's the analyst in me.

10

Play: Its Role in Child Analysis, Its Fate in Adult Analysis

Eugene J. Mahon, M.D.

Freud's masterful analysis of the little boy's play in *Beyond the Pleasure Principle* (1920) is so convincing that one begins to take the insight for granted, as if it were obvious even before genius stumbled on it. In the Freudian world we live in, originality and cliché often become confused, as if the original texts had been irretrievably lost and only jargon remained.

In *Beyond the Pleasure Principle*, Freud, like an anthropologist in a primitive setting (childhood in this instance), observed the social rituals and then tried to make sense out of what he saw. A boy confronted with the reality of temporary separations from his mother amused himself with an object attached to a string, a pull toy. He threw the object away from himself and then by pulling on the string retrieved it. The observation seemed simple enough. The interpretation, now well known to jaded psychoanalysts after many readings of this particular text, requires complex reasoning and is not at all obvious until eyes have become steeped in Freudian ways of looking. If the play is seen as a condensation of the manifest and the latent content, what is being "said" directly can be sifted from what is being implied. From this Freudian perspective the child's overt behavior and the covert inner dialogue can be reconstructed as follows:

> I am alone. Mommy has left me. I am suddenly sad, angry, bereft, but also hopeful of her return; and besides, I have resources of my own. What if I throw this thing away and pull it back again? As I throw it, I will release some of my anger. My sadness will diminish as I take control and lord it over a thing that is even littler than I am in relation to grown-ups. I can even pretend that I am the thrown-away thing about to be rescued by the heroic human (myself, to be sure, in one of my many alter egos) who controls the string. I can even pretend that I am throwing my mother away, and I may or may not rescue her, depending on how forgiving or unforgiving I feel. Play is won-

derful. Mother will never guess the intrigues I've been scheming up behind her back.

This partial reconstruction of the play reveals a wealth of complex mental mechanisms that may not be visible at first glance. The play's manifest gymnastics seem to express, but also disguise and even hide, the unconscious mental *activities* of the player. To do justice to the complexity of its meanings, psychoanalytic concepts such as identification, unconscious fantasies, symbolism, displacement, repression, the translation of passive experience into active, have to be invoked. Is play therefore a mélange of psychic activities that includes all facets of the mind, conscious and unconscious (symbolism, affects, defense mechanisms)? Such a comprehensive definition would tend to obscure what is unique about play, not differentiating it sufficiently from its mental bedfellows—fantasy, dream, defense. Before going any further, I shall attempt to define play, emphasizing its unique qualities rather than what it shares with other mental phenomena.

Toward a Definition of Play

Whereas the modern definition of *play* as "games, diversion" captures the ludic nature of the activity, the word derives from the Old English *plega*, which implied a less sportive intent—to strike a blow (*asc-plega* = playing with spears, that is, fighting with spears; or *sword-plega* = fighting with swords [Skeat, 1910]). How etymology shifts the meaning of a deadly earnest word used to describe warlike activity to the totally new sense that implies action as "only playing," so to speak, is one of the ironies of the history of language. Even *playing* the cymbals or the piano owes its meaning to violence, in the sense that one *strikes* the instrument. The history of the concept of sublimation may lie hidden in these shifting meanings: the psychological journey from swordplay to the bloodless percussion of musical instruments.

If we follow these etymological leads, play would seem to have begun with actions that were anything but "playful" in the modern usage of the word. *Action*, however, would seem to be the hallmark of play in ancient or modern usage, certainly common to swordplay or child's play—but action of a unique kind. *Action*, for a psychoanalyst, is a complicated, intriguing word. If we borrow one of Freud's early insights about source, aim, impetus, and object, new light will fall on this discussion. Freud (1915) said that human psychological events could be broken into components that would allow a dissection of the phenomena that might otherwise escape attention.

Human motivation has a source (in erogenous zones), an aim (in the actions that bring about satisfaction), an impetus (the quantitative factor), and an object (the least stable of the variables, according to Freud). The subject matter of play would seem to be primarily aims and their vicissitudes. This is not to say that play and action are synonyms. Sucking, one of the aims of the mouth, is not an example of playing. And yet an infant can "play" with food, much to the exasperation of mothers who overvalue nutrition and undervalue exploration. The difference between eating, sucking, and swallowing and activities of the mouth that might be called playful (such as blowing bubbles, whistling) surely lies in the *aim* and its vicissitudes. "You can't whistle and chew grain" captures the conflict between aims of instant gratification and aims in which postponement, delay, experimentation, detour, and compromise lead to other horizons of pleasure.

Although we can speak of play according to its multiple functions, or according to developmental aspects (presymbolic or symbolic), or according to its contacts with other mental activities (fantasy, drives), the essential ingredient in the definition from a *formal* point of view would seem to be *action*—not all of action, but discrete types of action in which immediate gratification of instinct is not the goal, and exploration and even creation of reality above and beyond immediate gratification take precedence over desire. In this sense, play, which ironically is not supposed to be "for real," is the greatest ally of the reality principle in its struggle with the pleasure principle.

A working definition of play, therefore, would suggest that play in humans or animals is actions that do not seek immediate gratification of desire or the obvious solution of a problem but seem rather to explore alternate or multiple possibilities of experience. If reflex is the shortest distance—a straight line between the two points, stimulus and response—play would seem to be the opposite of reflex, a protean defiance of the reflex arc in favor of expanded horizons, in which new meanings, new experiences, can be explored. In humans, as opposed to animals, play can explore its options with the assistance of thought and fantasy. It is this cooperation between the actions of play and the other psychic realms of thought and fantasy that makes play the great window into the psyche that the child analyst can exploit so profitably. In the strictest sense, however, play should not be confused with thought or fantasy, even when it is inextricably bound up with them. A psychoanalytic definition of play would narrow the meaning to the realm of aims and their vicissitudes. Even the concept of playing with words or playing with ideas (the hallmark of formal thought, according to Piaget) should not intimidate us or force us to relinquish the core of the definition, since these examples imply internalized *actions* (thought itself being compared to trial action by Freud). If action has a complicated history from its birth in the reflex arc to maturity in decisive behavior, becoming a slave of the unconscious all too often in periods of acting out, it nevertheless has a creative workshop called play where the future can be worked on before it happens. To confine the definition in this manner need not restrict it: if play is neither acting out nor fully realized action, it is nevertheless the crucible in which make-believe reaches toward belief and doubt advances toward conviction.

My thesis gets support from developmental facts: when the adolescent mind develops the more sophisticated hypothetico-deductive reasoning or, as Flavell (1963, p. 202) would put it, when preoperational and operational cognition yield to the higher level formal operations, play also recedes, and playful thought takes over. Play has become *internalized* as the action-oriented childish mind grows up.

To illustrate this definition in action, I shall construct a metaphor of the mind at play. Consider a pond in moonlight. The light plays with the surface of the water, illuminating facet by facet as it studies the subject (I have anthropomorphized the scene in the interest of making a point). Let us go a step further with this metaphor. Let us compare the moon with the mind and the surface of the pond with reality. Let us add one further complication and we will be ready to put this metaphor to work. Let us assume that the moonlight comes not only from the surface of the moon but also from hidden depths of the moon. The mind (moon) with all its conscious and unconscious surfaces (structures) explores (plays with) the textures of reality. One could argue that the essential element in play (whether mind or moonlight) is not moon or mind or light or pond but the action of the beam that allows multiple points of contact to be compared, contrasted, explored, integrated, processed, *played with*.

In strict psychological terms, the play of the boy in *Beyond the Pleasure Principle* is not the sum of the defense mechanisms (repression, displacement, identification) or the use of fantasy or symbolization per se but the *action* that creates a loss and then undoes it. If the boy were not two but twenty-two years old, the reaction to the loss would have been different. If we compare and contrast two- and twenty-two-year-old adaptations to reality, the meaning of play will become clearer. The twenty-two-year-old, confronted with separation from a loved one, will not represent his loss with a thrown-away inanimate object that can be retrieved by pulling a string. Why not? When we can answer that question, we will have gone a long way toward understanding the function and unraveling the mystery of play.

Before we can understand the maturity of the twenty-two-year-old, we need to consider the immaturity of the fifteen-month-old approaching the final stages of sensorimotor intelligence. Jean Piaget (Flavell, 1963, p. 85) defined six stages of sensorimotor intelligence between zero and eighteen months of age. A fifteen-month-old who is developing normally will be approaching stage 5 or 6, cognitively speaking. A description of one of Piaget's classical experiments will illuminate the essence of these critical stages of cognitive development. Picture a fifteen-month-old, a ball, a tunnel, and an adult testing the intelligence of the youngster. The ball is thrown through the tunnel. If the child has reached stage 5 on the sensorimotor development scale, she will crawl through the tunnel following the path of the ball to retrieve it. If the child has reached stage 6 on the sensorimotor scale, she will not need to trace the path of the ball by mimicking its journey through the tunnel with her own body. She will simply go around the tunnel and retrieve the ball at the other end. By eighteen months (stage 6 sensorimotor) the child's mind has achieved a simple yet astounding sophistication. It has internalized the action of the ball in the tunnel, deconstructed it sufficiently that it no longer has to retrace the ball's journey with the child's body; she can retrace the journey figuratively with the mind and save the body the extra effort. The eighteen-month-old mind has learned to grasp two displacements at once, Piaget would say, something the fifteen-month-old mind is incapable of.

It is this startling facility of the mind to juggle several ideas at once that makes human beings *the* symbol maker and separates them so dramatically from other species. (Even the most intelligent animals reach stage 5 on the sensorimotor intelligence scale, but never complete the leap into stage 6, which would put symbolism within their grasp.) What is symbolism, after all, but the mind's parsimonious way of getting one mental product to stand for many? Humanity's highest achievement, symbol production, has a humble origin in sensorimotor manual labor. If the symbol crawls out of a crucible of action when the mind is eighteen months old, what is its relation to action afterward? If thought is trial action, the mind seems to become more *thoughtful* as it matures, less prone to impulsive action. There does, however, seem to be a major transitional period from the dawn of symbolization at eighteen months to its full maturity in adulthood when the mind takes an intermediary position between impulse/action and symbol/reflex, which seems to be characterized by a symbolizing process that is half thought, half action.

Play and a child's deliberations about the nature of his own needs and the dictates of reality do not take place in some inner psychological theater that is removed from the experiential props of everyday life. On the contrary, a child sets up his proscenium arch in full view of parents and peers and rehearses his symbols and actions out in the open. In this prototype of all repertory theaters the mind rehearses the first drafts of dramas that will engage its attention in revised forms for a lifetime. If the mind at stage 5 of its sensorimotor life needs to drag the body through the tunnel for a period of time until at stage 6 it finally gets the point and learns to do it figuratively rather than literally, the mind, in this transitional period characterized by *playing*, insists on action as if symbol alone could not express the full story of the child's experience. The symbols, after all, are an *inheritance* and can seem to be passively received until the child acts on them, plays with them, and makes them his own.

In this intermediate, transitional period of playing, the child *takes action*. Everything that might be perceived or received passively has to be taken possession of *actively:* the Oedipus complex, for instance, to oversimplify it greatly, can be experienced as a *humiliation* at the hands of sexual aggressive giants or as an *education* by loving pedagogues, a leading forth of the child's sexual aggressive energies in a socially acceptable manner. The child relies on play to accomplish these active aims. The adult uses other resources.

The intermediate phase I am proposing has no boundaries, but by adolescence and adulthood, play as the significant mode that young Homo sapiens uses to titrate emotion with—play as one of the major yardsticks of reality—will wane and formal thinking, as Flavell (1963, p. 85) has called it, will take over. Formal thinking, or hypothetic-deductive thinking which is the hallmark of adolescent cognitive development, allows "action" to take place within the confines of the mind rather than partially outside the mind in concrete manipulations of the environment. If thought is trial action as Freud (1911) so felicitously named it, it is only in adolescence that the "trials" really take place in fantasy alone, not bolstered by the external props of the environment. That is not as absolute as these statements would suggest. I would like to introduce the reader to two examples of play, one in child analysis, the other in adult analysis, to extend this discussion further.

From the Analysis of a Five-Year-Old Boy

Consider action and affect and their development. The infant's major if not only communicative signals lie in this realm of action-affect. As Wolff (1967) has shown, the cries are orchestrated either to alarm the mother with an emergency appeal or to just nag her with fussy sounds. Out of these fussy or alarming appeals develops what Spitz (1965) has called the archaic dialogue, that preverbal mixture of love and mime out of whose soil basic trust sprouts and flourishes. Symbolism will inherit this protosymbolic world; ideally the archaic dialogue will pass the communicative baton to the much less archaic linguistic dialogue; and development will proceed, though not as smoothly as this outline suggests: the world of action-affect does not surrender itself so totally to its new master (language). Skirmishes, tantrums, even rebellions are the developmental rule, and these outbreaks get resolved in the courtrooms of play, a small claims court, if you will, where the Lilliputian Homo sapiens airs grievances and recovers pride.

The above paradigm of child development is a stick figure that bears about as much resemblance to the real thing as a child's figure drawing does to the complexity of anatomical structure. But I want to find a place for *action* in development, and I need to talk in caricature for a moment or the complexity of psychoanalytic detail will obscure my argument. Rather than talk of action-affect I could have focused on id-ego and the mutuality of influences or on instinct and its vicissitudes (aim primarily), but my intention is to stay focused on action for a moment and one of its tributaries—play. In a nutshell (a modest container that seems, however, to have little trouble holding immodest human-size ideas), my only point is that when archaic dialogue and linguistic dialogue go awry, the actions that support them feel false and a human being feels disenfranchised from herself, from her own center of action. The sole purpose of play is to recover this *sense of agency* so that the child feels rooted again in her own power to communicate effectively and adequately.

Alex was a boy whose developmental vessel got battered from all sides. His archaic dialogue with his mother was endangered from the beginning, his mother confessing that the ordinary acts of holding him, rocking him, reading him a bedtime story, were often in conflict for her, given her own memories of childhood. The maternal instinct was supplied vicariously by a loving primitive housekeeper who, however, left suddenly when Alex was three never to return despite promises to the contrary. The father was well-meaning, but his lifelong unresolved oedipal battle with his father found a new home in his relationship with his son, an arrangement that fanned the flames of Alex's preoedipal disappointments with the bellows of oedipal sexuality and aggression. When analysis began, this little boy was a boastful, hungry, hyperactive hellion close to expulsion from nursery school for grabbing the penises of his peers in a wild effort to find some power—some place to bolster his nonexistent self-esteem. He desperately needed to play with an adult and relearn how *to be* and how *to act*. His analysis, which was conducted in the classical Freud-Bornstein manner, could be described in terms of defense, resistance, transference, but again I wish to focus complete attention on play and action only, to the extent that this is possible.

Throughout the analysis, which lasted until he was ten years old, play with boats was a most significant activity that reflected his conflicts vividly. Their first appearance in the analysis was heralded as the transference began to take hold: the analyst was Dr. Doolittle, a wheelable bookshelf became a boat, and Alex at the helm of this makeshift vessel explored the foreign terrain of the playroom, taming the wild things that transference threw up on the shores of consciousness. The wild things that invaded his dreams at night could be leashed to play in this manner, calming this frantic child's anxieties considerably. A few months later, he brought a toy boat from home and began to play with it. A storm developed. The boat was in great danger. But we managed to get it to port—"the terminal," as he called it. Alex turned to me after the boat was safely in the terminal and said, "Maybe you can become a person terminal for me." This was Alex's most direct statement of trust in the transference to date.

As months went by, Alex began to trust me more and more, relying on play as much as language to carry the ball, emotionally speaking, for him. A major revelation, for instance, was introduced in linguistic form, but the working through in affect and action required play. Let me be clearer. The emotional revelation was that Maria, the beloved housekeeper, had left him, never to return. He counted the days. Analyst and analysand shared the poignancy of these revelations not only through dialogue but through play. Alex made a boat out of wood, carving it for many sessions, using the playroom as a miniature workshop. He carved, he painted, and then he named the boat *The Catch-up*, painting the red wood proudly with white letters. *The Catch-up* had multiple meanings, multiple voyages to sail into the past, so to speak, to revisit old psychological reefs and developmental rapids, to repair old wounds, and to plan new trips into the future. The analysis made several psychic voyages in the ensuing years and eventually termination was the last port of call, a very emotional final voyage. Alex was by now a socially competent, academically superior ten-year-old boy.

Termination was a graduation, an achievement, but it was also, when perceived neurotically, an abandonment, a rejection, a repetition of Maria's treachery. Once again Alex relied on play, not merely dialogue, to represent his conflicts. At first he thought he had no say in the matter of termination. He would be told after the fact. The analyst would abandon him. His rage at this state of affairs made him hate the analyst so much that he believed the relationship would be utterly destroyed. We would become strangers to one another. This is the way his relationship with Maria had ended, and he expected it would be the same with me. This murderous rage needed to be harnessed to language, to art, and to play. He made a portrait of me with a broken hand, a graphic attempt to hold onto me even while dismembering me. He also made another boat out of wood. With typical latency intrigue this boat was given a name in code—1160 5 413, numbers that represented his initials and mine and my office address. Significantly, this boat was left unfinished unlike *The Catch-up*, which had been modeled rather well and painted completely.

The boat surely had several meanings, all of which it is not necessary to analyze in this context. The point being stressed here is that making a "termination" boat was an *act* that gave Alex an extra modicum of control over the fate of his analysis that mere language would not have afforded him. Clearly, this boat did not hold as much emotional significance for Alex as *The Catch-up*. Language and thought were fast becoming the abstract "vessels" that could contain most of his affects and conflicts. The concrete boats of play would perhaps soon be unnecessary.

From the Analysis of a Twenty-three-Year-Old Man

If Alex was ready to relinquish his concrete hold of play, relatively speaking, Philip, at age twenty-three, seemed to be holding on to an aspect of play that was alarming to himself and a puzzle for him and his analyst to unravel.

As a boy, Philip had tried to resolve his considerable oedipal rivalry with his father and incestuous closeness to his mother with extreme passivity and masochistic tendencies: he seemed to relish being the butt of jokes, the victim of pranks. If there was a banana peel to slip on, he was sure to locate it. One game he loved to play in latency was "lost child." He would hide. A girlfriend would seek and eventually find him. When his girlfriend wished to reverse the order of the play and have Philip pursue and find her as the lost child, he was unable to relinquish his passivity even briefly and lost many a friendship because of his inflexibility. The alarming part was that now as an adult Philip was repeating his pattern in his relationship with women: he had three lengthy relationships with women who loved him for his many endearing qualities but became exasperated when the sole sexual activity involved going to bed and Philip quickly falling asleep, much to his partners' consternation and frustration as they attempted to arouse the lost child from his neurotic slumber. Massive castration fears, panic at the thought of the female genital, premature ejaculations, all were kept in abeyance by this insistence on a kind of foreplay whose sole purpose was to derail the more adult versions of sexual play with neurotic persistence of infantile games. The term *pathological play* could be assigned to this variant from the usual developmental waning of infantile schemas (Steingart, 1983).

For Philip *action* seemed inextricably linked to oedipal crime and massive oedipal retaliation. The whole subject was repressed so deeply in his unconscious that his abhorrence of the female genital was the mere tip of a hidden iceberg whose configurations were totally unknown to him for years of analysis. Again I am stressing action and its meaning rather than all the other components of this complex psyche. In this context it is significant that Philip remembered his childhood as devoid of football or baseball, as if he sensed that only in the rough and tumble of playful rivalry with his family could his oedipal demons have been exorcised. Whereas Alex could use play to redefine his own sense of agency, Philip's play seemed to betray a triumph of passive aims over active ones that would persist into adulthood.

Conclusion

One of the major developmental and psychological tasks of the human animal is to take action out of the realm of infantile omnipotence, strip it of its primitive magical qualities, and make it a tool of the rational mind. This developmental line could be called "from impulse to volition and decision." Action and symbolism seem to grow up together, so to speak, in the sensorimotor period of development, so well outlined by Piaget. But the story does not end at eighteen months obviously. The mind and the body continue to express themselves in symbols and in actions throughout life. Freud, in many papers, particularly in "Remembering, Repeating and Working-Through" (1914), outlined the links between memory recovered in words as opposed to memory repeated in neurotic action. The whole psychoanalytic theory of acting out is based on the connection between transference and memory, acting out being that portion of the transference that the patient is unable to put into words.

In childhood, play is the vessel into which affect and action can be poured when the vessels of language are not able to contain the entire psychic volume. In adulthood, play does not hold such a developmental urgency for the mind in conflict. It is, however, a psychological attitude that never vanishes completely and can probably be invoked by the human mind under normal or pathological circumstances whenever symbolism gets weary of pure abstraction and needs to remind itself of the action world of sweat and blood it sprang from.

References

Flavell, J. H. (1963). *The Developmental Psychology of Jean Piaget*. New York: Van Nostrand Reinhold.

Freud, S. (1911). Formulations of the two principles of mental functioning. *S.E.*, 12:218–226.

———. (1914). Remembering, repeating and working-through. *S.E.*, 12:145–156.

———. (1915). Instincts and their vicissitudes. *S.E.*, 14:109–140.

———. (1920). Beyond the pleasure principle. *S.E.*, 18:3–64.

Skeat, W. W. (1910). *An Etymological Dictionary of the English Language*. Oxford: Clarendon Press, p. 457.

Spitz, R. A. (1965). *The First Year of Life*. New York: Int. Univ. Press.

Steingart, I. (1983). *Pathological Play in Borderline and Narcissistic Personalities*. New York: Spectrum.

Wolff, P. H. (1967). The role of biological rhythms in early psychological development. *Bull. Menninger Clin.*, 31:197–218.

11

From Enactment to Play to Discussion: The Analysis of a Young Girl

Steven Marans, M.S.W.

With an increasing capacity to test and suspend reality, children in the oedipal phase of development are able to use imaginative play as a means of creating an illusion of wish fulfillment and invincible mastery. Children at this age can move fluidly through a range of themes in play that are determined by the urgency of what is uppermost in their minds, whether exciting, pleasurable, or fearful. The push toward mastery combines with curiosity to arrive at solutions in play in which theories about themselves in relation to others may be tested and explored.

The suspension of reality that is essential for imaginative play presupposes a child's ability to tolerate substitutions for more direct and immediate gratification of wishes and to rely instead on symbolic representations of impulses, affects, and fantasies. Although children recognize that reality may not yield to their wishes and aspirations, in the suspension of reality they do not need completely to relinquish their exploration either. In the domain of play—between fantasy and enactment—wishes and their consequences, conflicts and their solutions, can be manipulated or tried in multiple forms and configurations. When children are able to direct scenarios involving the displacements of their wishes and fears, they are no longer simply the passive victim of the attendant dangers and disappointing confrontation with reality. The experience of mastery in this transitional phenomenon of play allows the child to titrate fantasy and real life—wishes can be modified while reality limitations and age-appropriate capabilities can be better tolerated and appreciated.

Our assumption that imaginative play reflects and serves adaptation to inner fantasy and external reality is based in part on observations of young children in psychoanalytic treatment. The play activities, narratives, associated affects, and uses of the analyst are the data we employ in our attempts to understand the child's experiences and to facilitate new solutions to his or her conflicts. This process is by no means a simple one, and our task is even more complicated when the young patient steadfastly refuses to yield to a reality in which instinctual wishes will not be gratified immediately and is unable to play. When this occurs, there are few if any acceptable substitutes for or modification of the aims of instinctual urges. In this situation, the *suspension* of reality appears to be an inadequate substitute for the realization of intensely felt longings. Rather than pretending about wishes and consequences, conflicts and solutions, the child enacts them with the determination that the *real* objects of these longings will submit to his or her requirements. In the case of a child who cannot play we need first to understand why not and then to facilitate a move from enactment to pretend and from pretend to self-observation and perhaps discussion. These were the challenges when I began work with Emma.

Case Presentation
Background

At the time of referral Emma R. was four years eight months old. Mrs. R. complained that Emma was becoming "uncontrollably angry" and that every day began with a battle over the clothes she would wear and the food she would eat. She criticized almost everything her mother did and alternated between shouting that she hated Mother and that Mother hated her. She could not bear to see her sister, Sara, who was seven years older, talking with her mother and insisted bitterly that Sara was the favorite and had the best of everything. Emma's provocative behavior extended to peeling wallpaper and paint in the house, stealing, and swearing. In addition, although she achieved bowel control at two years, Emma was not dry during the day until she was three and a half and was still in diapers at night when referred for treatment. She was afraid to go to the bathroom on her own and frequently stained her underpants. Emma was also fearful of walking unaccompanied from room to room in the house, had difficulty getting to sleep, and had frequent nightmares. According to her mother, when Emma was not battling, she demanded close physical attention and was at peace only when curled up in her mother's lap, sucking her thumb. The mother was at her wit's end, feeling that there was little she could do to please her daughter.

Emma's parents separated when she was four years old. Mrs. R. had been desperate to have this second child "before it was too late" and gave birth to Emma when she was forty years old. Mrs. R. described the wish for this child both as an attempt to save her failing marriage and as a "selfish act," independent of the status of the marriage. At the time she became pregnant, Mrs. R. claimed, her husband was drinking heavily and they argued frequently. According to her account, when she announced the pregnancy, Mr. R. encouraged her to terminate it. Subsequently, Mrs. R. felt she received no emotional support from her husband. She became depressed and withdrawn during Emma's second year and relied on a series of au pair girls to take over much of her care. Despite Mr. R.'s earlier attitudes to the pregnancy and early infancy, both parents reported that around the time of Mrs. R.'s depression, the father became very involved with Emma.

As the marriage deteriorated, Mr. R.'s devotion to Emma increased. The mother described father and Emma as "inseparable." The father was indulgent with Emma, but his handling was inconsistent. Mrs. R. claimed that Emma had rarely heard the word "no" in her first four years. Discipline, she said, was the exclusive domain of her husband, as she had hoped this would reduce the ever-increasing marital battles. Mr. R.'s reprimands, however, invariably dealt with Emma's messiness, and at these times he could be harsh, sometimes shaking her violently. For example, it was common at mealtimes for Emma to sit on her father's lap and eat off his plate. When she spilled something onto him, however, Mr. R. would become enraged, shout at her, and put her down roughly. In addition, Mr. R. became especially distressed when the family dog urinated or defecated indoors. On such occasions he shouted and kicked the dog while Emma cowered, in tears. The mother claimed that these outbursts became more frequent as his drinking increased. While acknowledging his tendency toward fastidiousness, Mr. R. reported that tension in the home resulted from his withdrawal from the marriage and denied he had a drinking problem.

Following the separation, Mr. R. saw his children almost every week during the acrimonious separation and divorce. They frequently spent time with his steady girlfriend whom he subsequently married.

Emma's relationship with Sara was fraught with jealousy and insecurity. The rivalry went both ways. Sara resented the fact that Emma was their father's favorite and complained of being left out and ignored during their visits. The father readily acknowledged his preference for Emma, describing her as the "perfect companion" whom he loved to "cuddle and pamper." Sara taunted and denigrated Emma, viciously parading her own closeness with their mother and teasing her with her superior sexual knowledge. Although the mother accepted that Emma's feeling of being left out was justified, she persisted in demonstrating to Emma that her older sister was preferred.

At the start of the treatment, Mrs. R.'s attempts to set limits with Emma took the form of polite, restrained appeals to this five-year-old's sense of decency and propriety. Emma's responses to these appeals were anything but proper. At mealtimes, a request from the mother to sit at the table was often met with an angry "No!" and a piece of food being hurled at her. Mrs. R. tried to mollify her younger daughter by acceding to her demands. In one instance, Emma came down to breakfast and complained that she wanted butter on her toast. The mother sensed her battling mood and immediately buttered the toast. Emma threw the toast down and yelled that there was not enough butter. She then told her mother that there was not enough cereal in her bowl. When Mrs. R. put in a little more, Emma bitterly complained that there was now too much.

Treatment

When Emma and I met in the waiting room on the day of our first session, she peered at me from behind her mother's skirt. Her thick, long, dark hair framed bright brown eyes, a pert nose, and an impish smile. Her small but sturdy-looking body was dressed neatly in a school uniform. She shyly insisted on her mother's presence in the room on the first day and remained in her lap for most of the hour. She responded to questions about school and favorite playthings by nestling further into mother's bosom and demanding, "You tell him, Mommy." Mrs. R. told me about Emma's favorite doll at home and in a quiet exasperated voice tried to coax her daughter to speak for herself. With every angry refusal, Emma gave me a sidelong glance, sucked her thumb, and pushed against her mother's body as she maneuvered for maximum contact. I introduced two animal puppets and began a discussion between them about how hard it is to talk with someone you do not know and how much nicer it feels to make sure that the mommy stays close. Emma looked up at her mother and smiled, but she refused to take either of the offered puppets and again turned away. I began drawing and Emma joined me at the table. After many kisses and hugs she allowed her mother to leave the room.

As Emma drew a picture of her sister, mother, and herself, she calmly told me about seeing her dog, Sally, run over by a truck; about a cat that had just died; and about her grandfather who had died as well. She pointed out that the mother figure in her drawing was missing hands: "They were chopped off." She quickly left the table and pulled open the door of a closet that housed a water tank. Emma exclaimed that the room might be flooded and then raced to the window; she told me with considerable anxiety that it was dark outside and that she hated nighttime because that was "when the witches try to kill me." I commented that she might be trying to figure out whether or not she was safe in the room when her mother was not with her. Emma began jumping and said, "I can jump very high. How high can you jump? I can jump higher than you." When I announced that we would be stopping, Emma grabbed a small girl doll figure and tore its clothes off, complaining that the underpants would not come off. I told her that we would be able to play more the following day, and Emma raced out of the room.

Enactment. The next day, leading the way, Emma confidently climbed the stairs up to our room and announced with a smile, "I don't need Mommy to come any more 'cause now I know you." She immediately returned to drawing "nighttime" by covering a sheet of paper with black crayon and told me again about the witches that wanted to kill her. Rather than elaborate on this idea, she grabbed a pencil, sprang to her feet, giggled, and drew a "bottom" on the wall. She crossed it out and then erased it, saying that someone might beat her up if they saw it. I commented that she might be afraid that I would be angry and Emma agreed. I added that it seemed as though she was having worries about people becoming angry with her and about being safe. Instead of drawing on the walls, I suggested that we talk and play about her thoughts and feelings. With nonchalance Emma informed me that she had come to see me for her worries and that her worry was that she hated herself. "Everybody hates me . . . because I'm bad." For a moment she was subdued and nodded to my comment about how awful this must feel.

Her frenetic activity returned quickly, however, and she crumpled the drawing of nighttime and kicked it along the floor. Gleefully she described how she enjoyed getting her mother angry by calling her a fat pig so that her mother would chase her. "I like saying fuckee, fuckit, and stuff it up your nose. Sometimes I punch her boosies [breasts]—that's what Sally calls them." I replied that I thought she was trying to figure out whether I too would get mad and have scary chasing games with her. At the end of this hour, Emma told me that I did not need to clean up and that I should rest. As she put the paper and crayons away, she turned to me and dreamily said, "You smell like my daddy."

In the waiting room Emma's angry attacks on her mother were prominent. She often delayed coming to the playroom with tirades against Mrs. R. for not providing after-school treats, for not holding her coat properly (placing it on a chair instead of keeping it in her lap), or for failing to agree to buy a special gift on the way home from the clinic. These scenes often ended with a haggard, resigned expression on the mother's face and a softly spoken agreement to "discuss it later." In the consulting room, Emma's frenetic pace continued as she alternated between drawing pictures of ghosts and witches, describing nightmares about monsters that attacked her, and demanding to take playroom materials home with her. In addition, she attempted to engage me in exciting activities and quickly became enraged and frightened when I continued to suggest that words take the place of actions.

In a typical early session, Emma giggled when she told me her secret of "pooping on the back steps [of her house]. Mommy thinks it's a dog. . . . You won't tell, will you?" Before I could respond, Emma raced to the other side of the room and began peeling paint from the wall while looking at me with defiance and pleasure. I reminded her of the rule about peeling paint, adding that she seemed to need to find out if her worry about my getting angry with her would come true. This oft-repeated response to her provocations again had little effect on her actions. Emma ran across the room and poked me gently and repeatedly in the chest. As I moved away, she protested, "But I can touch you, I can!" Words and attempts to introduce play with puppets or family doll figures were no substitute for the exciting physical contact Emma sought in "real" action. Every intervention was met with an escalation in her provocative behavior and angry demands that I "shut up"—until finally Emma's fury turned to fear and she ran out of the room in search of her mother. The ghosts, witches, and monsters that had filled her drawings had now filled the room, and she again refused to return to her sessions without her mother.

For over a week, Emma used her mother as a haven that enabled her to continue to make provocative bids for intimate contact from me and to express her rage and frustration when these were not reciprocated. During one hour Emma again tried to make physical contact with me. When she approached with a felt pen poised for marking me, I stopped her, and she burst into tears, yelling, "That's all you say is No, No, No! You're horrid; everybody hates me!" She climbed into her mother's lap and sucked her thumb. While glaring at me, she asked if her mother would go with her to the waiting room to return a glass. Mrs. R. suggested that she wait, and with that Emma flew out of her mother's arms onto the floor where she wept. I commented on how awful she felt and added that even when she was very angry with me, I still wanted to be her friend and help her with her worries. Emma looked up at her mother and quietly said, "I want to be his friend." She insisted that we play a "happy game" to get rid of the bad feelings and taught me how to play her version of hide-and-seek.

This game was to be Emma's first play sequence of the treatment. But as I was to learn, what was play for Emma was never fully pretend but rather a mode of substituting an unwanted aspect of reality with a slightly recrafted version. In each of our games of hide-and-seek, Emma instructed me to become upset about not finding her and to become ecstatic when she finally announced where she was hiding. With this response, Emma beamed, delighted with this momentary proof that I liked her; I could again become the "good" man who smelled and looked like a daddy.

The reality this particular game sought to reshape had to do with the comings and goings of Emma's father, which were experienced by her as manifestations of his indifference and rejection. But hide-and-seek could not undo for very long the sadness and rage Emma felt about her father. In the transference, her buoyant response to the game was easily marred by the real interruptions of what Emma called "coming together as friends again." Following one of our early hide-and-seek games, I reminded Emma that the following day was a day that we did not meet. She exploded and yelled, "You're a daddy! Your stupid girlfriend. I'm not going to be your girlfriend and neither is Mommy!"

In spite of the ease with which she became enraged by the father-therapist who defied her wishes, Emma's longing for proofs of his love were powerful enough for her to persevere in treatment. In addition to frequent comments about her anger with me and worries about ghosts seeking revenge, Emma's powerful wish for an exclusive intimate relationship with the father in the transference prompted her to dismiss mother from the treatment room once and for all. The game of hide-and-seek was Emma's way of repairing the damage attendant to her rage when I would not allow both exciting bodily contact and an alternative but equally *real* form of gratification—proof that her longings and love were reciprocated. In the hours that followed, peaceful moments occurred when we played the game of hide-and-seek, when she sought my praise for drawings, or when she leaned up against me while reporting something of her day in school. In one such session, when I agreed to remove a splinter from her finger, Emma asked me to guess what it was thinking. I variously guessed, "It's angry; it's sad; it's scared." She quickly corrected me. "It loves you." Emma looked away smiling and said, "You're my daddy." Just as there was little pretend in the play about her loving feelings, Emma's aggression was as directly felt and expressed. When I announced the end of this particular session, Emma staggered around the room banging into me and, with a scowl, tore pieces of foam padding from under the rug and threw them in my face.

The brief play scenarios portraying separations could not contain the wishes or yield the gratification that Emma demanded in reality. Her separations from her father were a major source of pain and anxiety because they raised for her a crucial question that expressed the vulnerability of her self-esteem: how could she feel sufficiently valued and value herself when her objects found it so easy to turn from her? Her father's hellos and good-byes were out of her control, just as her mother's withdrawal had been, and Emma was enraged by her helplessness and sadness. The transference of these feelings onto me was swift, and she saw the interruptions in our contact as rejections. She returned from any separation, whether Wednesdays, weekends, or holidays, in a foul mood.

In a session following a vacation during the latter part of the first year of treatment, Emma entered the room with a scowl on her face and imperiously commanded me to get things from her locker. When I wondered about a possible connection between her anger and our time apart, Emma told me to shut up. She continued her tirade by telling me how much she hated me and wished she could get a gun so that she could kill me and everyone else that I saw. After threatening to kick and punch me, she stood by the window glaring at me until she wrote me a note that she crumpled and threw at me. It said, "I hate you . . . I like you." I joined her at the window where we watched the birds outside. Emma said that she wished that a bird would land and that if we made sure it got enough food, it would stay forever and eat. "Does this bird have a name?" I asked. "Yes. Happy Bird."

Emma continued to leave the treatment room in a mess but also began to elaborate on her concerns about separations in play; in this particular area words could begin to accompany and, in time, replace enactments. She initiated a series of games about sleeping that typically followed week-end breaks. Emma instructed me to be a "grumpy daddy" who repeatedly woke her with his snoring. In turn, she scolded me and finally threatened to punch me if I woke her again. "I'll show you. You kept me up all the other night!" In a rare moment, Emma allowed a comment "outside of the game" about how awful it felt when we did not meet. "Yes, I'll show you how it feels. See if you like it!" As Emma was able to express her frustration in the words, "I'm getting even," she could also occasionally talk directly about her unhappiness about difficult weekends and her wish for "affinity" (her word for *infinity*) days together. In fact, it was only in the context of turning passive into active and seeking revenge within the play that the longings and hurt feelings could emerge so clearly. After one holiday Emma became the therapist, and I was the child. I was kicked out of our room for "a very long time" and was instructed to feel very sad. But then I looked into the room and discovered that over the holiday the therapist was feeding other children. "And then you cried and got really angry," Emma exclaimed. Later in the same session, Emma became a wolf who wanted to eat me up, keep me inside, and take me home with her.

Although Emma could briefly take on a fantasy role, her play did not afford her any distance from the intensity of her need for real excitement and gratification involving her body and physical contact with me. In fact, the limited number of characters she began to introduce served the function of enactment. In turn, these scenarios were short-lived; Emma would quickly discard the assumed role but not the action. She was unable to relinquish the excitement of a more direct expression of her fantasies and was infuriated when I limited her activities. Emma's immersion in her fantasies, however, also made her feel vulnerable to the retaliation she expected from me as the object (in the transference) of both her excited, loving wishes and her enraged, aggressive ones. Emma could experience little if there was any distance between reality and fantasy or between her longings and fears. In time, it became more apparent that her sexually provocative behavior simultaneously served as an enactment of wishes and as a defense against their dangerous consequences.

Emma began initiating her sessions by sitting in a chair opposite me, momentarily lifting her skirt and giggling or pointing out the latest bruises and scrapes on her legs. She often responded to sympathetic comments about her having some concerns about her body by dancing a jig or drawing pictures of "beautiful women." With either activity, Emma repeatedly asked if I liked what she had done. Anything short of a direct exclamation of my admiration was met with an angry, "Just tell me!" or a sullen, "Never mind." In one such session, however, Emma became Godzilla, the giant who kills monsters. She tore paper into small pieces and threw them on the floor and then suddenly turned toward me and spat. I was stunned and angry, and attempted to control my voice as I told her that spitting was not acceptable. I quickly added that I thought she was again trying to make me angry. I had in mind continuing by saying that she needed to see what would happen, but Emma interrupted and yelled, "I want you to get mad at me and hurt me because you are awful!" She quickly emptied the contents of the trash can and climbed in to protect herself from being bitten by the angry snakes that now surrounded me. She sat in the trash can breathing heavily, looking both frightened and furious. I reminded her that I wanted to be her friend even when she was angry and said that she had been so worried that her scary thoughts about being hurt would come true that she had to find out. As I began to clean up the room, Emma got out of the trash can and on one of the rare occasions in this first year of treatment began to help.

In the next hour, Emma again began Godzilla's rampage in the room. I said that she was again showing me her anger, but that sometimes it was hard for her to remember that they were *her* angry feelings and not mine. Without a word, she abandoned Godzilla, and the exciting wish behind the fear of attack became clearer. She built a house out of chairs, pretended to go to sleep, and then awoke with a start, saying that she had had a bad dream. "I dreamed that I married you and kissed you on the lips." As she lay by the heating vent, Emma quickly changed her story, and now it was the heating vent that kissed her. "It put its tongue in my mouth and sent fire through my body which came out of my bottom." When I suggested that this was both an exciting and scary dream, Emma leaped to her feet and reached her hand inside the back of her skirt and rubbed her anus. She extended her finger toward my face and with a smile insisted that I smell it. When I declined, Emma pleaded, "Please, it smells very, very nice." As she began to cry, she added, "And it's *so* important." I told her that I could see how important it was to her and that it was as if she wanted to know whether I could really like her. In comparison to the intensity of her feelings, this response seemed to miss the poignancy of the moment. In retrospect, it seemed that Emma was at once trying to seduce me with the essence of how she felt about herself and perhaps trying to recapture a kind of intimacy that she knew from an earlier time in her life when the parents' care of her body and the exciting physical contact with her father were experienced as expressions of their love.

As treatment proceeded, the openness of Emma's wishes for physical intimacy and sexual excitement became a gauge of her feelings of worthlessness and reflected her attempts to undo the accompanying expectation of being unloved and rejected. A history of inappropriate limit setting in the home and overstimulation in the form of exposure to parental nudity and her father's seductive handling and open-door policy with his girlfriend seemed to have set the stage for this form of compensation. Although work with the parents during the first eighteen months of treatment significantly decreased their contributions to her overstimulation, the urgency of Emma's attempts to engage me in sexually exciting contact did not. She frequently invited me to look at her underpants, openly masturbated, and talked excitedly about "boosies," "hairy bottoms," and "men's things." Emma responded with disappointment and rage to my comments about her wish to have exciting times with me in order to feel that I liked her. A pattern began to emerge, however. When she stopped yelling at me to shut up and removed her hands from her ears, Emma frequently turned to brief play scenarios in which the characters' excited sexual activities were followed by frightening themes of bodily damage. For several months a game involving turtles made out of Plasticine was typical. In this game Emma expressed her fantasy of sadistic intercourse as she placed the boy on top of the girl. Amid excited laughter, she quickly began bashing the two together, careful that only the girl turtle "lost its body." Emma's laughter turned into nervous giggles as tail, legs, and then eyes went flying in pieces across the room. The boy turtle remained intact. Instead of commenting on the link between her excited, exhibitionistic, masturbatory behavior and her longings for closeness, I began pointing out how frightened she became when she grew too excited. Highlighting this dilemma, in addition to the frustration that I would not respond to her seductive behavior, heightened Emma's conflicts about the direct expression and enactment of sexual impulses. Enactment did not disappear entirely, but by the end of the second year of treatment, the sessions became dominated by elaborate, imaginative play.

Playing. In a move from direct action and immediate gratification, Emma could now introduce sustained and elaborate play scenarios. While she was capable of using displacement to express wishes and fears, Emma's control of the script and of our respective roles was absolute. Where she had previously pinned her self-worth on the direct enactment of sexual and aggressive urges, Emma now immersed herself in the wish fulfillment and reversal of fortunes possible only in play. Her angry demands that I "shut up and get back in the game" reflected both her wish to control me in reality and her fear that anything I might introduce would contaminate the suspension of reality in which she now sought gratification and refuge from disappointment.

Concerns about her "castrated state" illustrated Emma's worries about the consequences of her exciting sexual wishes for intimacy and served as an explanation for her feelings of inadequacy and failure in procuring the object's love. Having a penis was a symbol of strength and control that would protect her from attack and damage. In one game Emma became a puppy who closely guarded a pencil, which she referred to as her "special thing." I was instructed to make repeated attempts to steal this special thing as she slept, but each time the puppy awoke, growled, and frightened me away. Emma finally thwarted my attempts by placing the pencil between her legs, telling me she was hiding the special thing inside.

As Emma equated the penis with strength, we frequently played at being big, strong horses. Emma was not sure whether she wanted to be a girl or boy horse, but knew that she wanted to be the stronger of the two. I commented on the sexual differences, adding that sometimes girl horses feel awful that they don't have what boys have and are sad and angry. Emma asked me to repeat this and then gave an emphatic whinny and nod of her head. Just after this, the Emma horse had a fall in which her leg was cut and bled. Emma quickly gave up her role of injured horse and instead became Popeye, the strongest man in the world. At this time Mrs. R. reported that Emma was stealing pens and pencils, both at school and at home. Emma believed that somebody had stolen the one body part that would make her safe and whole and was determined to steal it back. Eventually she became able to express her feelings about her own body more directly. In one session, as she tried to hold water in her hands, Emma explained that it was escaping through gaps. I asked about these gaps, and Emma replied, "You know, where something's missing, like here." She pointed to her genitals. In other sessions I was instructed to steal pencils. I was always caught, however, and was sent to prison. Emma's explanation for the stealing was simple: in a whispered aside in the game, she said, "You don't have one, and you want it so badly!" When she understood the link between her wish to repair the "gap" and the games of stealing pencils, thefts outside the session stopped.

Emma's fear of being attacked and damaged continued as a central theme in her play, but she was no longer the helpless victim—I was. As the younger brother, I was fed and protected from snakes, lions, and tigers that wanted to eat us. Emma carried a big gun and was fearless as we made forays into the dangerous woods. In this game I learned that if only I were bigger and had a gun like her, I needn't be afraid.

Emma's conviction that she would be safer and preferred if only she possessed a penis became an essential aspect of the transference when she learned that her father was going to remarry. Her wish for an exclusive intimate relationship with him was intensified, as were her fears of the consequences. In addition, concerns that she might also lose mother's affection to another set the stage for defensive regression. These dilemmas were most apparent when Emma was scheduled to attend a party following our session. Here, though the enactment was not as dramatic, the intensity of her wishes and anxiety could not be contained in fantasy play alone. When she entered the consulting room, Emma announced that she was going to change into her party dress. After removing her school clothes, she looked down at her underpants and smiled at me anxiously. With her party dress on, Emma launched into a tirade about how silly boys are. She asked me to admire her dress but before I could say a word, angrily stated, "You don't know about girls; you think they're not as good as boys." Just as suddenly, Emma announced that the dress made her look like a prince. I suggested that she had become excited when she had taken off her other clothes and then worried that being a girl was more dangerous than being a boy. "Boys and princes have arrows that they shoot and they have snakes," she replied. She made thrusting motions with her arms to show me what arrows do. "Older girls know how to get away from the arrows which go inside and hurt." If she could not be a safe prince, Emma preferred to be a baby, avoiding danger because "they lie close to the ground and their mothers protect them."

The sexual fantasies and associated fears about her father became increasingly clear in Emma's developing story about a puppy. She invented a game in which I was the owner who took the puppy (Emma) on walks in the park. As I talked to strangers in the park, the puppy pulled at the leash and threatened to run away. Emma asked me to repeat my comments about the puppy feeling left out and unlovable. Over the course of this game, the stranger with whom I talked became more specific. "Who is it?" I asked. "A man." "Is he safe?" "Yes, I mean no!" she replied. "He's going to kidnap me and use his knife. He'll put it in my, um, stomach!" The puppy then scurried off, and I was to lock all the doors to keep the man out. This evolved into a story about a servant girl who felt left out as she listened at the door of the king and queen's bedroom. The servant girl heard screaming and then announced that the queen had died after being stabbed and that now she and the king would live happily ever after.

Although Emma did not make an explicit connection between the themes in her imaginative play and her longings for her father, she did begin to monitor her own levels of excitement in an attempt to forestall anxiety. In a departure from stories about kings and queens, she ran around the bases inducing me to tag her out. Suddenly she stopped and said, "I'm getting too excited. I'd better stop before I get worried." At home, she no longer engaged her mother in battles; she had stopped having daytime fears and nightmares; and her bed-wetting had ceased. The school reported Emma's greater ability to concentrate; they were pleased with her progress.

Her father's remarriage exacerbated Emma's feelings of being rejected and unlovable, but she was able to distance herself from these feelings. She sadly acknowledged that she could never marry her father because "I'm too young, and anyway, I'm his daughter." She spoke in philosophical terms about her parents' divorce, recognizing that it had not occurred because of her: "Sometimes people can't get along with each other and they divorce." Although she spoke with relative neutrality about her longings for her father, her wish to "grow up quickly" in order to marry me was intense.

In her third year of treatment Emma's oedipal fantasies in the transference began to flourish, as did their elaboration in sustained play. We started to take many trips together to exotic foreign countries. During one of these trips, Emma explained that babies come from eating special food and that girls can have them only after they become seventeen years old. Predictably, Emma became the seventeen-year-old who prepared special meals on our vacations. In other games, I was the king who admired the servant's prettier dress and her ability to jump higher than the queen. In the end, the queen died or "just went away somewhere." The king and servant girl lived happily ever after.

Emma began to woo me outside of games as well and wanted to show me all of the big-girl things that she could do. She dreamily talked about how nice it would be to get bigger so that we could be the same age. At the same time, Emma repeatedly asked if I was married and complained that I never took her anywhere nice. On several occasions she exclaimed bitterly that I had not attended a school event with her because "you were with your stupid girlfriend." She could begin to accept comments about how difficult it was waiting to grow up, but continued to associate the frustration of current wishes with her intrinsic belief that she was inadequate and unlovable. In a characteristic attempt to fend off or reverse these feelings, Emma introduced a school game in which she was, again, seventeen years old, the best at everything, and the teacher's favorite. The younger, stupid student was ignored by the teacher and was very upset when the older student announced that she was getting married the following day. As the older student, Emma teased the younger one about being too young to marry and about "not knowing what love is anyway." Emma instructed me as the younger child to become sad because "God made it so that you won't grow up and won't marry because you were bad! You'll be left by your mommy and daddy all alone." The older girl had never been bad and God rewarded her with "marriage, sex, and a baby nine months later." When this game was over, Emma was suddenly furious and stormed out of the room, exclaiming, "And you know *why* I'm angry with you!"

Outside of these games Emma asked many questions about other children I saw and worried that I might prefer them to her. She was steadfast in her conviction that there was nothing worthwhile about a girl her age when compared to the seventeen-year-old who could marry and have babies.

In spite of Emma's sensible views about her father's remarriage, it seemed that the only proof of being valued and loved would be found in a real proposal of marriage. The profound hurt that Emma experienced when this proof was not forthcoming from me was, for a long while, expressed in her frequent irritability and domineering in the sessions. During this phase of the treatment, Emma's intense criticism of me served to reverse her feeling that in refusing her wishes, I was criticizing her. In Emma's mind, I would not marry her because she was not "good enough," old enough, clean enough. In a further effort to compensate for this belief, she began to insist that I had neither a wife nor a girlfriend. In play Emma alone continued to be chosen as "the best and favorite." Outside of these games, she was highly critical of any of her real achievements, alternating between condemning her art, schoolwork, or athletic feats and deciding that it was I who thought they were "no good." The mother noted that Emma rarely showed her anything that she had made or spoke of what she had accomplished.

Play and Talk. In spite of her intensified feelings of frustration, Emma did not return to provocative enactment as a means of counterattacking or preempting expected retaliation. Instead, she could better tolerate the underlying affects that she expressed within the transference and her elaborate, imaginative play. Following a game involving the "best and favorite student," Emma again complained that it was not fair that I never took her anywhere nice. Her pain broke through in tears when I pointed out that her need to be the only "best" person in my life was the result of her never feeling sure that anyone could love her at all. She sat quietly during the remaining minutes of the hour, demanding that I stop looking at her.

In the following session, however, Emma initiated a new game about a time machine. In our multiple travels into the past, she set the stage in which a two-year-old girl was ignored repeatedly by her parents until she became messy. They would then yell at her, deprive her of toys as punishment, or simply kick her out of the family. The game abruptly ended as we returned to "now." In other games, the girl was now eight years old (Emma's age at the time) and got angry every time she was excluded from the activities of others. With a knowing look, Emma reminded me of the time machine but insisted that as a toddler the girl had been left out *because* she was messy and bad. That is, Emma's view was that the girl got what she deserved.

Although at first discounting my sympathetic questions about the girl's feelings, Emma began to make specific links between the game and her memories. In asides, she talked about her father's volatile response to her dogs and herself. She described how frightening it was to see him so angry when she or the dogs were "messy" and added with conviction, "It wasn't fair!" When creating the role of the inattentive mother in the game, she commented on the similarities to her own mother. In one session, as the two-year-old was again ignored, Emma suddenly departed from the play. "You know, I think my mommy used to get very unhappy about daddy and divorce and all that stuff." Returning to the game, she portrayed the toddler as confused and worried when the mother was unavailable. In subsequent time-machine games over a three-month period, the baby could be depicted in more sympathetic terms; she was sad and felt helpless, but was not necessarily bad and unlovable. Referring directly to herself, Emma pointed out that as a two-year-old she could only assume that her mother's lack of attention and her father's anger were in response to something deficient in her.

When Emma no longer took full responsibility for her father's departure from home, she was able to put her sadness and disappointment into words. She described feeling "very sad and angry" in her memory of father packing his bags and leaving. She said that she would always wish that her parents had not divorced but could enjoy time spent with both of them. The parents' relationship also grew more cordial, and Emma's sense of this helped diminish the intense loyalty conflict that she had felt in the past as well.

As Emma relaxed her critical view of herself from the past, she began to silence the "mean voice inside" that operated in the present. No longer needing to disavow painful feelings as "babyish" or automatically externalize self-criticism, Emma turned to me almost as a scientific colleague with whom she would check out new discoveries. Her imaginative play did not suddenly disappear in the last months of her treatment, but Emma spent more time with daily reports of "real" events. She was particularly interested in analyzing difficult or upsetting interactions with others, always checking her tendency toward self-criticism and resulting hypersensitivity. Her capacity for self-observation could be used to appraise situations that would have been very painful previously. She recognized, for example, that her sister's teasing, her mother's periodic inattention, or her father's sporadic irritability were not always the result of her behavior or a reflection of her work but were often due to "their own bad moods." She reported her sister's trying to frighten her with taunts about ghosts and witches. Emma replied, "You're just trying to worry me because *you're* worried! Well, we're different people, and I'm going to my room to read a book." When she had finished telling me the story, Emma beamed and said, "I really had her number, didn't I?"

Emma began to use this newfound insight in a variety of situations. When she became frustrated in her schoolwork, drawings, or games, she would nod her head, smile, and say, "I was needing to be perfect just then," or "I got so worried about being best, I couldn't practice." Although she still did not like her older sister's being allowed to stay up later, Emma no longer experienced this rule as mother's rejection of *her*. In a game, Emma, as the maternal figure, firmly but gently handled the young child's demands to stay up late: "You know that when you don't get enough sleep, you feel cranky and unhappy all the next day."

Having changed from a girl whose early sessions had been filled with provocative, overexcited, and obstinate behavior, Emma now preferred telling me riddles she had learned at school, practicing her italic writing, and occasionally describing incidents that made her angry. She now was established firmly in latency and, to use her words, wanted to "get on with it." Where separation once had spelled rejection and confirmed feelings of inadequacy, Emma now requested more time to spend with friends after school. She hesitated in asking to cut back the number of sessions, fearing that I would ask "all those questions about feelings and stuff," and was relieved to discover that I, too, recognized that "too many questions" were inappropriate. She was ready, indeed, to "get on with it."

Discussion

Over the course of treatment it became clear that the special attention Emma received from her father was not enough to sustain good feelings about herself. A history of confusing parental responses made it impossible for Emma to rely on a consistent internal source of positive regard. In the first instance, her mother's depression and emotional withdrawal during Emma's second year made it difficult for the child to feel adequately valued by her. Although the father stepped in at this point as an alternative source of affection and care, his inconsistent handling presented Emma with an equally confusing model for self-evaluation. His mercurial shifts in mood left Emma feeling valued and loved *only* when he overindulged her. When he became harsh and violent over messy play or eating, Emma felt bad and unlovable. The mother was unavailable to modulate these extremes, and, in the end, Emma never was quite sure that she was worthwhile or worthy of love. In the absence of consistent, appropriate parental demands and praise for the *delay* of gratification, Emma sought proof of love from her objects in their *immediate* gratification of wishes.

As a result, there was an open, insistent quality in her expression of wishes from each developmental phase. For a long while, to relinquish these wishes and their enactment was to give up hope of securing the proof of love she required so desperately. It was not until the third year of treatment that Emma could begin to recognize that her harsh criticism of herself interfered with her ability to take pride in her real achievements and to enjoy the pleasure of the praise that was available to her from external sources. It was only when fantasies could find representation in play that

Emma could begin to recognize the fact that the objects' refusal to accede to every wish did *not* mean that she was worthless and unloved. The transitions that Emma achieved from enactment to play and from play to talk were especially evident in a comment she made toward the end of her analysis. She reflected on how much she used to wish that she could marry her father and me and said, "I know I'll have a husband someday . . . but it's very hard to wait!"

During the analysis, Emma's ego capacities and their development were reflected in the move from (1) enactment or immediate gratification of impulses on her own body and in interactions with others; (2) to the development of a narrative in which the same impulses were given expression via other-than-self characters; and (3) to verbalization of self-observations both within the play and in discussions with the analyst. In her imaginative play the site of the discharge was no longer on her own body but on the bodies and activities of the characters in the story. The suspension of reality was required, as was an increased capacity to tolerate frustration, in order for Emma to elaborate and sustain narratives and central themes in play or in direct discussions. Over the course of her treatment Emma's inability to play could give way to her reliance on play as a replacement for reality, and finally to her ability to use play to express and work on the things she wanted and feared the most.

12

Play, Dream, Fantasy, and Enactment in Bornstein's "Obsessional Child," Then and Now

Mortimer Ostow, M.D.

In adult analysis, we attempt to learn about our patients' motivations by examining their overt behavior, that is, their actions within the world, their fantasies, and their dreams. We infer motivation in each instance ultimately from the dominant affects and the organizing fantasies to which they give rise. The process of free association provides us with these data by allusion or directly.

Since the capacity of children in analysis to give us free associations is much more limited than even the relatively limited capacity of adults, we encourage play during the child-analytic session, something that we do not tolerate in any form in adult analysis. We believe that play opens a window onto the child's world of affect and unverbalized fantasy, conscious or unconscious, and we are encouraged by the fact that what we see in play is congruent with the bits and pieces of behavior, fantasy, and dream that do reach us.

How do conscious fantasy, play, and behavior in the real world, including enactment, compare? In each instance affect achieves expression and seeks discharge in the fulfillment of specific and characteristic unconscious fantasies. These modalities differ in the degree to which they are constrained by considerations of external reality. Action in the real world is, of course, the most constrained of the three modalities. To the extent that action violates reality considerations, we consider it pathological. Conscious fantasying is not so constrained, but even though its pleasure is amplified by the absence of these constraints, it is nevertheless limited by the absence of actual, concrete, perceptible, gratifying experience, and by superego influences. Play combines the freedom of fantasying with the literal experience. Like fantasy, play need not conform to reality restrictions since it is so contrived that it leaves little enduring consequence. But like enactment, play offers concrete experience. To the extent that reality is permitted to intrude into play, play becomes more gratifying and exciting, but its freedom is encroached upon *pari passu* (Ostow, 1987).

In contrast, dreams are not at all limited by external reality. In dreams, the analyst perceives the affect that prevails and the attempts to regulate it. The affect in each instance is associated with Gestalten taken from the individual's repertoire of organizing fantasies. External reality is relevant only to the extent that it may determine affect; and day residue and associated memories offer images that conform to the prevailing unconscious fantasies.

Why affects and their consequences appear in dreams is not self-evident. The reason obviously relates to the psychophysiological function of dreaming. Does the dream act to contain the continuing motivational striving that would otherwise disturb sleep? Does the dream merely offer a window onto the continuing process of affect regulation? In any case, if dream contents did not faithfully reflect the continuing motivation that determines waking behavior, they could not be as helpful as they are in understanding the latter. Therefore, we assume that they do.

If these considerations are valid, then we should expect to find the same affects, the same pattern of affect regulation, and the same organizing fantasies in dream, fantasy, play, and enactment.

Bornstein's (1953) case report of Sherry, an obsessional eight-year-old child, furnishes an excellent data base for testing these suggestions. It also permits us to discern a difference between play in analysis and play outside analysis. Finally, on the basis of my years of work with this patient since Bornstein's death in 1971, I shall demonstrate that the affects and fantasies that prevailed in the eight-year-old child have continued with little change into adult life. In other words, I shall try to demonstrate that there is a continuity in manner of expression at any given time and a continuity in time.

Bornstein's report, however, is not ideal for my purposes. She tells us that her presentation focuses on the vicissitudes of the child's aggressive impulses and Sherry's defenses against them, so that we do not get a true cross-section of the analysis. Second, from the data that she provides as well as my own observations, I infer that the proper diagnosis is cyclothymic personality and that Sherry came to Bornstein with a syndrome of childhood depression. Its manifestations then were insomnia and preoccupation with thoughts of death, which pervaded much of the analytic material that Bornstein cites. The aggressive impulses to which Bornstein refers are component manifestations of the depressive complex. In the twenty years that I have known this patient, she has presented no obsessional symptoms.

The obsessive thoughts to which Bornstein referred were depressive thoughts, essentially about death. That is, they were expressions of her depression. (I am informed by colleagues who treat children that obsessive thinking is an age-appropriate defense that serves to ward off depressive affect in children of this age, and not ordinarily a precursor of obsessive-compulsive neurosis or personality disorder.) The child speculated about the nature of human life and existence, but these speculations hardly achieved obsessional intensity or persistence and reflected merely a philosophic inquisitiveness on her part. She has always been thoughtful, but her speculations have never seemed obsessive.

I favor the diagnosis of cyclothymic disorder because during the adult years that Sherry has been with me she has exhibited a continuing succession of mood swings, mostly depressive but occasionally hypomanic, and on at least one occasion she became sufficiently high to entertain frankly delusional ideas, though for a few hours only. Her episodes of depression achieved expression as dysphoria of moderate degree, intensification of her insomnia, and irritability, which she tried to control. Occasionally, these recurrent depressive episodes were entrained by her menstrual cycle, presenting as premenstrual tension, but they did not all follow this temporal pattern, nor was every menstrual cycle preceded by depression or its derivatives. Bornstein's data did not preclude a diagnosis of cyclothymic personality, but they are not so organized as to suggest it.

Nevertheless, the data are adequate to permit me to examine the structure of the episodes of play and its process, and to compare it with the structure and process of other psychic products in which impulse and defense can be expected to become visible, principally dreams, but also fantasy and enactments.

I have observed elsewhere (Ostow, 1989a) that cyclothymic individuals, as well as borderline personalities and patients with adult attention deficit disorder, frequently exhibit dreams that display alternation of mood, a sequence of death and rebirth scenarios, as do patients with any mood disorder who are struggling to control it. It is these alternations of mood, or rather the struggle to regulate mood, that I find readily visible in the various materials presented by Bornstein. In addition, I shall try to discern in the materials the various themes and fantasies that organize the patient's mental life.

Affect Correction

Sherry had developed insomnia and fear of death shortly after the birth of a sister when she was just over four. These symptoms and a preoccupation with death in general persisted during the entire period of treatment reported in Bornstein's essay. I shall start with the first play episode that Bornstein described.

Play item 1

At the very outset of treatment, Sherry attempted to display to Bornstein a scene in which "a married couple" was injured in a car crash. The participants were given the names of her own parents in some versions of the play. As the inevitability of injury became more apparent, the child's distress caused her to terminate the episode and try a modification.

I infer that the depression syndrome included not only anticipation of the child's own death but a quantum of anger that was directed against the parents, probably because they were seen as the causes of her depression.

Reparative efforts—or rather, in this case, efforts to control the aggressive intent—consisted of including in the scenario a doctor who declares that the crash has seriously injured no one; depersonalizing the participants, that is, attributing responsibility to the cars rather than to humans; challenging the seriousness of the play episode (it was a joke), or its reality ("Does a car know whether it is real or not?"); or terminating each episode as it seemed to be progressing to the point of visualizing the parents as seriously hurt. It is clear that in each of the efforts the child made to express her anger, anxiety caused her to arrest the process that she had set in motion and to undo whatever damage she might have thought she had done. The initial phase of each effort to arrange a car crash may be thought of as a death fantasy, and its arrest or undoing as a corrective rebirth.

Let me illustrate the same alternating death and rebirth pattern in another analytic product. Here is some material that Bornstein includes with two drawings made by the child, presumably during an analytic session. The child quoted a well-known ditty and illustrated it:

I had a little duckling
His name was Sunny Jim
I put him in the bathtub
To teach him how to swim
He drank up all the water
He ate up all the soap
He died last night
With a bubble in his throat. (legend to fig. 7)

She then elaborated the ditty into a fantasy:

> Once upon a time there was a little girl who had a very nice mother. The mother was so nice that she got the little girl a duckling. But the duckling was so young that he didn't know how to swim yet. So the little girl decided to teach him how to swim. Twice she filled her tub full of water. Then she put the duckling in. But the duckling has been so far away from water that he did not know what the water was. So he ate up all the water and drank up all the soap and he was very ill. So ill that no doctor could cure him. And he became so sick that he died the very next day. In came the doctor, in came the nurse. In came the little girl's mother and also the little girl. The mother said, "Don't cry, little darling, I will buy you a duck that will know how to swim." The little girl cried anyhow. But then when the other duck came, the little girl was happy and her mother was happy. But the thing that was most happy was the other duck.
>
> The little girl was so happy that she has gotten another duck that she called him "Hero." And then everybody was happy and nobody could be more happier than that family was that day. By now the little girl may be 21 or 22, but I'm sure that her duck is dead. (legend to fig. 8)

In the fantasy, the child, enjoying and attempting to care for her baby, the duckling, inadvertently kills it. (I shall not develop the implications of this fantasy for her ambivalence toward her younger sister and her mother.) As in the initial play episode cited above, the child calls upon the doctor and nurse to rescue the duckling, but to no avail. Here then is the effort to undo the murder, an effort that fails. However, the child's mother now provides a new duckling; essentially the duckling is reborn, thanks to the mother's kindness. In the end however, the child muses that this duckling is dead. Here we have a sequence of birth, death, rebirth, and finally death again.

In two episodes, having engaged in serious and troubled conversation with the analyst, the child abruptly began an activity that expressed her desire to reverse her negative feelings.

Play item 2

During one depressive session, the child feared that her mother might die, and that then she must die too. This sad sentiment was followed by her cutting pictures of men and women out of a magazine and arranging kissing scenes. "I like them when they flirt," she said.

In that one act of play, the depressive fear of death for herself and her mother was corrected by the fantasy of her presence at a primal scene.

Play item 3

In one episode, following a talk with the analyst about her father's attempt to reconcile with her after a misunderstanding in which the child had been frightened, she abruptly began a drawing entitled, "Hard-working Man in Pioneer Times" [p. 320]. That moment captured her switch from anger and fear to love.

In these episodes of play (I call the latter play because of the drawings that the patient made during the session) we can recognize shifts in affect from negative to positive. The negative affects are associated with thoughts of death, and the positive affects with thoughts of rebirth in one form or other. In each instance, it is the discussion with the analyst that facilitated the switch in affect—a truly psychotherapeutic intervention.

Study of the dreams that Bornstein presents from the same period of analysis discloses a similar phenomenon. The following dream is given as the explanation for a drawing. It was reported some time after it had occurred and in Bornstein's essay is labeled an "Old Nightmare."

Dream 1

"Once upon a time I dreamed I was a princess. And I went walking with a prince. And on the way I met a few elfs. And then I met a joker of a pack of cards walking up to me. And then I woke up.

And when I woke up, I was not so sure what the dream was about. From then on I tried to remember what that dream was about. But I can't remember.

The dream was at a time when I had the falling downstairs dream." (legend to fig. 3)

The reference to a "falling downstairs dream" tells us that the dream dealt not only with her oedipal conflict but also with the depressive feelings that had been generated. The elves and the joker interfere with her romance. They can be interpreted as symbols for her sisters and her nurses. The subsequent falling downstairs reveals that these were merely representations of internal corrective influences initiated by a punitive superego. The dream displays clearly the conflictual interplay between erotic and punitive depressive forces. Here the dream starts with the oedipal gratification, which is interfered with by the elves and the joker. The falling downstairs, which is illustrated in the same picture as the interrupted walk, definitively terminates the oedipal gratification and symbolizes the onset of depression.

We can detect this same tendency to alternating, sequential affect correction in the child's fantasies. Sherry reported to Bornstein that she tried to make up good "thinking stories" when she went to bed—that is, fantasies intended to overcome the depressive fears that created her insomnia. But she always ended up thinking about death; the depression was not easily overcome by the deliberately cultivated optimistic fantasies.

I shall call this phenomenon of alternation of negative and positive affects associated with ideas of death and destruction, on the one hand, and rebirth, on the other, an apocalyptic pattern. Apocalypse appeared in the ancient Jewish and Christian worlds as a prophecy presented as a revelation to a seer or prophet by a divine agent. The revelation always dealt with death and rebirth, a common concern at all times. The typical, classical apocalypse incorporates other features: dualism (good and bad); pseudepigraphy (i.e., false attribution); a tour of heaven or hell, usually by means of a vehicle, animate or inanimate; allusions to heights and depths, rising and falling; and prodigies of nature, including the expectation that at the "end" (the eschaton), time will stand still and nature will be altered. Each of these elements has dynamic significance. I use the term *apocalyptic* in connection with the death and rebirth sequence because that is, in my opinion, the essential dynamic of apocalypse and the psychobiological basis of the almost universal promulgation and acceptance of apocalyptic ideas (Ostow, 1986).

These observations apply to the individual, solipsistic *Weltuntergang* fantasy of schizophrenia and schizoaffective psychosis as well as to the socially circulated apocalypses that achieve wide public credence. Close inspection of both individual and group apocalypses, however, discloses that in some instances one detects a success phase at first followed by a destruction phase, in which case the latter can be and frequently is interpreted as punishment for the improper ambition of the first phase. The issue of sequence becomes less problematic when these phenomena are inspected more closely. For example, in the duckling story, I see four phases: initial gratification (possessing, enjoying, and raising the duckling), followed by its death and the child's disappointment, followed by rebirth (acquisition of the new duckling), and ending with the expectation of the death of the new duckling. In many circulated apocalypses, we hear of anticipation of several alternations of defeat and victory before the final triumph. It is not uncommon to find several alternating affect corrections in dreams. I shall quote one below from the patient's adult life.

Affect alternation of this type occurs frequently in the dreams of patients whose illness is based upon affect dysregulation. I include here not only the manics, hypomanics, depressives, and cyclothymics but also—and especially—the borderlines and children and adults with attention deficit disorder, as well as the phobics and the patients with depressive character. I find descriptions of apocalyptic dreams in the accounts of patients with posttraumatic stress disorder as well. What I am not sure about is how frequently such dreams and fantasies occur in individuals other than those with these syndromes. Moreover, do they occur more commonly among children than among adults?

Affect Dysregulation and Neurotic Conflict

From a psychodynamic point of view, one can interpret each switch from gratification to deprivation or frustration as punishment, especially in an oedipal context, suggesting that the gratification was improper; and each switch from disappointment to gratification can be interpreted as reconciliation or vindication. Nevertheless, from a purely descriptive point of view, these switches can be seen as automatic mutual corrections, serving as a homeostatic mechanism to regulate affect. It is reasonable to suppose that when this affect-stabilizing mechanism functions well, its function is invisible. It becomes evident in dream, fantasy, play, and enactment only when it loses its precision and fails to correct, or corrects too soon or too late, or corrects excessively. From this point of view, one may deduce that in each of the psychic creations of this child, her play, enactments, fantasies, and dreams, we find a window onto the function of this homeostatic mechanism.

Am I speaking here of neurotic conflict as that term is ordinarily understood in psychodynamics? I believe that the apocalyptic sequence of death and rebirth differs from neurotic conflict in two significant ways. First, in neurotic conflict, resolution is sought by countering an inadmissible impulse *concurrently* with defense and achieving a compromise. Two dreams recorded by Bornstein illustrate in graphic form the contamination of gratification by defense, yielding frustration.

Dream 2

The child dreamed that she was forced to dance with a rooster "who had an awful grip" on her and was squeezing her hand.

Dream 3

A "poisonous snake, terribly slimy and cold," is laid in her hands. (p. 323)

In each instance the desired sexual object is presented in a repulsive manner. Moreover, the mention of hands in each dream suggests that the conflict involved concern with masturbatory gratification. Masturbation and its baleful consequences were mentioned by the child explicitly, later in the analysis. The death-rebirth sequence that I am describing presents impulse and its counteractive impulse as two *successive* phases.

Second, the neurotic defense against an unacceptable impulse relates specifically to its ideational content. For example, in the two dreams just cited, the disagreeable and frustrating aspect of each of the two potentially gratifying experiences complied with the nature of that experience. Touching the phallus loses its gratifying quality and becomes frightening or disgusting. On the other hand, the death-rebirth sequence presents as a contrast of affects—despair versus hope, destruction versus construction—in which content is appropriate to the affect but not necessarily specific to the idea.

Apocalyptic Archetypes

The relation between the polar affect reversals and apocalypse transcends their common concern with death-rebirth fantasies. Among the various apocalypses, classical and modern, scriptural and apocryphal, the rebirth fantasy assumes different forms. Within these rebirth fantasies certain archetypes can be recognized (Ostow, 1986). Some of these archetypes appear in the material we have before us. Almost all apocalypses include the image of a messianic savior as well as a seer and divine or semidivine informant. Frequently these roles are combined. Sherry regards her psychoanalyst as rescuer, guide, instructor, and revealer of secrets. In addition, both in the initial play episode in which her parents are endangered and in the duckling story, the doctor and the nurse are archetypically called upon to rescue the victim.

Many apocalypses envision the rebirth or the revelation as starting with a journey, and usually a vehicle is specified. In an earlier paper (1986), I observed that the vehicle represents psychologically both the maternal claustrum and the method of reaching it. The first play episode describes the parents as endangered by the vehicles in which they are riding. In this case the vehicle not only fails to protect or to rescue but itself becomes the source of danger.

The rebirth fantasy may assume any of a number of forms, from simply reuniting with mother or a mother surrogate to becoming a member of a fraternal cultlike community. Reactivating an oedipal relationship is a favorite technique.

The preferred device usually retains its promise during most of the individual's life. As such it becomes an *organizing fantasy* that imposes its signature upon many forms of behavior subsequently. Individuals may deploy one or more such organizing fantasies throughout their lives. Although the emergence of the organizing fantasy is seen most clearly as a reaction to some frustration, in fact, in many individuals we can detect its continuing but subtle influence in a large number of activities in which it attempts to achieve enactment over long periods of their life span.

Commonly, the rebirth fantasy consists of entering into a closed area where a deity may be seen sitting on a royal throne (Ostow, 1989b). By returning to a maternal claustrum, the visitor hopes to glimpse the father and especially the paternal phallus. The attempt to enter a claustrum and there to encounter father appears several times in Bornstein's case. She describes the following dream:

Dream 4

"I saw a crocodile or alligator and I was in a small sort of cabin. The crocodile stuck his head between the bars and that looked funny. And the crocodile kept on moving from side to side and I kept on jumping from side to side too. And finally he got me. And instead of biting a chunk out of me, a sort of tooth stuck in me. And I tried to pull it out and I did not succeed. Then we went to supper and then I woke up."

Later, Sherry added, "In that cabin there was a little girl with me. I don't know her name. She was about the size of me and eight years old. But we were very small, a little bigger than a baby." (pp. 317–318)

The dream followed some agitated and unaccustomed flirtation with the father on that day, Sunday. Previously, the parents had withdrawn into their bedroom, excluding the children. The patient had often tried to invade the parental bedroom and incurred the resentment of her father, who blamed the mother for not keeping her out. That afternoon she had, in play, grabbed his leg as if she wished to hurt him. In the dream, it is the crocodile that is attacking her. The second part of the dream report, about the twin, came almost as an afterthought, after discussion of the dream had begun. She speculated what it would be like to have a twin, or even to be one of triplets, and wondered whether these quarreled as much as ordinary brothers and sisters. In this context the child reported playing with a friend and that the doll of each of them had given birth to twins. (See play item 4.)

Finding herself in the cabin represents return to the maternal claustrum, which had always been, in childhood and later in adult life, one of her most common dream wishes. The quadrangular claustrum configuration recurs frequently in her dreams: cabins, cars (compare the first play episode), railroad cars, chairs, beds, couches, tables, rooms, buildings. (I have elsewhere [1986, 1989b] commented on the number 4 as a universal symbol of mother's body, a desired goal.) The crocodile intruding between the slats represents the father's penis intruding into the mother's body. The reciprocal, alternating dance represents her understanding of sexual intercourse. The subsequently recollected fragment about the twin sister suggests that if the sister were a clone of herself, there would be no rivalry: they could both inhabit mother's body and play with father together. The tooth play, as Bornstein indicates, represents an impregnation fantasy. This dream seems to represent the wish gratification alone. We see no antecedent or subsequent death fantasy.

Dream 5

In a dream that I see as related to the theme of encountering the paternal phallus in the maternal claustrum, the child had "ears like Pinocchio," who, she added, "met his daddy in the whale's stomach." (p. 323)

That association suggests the image of encountering the crocodile's snout in the log cabin—that is, again the father's penis intruding into the maternal claustrum. For her, that image meant sexual contact with father with mother's sanction. She did not have to choose between the two. She achieves the reconciliation of what would ordinarily be incompatible wishes. Note that the same configuration occurs in Edgar Allan Poe's "The Pit and the Pendulum," in which both the female genital pit and the phallic pendulum are terrifying and life threatening. It is interesting that the child did not refer to Pinocchio's nose, a phallic element with which she identified. The conflict between masculine and feminine identity was explicitly stated elsewhere in the analytic material. As an adult, she selected a career and performed in a way that accorded her power and that gave her command over men, although she strove consciously and successfully to be and to appear feminine. This dream too is a conciliatory dream, combining love for her mother, sexual attraction to her father, and phallic identity. The corrective or punitive elements include the trauma of having been swallowed by the whale and of the image of herself as deformed—that is, with Pinocchio's ears, representing a paired, deformed phallus.

In the child's external behavior we can recognize some symptomatic acts—enactments—that give expression to the same needs.

Enactment 1

On one occasion, Sherry's father locked the door to his study to prevent her from using what Bornstein called his gadgets. She apparently obtained and hid the key, returning it to him only after he gave her a copy of that key, which she then wore as a pendant.

Enactment 2

Sherry began nightly visits into her parents' bedroom shortly after the birth of her sister when she was a little over four.

I interpret this need as a variant of her longing for the maternal claustrum, a longing that was represented most explicitly in the cabin dream and also elsewhere. The fantasy of entering the maternal claustrum and often encountering father there appears in dream, fantasy, and enactment. Bornstein cites no play material that specifies it.

In the case of Sherry as reported by Bornstein, the organizing fantasies that we encounter include (1) the return to the maternal claustrum, usually with the hope of encountering the father's phallus there, leading to identification with the phallic father; (2) the avoidance of exposure to strangers, but also occasionally erotized flirtation with them; and (3) an exaggerated concern with danger to the point of making strong provision for medical care.

Dream, fantasy, play, and enactment constitute a series of modes of behavioral expression. They all exhibit responses to external opportunity and demand as well as to internal demand. In that order they are characterized by increasing contact with reality, increasing action upon the real world and increasingly literal experience of it, increasing intensity of feeling, and decreasing freedom from the limits of hoped-for gratification. All are susceptible to interruption by anxiety. In Bornstein's material we find that the first three exhibit succession of death and rebirth fantasies. We also find in all of these the dominant rebirth fantasies that shape much of the child's ordinary as well as neurotic behavior.

Play in and out of the Analysis

Bornstein cited two instances of play that had taken place outside the analysis but that had been reported to her:

Play item 4

In the one she and a friend had played that their dolls had each given birth to twins simultaneously, and the two dolls agreed that "I'm so glad that I have twins!" (p. 318)

The episode of play does not incorporate affect correction in its course. It replies to the envy of her sisters and jealousy of their relation to her mother. In the game each newborn has a twin sibling. Twins, she thinks, may not quarrel the way nontwin siblings do. Moreover, playing the game with her friend who shares an identical experience simultaneously makes of the friend a twin of hers.

Play item 5

The second instance of extra-analytic play is a negative instance in a sense. The child reported that some children had accused her of not wishing to play with them, "just because they were new." She acknowledged that she did not wish to play with them, but it was because she could not see any fun in doing it their way. But she denied that she could be mean enough to exclude someone merely because of the recency of the child's arrival. Bornstein reminded her that she had teased her younger sister, Ann, saying that their father did not love her because she was "new."

We see no affect shift in the course of either of these two episodes. Playing itself became the issue. I do not know why she refused to play with the other children or whether the issue had to do with her rejection of her sister. Moreover, despite her profession of wishing to have a twin, she insisted on having things done her way.

A priori one would see no reason why play outside the analysis would differ in its affect-regulating function from that within the analytic session. We may, however, consider the possibility that the presence of the analyst and the desire to invite her assistance emboldens the child to contemplate impulses that would otherwise be repressed. Such boldness does not occur in play that takes place outside the analysis and is reported to the analyst after the fact.

In the instances of play taking place during the analytic session, we can discern two separate but related aims. In the first place, the child is trying to engage the analyst in her daily life by presenting it to her, describing what is going on, drawing pictures, and enacting the fantasies that accompany her affects. Having the analyst's attention and concern, she acquires the courage to confront her angry fantasies by turning them into dramatic play. When anxiety appears, she terminates the game and reassures herself that what is happening is not real. The analyst's assignment in this case is implied in Sherry's introductory statement that she is asking for help because "Mommy cannot do anything much about it either" (p. 314).

Second, at each point of elicitation of powerful negative affect—anxiety or sadness—she looks to the analyst for an act of rescue. The designated victim is rescued from danger, and the patient is rescued from anxiety. In the car crash game, the doctor assures her that no one has been injured. When, after her grandmother died, she beheaded a doll, Bornstein was there to sew it up, and that repair was all that the child remembered of the play two years later.

The two extra-analytic episodes of play differed. They did not deal with anxiety-provoking material, and they did not require rescue. The analytic play dealt with the child's depression and its consequences; the extra-analytic play dealt with her inability to relate to peers. Only if the other child was a literal or symbolic twin, another self, would she be able to contemplate friendship. Because the analyst was not there, she confined her extra-analytic play to matters that did not provoke anxiety. Yet she brought the material in to promote the analyst's caring interest in her. The play that took place in the presence of the analyst dealt with the patient's illness, with the fantasies with which she was obsessed, and with the anxieties that she could not control. The doll play with her friend dealt with relations between children of the same age. It seems reasonable to see these observations as demonstrations of a general principle that the content of an act of play is likely to reflect the issues that arise between the player and his or her companions in play, especially when the object relations are problematic for the child.

The two episodes of extra-analytic play present an issue that otherwise does not come up in the material presented by Bornstein but has troubled Sherry throughout her life—her discomfort with others her age. As we can see in play item 5, she becomes anxious when called upon to associate closely with others. To deal with this discomfort, she has developed a number of strategies. She avoids close associations, except with a few people whom she thinks pose no threat to her. She appeases others by kindness and gifts and reassuring appreciation. In her pubertal and adolescent fantasies, she erotized the experience of attack by dangerous strangers. On infrequent occasions, she has become slightly paranoid. In her analysis she has frequently expressed the wish to overcome this problem and in recent years has done so to a certain extent. It would not be relevant to the major concern of this essay to discuss the pathogenesis of this issue; I just want to point out that the issue appeared in childhood and has persisted to this day.

In a sense play in analysis is not free play at all but a means of communication with the analyst. The child is told that the analyst will help with his or her concerns and fears, and is brought to the consulting room and placed before some materials that lend themselves to play. In that way the child is implicitly instructed: let me see what you would like to do. The youngster will sometimes make the situation more explicit by using play activities to illustrate spoken communications. At least when the child is in the mode of apocalyptic thinking, he or she sees the analyst as a rescuer, a savior, and proceeds to inform the person of the problem by acting it out. When the acting out becomes too realistic, the play must be modified or terminated. Play in analysis, whether a respite from stress, a novel occupation, or a "trying on" in anticipation of the new, is also a communication. It is more likely therefore to include pathological material than play and other mental processes that take place outside the analysis. It is driven by the child's hope for relief from distress and by the response to the therapist as a savior and a rescuer. Both the hope and the rescue fantasy are facilitated by apocalyptic thinking.

Bornstein's Patient as an Adult

When we consider Sherry's adult life, we find the same elements that we found in the childhood material. The initial complaints of insomnia and concern with death continue but are now quite tolerable. She manages the insomnia by getting out of bed and doing her work at her desk or reading. The concern with death has to a large extent been replaced by concern with aging, but both are included in the apocalyptic fantasies now as they were then.

As noted above, during the entire twenty years of her analysis with me, she has exhibited frequent oscillations of mood from mild depression to mild euphoria and back. Apocalyptic fantasies and themes have continued to appear frequently in the analytic productions and in her daily life. During the period when her mother was fatally ill, Sherry reported a number of frankly apocalyptic dreams. Here is one of them:

The world was being flooded. The water was reddish and grayish. It was turbulent with white crests. I saw rocks and houses. People were drowning. We were on a high level where there were white houses. I was on a boat, a nice boat, large with blond wood lacquer floors. There was a kitchen on the boat. I became concerned that it would capsize. We landed at a house on some land. We brought things onto the boat, glasses, no, plastic cups for fear that they might break, and food.

What's the point of living if you're going to drown? I thought of suicide and became calmer. No, I said, there is always hope. If you die now you eliminate hope.

I saw some people drowning, some with their hands raised, some protesting, some peacefully.

The specific details of this dream are of interest for the patient's analysis, but irrelevant to the argument I am considering here. What we see is a prevailing depressive mood and recurrent attempts to overcome it: the high level, the boat, the kitchen, the food. All to no avail. The depressive process is not overcome. In the end, suicidal thoughts are pushed aside by displacing the prospect of death onto others. "Some protesting" suggests an explanation for the anger that disturbed Sherry during the segment of analysis reported by Bornstein.

The alternations of mood have served her well in her work as a business executive. The experience of these alternations has encouraged her to make decisions and to review them from different perspectives. The expression of apocalyptic anger is usually limited to scolding and shouting at home, which she regrets and tries actively to avoid. Occasionally she will turn against employees, associates, or acquaintances when she feels she has been wronged, but aware of this tendency, she reviews all such inclinations critically before acting upon them.

The organizing fantasies of her life that were detected in the early analytic material have continued to play important roles. The need to find her way into the maternal claustrum and to encounter there father's phallus so that she could identify with him has been recognizable in a number of activities. With his concurrence, she took over her father's office in the family business as well as his functions, just as in childhood she once stole the key to his study at home and would not return it until he gave her a copy of it to wear as a pendant around her neck. Her city and country homes have been important to her and were renovated and decorated attentively. In analytic sessions, she frequently has sat opposite me on the couch. Dreams have indicated clearly that this practice expresses her need to repeat her viewing of her father's phallus to which she was inadvertently exposed from time to time in childhood.

Sherry's need for messianic rescuers has found expression in her prolonged continuation in analysis. She has come not only for what she calls "real analysis" but also for help in resolving all kinds of problems with her children, husband, parents, friends, and business associates. In addition, she has promptly found competent analysts for all her children when the occasion arose and has been assiduous in finding proper physicians and adhering to their recommendations. At work, she has tried to provide herself with reliable advisers, though she never shirks decision making.

The theme of relating to others has been dealt with least satisfactorily. She tries to cope with her problem by deliberately reaching out to make and keep friends. Nevertheless, the friendships never become very deep and are usually limited to courteous, gracious social contacts. In her philanthropic work, she is often put off by clumsy attempts to use her as a rubber stamp and to ignore her input. Infrequently, her fear of close associations escalates into paranoid attitudes. When this mechanism is demonstrated to her, she is quickly able to overcome it.

The issue of play does not arise in adult life. Her leisure-time activities are usually solitary such as reading or organizing family photos and films. She spends as much time as she can with her children and with her husband when he is available. She plays tennis only with members of her family and indulges in no other sports. She enjoys traveling, usually with her husband and her children, associating her trips with memories of being close to her mother and being loved and fed by her. The analytic play of childhood finds no homologue in her adult analysis, except perhaps in those sessions in which she consults me about specific problems.

Although it would have been difficult to predict this patient's career and interests from the data of her analysis during childhood, given that information, we find no surprises. Her cyclothymia, her apocalyptic mode of thought, and her organizing fantasies all continue unchanged. I believe that it is fair to say that the affective swings that are visible in the childhood material continue into adult life where they are clearly discerned in dreams and less obviously in fantasy and in conscious symptom change. The organizing fantasies that we saw in the material from age eight continue to find expression in the patient's dreams and in her symptomatic acts and career. So reliable is this continuity that on occasion when I am baffled by some problem in the current analysis, I can often find a precursor of the issue in the data that Bornstein provided. Given the profound alterations in condition, interest, influence, and physical structure that time brings, this continuity and consistency are impressive. As a result of analysis, she has been made acquainted with all these tendencies and has been helped to achieve sufficient control over them so that they lend spice to her life but do little damage.

References

Bornstein, B. (1953). Fragment of an analysis of an obsessional child. *Psychoanal. Study Child*, 8:313–332.

Ostow, M. (1986). Archetypes of apocalypse in dreams and fantasies and in religious scripture. *Israel J. Psychiat. & Related Disciplines*, 23:107–122.

———. (1987). Play and reality. *Psychoanal. Study Child*, 42:193–203.

———. (1989a). The interpretation of apocalyptic dreams. Presented to the panel on "The Significance of Religious Themes and Fantasies during Psychoanalysis," American Psychoanalytic Association.

———. (1989b). Kadosh, Kadosh, Kadosh: The psychodynamics of Merkavah mysticism. Presented to a symposium on "Jewish Mysticism and Psychoanalysis," Spertus College of Judaica.

Part III
Developmental Dimensions

13

The Developmental Dimensions of Play during Treatment: Conceptual Overview

Samuel Abrams, M.D.

The developmental process may be described as an emerging sequence of progressively differentiated, hierarchical organizations that lead to progressive changes in behavior. The sequence, driven by an underlying maturational program, unfolds in steps or phases, each evolving within a limited time frame, each characterized by a transient disequilibrium or crisis, each to a greater or lesser degree reorganizing antecedent phases, and each yielding novelties. The appearance of the novel suggests transformations or qualitative alterations in underlying structures. Each step requires experiences to concretize the interaction between the underlying program and the surround, thereby providing nuclei for the nascent structures. Play promotes the developmental process since it is one source of those experiences.

The analytic process may be described as a sequence of steps designed to induce progressive changes in behavior by integrating unrecognized entrapped pathogens into the more mature organizations. The pathogens, residues of antecedent developmental periods embedded by defense, remain entrapped until they are freed by the tool of interpretation and the effect of insight. Once freed, they can be brought into the more mature psychological organizations. The steps in the analytic process include resistances of character, of transference, and of the affective past. The appearance of insights implies success in the integration of pathological aspects of past developmental organizations into the more mature hierarchies. Play promotes the analytic process by facilitating access to the unrecognized pathogens.

Play, therefore, serves both developmental and analytic goals. It serves the former best when it is allowed free reign to proceed toward consolidation, and it serves the latter best when the activity of play can be converted into verbal channels. As a consequence, the child clinician is often confronted with the task of determining when to sustain play as play in order to provide the necessary concrete experiences that establish nuclei for the emerging hierarchies and when to shift play into words to facilitate access to the unconscious. The pacing is not inconsequential, since new hierarchies bring new psychological capacities into existence; some of the capacities enhance access (for example, during the oedipal organization), whereas others usher in features that abet the repressing forces (for example, during latency). Such actualities intensify the dilemmas of the clinician.

The focus of this chapter is on play during the emerging oedipal organization, a period between the ages of four and seven when the foundation for the subsequent, mature, psychological structures is established. It is an especially felicitous time to study the relationship between the developmental and analytic processes and the effect of play upon both. It is a time when children's play becomes strikingly distinctive, assuming the form of imaginative dramas, different from the somewhat more unidimensional playing that has preceded and the play with games defined by rules that will follow.

Play and Oedipal Organization

The oedipal organization is a broader concept than the oedipal phase and the oedipal conflict. The oedipal phase highlights the fate of the instinctual drive derivatives; the oedipal conflict describes the psychological nucleus that is at the phase's center. The oedipal organization contains both the phase and the conflict, but, like all developmental organizations, it also describes a specific plateau during the progression when instinctual drive derivatives are integrated with the emerging self and object representations and the ego and its equipment.

The oedipal organization provides the foundation for the personality as a whole. It, too, is characterized by novel yields. One structural novelty is the consolidation of the superego; one functional novelty is the appearance of a new regulator of behavior, guilt. Antecedent developmental organizations provide the necessary building blocks for the foundation as well as such precursors of conscience as pleasure and pain, power and helplessness. The play of younger children often betrays the shape and character of these emerging building blocks and precursors and also provides necessary experiences for them to consolidate. The integrity of the antecedent building blocks will be one of the influences that effects the degree of success of the assembling of the foundation during the oedipal period.

Clinical observations of play during the emergence of the oedipal organization can reveal the status of the drive components, ego functions, ego apparatuses, the residual consequences of antecedent and ongoing object relationships, potential growth disparities, and the effectiveness of the new assembling. The play is also a window upon the formative unconscious fantasies that are achieving ascendancy during that time. The play, however, is more than simply evidence of the various ongoing psychological activities; it also provides experiences, necessary nuclei for consolidating components of the emerging oedipal organization—structural components such as the superego and functional components such as guilt—as new regulators of behavior. In this sense, play is an intermediary between meaning and structure. Therefore, interventions that aim at prematurely converting play into words to facilitate understanding may interfere with the requirements of the developmental process, whereas those that facilitate the consolidation of ongoing roles and dramas through play may promote and help shape it.

The example that follows is an attempt to describe how play may be used to enhance the mutual relationship between the developmental and the analytic processes.

Clinical Illustration

Leslie came for treatment when he was three. He was difficult to control at home and had trouble establishing limits to his behavior while interacting with adults or other children. In addition, he often insisted that he was a girl.

He was the second child of ambitious parents who feared at first that treatment might injure his self-esteem. This led them to defer therapy for a time until his imperiousness became unbearable and his gender confusion too worrisome. He increasingly preferred wearing girls' clothing and playing with dolls and was attracted to television and comic-book female super-heroines.

Soon after the treatment got under way, Leslie became involved with puppet play. The puppet expressed aspects of the way he represented himself, features of his past life, and components of his relationship with me. Play, therefore, provided access to the status of his self representation, his ego functions, ongoing unconscious conflicts, and the integrity of the existing developmental organization. After a time, however, I began to view some of his play as ways in which Leslie shaped and engaged experiences needed for his growth, in addition to its representing how that growth was proceeding.

Initially, he practiced constraints and limits through the puppet. He would caution it that it could not do certain things. To reinforce the injunctions, Leslie often treated the puppet in a punitive manner, spanking it or constraining it or threatening it in ways never experienced at home. These isolated moments of play led to interpretations of his own impulsiveness and the extent of his rage expressed both in the impulsiveness and in the controls. He accepted the comments and sometimes modified the play action, making it less cruel. But it also occurred to me that the play was providing experiences for Leslie to establish the necessary internal structures to exercise restraint over his own behavior; what seemed worrisome was the sadistic quality of these budding repressive structures. While attempting to have him understand what he was doing, I also hoped to convey the impression that constraint could be achieved by less cruel means, an idea that was often implemented by a change in the way he taught constraints to his puppet.

At other times Leslie would play at engaging in housekeeping chores—sweeping floors, washing dishes, cooking meals. I recognized that he was also moving toward consolidating stereotyped female roles through this play. I noted that this provided an area to express some of his "girl" feelings. I also tried to follow the relationship between the cruelty and the female behavior as each appeared in his hours. There was a crude linkage between sadism and masculinity, on the one hand, and slavish submission and femininity, on the other. Being a girl was one way to control his cruel feelings.

After a while, the play became elaborated into more extensive dramas, often with a compelling quality. At these times, he would brush aside explanatory comments in a determined attempt to carry the play forward toward some specific outcome. At those moments it seemed as if the experience of engaging in these dramas was more vital than access to their multiple meanings. I restrained myself from interpreting them and watched them consolidate instead.

A rescue theme became evident between the ages of four and six. Three figures were assigned changing roles in his drama—I, the puppet, and Leslie himself. One role was that of a girl or woman who had been stolen away by a second character, a monster, who intended to devour her. The third participant was a heroic rescuer whose aggressiveness was ultimately inflicted upon the villainous monster. Leslie repeated the drama many times, frequently changing parts. Was the rescuer to be male or female? He often used a twig to implement the rescue, pausing briefly to decide whether he was a good witch on a twig-broomstick or Robin Hood brandishing a twig-sword. I recognized the overlap of antecedent libidinal phases, the oral in the devouring, the phallic in the twig, and the surfacing oedipal in the form of the rescue of a damsel in distress. In terms of ego development, the capacity for differentiation had improved during treatment, but a fluidity still persisted in the ease of his shifting roles and in the uncertain gender of the rescuer. He moved too readily between active and passive, rescuer and being rescued, monster, damsel, and hero, while expressing manifest pleasure in each role. He threatened to devour with sadistic glee, anticipated attack with anxious excitement, and enjoyed the heroic rescue with exuberance.

For the most part I chose to allow the drama to consolidate, while pointing out the changing roles and themes. I participated as he directed, although through activities and comments I tried to promote differentiation, mute the aggressiveness, and reinforce the pleasures of the rescuer as contrasted with those of the villain or the victim. Despite the manifest oedipal theme, I did not choose to interpret desire or competitiveness; rather, by promoting these features of the play, I hoped to have desire and competitiveness consolidate within settings that were more felicitous for further growth. I especially had in mind the nature of the superego that might precipitate out of all of this, his available defensive repertoire, his gender preference, and the regulators of his self-esteem.

After some time, despite some residual leaning toward Leslie's interest in being the monster, the drama increasingly consolidated around his choosing to be a heroic male rescuer. Also promoted was differentiation between male and female, sadism and assertiveness, good and evil.

The dangers that he perceived and that required protection also overlapped from different time periods and underwent further differentiation. The rescue of the girl enhanced him as did the successful vanquishing of the monster, although there were brief times when he called up the old feelings of being enhanced as the monster or the damsel in distress. From the standpoint of regulation of self-esteem, the fact that he felt enhanced by doing good through rescuing rather than exerting power through imperiousness seemed to bode well for his progress.

After some time and following some cautious interventions about the dangers faced in rescuing, the drama became somewhat stereotyped along expectable lines. This coincided with a diminished interest in dolls and television heroines and an increased interest in wearing clothing that was clearly boyish. He began to deny that there had ever been a time when he had said he was a girl, and he denied it with the vigor that had characterized his early imperiousness. I understood this change to reflect shifts in internalized structures as a result of the mutual relationship between the analytic and developmental processes; the analytic work had used the play to gain access to understanding pathogenic elements, which in turn modified the play, leading him toward play actions that permitted his consolidating more differentiated structures and more adaptive strategies for his ongoing and future development. Superego development could be inferred, and guilt and shame emerged as more obvious regulators of behavior within the play setting.

The compelling quality of these new restraints soon revealed itself in his real life as well. In school he began participating more actively with class-mates. Despite minor displays of imperiousness at home, his deportment at school was exemplary, although learning difficulties (suspected earlier be-cause of his many deficiencies in ego functions) surfaced. His parents became concerned about this new threat to his self-esteem as he was increasingly relegated to a group of less competent students.

Reflecting the difficulties at school, his play underwent some change. Leslie became a tyrannical ruler of his puppet, cruel in his judgment and decisive in implementing punishment for transgressions. The transgressions, however, became academic failures. The puppet was asked questions, often simple questions such as guessing a number between 1 and 100. When the puppet's answer was incorrect (it almost always was), some cruel punish-ment was implemented. The puppet was cut into pieces, despite its objec-tions about the unfairness of the penalty. In asides, Leslie and I agreed that such cruel punishment for not knowing answers was patently unfair. For some time, however, this recognition did little to modify the penalty because the pleasure in cruelty had once again become more compelling partly because the pleasure of achievement had become more elusive. The cutting apart of the puppet usually began or ended with castration, apparently the harshest of the actions and the unfairest of them all.

As tyrannical judge, Leslie periodically tossed protestations aside, taking a certain pride in his renewed capacity for sadism. In a flash of inventiveness, he looked to devise more unreasonable penalties. After some time he intro-duced what he and the puppet agreed was the weirdest. When the puppet failed to answer correctly or misbehaved in any way, a live snake was inserted into his bottom. As it writhed about inside, the puppet emitted agonized screams.

I recognized the further consolidation of moral values influenced by the earlier gender disturbance and the intense aggressiveness now fused with libidinal aims. The latent wish to receive the brutalizing penis was obvious, as was the fact that this wish—enacted in play—was an intermediary be-tween unconscious fantasy and the consolidation of the potentially sadistic superego. Since the crimes that induced such punishment included giving wrong answers to questions, there was the threat that Leslie might pull his deficiency of ego apparatus into the meaning of an offense. His being a learning-disabled boy could be converted into his being a bad boy. Furthermore, homosexual desire was being realized in the form of the punishment. Leslie might be tempted to retain the disability to serve that desire in its new form. It was a demonstration of a form of moral masochism in the state of being born. Leslie was assembling his drive development, features of his ego development, and his self-regulating functions into a firm organizational climax, and he was bringing all these components together in a very specific way. The assembly was producing a coherent foundation for new psychological structures, but the way some of the components were pulled together still seemed problematic for future development.

I intervened in this with interpretive efforts. I tried to distinguish a learning disability from a criminal act in the play. I called attention to the harshness of his punishment and connected it to his earlier imperiousness and interest in the power of hurting others. I even tried to suggest that the snake-in-the-bottom punishment was related to his view of how a girl might feel when making love and, by inference, to his own girl feelings. Over time, clinical improvement was heralded by the appearance of a state of fearfulness. He became worried that one of his parents might be killed by a robber or mugger and, for a while, needed to be with them to feel reassured about their safety. This further internalization of the various conflicting elements seemed more manageable by the customary therapeutic techniques alone.

Discussion

The therapeutic efforts aside, the illustration indicates the interaction of the different areas of discontinuous growth—drives, ego, and object relationships—as they emerge and are assembled during the oedipal period. The specific illustration is one of a child whose developmental process is characterized by a degree of dominance of drives over a relatively less endowed ego and a somewhat limited success in the expectable achievement of object relations. The drive endowment is high—both libidinal and aggressive trends are of a high order and each poorly distinguished from the other; the ego is somewhat deficient in capacities for differentiation and quite limited in some of its apparatuses; and the definition of self and objects is faulty, while the acquisition of self-esteem is excessively invaded by drive influences. The pull forward into the expectable oedipal organization occurs in the midst of these disparities in the development of drives, ego, and object relations; consequently, drive expression has a greater influence upon shaping the character of development than might be the case with children having more evenness. This kind of inherent disparity between drive endowment as contrasted with the other subordinate discontinuities may be one of the sources for psychopathological disorders of the kind that Leslie displayed.

The shifts in his constructed dramas can be understood as not only providing access to understanding but also creating experiential nuclei to consolidate an ongoing developmental organization in a more felicitous way, one with greater differentiation and more adaptive regulators of behavior.

Summary

I presented a clinical illustration of play in the process of development, especially in helping create nuclei for consolidating the foundation of the mind. There is an overall sequence of developmental organizations that is useful to follow clinically, as is the expectable progression within three areas subordinate to the larger developmental organizations: drives, ego functions and apparatuses, and the representational consequences of object relationships.

I contrasted the use of play in aiding the developmental process and the use of play in promoting the analytic process. The child clinician is often confronted with these different aspects of play within the treatment setting. In the clinical example, focused on a child during the oedipal period, I illustrated how it is possible to shift between these various uses of play to facilitate the mutual interaction between the developmental and the analytic processes.

The play of children between the ages of four and seven provides necessary experiences to actualize the potential for the oedipal organization. In the play, the intensity of the pull forward can be observed, as can disparities between subordinate areas that influence the nature of the superego as it evolves, one of the novel yields of this developmental hierarchy. I also illustrated a technical approach that induces changes within a sustained play action, as contrasted with shifts into a verbal channel to facilitate interpretation and the acquisition of insights.

Children require play to promote the developmental process. Clinicians generally use the multiple windows available during play to evaluate underlying psychological activities in order to propose more accurate interventions and interpretations to profitably propel the treatment forward. Interventions that hold a child within the play action, however, may serve treatment needs equally well without compromising developmental ones.

14

Play, Parenthood, and Creativity

Eugene J. Mahon, M.D.

If we define play as one of the unique communicative modes of childhood, a semiotic skill that merges action and symbolism, the link between play and parenthood will not seem obvious at first. But if we define parenthood as an object relationship in which a mature person gets down on the floor to meet the needs of an immature person, it will quickly become obvious that without play and playfulness the dialogue between Gulliver and the Lilliputians could never take place.

What parenthood is is probably as difficult a question to address as what childhood is. Should we define it as a category of object relations or a unique amalgam of ego functions in the service of child rearing, or from a libidinal point of view, as Therese Benedek (1959) suggests in her paper "Parenthood as a Development Phase"?

If the history of parenthood could be told, it would probably be as frightful and frightening as the history of childhood itself, a nightmare we have only begun to awaken from, with any relative awakening owing largely to the efforts of psychoanalysis in this century. Parental attitudes and convictions, like character traits, must have pedigrees that defy analysis, so deep are the identifications and reaction formations that support them. I mention identifications and reaction formations, but if all the psychological components of parenting skills or deficiencies were to be outlined, which defense mechanism, which aspect of the tripartite mind, could be left out of the reckoning?

From a libidinal point of view one could address all the love and hate that children stir up in the parents—incest, postpartum depression, and the Laius complex being obvious examples of libidinal and aggressive instincts dealt with pathologically rather than adaptively. In more normative examples of parenthood one could cite the love, tolerance, and educative principles that guide good enough mothers and fathers as examples of pleasure and compromise that come from libidinal strivings channeled in the service of society.

From a structural point of view one could argue that parenthood makes demands on all three facets of the tripartite mind. The id of a parent requires continuous nourishment from spouse and other object relations to keep it from turning against the child as frustrater. Child abuse is surely in part a reflection of unfulfilled parenthood acting out its frustrations on the perceived frustrater, the child. The ego of the parent will be tested constantly, day and night from infancy through adolescence. The resourcefulness, the frustration tolerance, the ingenuity of conflict resolution, the sheer energy required to meet the needs of the developing nation called childhood would tax the diplomatic and political skills of the most seasoned arbitrator. The ego will need to be able to titrate empathy and discipline, gratification and frustration, laissez-faire and authority, love and hate, in its arduous role as lover, educator, taskmaster. The parental superego will have to regulate the sense of guilt and pleasure with great flexibility and fairness as it not only frustrates and disciplines but also forgives child and parent with tact and timing. One way of focusing and perhaps simplifying the discussion of parental attributes and the mental structures that inform and sustain them is to introduce the concept of play and its role in parenthood.

First let us look at some examples of parents at play and other parents who seem unable to play.

1. A parent who has been away on a trip returns to a five-year-old who hides behind the kitchen door several times until the father, a humorless man, eventually "spanks" her for being naughty. This parent seems to be unable to enter into the spirit of the child's playful communication. The child is surely speaking in a ludic voice, saying, "If you go away, I can go away. I can make you feel what I felt in your absence." A playful father would join in this play, reading the ludic code accurately and thereby giving the child the feeling that his or her voice was heard.

2. A three-year-old bumps his head on a table top. The mother spanks the table, saying, "Don't you ever touch my child again." The child's trauma is relieved by this magical drama. This "good enough" mother knows intuitively that the three-year-old lives in an animistic world where "bad" tables hit "good" children and mothers who attempt to make the world "child proof" will fail but then try again to create the illusion of a protected child-proof world until children can gradually be weaned from such illusions as development proceeds.

3. Let us return again to that most celebrated example of child's play— Freud's grandchild in "Beyond the Pleasure Principle." Even though Freud (1920) does not describe the parental or grandparental reaction (except for his own brilliant interpretation of its meaning!), we can

imagine what an appropriate parental response could have been. The child throws the stringed object away and retrieves it, thereby depicting and mastering his loss in play. If the mother returned and saw this play taking place, how might she have joined in the play interaction? Depending on the amount of language available to the child, the mother might play peek-a-boo or join in throwing and retrieving the inanimate object, mixing language and play in an attempt to get across to the child that his affects of sadness and anger and loss and love were being heard. If the child punched the mother playfully, this might be viewed as confirmation that the mother's playful communication with the child was "getting through." I have "constructed" one possible playful interaction between child and mother. Play is inventive: the other possible interactions between mother and child are as endless as the limits of the imagination itself.

I believe that the links between play and parenthood are subtle but crucial for an understanding of the parental role in development. Since play tends to diminish as symbolic development proceeds from childhood to adulthood and human semiotic skills rely less and less on action and more and more on abstraction, the return of this relatively repressed secret garden of playfulness is mandatory if parental regression in the service not only of the parental egos but also of the collective egos of childhood is to reach its full creative potential. I am suggesting that the creativity of parenthood is a totally neglected issue, its lack of glamour as a research topic owing probably to countertransferencelike affects in the research community.

If creativity can be defined by the scope and ingenuity of the ego's multiple and resourceful regressions in the service of the ego, where is the call for creativity more urgent or more enduring than in the parent-child relationship; and where can one find a developmental canvas more varied in psychological nuances and pigmentations or more challenging for the artist-parent to play upon; and where else can one find an artistic work-in-progress that takes at least eighteen years for the developmental paint to dry? And even then many further masterful touchings and refinishings are required before the artist can relinquish the developmental brush and rest a little from the labor in some midlife oasis of satisfaction (why do we tend only to describe the crises and rarely the satisfactions of the unfolding stages of the human condition?). I would suggest that the capacity to play is one of the essential components of this parental artistry.

I want, however, to focus on one feature of play only: its relation to regression. Play may well be the first aesthetic exercise of the human mind as it struggles with conflict. The regression in play is of course a calculated regression, ego dominated rather than id ridden, an aesthetic detour in Hartmann's sense (1939) rather than the mind out of control or gone astray. Since *analysis itself* can also be depicted as titrated regression, an analysand's willingness "to play the transference game," as one of my patients put it, *play in* childhood, *play in* parenthood, and *play in* analysis can be compared and contrasted from this point of view. An analyst is interested not only in how the analysand deals with the transference-fanned flames of regression in the psychoanalytic situation but also in the patient's creative handling of regression in all other aspects of life—play, foreplay, aesthetic pursuits, fantasies, parenting, and so on. The creative handling of regression is a euphemistic phrase that makes the analytic process or the parental process sound a lot easier than it is in reality.

There are powerful resistances both in analysands and in parents that derail the creative process, and the bulk of analytic work lies in exposing them and thereby diminishing them: (1) when Winnicott (1981) compares psychotherapy and playing, stating that if the patient is unable to play, the analyst's job is to get the play going again, he oversimplifies (not unwittingly, given Winnicott's impressive clinical savvy) a process of defense analysis and resistance analysis that is arduous and laborious; and (2) if a parent walks around the house naked, overstimulating the child, confusing domestic exhibitionism with the parental responsibility for the sexual enlightenment of the child, regression is being abused and indulged rather than being tamed and tempered in a more creative parental attitude.

In chapter 10 of this book, I argued that play, the essential communication mode of childhood, recedes in importance as the developing psyche weans itself from its action-packed infancy and embraces the abstractions and conceptualizations of adulthood. This is a relative issue obviously. If the mind never relinquishes anything, as Freud argued, but secures a permanent albeit repressed place for abandoned psychic products in fantasy, it is unlikely that play could ever be totally abandoned either. A parent makes a good example of an adult who must rely most of the time on the formal thought processes outlined by Piaget as the hallmark of adolescent and postadolescent cognitive achievement (Flavell, 1963). But if the parent is to be empathic and effective as a caretaker of children throughout their developmental cycles, he or she must revive the play mode that was temporarily rejected in the service of other more adult modes of being and thinking and behaving. The parent who never learned to play even as a child will obviously have a difficult time speaking the foreign language of play with a citizen who knows no other tongue for so many developing years.

The concept of creativity, that much-written-about province of the mind, is rarely used in the same breath with the concept of parenthood. Is it perhaps some pathology of the collective ego ideal that can sing the praises of creativity in childhood but never even conceive of creativity in a parent? In an age of abstract expressionism, is it not ironic that we insist on concrete marks on canvas or paper before we call it art when the indelible but invisible marks of parenthood on the evolving canvas of childhood clamor for equal attention? In a sense competent parents are the unsung artists of generation after generation, their canvases not honored in museums, their subtle artistry invisible in the complex fabric of society. Is some form of recognition not long overdue for this creative parental playing?

References

Benedek, T. (1959). Parenthood as a developmental phase. *J. Amer. Psychoanal. Assn.*, 7:389–417.

Flavell, J. H. (1963). *The Developmental Psychology of Jean Piaget*. New York: VanNostrand Reinhold.

Freud, S. (1920). Beyond the pleasure principle. *S.E.*, 18:7–64.

Hartmann, H. (1939). *Ego Psychology and the Problem of Adaptation*. New York: Int. Univ. Press, 1958.

Winnicott, D. W. (1971). *Playing and Reality*. New York: Penguin, 1980.

15

Play and Illusion

Samuel Ritvo, M.D.

The roots of play are to be found in the conflicts between conscious and unconscious desires, on the one hand, and the frustrations and demands of the external world, on the other. The task for the developing ego, the organization in the mind to which we assign regulatory and adaptive functions, is to find creative solutions or compromises for the conflicts arising from unfulfillable desire. In play the ego makes an attempt at resolution by the creation of a world of illusion that attempts to meet the demands of both the desire and its prohibition. In Freud's phrase, "Every child at play behaves like a creative writer, in that he creates a world of his own, or, rather, re-arranges the things of his world in a new way which pleases him" (1908, p. 143f.).

In the human being, play and its attendant illusion formation do not develop adequately or flourish without a close and extended relationship with a nurturing person. Adequate functioning of the innate biological fit between the infant's need and desire for nurturing and the mother's antic-ipation and supplying of the need is essential. In their studies of infants in institutions, Provence and Lipton (1962) observed that those infants who were not cared for by a single person to whom they had an attachment did not show an interest in toys, were unable to play, and lagged seriously in their mental and physical development.

The beginnings of illusory experience can be inferred from behaviors in early infancy. Winnicott (1953) placed the earliest illusory experiences in the first few months of life between the first use of fist, fingers, or thumbs in place of the breast for stimulation and satisfaction and playing with dolls or some special object to which the mother expects the infant to become attached or addicted for satisfaction in her absence. Between the thumb and the teddy bear, as he put it, Winnicott (1953) studied a wide variation in the sequence of events and filled in the steps in the process by which the infant goes from oral excitement and satisfaction

Freud Lecture, Muriel Gardiner Program in Psychoanalysis and the Humanities, read on November 21, 1991.

with the breast to what he called the first "not me" object, which may be the infant's own fingers or sounds, the edge of the blanket, or a toy or doll offered by the mother for soothing. The infant makes use of objects that are not part of the infant's body, yet are not fully recognized as belonging to external reality. Winnicott termed these *transitional objects*, and the behavior associated with them, *transitional phenomena*.

The transitional object belongs to an intermediate state and realm of experiencing between the inability and growing ability to recognize and accept reality, an area of experiencing engaged in the perpetual task of keeping inner and outer reality separate yet interrelated. It is an intermediate area between primary creativity and objective perception based on reality testing. The transitional phenomena that are its behavioral manifestations represent early stages of the uses of illusion without which, according to Winnicott, there is no meaning for the human being in the idea of a relationship with an object perceived by others as external to that being. The intermediate area of illusion is the indispensable bridge between the internal representation and the externally perceived object.

The infant's dependence on the nurturing adult is a basic motive force in the development of illusory experience. Freud hypothesized that the infant, in a state of unsatisfied need, hallucinates the breast. Winnicott extended and elaborated this idea, stressing that illusion is created out of the experience between mother and child. At the start, the mother's nearly total adaptation fosters the illusion that the breast is part of the infant and is under the infant's omnipotent control.* Initially, the mother has to disillusion the infant gradually. But to accomplish this successfully she must first provide sufficient opportunity for illusion. The breast can be said to be created by the infant again and again out of need. This intermediate area of illusion is necessary for the beginning of a relationship between a child and the world and is made possible by adequate mothering at this early critical phase. The capacity to love—to turn to another for satisfaction of a need—may be significantly determined by the outcome of the early illusion-disillusion experience. In this view the human being is from the beginning confronted with the problem of the relationship between what is objectively perceived and what is subjectively conceived of. The intermediate area of illusion exists between the infant's primary creation and the objective perception based on reality testing.

Implicit in the transitional phenomena as described by Winnicott are the precursors of intrapsychic conflict and transference. Intrapsychic conflict

---

* Here breast stands for the act of mothering as well as the mother's body.

arises with the development of internal prohibitions against the desires, prohibitions that at first come from the mother and the external world. Freud's basic concept of transference—discovered in his study of the psychology of the neuroses and of dreams—holds that an "unconscious idea is as such quite incapable of entering the preconscious and that it can only exercise any effect there by establishing a connection with an idea which already belongs to the preconscious, by transferring its intensity on to it and by getting itself 'covered' by it" (Freud, 1900, p. 562). In turn, the preconscious idea that takes over the intensity of the unconscious idea may be altered by it. If the outcome is the creation of an illusion, the illusion is shaped by the unconscious idea or desire that is repressed.

Apparently unnoted by Winnicott, Freud described the transference in the psychoanalytic situation in the identical terms that Winnicott used for the transitional object. In 1914 Freud spoke of admitting the compulsion to repeat into the transference as "a playground in which it is allowed to expand in almost complete freedom. . . . The transference thus creates an intermediate region between illness and real life through which the transition from the one to the other is made. The new condition has taken over all the features of the illness" (p. 154).

The transference illusion is created out of the opposition between need, desire, or wish and external reality or internalized prohibitions, and is mediated by the operation of transference. The rudiments of the same mental operation can be discovered in the transitional phenomena where the infant, upon the mother's inevitable failure to adapt perfectly, transfers the need to the illusory transitional object, to which the infant can then adapt his or her desire.

The infant who can achieve this transference to an illusory transitional object has taken a crucial step toward mental health. Via transference the baby is then able to develop toward detoured discharge of instinctual drive derivatives so necessary to the development of adaptive defenses and toward a tolerance for partial or substitute gratification essential for compromise formation in the resolution of psychic conflict. The burden of reality acceptance is never removed, and no one of us is free from the task of having to relate inner and outer reality. The intermediate illusory area of experience that provides unchallenged relief from this strain not only in childhood but throughout life is also the area of creativity, the area of imaginative experience in which the mysteriously gifted produce their world of art.

Although he eschews psychoanalytic explanations, Huizinga (1955) in his book, *Homo Ludens* (man the player), studies the play forms in culture and places them in the same intermediate area of experience. The consecrated spot of ritual cannot be distinguished from the playground. The arena, the magic circle, the temple, the stage, the court of justice, are all, in form and function, playgrounds within which special rules reign. In Huizinga's words, "All are temporary worlds within the ordinary world, dedicated to the performance of an act apart. Through this playing society expresses its interpretation of life and the world." He means not that play turns into culture but that, in its earliest phases, culture has the character of play. In the twin union of play and culture, play is primary.

There is a direct line from this intermediate area of illusion to the child absorbed in fantasy play. Bridging the internal and external worlds and partaking of both, play has a crucial developmental role throughout childhood. Via the creation of illusion and the suspension of disbelief, play offers opportunities for more direct discharge of instinctual desires than stringent reality testing would allow. The play realm offers the special feature that the gratification or discharge need not be governed by the external constraints and restrictions of the parents or, later, by the internalized prohibitions of the parents. At the same time, play does have a function in establishing and securing the prohibitions that are eventually internalized when play, for example, reaches the point at about age seven or eight when the rules of the game become sacrosanct.

Play has an important role in relation to the aggressive drives that carry dangers if expressed directly toward the parents. Their expression in creative illusion and fantasy not only seeks to avoid punishment and guilt but is given forms accepted by the culture and prepares the way toward sublimated transformations of aggression and the mastery of external difficulties.

Play serves like a theater workshop. Elaborations in play provide the child with a safe modality for integrating new maturational achievements. This can be observed most clearly in the new modes of play that accompany the acquisition of skills and capacities—for example, eye-hand-mouth coordination in the infant, sphincter control in the toddler, or the rapidly expanding ego capacities in latency. In this manner, play accompanies psychosexual development and is invaluable to the clinician in appraising whether a child is developmentally regressed and in gauging the nature and severity of the regression. Over the course of psychosexual development, play, with its synthesis of illusion and fantasy and by virtue of its position between the inner and outer worlds, provides the opportunity for the individual to employ his or her maturational endowment to develop and organize defenses and compromise formations and thus create his or her own way of coping with normative developmental crises. It is in this context, too, that special

gifts or endowments may make their appearance as unusual creative subli-
mations.

As the child's reality testing advances, fantasy play increasingly requires
the suspension of reality and disbelief. The ability to regulate this capacity
is one of the limiting factors in play. The child who is anxious about being
able to control his impulses may defensively be too reality-bound and thus
unable to play. The child who too readily or too completely suspends reality
may likewise be unable to establish a safe and gratifying middle ground on
which she can play.

Play is an essential psychosocial medium for integrating new maturational
steps into the total personality. Developmentalists and educators are well
aware that preschool-age children who are unable to play because they have
been deprived of adequate nurturing and have not established gratifying
ties with adults or because they suffer maturational lags and deficits can
make impressive gains in their overall development if they can be taught to
play and encouraged to fantasize via the relationship to a teacher or therapist
who may substitute for the failed relationship with the original care-giver,
the so-called primary object. Once the teacher is accepted and established
as a person who can satisfy the child's needs, the child may be able to create
an illusory play sphere to serve normal developmental functions.

Although play originates and develops in the nurturing setting of primary
object relationships, play with other children also serves an important function. When observing children who have been with adults exclusively for
extended periods of time, one can detect something like a hunger to be with
other children. There may be a burst of energy and a palpable air of relief
when they finally have the opportunity to play with others their age. They
are relieved to be free of the expectation of impulse control and the restraints
of reason and reality imposed by adults. Play companions do not impose
the same requirements. They provide a setting that encourages and joins in
with illusion and fantasy.

Although children play more freely with one another when the adult's
restraining influence on drive expression is absent, they can invoke parental
controls against a playmate, giving a clear indication that they have internalized parental prohibitions, particularly against the expression of aggression. For example, a four-and-a-half-year-old boy playing with his friend
of about the same age killed his own pet fish by removing them from the
tank and piercing them with a pointed object. His playmate became upset
and rushed to tell the mother what her son had done. When the play had
exceeded his internalized standard of what the adults permitted, the visiting
child broke off the play and called on the external parental authority.

As soon as language is discernible, we can speak of articulated fantasies with identifiable ideational content and we can recognize a narrative quality in the play. In examining the psychological phenomenon of narrative, we should keep in mind the conventional definition that narrative is "a discourse designed to represent a *connected* succession of happenings usually with descriptions of personages and their environment."* We can bring to the understanding of narrative play and narrative in general what we have learned from the psychoanalytic process—that the narrative the analysand proffers is a creation of the ego, which silently exercises its defensive, integrative, and synthetic capabilities in response to the danger from the continual pressing forward of the drives for discharge. In the analytic situation the danger is from the transference to the analyst of the analysand's own opposition to the instinctual drives and their derivative wishes, that is, in a reexternalization of the parental prohibitions.

Children creating a story to go with their play are formulating a discourse that varies in degree of logic and reason with their level of development. Their play gives individual expression to their perception of their wishes, influenced by the actual or anticipated attitude of the immediate listener or companion or by the transferences the children make to these persons. The narrative is constructed of a succession of connections and transferences created to give masked expression to the instinctual drive. The narrative provides forms of expression deemed acceptable to both the narrator and the narratee, to use Peter Brooks's term (1989).

This secondary process elaboration, in which illusions may abound and which may be the most creative part of the narrative, tries to present a seamless tale. But, as in the analytic hour or in the construction and telling of a dream, the joints, connections, and transitions indicate switch points where a defense or resistance is instituted against the threat of a break-through of warded-off drive derivatives. The creativity of the narrator is not in the representation of the instinctual drives that simply keep pressing forward but in the creative achievement of the ego which, via transferences, invents ways of giving expression to them or weaves a tale that disguises or hides them from open view.

As Brooks (1989) pointed out, all narrative is dialogic and the transferences to the listener are vital to its construction. The responses of the listener or reader in turn contain transferences to the narrator and the tale, which influence the narrative as perceived and constructed by the narratee.

* *Webster's New International Dictionary*, 2nd ed. Springfield, Mass.: G. & C. Merriam-Webster, 1956.

An examination of narrative fantasy play in the psychoanalytic situation—almost always accompanied by some form of enactment—gives us access to the inner lives of children. Influenced by some degree of understanding that they are there for the analyst to relieve their distress, children offer the story of their life shaped by the necessity to keep conflicted desires out of consciousness because of the painful affects associated with them. The analyst has the task of unraveling the meanings of the play in the mental and emotional life of the child. Since a direct line of questioning will get nowhere, the analyst tries to ask questions indirectly via the way he or she participates in the play—for example, in the way an assigned role is carried out or the motives of the characters are queried. The direct interpretation of meanings within the play carries the risk of intruding upon or challenging the illusion and depriving the child of the safe haven of the intermediate play space.

Play, Character, and the Development of the Play Signature

Although all play shares the intermediate region of transference, illusion, and narrative, the play of each child becomes distinctive, individualized, characteristic for that child; it carries his or her play signature.

What forces shape this individualized development? And how does the evolving style of play contribute to personality, character, creativity, health or neurosis? The variables are myriad, but for the sake of study we can divide them into two broad categories—endowment givens, or constitution, and experience.

The constitutional givens, though difficult to define, describe, or quantify, are nevertheless powerful determinants of individual differences in development. Psychoanalysts have thought of constitutional givens in terms of gender, temperament, energy levels, perceptual sensitivities, or discharge thresholds and rhythms.

Although the endowment qualities can be regarded as givens and carry potentials, their expression, whether exaggerated, distorted, or muted, is powerfully influenced by children's experience with the primary objects upon whom they are dependent for survival. In the interaction with the primary objects, children establish their individual, characteristic synthesis of internal needs and external excitation or restraints, creating their own modes of adaptation and defense in which play has a major role. Frustration and conflict generate anxiety, and the individual—child and adult alike—creates neurotic symptoms when the defenses and compromise formations fail. We need to bear in mind that a neurotic symptom—phobia, obsession, or hysterical conversion—is basically an illusion, a false perception treated as real. Because internally there is no barrier against impulses or desires, unacceptable ones can be avoided, attacked, or repudiated, as in a phobia, if they are perceived as belonging to the outer world.

As the mode of coping with the internal pressures and external stimulation or constraint becomes structuralized, the child's play, which is both a generator and a product of these processes, takes on particular characteristics that can be observed in preferred patterns and modalities of excitement and discharge, affective responses, repetitive themes, favorite characters, and the structure and outcome of narrative. The child's play incorporates the fantasies that represent the specific, individual conditions of pleasure for his or her desires, reflecting the individual bent of the child's psychosexual development.

If the conflict becomes intense and protracted and is accompanied by regression and symptom formation, the play, too, tends to become fixed, repetitive, impoverished, dominated by defensive phenomena. It loses the richness of creative illusion and imagination that nourishes progression in development. For the clinician these features of play provide useful and reliable information for diagnosis and the planning of treatment. In the treatment room, we offer the child the opportunity to relate his or her narrative with or without play. The child most often chooses play for communication because the allusive and illusory nature of play provides rich means of representation, and the suspension of reality in play provides relative safety and control.

To illustrate the interactions among endowment, maturation, and the relationship to the primary objects and to examine their influence on the development of individual characteristics of play, I offer observations on Evelyne and Jerry, two children from a longitudinal study of child development initiated by Ernst Kris and Milton Senn at the Yale Child Study Center in 1949. Since Evelyne and Jerry were followed from the prenatal period to the ages of thirty-three and forty, they provide a unique opportunity to examine how the play signature derived from early interaction of constitution and experience contributes to personality and character formation and influences the course of life.

The study was an action research, a service-centered study in which a group of children and their families were provided pediatric, educational, and psychological services as needed from the prenatal period through the first five years of life. Educators, pediatricians, psychoanalysts, psychologists, and social workers collaborated as expert observers of child life and specialists in their own field, making direct observational data available for both prospective and retrospective examination. As formulated by Ernst Kris, such a study would advance our understanding of the way certain personality characteristics arise and how they persist—how the sameness of personality manifests itself despite developmental changes. I should add that our knowledge of Evelyne and her family is much more extensive than that of Jerry, as she was in psychoanalytic treatment with several interruptions from three until ten.

Evelyne

Evelyne's father was a steady, responsible, obsessional man, constrained in the expression of his feelings. A major issue in his life was his deep resentment of his own father's preference for his sister who was two years older than he. The resentment he bore toward his sister was transferred to Evelyne, who in his mind increasingly became the older sister. Evelyne's mother lived in an all-female household after age ten, when her father died. Shortly after her older sister married and moved away, she avoided being left with her mother and spinster aunt by marrying, replacing her sister with her husband and then with her first child. An introspective, imaginative woman with artistic talents and a strong interest in teaching her children, she suffered from depressive moods sometimes accompanied by obsessional symptoms and at times had difficulty controlling impulsive, angry outbursts.

From birth, Evelyne and her mother seemed well suited to each other. The parents had hoped for a boy but were very happy and pleased with the baby. This sensitive, introspective young woman was paired with an infant who was receptive to the mother's care, easily satisfied and pacified. The mother had a strong empathic tie to Evelyne and constantly tried to be aware of the infant's feelings, carefully gauging and responding to her needs. The sensitive interactions between mother and child were observable in the early feeding and in the toilet training. Throughout the early feeding, the mother carefully exerted varying degrees of pressure on Evelyne to mold the child in the form the mother preferred. Evelyne seemed to adjust quite well to the mother's pressures, aided in this by her receptive temperament, which left her relaxed and relatively easily pacified. In terms of Winnicott's model, one could say that Evelyne's experience was of creating a breast almost whenever the need arose. The mother provided opportunity for the creation of illusion, and the disillusion was gradual enough that the infant could adapt to it without a major disruption.

In toilet training, the mother was much more ambiguous in her demands. When Evelyne did not comply readily to a mild pressure, the mother was unable to make a more forceful demand partly because of her guilty feelings about her own aggression, which the child manipulated with great skill.

The receptivity noted early in response to her mother's care was a prominent feature elsewhere as well. In her early motor development she was receptive and reactive in her response to the adult rather than the active initiator. She did not use activity for discharge of tension. The mother contributed to the relative underdevelopment in the motor area by her preference for visual contact over physical handling. Consequently she predominantly presented the face and eyes in her contacts with Evelyne, fostering visual alertness and discrimination, as well as an early, pronounced, and persistent interest in the human face.

Evelyne's interest in dolls and toys with faces, encouraged and shared by her mother, led to very early fantasy play with imaginary companions in which Evelyne assumed many roles. The fantasy play went quite beyond the domestic mimicry usually seen in the second year, and Evelyne used it as an effective means of coping with the arrival of a new sibling and the concomitant separation from the mother at age two. By pretending and role-playing she was able to bridge physical separations, an impressive early demonstration of the adaptive function of play.

When Evelyne entered nursery school at two and a half years, she was the most mature and predictable child in the group. Although the other children were important to her, she was demonstrative and energetic in her independence and was the least forlorn child when her mother left. Although she found little enjoyment in physical activity, her capacity for fantasy play was an asset, and the group got on better when she was there as the initiator of dramatic, narrative play.

But Evelyne's world had been severely shaken with the birth of her sister, Wendy. Both parents had wished for a boy, and the father's shame and disappointment were so great that he did not announce this baby's arrival. He soon identified her with himself, however, and saw her as a symbol of the masculinity he wished for, often calling her by a boy's name.

Within months, the father shifted his affection from Evelyne—now identified with his own disliked older sister—to Wendy. The changes in the family had a disturbing effect on Evelyne, and she developed a number of symptoms. At two and a half, she was severely frightened when, on Halloween, her great-aunt appeared as a ghost with a face cut from a white sheet. The fear spread to pictures of clowns and people in masks on television and in books. She was afraid of the dark and of her bedroom at night. All toys with faces and paintings on the wall had to be removed before she would go to bed. She was also distressed by loud noises like the doorbell, by the aggression of neighborhood children, and by her parents' arguments. It was unmistakable that the fears were related to her conflict over her own aggression and the aggression of others, primarily her parents'. Her mother stressed that Evelyne had a mind of her own, was slow to anger, but could be fierce when she became angry. Quite aware of the shift in her father's affections to Wendy, Evelyne was reluctant to go out alone with him or remain in the house with him. The mother was delighted but sometimes awed by Evelyne's very rich fantasy life. She liked to play alone with her toys and to act out favorite stories.

The same fantasy play with special interest in the face now became the preferred means of representing the conflict and the anxiety arising from her own aggression and determined the features of her symptoms. In her fear of faces and the avoidance of situations where they were perceived, Evelyne was trying to cope with her aggression by externalizing it and then trying to avoid the externalized representation. What had been freely creative play and fantasy was now fixed in coping with neurotic conflict.

Because of the persistent anxiety and phobias, psychoanalytic treatment three times a week was started at three years four months, when Evelyne was in nursery school. Her aversion to being alone with her father was transferred to the analyst, and she was quite explicit that it was because the analyst was a man. At first she was unable to use her capacity for fantasy play to establish herself comfortably with the analyst. For the first six months she refused to come to the treatment room alone with him, insisting her teacher accompany her and remain in the room with her. In her play, her drawing, and her relationship to the analyst, she made it clear that she preferred the woman and had no room for the man. Yet there were times when she was coquettish and teasingly contrary.

After six months, in recognition of the analyst's steadfastness, Evelyne, though still declaring to the nursery school teacher that she did not want to stay with him, began to be close and cuddly, reading a book with her head in his lap and letting him know she thought about him at home. She was able to tell the teacher that she loved her analyst. After her second sister, Tammy, was born when Evelyne was four and a half, she told the analyst she had not liked him the year before but did not feel that way anymore. This declaration ushered in a positive oedipal transference that became more intense as time went on. She confided the secret that the analyst was her best friend. She played marriage games in which a new doll became her new baby while the analyst was sent out to work.

Evelyne's high capacity for gratification through illusion and fantasy in the transference during the oedipal phase when her father had turned away from her was beneficial for her feminine identity and development, as was the birth of Tammy at that time. About her birth, Evelyne said, "That is when I had *my* baby." Tammy continued to be "her child." They drew closer to maintain a common front against Wendy—who became increasingly hostile and unruly—and their closeness has continued. As an adult, Tammy chose to live near Evelyne, looking to her for guidance, support, and intimacy more than she did to their mother; Evelyne enjoyed mothering her.

Through Evelyne's analysis we learned of the subculture within the family, formed by the three sisters, which created its own play traditions and narratives, accurately reflecting the fantasies and desires of the parents without their ever having been openly communicated. The shared fantasies shed an interesting light on mythopoesis in a particular culture. One myth, which involved gender change by metamorphosis, said that the younger the child, the greater chance she still had of becoming a boy, even if not born one. By then, at seven, Evelyne had already given up that hope for herself and Wendy, but Tammy might still achieve it. In their joint fantasy play Tammy was cast as a male. In their doctor play Wendy was the male doctor, despite the fact that their pediatrician was a woman. Evelyne was the nurse, and Tammy was a prince or other royal personage, accurately reflecting their perception of how they were identified in the minds of the parents.

Between the ages of six and eleven, Evelyne's position in the family improved as Wendy's kept sinking because of her aggression and unruliness. Evelyne's artistic activities in school were commended glowingly. Her characteristic ability to tolerate disappointment and gain the ultimate reward of mastery through persistence served her well.

In her twelfth year, on the threshold of puberty, she seemed to be considerably less imaginative and derived little satisfaction from feminine interests, a turn to concreteness frequently observed at that stage as a defense against the early intensification of the instinctual desires in preadolescence. At the age of fifteen, she gave the impression of docility, compliance, and inhibition with no hint of rebellion. There were no outward signs of imaginative or creative activity, and her fantasy life was not accessible in the interview setting. At eighteen, after her freshman year in college, she actively tried to overcome her inhibitions. She spoke of having a strict superego and of feeling guilty if she failed to please others. She wanted to feel less opposed to her desires. In this meeting with the analyst, she spontaneously expressed the realization that her father could never be close and loving toward her because he identified her with his own older sister.

Over the next several years she made the transition to adulthood with the aid of illusion and fantasy, this time in the form of religion. She joined an evangelical group led by a charismatic male teacher. In this setting, she met her future husband, an evangelical churchgoer. From this point on, she felt secure that, through her actions and feelings, she was carrying out God's will. By finding God, loving God, and being loved by him, she replaced her rejecting father with a loving father, as she had in fantasy in the transference replaced him with the analyst in the oedipal period. The sublimated oedipal gratification via religion enabled her to be more independent of both her parents without feeling guilty.

At thirty-four, Evelyne appeared to be leading a satisfying and fulfilling life, although in straitened financial circumstances because she had decided to stay at home and care for her four young children. She was in a satisfying marriage and had the close relationship with her husband she could never have with her father. She was imaginative, playful, and creative with her children. In planning to return to work, she considered changing to a field that would give her more opportunities for creative expression.

Jerry

Jerry started with an endowment vastly different from Evelyne's and grew up in a family that compromised the possibility of healthy development and did not nourish play and fantasy.

After a predelinquent childhood and a roaming, adventurous adolescence, Jerry's father, a shrewdly intelligent, compulsive gambler, enlisted in the military, where he continued his gambling. Upon discharge, a routine X ray disclosed a chronic, recurrent pulmonary infection that required several long hospitalizations and left him a semi-invalid irregularly employed.

Jerry's mother was a physically active, emotionally labile woman with shifting, tempestuous moods and poor impulse control. Her father had repeated psychotic episodes, and her mother had a history of sociopathy with several periods of protective institutionalization in adolescence.

As a newborn infant, Jerry was hyperactive and vigorous. He reacted to external stimuli and physical discomfort with massive discharge movements. Breast-feeding was distressing for mother and infant. Feeling Jerry was not satisfied, the mother's frustration, combined with disgust at the messiness of dripping breasts, reduced her to exhaustion and tears. She was relieved when the pediatrician recommended bottle-feeding.

Both parents handled Jerry in exciting, stimulating, seductive, and punitive ways. His first words were "bad boy," and a wooden cooking spoon was the signal for an imminent spanking. The mother's furious outbursts were immediately followed by reconciliations in which she cuddled him quietly and affectionately. Rapid alternation between violent activity and quiescence later became a feature of Jerry's behavior in nursery school and in his treatment.

Neither parent was ever observed to play with Jerry. Although the objects forbidden to him were in full view in the home, his own toys were kept out of sight in a toy chest and were offered to him only in his playpen out of doors. The mother was never observed to make a toy attractive to Jerry by investing it with her own interest. On the contrary, she repeatedly interfered when Jerry engaged in play with the interviewer or when he attempted to play with an object independently.

Disturbances in Jerry's capacity to play began to appear in the developmental tests in the first year. Although earlier tests had been satisfactory, he showed increasing signs of developmental difficulties between nine and twelve months. He tended to hold or manipulate only one object at a time and did not do well on test items requiring that he combine objects or handle multiple stimuli. He had much less interest in the test materials than he had shown earlier. He accepted and explored them briefly but without the interest and energy shown before. These adaptive items reflect the infant's integrative functioning, and for the first time this aspect of Jerry's functioning was in question. On subsequent tests, his extreme activity was combined with a lack of interest in inanimate objects and an easy distractibility. By precipitating and facilitating massive discharge, his mother contributed to his decreased ability to tolerate tension. From nine months on, his failure to use toys and test materials adaptively was striking. A lost toy did not seem important enough to look for, and any obstacle made him turn away to some other object or activity. The deficit in his play with toys foreshadowed his later disturbance in play and learning.

In strong contrast to Evelyne's mother, Jerry's mother was unable to relate to him in a way that would foster the establishment of that intermediate area of illusory experience essential to the development of play and fantasy. Because of the serious portent of Jerry's inability to play, his pediatrician recommended that he start nursery school at twenty months where he might be taught to play and would be in an environment that would mitigate the adverse effects on play and learning of the fighting and overstimulation by both parents.

From the first school session, he was hyperactive, impulsive, poorly controlled, reckless, negative, and aggressive. His only interest in play materials was to snatch, throw, or brush them out of the way. He had none of the two-year-old's sense of the possibilities of a toy for manipulation or adaptation to dramatic play interests. He was so poorly organized both in play and in behavior that it was difficult to say when ideas were at work or to study the nature of them.

By the end of the second year in school, with the aid of his gifted and devoted teacher, he began to make friends and to show an interest in manipulating materials and in quieter play. Dramatic play of an active nature became a source of pleasure and an avenue for expression of ideas, as well as for discharge of energy and tension.

This changed the following school year (three years five months) when he was very disruptive, moody, and generally ill-humored. The organization and control he had shown the previous year were lost in wild, disturbing behavior. His aggressive attacks on other children were much more directed and damaging. It was clear that anxiety played an important part in his unrest and that he was attacking head-on any object or situation that frightened him. He once bit a rabbit as if to keep it from biting him. It was evident that he was reacting strongly to the birth of a brother when he was three and the consequent loss of his exclusive relationship with his mother. Analytic treatment was begun at this time.

After his therapy was under way, his fighting diminished in frequency, but he was otherwise disorganized and difficult to handle much of the year. The content of his play was meager, and his investment in materials, low. In his final year (four years five months to five years two months), although he was functioning better, it was clear he had a learning problem. He lacked the capacity and interest to manipulate symbols or to use symbolic representation essential for play. He showed little interest and productivity in the elaboration of self-initiated play and dramatic activity. His dramatic play, which in the early months in school could only be described as "gymnastics with sound effects" and which was merely suggestive of his fantasy, now included some identifiable fantasy around such realistic activities as housekeeping play, repairmen, cowboys, bandits, and so on. Even at five, his impulsivity and hyperactivity were predominant rather than ideas, continuity, planning, or purpose. Regression under the impact of stress was as extensive and rapid at five as it had been at two.

In the treatment room, the hyperactivity and the sexualized, exhibitionistic mode of relating to the adult were immediately in evidence. The play was a literal and direct repetition in action of scenes and sequences from his home life without much disguise or elaboration in fantasy. The most sustained play in the beginning was cooking and feeding, giving a nursing bottle to the doll, then drinking from it himself, and ending either with smashing the bottle against the wall or throwing both the bottle and the doll out the window, enacting his wish either to be in his brother's place or to be rid of him. He vividly portrayed primal scene experiences that were abundantly stimulated at home, as his crib was next to his parents' bed in the tiny bedroom.

Jerry's mode of coping with the increasing anxiety over attacking and being attacked was to develop a phobic symptom in the treatment room. He feared there was a monster in the next room who would bite, scratch, and yell. The symptom also incorporated the paranoid grandfather on the other side of the wall in the next apartment. With the creation of the symptom and the illusion of the monster on whom he concentrated his aggression, his attitude toward the analyst became more friendly and less attacking. To the interpretation that he liked to be noisy and act big and strong (identify with the aggressor) because then he did not have to be afraid of the monster, he acquiesced and shouted that he was Superman.

Throughout the study the staff was concerned for Jerry's future. The prediction was delinquency stemming from impulsivity and conflict over passive homosexual strivings. Projective tests at nine years showed an increase in his fantasy life. This might have been due to his having been hospitalized and immobilized in traction for more than a month because of a leg fracture sustained in a fall from a fence while fleeing from a policeman who was pursuing him because he and his companions were trespassing on railroad property.

When a staff member visited his home when he was fifteen, the family situation appeared more stable than at any previous time. They had moved to the suburbs and both parents were working. Jerry was limping along academically in high school but getting much recognition from the community for his athletic skills. He had a close, supportive relationship with a teacher who was also his athletic coach, reminiscent of the devoted nursery school teacher who had coached him carefully. We learned much later, however, that under the influence of an older boy he was already involved with drugs and in difficulty with the police.

At twenty-three he initiated a visit, expressing nostalgia for the Child Study Center. In dress and manner he conveyed a self-conscious image of a relaxed, confident man of the world, but he told of the hurt of being turned down by a sixteen-year-old adolescent with whom he was in love. What we learned only later was that he had come because of trouble with the law over activities in which he engaged under the influence of an older man, just the kind of outcome the study had feared.

After extricating himself at the age of thirty-two from his dangerous illicit activities and recovering from a life-threatening illness, which he was convinced was caused by an attempt by his associate to poison him, he was left without a vocation, only a marginal position in the community, and feeling trapped in a hopeless, troubled marriage. His capacity for self-reflection was very limited. He seemed unable to take an imaginative or creative approach to planning the next steps in his life. His views of the world were cynical and concrete. What he idealized most was power. He had retained some of his early appealing qualities but seemed colorless and lacking in depth.

At forty he had a semiskilled trade but was temporarily laid off, living amicably with a divorcée and her children and engaged in a bitter custody battle with his former wife over their two children. Indicative of his limitations in imagination and empathy was the difficulty he was having with his own lawyer in understanding that the court was not interested in meeting his wishes and needs to have the children but was guided by what was in the best interests of the children. For him the two were identical.

Conclusion

The prospective and retrospective views of personality development afforded by the longitudinal study of Evelyne and Jerry from the prenatal period through the fourth decade allow us to appreciate the origins of their different styles of play and fantasy in the early interactions of constitution and parenting. Although they changed with time as individuals, we can discern how the style of thought and fantasy persisted. It was for Evelyne a continuing source of enrichment of her mental and emotional life, whereas for Jerry the impoverishment of play and illusion deprived him of resources for coping more creatively with the vicissitudes of life.

The contrast between them stands out in their utilization of religious experience. Only when desperately ill did Jerry pray to God. After his recovery, religious illusion had no significant role in his life. Play had not been available to him as a child, and as an adult he was unable to create an adaptive illusional or fantasy bridge, via religion or otherwise, between the demands of his inner world and the world outside. For Evelyne, finding God through the father image in a teacher enabled her to remove childhood ties to her parents and transfer them to husband and new family—a transition from adolescence to adulthood that had been difficult for her. Religious illusion continued to be a guiding, creative spiritual force in her life with family, friends, and community.

References

Brooks, P. (1989). Changes in the margins: Construction, transference and narrative. Unpublished paper.

Freud, S. (1900). The interpretation of dreams. *S.E.*, 4 and 5.

―――. (1908). Creative writers and day-dreaming. *S.E.*, 9:141–154.

―――. (1914). Remembering, repeating and working-through. *S.E.*, 12:145–156.

Huizinga, J. (1955). *Homo Ludens*. Boston: Beacon Press.

Provence, S., and Lipton, R. (1962). *Infants in Institutions*. New York: Int. Univ. Press.

Winnicott, D. W. (1953). Transitional objects and transitional phenomena. In *Collected Papers*. New York: Basic Books, 1958, pp. 229–242.

16

Play Modes in Child Analysis

James M. Herzog, M.D.

Play in child analysis is a complex and changing phenomenon. It may involve displacement, enactment, or direct interaction with the analyst. It may feature only one mode of activity, an unvarying, identifiable series, or a collection of activities under the sway of differing developmental and dynamic pressures. It may shift in terms of stages and techniques within the same child. This capacity for play, as well as the necessity for variability within the play process, is an important feature of the child's ego structure. Within each analysis, it is possible to use observations about the consistencies and variations in the play process both to reconstruct early experience and trauma that have affected ego development and to gauge the process of the analysis itself.

I shall present material from several child analyses to illustrate the ways in which play modes vary or remain stable. In doing so, I hope to document an important variable in this critical human ego function—the capacity to play—and to demonstrate its vicissitudes within the analytic situation.

I conceptualize play as the action language of doing, redoing, and undoing. It is a mode for representing, communicating, and trying on, both within the evolving self system and between the self and others. It is first and foremost a linguistic system for constructing, organizing, trying out, and revising meaning. The exercise of play involves taking oneself and one's agenda—cognitive, affective, and putative—seriously enough to be playful. The capacity for play appears to be innate, but as with almost every other human ego function, the *Umwelt* must provide a suitable haven for and response to the inchoate capacity. Just as there is no vision without stimulation by light, so play does not fully develop without an adult taking it seriously. Developmentally, this task of endorsing the child's play is

The work described in this chapter was conducted in part at the Clinic for the Development of Young Children and Parents, Department of Psychiatry, Children's Hospital Medical Center, Boston.

performed by both parents, each with a somewhat characteristic mode of play interaction.

As analysts, we know that this average, expectable, interactively contingent development features more permutations and deviations than easily predicted and smoothly functioning sequences. Such contingencies, exigencies, and actual experiences often constitute the determinants of a child's play repertoire—its limitations and play mode predilections.

To explicate these concepts, I shall present some play material derived from the evaluation of an extraordinarily distressed family with three preschool children. As these children were later seen in an analytic situation, it will be possible to advance certain hypotheses about the origins and variability of what Ritvo (1985) has called "play signatures"—in this case, individual as well as familial. The role of endowment, experience, responsivity of the Umwelt, and trauma will be explored in an effort to unravel the constituents and the dynamics of play.

Clinical Material

Every night at around 11:00, Jack, thirty-three months old, gets up from his bed, cries a few unintelligible sounds, and heads for the window. His parents say that his behavior is as regular as clockwork. His younger sister, Kerry, is like a whirling dervish. Her mother says that Kerry is tough, nasty, and, at twenty-three months of age, the most difficult of her three children. Robby, who at forty-three months is the oldest, clings to his father. He literally will not let go except to clobber Jack.

At the Clinic for the Development of Young Children and Parents at Children's Hospital, we were asked to evaluate and assist this young family. The referring social worker told us that the father, who is twenty-four, has a hereditary cardiac condition. He has already suffered several heart attacks and is a virtual invalid. He cannot work. Moreover, the family has been reported for child abuse, and our evaluation is to be part of the social service agency's assessment of this issue. Interestingly, the initial referral made no mention of the mother. The family's first appointment was almost canceled: the problem had been solved, we were told, because Jack had not awakened at 11:00 for two nights in a row. Tactfully, we suggested to the parents that it might be useful for us to meet anyway. Mrs. T., twenty years old, agreed and added that maybe we could help her too. Her mother, she told us, insists that she is retarded. Can we give her some tests? Then she'll show her mother a thing or two.

In our initial meeting with the family, we were impressed by how thin, ill, and wan Mr. T. was. He smiled and told us that his illness was nothing. His mother had it, and so did his son Jack. He was not afraid of dying. "When your time comes, your time comes," he said with a smile. Although he was twenty-four, his manner and appearance suggested a fourteen-year-old, while something else in him suggested a very old man.

He illustrated his attitude about mortality and something of his cognitive style and capacities by telling us that his mother had "died" on the table during a cardiac catheterization, but because it was not her time yet, she came back to life and was now fine. Mrs. T. did not appear to listen as her husband talked. She wanted to speak only about her mother. She was quite adamant. What does it mean to be retarded? Could we tell whether or not she was? She was not much concerned about her husband's health but did say that it took him longer than any of the three children to climb to their third-floor flat. In contrast to her husband, who seemed affectively attuned and present, Mrs. T. had a somewhat preoccupied and absent quality. Her face seemed blank and without emotion. For example, when Mr. T. told us that there was no heat in their apartment, that they were cold, and that it was nice to be in the clinic because it was warm, Mrs. T. merely shrugged her shoulders and grinned.

As we spoke with the parents, the behavior of the children was most noteworthy. They were absolutely silent. Jack and Robby clung to their father, one on each leg; Kerry sat on his lap. It was almost impossible to see Mr. T. as he was completely covered with children, but it was possible to hear him. He spoke about how difficult the children were. They were always naughty, he said, and he had to use the belt on them a lot, especially on Jack. He didn't like to do it—children were to be loved, not hit—but what could you do? It was strange, he said, that there was much more trouble since he was home full time after his last heart attack. He didn't know what got into the kids, what made them so difficult. Again, Mrs. T. did not pay much attention. From time to time she muttered about her mother, who was called Angel, but she was "hell on wheels." When Mrs. T. was a child and her mother got angry with her, she would burn her with matches. Maybe, Mrs. T. wondered, she should burn Robby and Jack and Kerry. Her husband burst in: "We don't want to do that. That's why we are here. We love our children and don't want to hurt them." Throughout all of this, the children were literally frozen to their father and watched him like a hawk. When at one point, Mr. T. coughed and put his hand on his chest, an expression of concern appeared on Robby's face and then on Jack's and even on Kerry's. Mrs. T. appeared not to notice.

As is our protocol in the clinic, we then observed the family interacting behind a one-way mirror. Mother and father conversed a little bit. The subject was Angel and her cruelty to Mrs. T. Mr. T. seemed sympathetic. As his wife's anger grew, so did his own excitement. Mrs. T. began to cry as she described her mother's threats against her; Mr. T. became so upset that he said he would strangle Angel. The emotion was apparently too much for him. He clutched his chest and became silent and pale. The children, who had been playing on the floor, immediately stopped and stared intently at him. Robby said, "Ma stop," but Mrs. T. continued what had now become a monologue about her mother. We interrupted the observation at this point, concerned about Mr. T. He said it was nothing, it happened often (which his cardiologist confirmed), and he took some propranolol. The children's watchful wariness and the mother's obliviousness were particularly noteworthy to us.

After we left the room and the observation recommenced, little Kerry launched into action. She got the boys to join her, and the three began first to throw things and ultimately to fight with one another. Jack, after much provocation, pulled Kerry's hair. At this point, Mr. T., who was again looking very upset, threatened Jack with his belt. We once again intervened when Mrs. T. told Jack he was going to get it and grabbed him while Mr. T. took off his belt and prepared to strike his son. As we entered the room for the second time, it was clear that in some way Mr. T.'s gesture had decreased the tension rather than increased it. All the children, including Jack, the would-be victim, now seemed relaxed. Robby smiled, as did Jack, and little Kerry sang, "Daddy here, Daddy here."

In this segment of the observation, the interaction between the children and their parents had markedly increased. Kerry had initiated the "naughty" activity about which the parents had complained and had elicited a response from Jack, which led to their father's taking physical action. We hypothesized that her triumphant singing, "Daddy here, Daddy here," represented her reassuring herself that her father could still respond—that he was still alive. Although the concept of alive or not alive is in many ways beyond a twenty-three-month-old, her later play seemed to substantiate the notion that her father's reactivity was a central concern. Her two brothers were equally concerned with this issue.

Each of the children was seen in an individual play interview. Kerry played with some teddy bears of differing sizes. She made the little teddy bear poke the big teddy, which stayed still and did not react. This sequence was repeated several times. I brought in another big teddy and asked, "Who is this?" "Mommy," said Kerry. The little teddy kept poking the first big teddy. "What will Mommy do?" I asked. "Lone, alone," said Kerry. After what seemed like interminable poking, the first big teddy (Daddy?) made a loud noise and started to hit the little teddy. Kerry smiled. "Good, good," she said.

Jack played at a more advanced level. He created a doll family with puppets. A big doll hit a truck. He was badly hurt and could not move. Jack thought that the truck had hit his legs. The doll mother would not or could not talk. Jack thought that the truck had maybe hit her too. Maybe it had hit her mouth. The little boy in Jack's made-up family didn't know what to do. He couldn't go to bed. What if a robber came? His father couldn't do anything; his mother couldn't say anything. The little boy puppet got up and stood by the window. Eventually, I persuaded the puppet to go back to bed. I taught Jack a lullaby and we sang the puppet to sleep. Jack turned to me and said, "Move, move, talk, talk." (I wondered if I was being asked to be both mother and father.) Finally the little boy puppet fell asleep. I took out a pen that I called my dream machine, which allowed us to look into the puppet's head. I showed Jack how to place it on the sleeping toy. Jack announced that the little boy was dreaming of a monster with a big mouth. It would tear up, eat up the little boy. I asked how the boy felt. "Scared," was the reply. "Let's get help," I suggested. "Shall I get a daddy?" "Daddy can't, he's hurt," said Jack. "I'll get a mommy," I suggested. "Mommy can't," said Jack. "Why?" I asked. "Mommy can't," he repeated. Then Jack had the little boy awaken, go over to another puppet, and hit him. Then the daddy moved his arm to hit the boy. "Is the boy still scared?" I asked. "No," beamed Jack. "Daddy better."

Robby played on the most advanced level. His was also a family scene. Robby's puppet family had a lot of trouble. The parents were both sick, and Robby told me that their mothers were to blame. Mother's mother had hit her on the head and made her sick; father's mother had fed him something bad and that had made him sick. The mother's ailment rendered her incapable of doing anything, and the father's condition was even more serious. Because of the parents' illnesses, the children had to be very quiet and do all the work in the household. The affective tone of the play was very grim.

I introduced a television reporter from "Sesame Street" into the play, using a puppet, to help Robby reflect on the action. He had come to do a report on this unusual family where the children took care of the parents and had to be quiet all the time. (Robby told me that he had seen "Sesame Street" at a friend's house; the T. family did not have a television set. Robby said it would be nice if they had one because his dad, who must rest, would like to watch it.) When the play resumed, Robby had one of the little children begin to cry. A bigger child went over to comfort his sister. "Daddy, Daddy," Robby had her wail. "You know Daddy is sick," the bigger boy told her. "I will take care of you. Don't be sad." Then Robby had the little girl hit her brother. He started to laugh and told me he could see all the children smile. "They are saying, 'good,'" he told me. I expressed surprise. "Is it good to hit?" I asked. Robby grinned at me and said, "When we hit, then Dad hits us. Then we have a daddy." "And the rest of the time?" I asked Robby. The little boy stared at the floor. He looked very sad indeed.

This play material is, of course, not analytic. It was elaborated in a diagnostic format designed primarily to elicit information regarding the children's safety and secondarily to foster the development of a plan to aid the entire family. Nevertheless, each child's play style does tell us much about his or her most pressing individual conflicts. The play scenarios seem closely related to reality concerns as they might be conceptualized by an outside observer. The variation from one child to the next is more in the realm of causation—theory making—than in the basic dilemma depicted. Moreover, in our cursory diagnostic examination, the children were neither invited, nor did they attempt, to evolve the play beyond their most pressing real-life concerns.

After our initial interventions, which were aimed at assisting the family, decreasing the beatings, and simultaneously arranging in-home care for all five family members, each of the children entered an individual treatment situation. Mr. T. died six months after our plan went into effect, and despite serious consideration by the responsible authorities of the recommendation that the children remain together, they were separated and each went to a different new home. Their individual treatments continued for about six months following the relocations and ceased thereafter. The boys' therapists, who were not child analysts, reported that the two, seen separately, played out age-appropriate cops-and-robbers scenarios and seemed to be concerned with aggressive themes and matters of right and wrong. Kerry's therapist stated that the little girl displayed the disturbing symptom of pinching herself with resultant ecchymoses. In contrast to her play facility during the diagnostic workup, she did not play and was often withdrawn and difficult to reach in the therapeutic situation.

I was able to monitor the ongoing experiences of the children, albeit distantly, through the good offices of the Department of Social Services, which held their guardianship. It was through this channel that Kerry, who had been adopted by a concerned family, came to me at age six. Similarly,

I was able to assist the two boys, Jack and Robby, in finding child analytic placement.

Kerry's new parents introduced her to me by stating that she was a great success in school but seemed miserable at home. She pinched herself frequently, was quiet and withdrawn, and did not seem to want to have anything to do with their two older children, a boy and a girl, both also adopted, who kept reaching out to their new sister. The parents were also concerned about her extreme politeness. "If only she would have a tantrum or just cry," her adoptive mother said. "They love her in school because she is so good and compliant, but we see this as a liability, not a strength."

Kerry did not appear to recognize me when we met. She was indeed a picture of great sadness, with many visible black-and-blue marks, and of doll-like obedience and compliance. She waited for directions before taking any action and then repeated what had been said to make sure that she got it right. After five or six meetings with me, she began to explore my play cupboard. She took out some teddy bears, not the same ones that she had used at the hospital some four years earlier, and initiated an interaction between two of the bears. One bear did something to the other. The second bear screamed. The first bear laughed. Kerry had a hard-to-decipher look on her face and played on. The two bears were given names: Abra and Kadabra. It was established that they were both girls. In the second week of the analysis, I was asked to "do it to Kadabra." In response to the query, "Do what?" Kerry tried to take my foot and smash it down on Kadabra. I attempted, probably unwisely, to explore this scenario rather than to enact it. Why should Abra do this? What was Kadabra thinking, feeling, wanting? Kerry continued, "Do it!" and substituted Abra as the doer when I did not comply with her request.

The play did not seem to move forward. The sequences were repeated without any deepening of insight or understanding, and my attempts to question their meaning were not productive. Eventually Kerry began to look ever grimmer and to pinch herself during the hours. This alarmed me, but it seemed to calm her in much the same way as the father's beatings or threats of beatings had a calming effect during the diagnostic interviews. The child then wondered if I would pinch her. I declined and asked if I should "do it to Kadabra." "Yes, yes," Kerry responded. "But what is 'doing it'?" was my next question. Kerry proceeded to stomp on Kadabra, causing the teddy to scream, just as had occurred in the initial analytic play sequence. She then touched (gently) my foot, clearly guiding it into stomping position. I allowed my foot to be so guided. Kadabra was stomped upon and once again screamed. Over the next several months, this play expanded significantly. It appeared that the partially displaced mutual enactment was required before further elaboration was possible. It is important to note that Kerry moved from the request that I do it to Kadabra, to allowing Abra to do it, to doing it to herself, to asking me to do it to her, to redoing it to Kadabra, and then to requesting again by physical gestures that I do it to the bear.

What was happening and what kind of play was this? The child allowed me to do what needed to be done to the bear rather than to her, but she insisted that I actually "do it." Could I have forestalled this event by an interpretation? Should it have been forestalled? I think that the answer to the first question is probably yes, and the answer to the second question is probably no.

It is possible that I could have posed questions or offered possible meanings of the request and attendant play that would have interrupted the ongoing process. If my thoughts about the origins of enactment in the play process and their interactive component possess validity, then my acquiescence facilitated the subsequent playing out of material—not only deepening it but also elaborating the modes by which it could be expressed and thus become accessible to consciousness and to analysis. I realize that as the analyst, I must abstain from most forms of requested gratification for ethical and technical reasons. I am positing, however, that this kind of pressure for mutual enactment represents a frequently encountered and repetitively experienced aspect of some children's play repertoire. It is always imperative to explore the meanings of the request, though it does not disappear by interpretation alone. Its origins, as in the case of the T. children, are often tragically apparent. Yet it is sometimes necessary to decline outright, as in requests to touch, hurt, and so on. But it is also often possible to accede, to enact in displacement, to "do it," and thereby allow the material to flow and the process of exploration to continue.

Material from the separate analyses of Jack and Robby came to me in a more indirect fashion. Jack's analysis began when he was seven and a half and lasted for three years. His female analyst communicated with me only after the treatment had been completed. She described an active, affable boy who suffered from nightmares and exhibited provocative behavior toward male classmates at school.

In the analytic situation, he had elaborated syntactical play, which the analyst understood to be primarily oedipal. In a variety of forms its focus had revolved around overcoming the father, winning the mother, and then fearing castrative retribution. Interpretation of this dynamic constellation and subsequent working through had proven ameliorative, according to the analyst. I wondered if there had been much enactment or press for particular interactive participation in the analysis. Jack's therapist reported that the play and discussion would occasionally be interrupted by an upsurge of tremendous depressive affect. Attempts to explore or to interpret these occurrences produced neither clarification nor resolution. On one such occasion, while in the grips of this "awful feeling," Jack had come over to hug his therapist. Somewhat to her surprise, but eventually with comfort, the analyst returned the hug. Following this "parameter," Jack's behavior in school improved dramatically.

With appropriate reserve reflecting my distance from the primary analytic data, I speculate that the analyst is describing a press for interactive enactment (mutual enactment) emanating from Jack and eliciting a "necessary response" from her. Jack does not "insist" that his analyst do something in displacement. Rather, a recurrent, refractory, affective state is eventually discharged in action, and the analyst finds herself "going along with it." Apparently, the important play that took place within the analysis did not lead to a deepening of the exploratory and reconstructive processes (although it may have happened and was just not shared in the postanalytic communication), but there was a dramatic and decisive change in Jack's behavior.

Robby entered analysis at age ten. Like his brother, he lived in a city different from the one where he had grown up. His difficulties seemed to be primarily in learning; he had particular troubles in maintaining a narrative. He apparently experienced a kind of blackout or absence, which led to his being worked up for petit mal and then receiving the diagnosis of attention deficit disorder and being started on Ritalin. Failure to improve after a trial of pharmacotherapy led to referral to a child analyst and to a subsequent four-year treatment. Robby's analyst contacted me during the treatment, but, to the best of my knowledge, I did not influence the analytic process while it was underway.

Robby complained bitterly to his analyst about his "blackouts," and the two of them set out to understand them. An early play mode involved some shenanigans of Big Bird and Mr. Hooper. (The "Sesame Street" motif reappeared, but now in the play of a ten-year-old.) Robby asked his analyst to play the role of Mr. Hooper, who was portrayed as warm, loving, and supportive. He never became upset with Big Bird. The shenanigans appeared to be quasi-aggressive, quasi-sexual attacks or forays that always "knocked the wind out of Mr. Hooper." These scenes were played over and over again. Mr. Hooper survived in contrast to events on the actual television program. The analyst participated in his assigned role while trying to learn more about the shenanigans.

During the play Robby often asked questions such as what time it was. When the analyst answered either by exploring the meaning of the question or by answering it forthrightly, Robby blacked out. He would not or could not or did not hear the analyst's reply. In the second year of their work, Robby began to observe that the blackouts occurred only when he and the analyst conversed, not while they were "playing." "It has to be with you," he stated. "Aren't we together when we are playing?" the analyst inquired. "It's not the same," was the boy's reply.

In the third year of the analysis, Robby asked the analyst to call out, "I'm here, I'm here," when the blackouts occurred. This was explored for a long time. Various substitutions were attempted, and eventually the analyst complied. There was no symptomatic relief, but Robby was "very happy."

The "Sesame Street" play was resumed after a long hiatus, and it was learned that Big Bird was enraged at Mr. Hooper for smoking cigarettes, which was bad for a bird's breathing. In his direct interaction with the analyst, Robby now began to ask for a new behavior: would the analyst take his hand if he reached out to him during a blackout? Once again the request was explored and attempts were made to displace and to understand. The analyst even suggested that Robby was longing for someone who was no longer there and that the blackouts were, quite literally, exactly that— the blocking or blacking out of a very sad feeling, the feeling of loss. Just as before, Robby could not hear. His blackouts increased in frequency and duration, and he began reaching out to the analyst. One day (Casement's paper [1982] notwithstanding) the analyst took Robby's extended hand and held it. In the next hour the play reverted to displacement, and Mr. Hooper died. The analysis concluded the following year. The blackouts had been understood and no longer occurred either at school or in the treatment hours. It was necessary that the analyst and Robby physically connect, as Robby and his father had done much earlier. There were no further presses for interactive enactment.

Kerry's analysis, which lasted for three years, featured subsequent requests for me to "do it." At first these were all in the displacement mode— that I stomp on a play character—but then they overflowed into real life. Kerry wanted me to stomp on a classmate who was annoying her. Together analyst and analysand learned about the offending Samantha. I was assigned the role of Herlock Homes; the name was less suggestive of "Sherlock" than of being "locked out of her home." During this time, Kerry's agitation and distress were very great. She berated me for my unwillingness to stomp on

Samantha. She clearly recalled the episodes with Abra and Kadabra but made no connection. She felt miserable.

Eventually, to the accompaniment of several self-attacks and a few swipes at me, she changed my name first to Furrock Homes and then to Kick Out Kid. Kick Out Kid was asked to kick Sam, another classmate, in the pants, again and again. Kick Out Kid, now represented by a doll, did this to another doll named Sam, and it became clear that it both delighted and terrified Sam. The play led to the analysis of a number of sexual and aggressive fantasies that appeared to be linked to the original "sadomasochistic" sibling play in the T. family and to our understanding why Sam had been incorporated into the analysis. At the conclusion of this phase of the analysis, it appeared that the capacity to tolerate painful affect and to explore earlier formulations in displacement were developing.

Discussion

The depth of material available from these three cases varies greatly. In each, however, the emergence and handling of the press for interactive, or mutual enactment as one form of play can be detected. What is this press? What are its origins? How ubiquitous is it in children—in children in analysis? What are the implications for understanding it and handling it technically within the child analytic situation?

I have chosen to present the T. family and to describe the presence of what I am calling mutual, or interactive enactment in each of the children's analyses because of the unique opportunity afforded by prior contact with this family and an ongoing tracking of each child's analysis. It would appear that some aspect of each of the children's experiences or of their shared experience might be involved in the genesis of, maintenance of, or necessity for the mutual enactment mode in their analytic play.

Much has been written about the role of trauma in psychological development (Furman, 1986; Kennedy, 1986; Yorke, 1986). For the purposes of this discussion, I should like to suggest that trauma occurs when what actually happens or does not happen overwhelms the ego's capacity to play—to try on, take off, orchestrate, and reorchestrate, changing both key and meter at will. The presence of trauma, so defined, can be seen either retrospectively or pari passu to coopt the play function, as in the case of the T. children, in the early diagnostic interviews—or to deform the play function as in a "shift to the left," namely, from displacement to enactment to an obligatory mutual enactment. This "shift to the left" may be conceptualized as a regression in an ego function that is the reciprocal of the original developmental sequence.

It is immediately obvious that the pervasiveness of the play interruption and the overwhelming of that function in the three children are not totally apparent by observing their initial play styles or capacities. Nor is it solely a function of their individual developmental positions before and including the loss of their father and the separation of the siblings. More information about the nature of the trauma for each emerges in the analytic situation; but here, too, it can be seen that what is learned is deeply affected by the combination of what comes from the child and how it is regarded, understood, and responded to by the analyst. In terms of what is often called the widening scope of analysis, it might also be noted that Jack's treatment did not seem to focus so much on his earlier life experiences, whereas the work with Robby and Kerry could not steer clear of them even if the analysts had been so inclined.

In a number of earlier publications (Herzog, 1984, 1985, 1988), I have considered maternal and paternal play styles with infants and toddlers in the second year of life as possibly pertinent to evolving modes of experiencing affect, sensation, and interaction. I am inclined to wonder further about the father's role, his particular use of disruptively attuned, nonmatching play, as a provider of gear shifting and intense affect experiences in the construction of a part of the ego's capacity to roll with the punches, specifically, to resist the overwhelming, interrupting, traumatizing intrusion of actual hyperstimulation or hypostimulation on the play function. Might it be useful to consider that the paternal rough-and-tumble play mode might also allow experience with disruption against a maternally provided background safe enough to prevent the experience of what Winnicott (1971, 1974) called an "interruption of its going on being"? That the father's mode of interacting in play with his child might help to construct a protective shield against traumatogenesis is a way of stating this proposition. Were this hypothesis to be further elaborated and explored, it might lead to a nosology of paternal-child play repertoires that could be implicated in susceptibility to traumatic play disruption and to subsequent patterns and deformations (pathologies?) in each child's play.

Mr. T.'s capacity to participate in rough-and-tumble play with his children was severely constrained and sometimes nonexistent. He could not provide experience with the intense affect paradigm, with gear shifting, and with the experience of asking his children to match his style rather than his matching theirs. When he was roused to interaction with them, it was to strike them with his belt, an experience that must have elicited a wide range of responses in both the somatosensory and associational (meaning) areas of both brain and mind. The children were thus deprived not only of the normal paternal contribution through play of affect modulation and perspective shifting but also of the establishment of a zone of comfort with disruption and derailment that is posited to act as a protection against trauma.

Mrs. T.'s contribution is equally pertinent. Her lack of "homeostatically attuned" (Herzog, 1984) maternal interaction deprived the children of the "background of safety" (Sandler, 1960) against which the father's more active and disrupting play style could be profitably juxtaposed.

I hypothesize that these factors—the maternal deficiency, the lack of "disruptively attuned paternal play," and the desired but painful repetitive beating by the father—combined to lead to the occurrence of trauma, namely, the overwhelming and disrupting of the play function and then its subsequent deformation, the shift to the left, and the press for mutual enactment. Pathogenesis and play deformation can be seen to develop as two sides of the same coin.

In every child analysis, and in most if not every adult analysis, displacement, enactment, and some press to mutual enactment and the defenses against each are encountered. In the analysis of children, where the play mode involves physical action as well as verbal play, it is particularly easy to identify these modes and to study the analyst's role in conceptualizing, utilizing, exploring, rejecting, modifying, and accepting each of them. The analytic situation as *Spielraum* then becomes a place in which the ego function of play both reveals the prehistory by which it has been shaped and reshaped and invites opportunity for repair through repetition, alteration, formulation, and interpretation. The individual's developmental line of personal meaning can be reconstructed not only by analyzing the meaning(s) of that which is played out but also by studying the modes of play encountered and the necessity for the individual child to do, redo, do differently. The work, then, involves not only mourning the losses of the past in fantasy and in fact but also assaying the state of the play function itself. The intertwining of traumatic deformation of the play function with subsequent press for interactive (mutual) enactment and concomitant experience in object relations and the vicissitudes of drive endowment and discharge opportunity all contribute to a particular constellation of adaptations, defensive patternings, and psychopathological equilibria. Whether this ego function, play, can be restored to fuller capacity or not, and if restored, how it still features its antecedent course, may be debated by those of differing theoretical or technical persuasions. The child's persistence and the very nature of the play function at least compel us to ask the question and to note that reversibility and alteration are built into the function even when developmental arrest has occurred. Thus, careful attention to play modes encountered in the child analytic situation may aid the analyst in conceptualizing pathogenesis, analytic technique, and therapeutic action.

References

Casement, P. (1982). Some pressures on the analyst for physical contact during the reliving of an early trauma. *Int. Rev. Psychoanal.*, 9:279–286.

Furman, E. (1986). On trauma: When is the death of a parent traumatic? *Psychoanal. Study Child*, 41:191–208.

Herzog, J. M. (1984). Fathers and young children: Fathering daughters and fathering sons. In *Frontiers of Infant Psychiatry*, ed. J. Call, E. Galenson, and R. Tyson. New York: Basic Books, 2:335–343.

———. (1985). Suffering, perception, and adaptation. *Int. J. Family Psychiat.*, 6:275–284.

———. (1986). So sad you'd think the world was about to end: Perceptions of and adaptations to suffering in three preschool children, zero to three. *Bull. Nat. Cent. Clin. Infant Programs*, 6:6–10.

———. (1988). Preoedipal Oedipus: The father child dialogue. In *The Oedipus Papers*, ed. G. H. Pollock and J. M. Ross. Madison, Conn.: Int. Univ. Press, pp. 475–493.

———. (1990). Trauma and creativity. Presented to the "Psychoanalysis and Culture Seminar," Harvard University, Cambridge, Mass.

Kennedy, H. (1986). Trauma in childhood. *Psychoanal. Study Child*, 41:209–219.

Ritvo, S. (1985). Personal communication.

Sandler, J. (1960). The background of safety. *Int. J. Psychoanal.*, 41:352–356.

Winnicott, D. W. (1971). *Playing and Reality*. New York: Basic Books.

———. (1974). Fear of breakdown. *Int. Rev. Psychoanal.*, 1:103–107.

Yorke, C. (1986). Reflections on the problem of psychic trauma. *Psychoanal. Study Child*, 41:221–236.

17

Childhood Play and Adult Life

Martin S. Bergmann, M.D.

Man is made of God's playing and that is the best part of him. Therefore
men and women should live life accordingly and play the noblest games.
—Plato, *Laws*

All the world's a stage
And all the men and women merely players:
They have their exits and their entrances;
And one man in his time plays many parts.
—Shakespeare, *As You Like It*

At a specific point in the child's development the term *make-believe* becomes
significant. It is a wonderful term, to my knowledge not found in other
languages. It connotes an activity that achieves a temporary suspension of
disbelief without endangering the capacity of the ego to test reality. In
adult life this capacity leads to our enjoyment of the theater. Kris (1943)
called this "regression under the control of the ego." It matters a great
deal whether the realm of make-believe is separated from what children
know to be real and whether it is associated with pleasure. Only then can
children make full use of the human capacity for symbolization. They can
relive what has disturbed them without being overwhelmed once more by
the trauma.

To the child's therapist, play offers two ways of intervention. The
analyst can interpret the play by telling the child in secondary process
language what the symbolic meaning of the play is. Or he or she can enter
the play and suggest modifications within the play itself. Ekstein (1954)
called this type of intervention "interpretation within the metaphor." Many
disturbed children who cannot respond to interpretations can accept them
when they are made "within the metaphor." A rereading of Berta Bornstein's (1949) classic Frankie case suggests to me that she might have been
more effective with her young patient had she entered into his hospital

This chapter was a paper read at the Division of Psychoanalysis (39), American
Psychological Spring Meeting, Chicago, April 10–14, 1991.

play where mother and children got burned rather than attempted to interpret the play to him.

Psychoanalysts are particularly sensitive to this point in development because, as Loewald (1979) has pointed out, the analytic relationship has a close relationship to play: "it seems to exist for its own sake and at the same time to be a rehearsal for real life" (p. 156). To undergo psychoanalysis, the analysand must be capable of participating in the analytic process, at the same time remaining aware that transference has a make-believe aspect.

Play and Work

After latency sets in, the capacity to play gradually fades. Rule-governed games replace the free play of earlier childhood. The games of latency children increasingly become adaptations to reality. Anyone who has played checkers or chess with children during the latency period will have noticed how tempted they are to move their figures in ways other than prescribed and how often they cheat. These tendencies represent a difficulty in transition from the realm of fantasy to the world of reality.

Unlike play, work requires a greater capacity to function according to the reality principle. The first five years can be considered the years of play, but after school begins, the area of work increasingly takes on a greater significance. We obtain evidence that the transition has not been successful when learning disabilities set in or the child is unable to concentrate or has a short attention span. Reports of analysands who have these difficulties usually indicate that psychologically they were not engaged in the school activity, but as a rule they cannot tell us about the fantasies they had. We surmise that in such children the capacity to fantasize was not conscious.

I must add, however, that fantasy is not as a rule absent from work. We know how important it is for many students that they are their teacher's favorite and how relationships to other children are governed by sibling rivalry. We also know how frequently oedipal fantasies are transferred to the workplace. But important differences remain. Work must yield a usable product. It has a coercive power by itself and disregards our wishes for pleasure. Nor can it be terminated at will like play.

Clinical Examples

How do we trace childhood play into adult life as related in clinical practice?

Case 1. The mother of a two-year-old son sought analysis for a variety of somatic complaints, phobic reactions, excessive drinking, and marital tension. What emerged in the course of the analysis was her inability to play with her child. She could minister to his bodily needs, but she could not play with him. She also recalled disliking the nursing experience and curtailing it as soon as possible. In the third year of her analysis she recalled the following dream: I am taking her out of the consultation room into a room full of boys' toys, trains, guns, and so on. As we are standing there, I begin to *play* with her breasts. She notices to her surprise that my advances are not as horrifying to her as she would have imagined and even to some extent are welcome. Associations to this dream revealed that the room was the room of her twin brother, a twin that she had felt was preferred by both her mother and her father.

The patient reconstructed her past as having been physically cared for by her mother and a housekeeper but was put into the playpen with her twin brother without anyone paying attention to them. A photograph existed in which the two of them were looking out of the playpen with a forlorn look. She did not believe that they ever succeeded in playing together; as far as her memory allowed, he played with guns and trains while she played with a dollhouse. For this patient, playing was associated with separation from the brother and the establishment of her own gender identity. Playing was a solitary activity associated with the pain of not being a boy.

In her adolescence, when the brother became rebellious, her own relationship to her father greatly improved and she became his favorite. She recalled envying her brother's toys, and we were able to connect her inability to play with her child to this early envy. As an adolescent she had won the love of her father, and my "playing" with her mitigated the envy. She herself did not "play" sexually with her husband, nor did he with her. The dream may have been a link between forgotten childhood play and her inhibited adult sexuality.

As an adult she was a lawyer by profession but awkward in company, relying on her husband for social contacts. I was impressed by the fact that the early failure to play with her brother reappeared in adulthood as an inability to initiate discourse as well as sexual relationships.

Analysis showed that the patient's husband was a displacement from the twin brother she envied and wished to control. She recalled feeding and putting her dolls to sleep, and indeed she was a more devoted mother than her own mother had been. In analysis her capacity to care continually for children markedly improved, but I was unable to confirm Kestenberg's observation (1968, p. 471) that the recovery of doll play heralded a change in sexual frigidity.

Among analysands who are also therapists and parents of young children we encounter the opposite problem. Fearful lest they block their child's future creativity, they permit play to encroach upon reality. They do not tell their children that there are conditions under which splashing of water is not allowed or that going to bed cannot always be treated like a game.

Case 2. A young woman had led a life of stern duty, spending her days in the library while other children played. Eventually she succumbed to depression and was helped out of it by an older man. They established both a sexual relationship and a partnership. Recalling the first year of this relationship, she spoke of it as a year of play. Whatever they did together was considered not work but play. The case suggests that in a state of being in love, with regression back to childhood, the dichotomy between work and play so characteristic of adult life is undone.

Case 3. A middle-aged, professionally successful man had difficulty in arriving at work on time. He was tempted to read science fiction instead of attending to his professional duties. He recently had bought a computer and was trying to master it. He felt interested in the computer only as long as it was a toy, but when it came to solving a problem he lost interest. Whenever he was not working, he felt he was "stealing time." As a child he was burdened by the need to take care of severely traumatized parents. He did not recall having had any toys or engaging in any childhood play. In the course of the analysis he recognized that when he was "stealing time," he was making up for lost opportunities to play during his childhood. It slowly dawned on us that the computer represented a toy he wanted to play with, not share it with others and not allow it to become a tool for work. Claude Shannon was his hero. He brought me the following excerpt from the January 1990 edition of *Scientific American:*

> Claude E. Shannon can't sit still. We're at his home, a stuccoed Victorian edifice overlooking a lake north of Boston, and I'm trying to get him to recall how he came up with the theory of information. But Shannon, who is a boyish 73, with an elfish grin and a shock of snowy hair, is tired of expounding on his past. Wouldn't I rather see his toys?
>
> Without waiting for an answer, and over the mild protest of his wife, Betty, he leaps from his chair and disappears into the other room. When I catch up with him, he proudly shows me his seven chess-playing machines, gasoline-powered pogostick, hundred-bladed jackknife, two-seated unicycle and countless other marvels. Some of his personal creations—such as a juggling W.C. Fields mannequin and a

computer called THROBAC that calculates in Roman numerals are a bit dusty and in disrepair, but Shannon seems as delighted with everything as a 10-year-old on Christmas morning.

My patient envied Shannon; he saw genius as never having to give up play in favor of work. It may well be that the high value we all assign to creativity is at least due in part to the fact that insofar as we are creative, we do not have to go through the painful process of giving up play in favor of work.

Case 4. A professionally successful woman had great difficulty in doing the paperwork necessary for billing. Other activities that dealt with numbers also caused extreme displeasure. The symptom was overdetermined, but one of the relevant issues was that dealing with figures represented reality without any fantasy compensations. She eventually found a way of doing these chores provided she could listen to music at the same time. The case illustrates the difficulty many have with an activity that is entirely devoid of pleasure or one that is undertaken only on behalf of the reality principle.

Other Cases. My next two samples are composites of a number of cases. They pertain to the problem of the regulation of leisure in the life of a couple. A woman said, "It's the baseball [or football] season. He's glued to the idiot-box yelling and screaming. You can't speak to him and sex is out of the question until the season is over." Another woman: "I like to go to museums and would love to go to Paris, but he hates museums with a passion and can't stand visiting a country where he doesn't speak the language, so it's back to the boring seashore. I know from experience that if I fight him on this point, we will stay in the city and there will be only work."

Here are basic differences in the way couples use their leisure. Leisure is the adult's area of play. Many couples settle the problem of how leisure is to be spent before their wedding, but there are circumstances in which the choice of the partner based on pressing intrapsychic needs cannot be determined by similarities of interest, and this factor becomes a source of marital difficulty only later. In common parlance, the term *toy* has undergone expansion. Computers, cameras, and even cars are referred to as *toys*. If the partner does not participate, the term *toy* is often used with derision.

Discussion

Psychoanalysts today are heirs to two traditions. One comes from Freud (1920) and was reemphasized by Anna Freud (1965). Here play is in the service of mastery. In this view the main difficulty many people have is in relinquishing play and its manifold satisfactions for work under the jurisdiction of the reality principle. The other tradition comes from Winnicott (1971), who emphasized that play is a precious possession in danger of being overwhelmed when the environment of the child is not responsive. In his view, play is the beginning of all creative capacities. One of the functions of the analyst is to help analysands who have lost the capacity to play regain it. These patients can work, but they cannot enjoy life outside of work. With the loss of the capacity to play the ability to enjoy leisure has also been curtailed. The cases I have presented show difficulties in both directions.

I am led to differentiate four types of problems that therapists encounter in the area of play and fantasy. In the first group are very disturbed patients who never developed the capacity to use symbols or who lost the capacity to differentiate between signifier and signified. Among those will be the children who never reached the capacity to play on a symbolic level. Survivors of concentration camps often reported the cessation of all fantasy life. With the abandonment of hope fantasy ceased.

In the second group are those who repressed fantasy in their childhood and who, in order not to recognize the amount of hostility directed at them from their caretakers, repressed fantasies in favor of a monotonous existence. It is in this category that I would place those patients—often but not necessarily always perverse—whose sexual activity has a rigid form from which no deviations are allowed.

In the third group I would place those who function in real life, but reality pales in comparison to the world of fantasy. They must continually sacrifice possible real satisfactions to fantasy satisfactions.

In the fourth group are the healthy, who do not fear their fantasies and yet are not unduly dominated by them; by their capacity to use symbols, they can maintain a connection between the unconscious and the rest of their personality. In this group I would expect to find a capacity to use humor that is not a disguise for aggressive wishes.

Fantasy

One of Freud's important contributions to the understanding of human nature was the awareness of the difficulty with which humanity makes the transition from the pleasure principle to the reality principle. The change takes place slowly, painfully, and incompletely. If we are better psychologists than the thinkers of the nineteenth century, it is due in no small measure to our understanding of the equilibria and disequilibria that take place in most people in their struggle between the pull of fantasy life and the push of reality pressures. As early as 1908, Freud noted that fantasies proceed from deprivation and longing. He observed that such fantasies can become unconscious; and once unconscious, they become pathogenic and find expression in symptoms. Such unconscious fantasies have a close relation to the sexual life and provide sexual satisfaction during masturbation.

Arlow (1969a), continuing Freud's trend of thought, concluded: "In one part of our mind we are daydreaming all the time, or at least all the time we are awake and a good deal of the time we are asleep. . . . Every instinctual fixation is represented at some level of mental life or by a group of unconscious fantasies" (pp. 5–6). In another paper (1969b) Arlow suggested that the outside world conveys to us a continuous screen of perceptual data, but at the same time another screen passes before our inner eye from our inner world. Because both coexist, outside reality can often be misinterpreted by the pressure of inner reality.

In discussing fantasy we face the same problem we encountered when I discussed play. At what level of development should we speak of fantasy? Must the child know the difference between fantasy and reality before we call his or her activity fantasizing? Melanie Klein and her followers such as Susan Isaacs (1948) and Joan Riviere (1936) speak of infants as fantasizing. At that stage they are clearly not capable of differentiating between fantasy and reality.

I would like to follow the lead of Sandler (1963, 1970), who emphasized that to deserve its name fantasy can only take place through the intervention of the ego. Only the ego can differentiate fantasy from hallucination. This differentiation is relevant not only for the Kleinian concept but also for Arlow's concept of unconscious fantasy. As long as the fantasy is unconscious, no differentiation takes place between fantasizing and hallucinating. Only when the fantasy is made conscious and the powers of the ego are brought to bear upon it can an individual accept that some images are memories and others only fantasy. Clinical experience teaches us daily how painful it is to recognize that what is psychically real can nevertheless be a fantasy.

Along the same lines Sandler (1970) indicates that the sexual fantasies of children are not really fantasies but beliefs. When they undergo repression, as Freud had discovered, they retain in the unconscious the status of belief. Only when they emerge from the unconscious can they be worked over in such a way that the ego accepts, and then forces the id to accept, that these are fantasies and not reflections of reality.

Although the typical analysand's fantasies are connected with current or future wishes, this need not always be the case. I am familiar with a patient in whom narcissistic injuries played an unusual role: all his fantasies were directed toward the past. Typically he would recall a situation in which he behaved in a cowardly fashion or was rejected by a woman, and rework it to give it a happy ending. If this process is successful, it transforms painful memories into screen memories. Nietzsche's dictum, "Yes says my memory, no says my pride; my pride wins," is relevant here.

I recall a patient who had the fantasy that he would win a Nobel Prize. It took a great deal of work for both of us to realize that though in deference to me and the reality principle he called it a fantasy, it was in fact a belief. He expected to be treated by me and his coworkers as if he had already won the prize.

Neither Freud nor Arlow drew a sharp line of demarcation between fantasy and imagination. But to Winnicott fantasy is sterile, whereas dream and play and imagination are productive. An account by the Portuguese poet Fernando Pessoa throws light on this difference:

> I have always, since a child, had the compulsion to augment the world with fictitious personalities, dreams of mine rigorously constructed, visualized with photographic clarity, understood right into their souls. I was only five years old when already, as an isolated child who wanted only to be so, I used to take as my companions various figures from my dreaming—one Captain Thibeaut, one Chevalier de Pas—and others whom I have now forgotten, whose forgetting, like my imperfect recollection of those two, is one of the great regrets of my life.
>
> This looks like simply the kind of childish imagination which amuses itself by attributing life to dolls. But it was more: I did not need any dolls to help me conceive those figures intensely. Clear and visible in my constant dreaming, realities precisely human to me—any doll, being unreal, would have spoiled them. They were people.
>
> What is more, this tendency did not go away with childhood. It developed in adolescence, took root as that grew, became finally the natural form of my spirit. Today I have no personality: all that is human in me I have divided among the various authors of whose work I have been the executant. I am today the point of reunion of a small humanity which is only mine. (Gibbons, 1979, p. 10)

To judge from this excerpt, imagination is not only more intense than fantasy but also populated with people. To imagine is to have an object relationship, albeit a purely internal one. This capacity must be developed not only among artists but among those who read fiction for pleasure, listen to music, or go to a museum; in fact it may well be the bridge between the play of childhood and the creativity of adults.

References

Arlow, J. A. (1969a). Unconscious fantasy and conscious experience. *Psychoanal. Q.*, 38:1–27.

––––––. (1969b). Fantasy, memory and reality testing. *Psychoanal. Q.*, 38:28–50.

Bornstein, B. (1949). The analysis of a phobic child. *Psychoanal. Study Child*, 3–4:181–226.

Ekstein, R. (1954). The space child's time machine. *Amer. J. Orthopsychiat.*, 24:492–506.

Freud, A. (1965). *Normality and Pathology in Childhood*. New York: Int. Univ. Press.

Freud, S. (1908). Hysterical phantasies and their relation to bisexuality. *S.E.*, 9:155–166.

––––––. (1920). Beyond the pleasure principle. *S.E.*, 18:3–64.

Gibbon, R. (1979). *The Poet's Work*. Boston: Houghton Mifflin.

Isaacs, S. (1948). The nature and function of phantasy. *Int. J. Psychoanal.*, 29:73–97.

Kestenberg, J. S. (1968). Outside and inside, male and female. *J. Amer. Psychoanal. Assn.*, 16:457–520.

Kris, E. (1943). Some problems of war propaganda. In *The Selected Papers of Ernst Kris*. New Haven: Yale Univ. Press, 1975, pp. 433–450.

Loewald, H. W. (1977). Reflections on the psychoanalytic process. *Psychoanal. Study Child*, 34:155–167.

Riviere, J. (1936). On the genesis of psychical conflict in earliest infancy. *Int. J. Psychoanal.*, 17:395–422.

Sandler, J. (1970). Sexual fantasies and sexual theories. In *From Safety to Superego*. New York: Guilford Press.

Sandler, J., and Nagera, H. (1963). *The Metapsychology of Fantasy*. New York: Guilford Press.

Winnicott, D. W. (1971). *Playing and Reality*. London: Tavistock Publications.

18

Aggressivity in Play: Discussions with Oedipal Children

Steven Marans, M.S.W.

E. Kirsten Dahl, Ph.D.

Wendy Marans, M.Sc.

Donald J. Cohen, M.D.

Aggressivity denotes hostile or destructive actions that attack, hurt, damage, or destroy persons or things. In this chapter we do not attempt to link these observed behaviors to notions about underlying drives, or to tackle the larger theoretical issues concerning aggression that destroys versus aggression that binds or contributes to structure building. Nor do we deal with the treatment of children who come into psychoanalysis because of destructive and oppositional behavior that is typically described as "aggressive" in nature. Instead, we focus on ways in which aggressivity is represented in the child psychoanalytic playroom through language, narrative structures, and play transformations. These surface presentations are markers for, but not isomorphic with, mechanisms that include inner representations and fantasies. In a previous paper (Cohen et al., 1987) we focused on the libidinal aspects of the oedipal phase; in this chapter, we ask: what can be understood about the child's inner world through an examination of these surface presentations, both direct and transformed, of destructive aggression? Are there common elements, themes, and dilemmas as well as characteristic modes of presentation for the "normal" oedipal boy? If so, what is the range of individual variation?

Methodology

As we described in a previous paper (Cohen et al., 1987), twenty children, about five years old, were recruited from a nursery school for a study of children's play during a clinical interview. Each child attended three forty-five minute play sessions with child analysts who knew nothing about the child's history, background, or developmental status. The sessions were videotaped from behind a one-way mirror and transcribed; videotapes and transcriptions were then examined by the research team, composed of five child analysts and a communications/language specialist. The interviews were analyzed for manifest and latent themes; the construction of the hour was assessed along behavioral, linguistic, and narrative lines.

Although specific presentations of aggressive components varied with the individual child, a number of shared characteristics were apparent. Themes of bodily damage, transformations of the body, and issues of "good" and "bad"; the use of the analyst; sites of displacement; specific language patterns—all emerged as modes of representing aggressivity. Most striking were the boys' attitudes toward their own aggressivity. Each boy relied on a moral construct that operated on the basis of external consequences. There was nothing inherently "bad" or "immoral" about their destructive urges as long as they did not suffer the retaliation of the objects of their aggressivity. Each boy's pleasure in attacking and destroying was matched only by the wariness about what danger he might incur as a result. In order to illustrate these, we will first describe the second research sessions of three five-year-old boys. The second sessions of the series of three were chosen for closer examination because of the relative familiarity of the child with the analyst in the absence of an impending dissolution of this new relationship. Following the descriptions of individual sessions, we will discuss central characteristics of each of the boys and comparisons of the findings.

The three boys, Bobby, Eddy, and Jim, were all five years old, but demonstrated in their play three very different approaches to the presentation of aggressivity.

Bobby told a very coherent story in which his aggression was presented as a highly controlled and justified response to dangers coming from the outside. His story emphasized the harmonious male dyad in which the partners were equal and good; he used himself and the analyst to play the central characters.

Eddy played a series of rapidly shifting stories in which the body and bodily transformations were central themes; in his play the body continually threatened, but the danger was warded off through the construction of larger than life characters. Eddy's operative assumption seemed to be that it was all right to be aggressive as long as you were punished for it. Eddy controlled the analyst, either keeping him outside the play as audience or using him to carry out Eddy's commands.

Jim's play was the most fragmented and unsustained of the three. His play contained eight consecutive sequences in which the theme was his wish to be powerfully destructive and his fear that the expression of the wish would inevitably bring retaliatory injury and punishment. Jim seemed to feel continually threatened from within and without by his aggressive urges. Although directly threatening and attacking the analyst during his play, he viewed the analyst as a powerfully dangerous punisher of his aggressive wishes.

Clinical Material
Bobby

Bobby held onto his father's hand, maintaining physical and verbal contact with him for the first four minutes of his second play session; during this time Bobby spoke in a low voice to his father about various play materials. He then looked at the analyst for the first time and announced, "I still remember what we were playing last week." In a whisper, Bobby told his father that he and the analyst had played robbers. (They had, in fact, built a bank out of cardboard blocks and had protected some play money given to Bobby by his father by shooting at imaginary robbers.) Bobby then picked up a toy eggbeater and warned the analyst of the dangers of "someone's shirt getting caught in it." When the father left, Bobby continued his commentary on the eggbeater. Suddenly Bobby reminded the analyst: "We weren't finished with the game" from last week. Instead of returning to the theme of robbers, however, Bobby found a second eggbeater, compared the sizes of the two, and suggested that the analyst could use the larger one. Moments later Bobby again reminded the analyst of the shooting game of the previous session, but turned instead to a four-minute play sequence of cooking a meal; he maintained a running commentary on the relative sizes of various pots and pans, making sure these were equally divided between the analyst and himself. This cooking sequence came to an abrupt end when Bobby, searching for more cookware, looked over at the building blocks and announced, "Oh, here's the shooting place."

For the next five minutes, Bobby was busy rebuilding the bank. In contrast to the cooking sequence, Bobby was not satisfied unless the analyst was actively involved in his preparations. As he built the protective wall, he asked the analyst, "Aren't you going to help me?" and described all the preparations for the shooting play in terms of "we"—what he and the analyst needed to do together. Bobby was pleased to find the gun he had used the previous week but then warned the analyst about its potential dangers. As he put his gun into his back pocket, he explained, "We'd better not put guns in our pockets because you might shoot and go right through the pants." Although Bobby assigned the analyst and himself positions behind the protective wall, he seemed uncertain about how actually to enter into the shooting action of the game. After several moments of aimless movement as he talked about the play, Bobby abandoned the story line. The carefully built fortress was turned into a house in which Bobby and the analyst were to cook a meal together.

In the middle of the second cooking sequence, Bobby discovered the second gun and exclaimed excitedly, "Now we both have guns!" and he invited the analyst to return with him to the story about shooting the robbers. Bobby explained that he had better put away the eating utensils quickly because "we're being robbed." At this point Bobby once again insisted on the analyst's active participation, and they both hunkered down on the floor behind the protective wall. Bobby explained that the robbers wanted their money and that the analyst better start shooting or he would get shot.

The shooting game, lasting thirteen minutes, constituted the longest play sequence in this session. The theme of big and little, seen in the earlier cooking sequences, was now expressed in the context of power and safety. Bobby explained to the analyst that they could not use their fingers because "fingers don't shoot anything." With gun in hand, however, Bobby quickly "ran out of bullets." In an apparent effort to maintain parity with the analyst, he suggested, "I think you ran out of bullets, too." A remedy was found when Bobby discovered that he not only had extra bullets, but they were also special "blowing-up bullets"; he shot one of the robbers who then blew up. Throughout the shooting, Bobby continued to run out of ammunition, each time discovering increasingly greater supplies, the destructive potential of which grew exponentially. When the analyst commented on how powerful his gun was, Bobby suggested they take a brief break from the shooting; he reported that most of the robbers got killed but added, "I think my arm got shot." Again, maintaining equality, he proposed that both he and the analyst had sustained the same kind of wound. When the analyst pointed out how dangerous the robbers were, Bobby agreed, referring to his diminished supply of ammunition.

Throughout the shooting sequence, Bobby compensated for danger and vulnerability by introducing increasingly powerful armaments. Soon he not only owned a much larger gun than the analyst, but in the face of diminishing supplies of ammunition he discovered an inexhaustible and potent source. Moving to another part of the room, Bobby spied a lion and decided that the lion's sharp bones and sharp teeth would be even better, more destructive than the bullets. He not only easily defeated the dangerous lion but became a robber himself, in order to steal its teeth with which to load his gun. With the bigger gun and more powerful ammunition, Bobby's fantasies about his destructive power and any possible dangers grew more elaborate. He now explained that his gun shot ten thousand bullets, teeth, missiles, and special dynamite caps, adding as an aside to the analyst, "We have different guns." He turned his attention from shooting robbers to killing poisonous snakes. He warned the analyst, "You need to shoot them when they're not looking and to shoot them ten times," because, he added with much gravity, "I think they have five hearts." Bobby then combined the two sources of danger that he needed to overcome and shot at bad guys who had poisonous snakes as pets.

Finally, the scene was set and all dangerous contingencies appeared to be covered adequately. Bobby could move from narrative preparation into the action of the fight. He lay on the floor with the analyst next to him and fired his gun furiously from behind the wall. After forty-two seconds of shooting, Bobby stopped and announced, "That's enough shooting for to-day." For a moment just prior to his return to cooking play, Bobby became a robber himself, stealing a doctor's kit in which to keep his money and guns.

Bobby now returned to the kitchen to prepare food for guests who were to join him and the analyst for dinner. In this final play sequence using the last nine minutes of the session, Bobby again became the sole player, although he kept the analyst informed of his progress in preparing for his guests. While searching for more plates, he spied a small piece of Plasticine on the shelf and told the analyst, "There's only one thing; there's some kind of doo-doo in there. Look for yourself." He immediately announced that the guests were not coming after all: "They changed their mind." Explaining that there would have been too many guests anyway, Bobby now set the table for two. The dinner partners ate their meal until the analyst announced the end of the session.

Bobby reminded the analyst, "We have to put everything back where it was," and before leaving, he surveyed the room to be sure they had done the job right.

Analytic Perspectives. Bobby utilized two very different modes in representing the aggressive fantasies of his inner world. These two modes or domains were distinguished by play themes, his relationship to the analyst, and his use of language and affect. The two were also quite different in the degree to which aggression was shown directly. The cooking play appeared to be "nonaggressive": Bobby's main concern in this play was cooking for the analyst; the analyst was clearly a grown-up and Bobby was clearly a child. The world in this play was neat and orderly, with the emphasis on the equal distribution of supplies. Bobby's fantasy seemed to be of a harmonious dyad in which concern with good, bad, and dangerous intrusions was unknown. Although the story narrative emphasized the harmonious dyad, Bobby's affect was subdued and he made little eye contact with the analyst. We thought the constricted affect and limited eye contact hinted that the cooking play and the shooting play might be linked at a latent level. The effect of the cooking play was to keep the analyst carefully controlled in space and in his relationship to Bobby. It was as if this play functioned as a denial in fantasy of the aggression given more direct expression in the shooting play. Bobby's sense of the potential danger of more direct aggressive expression was suggested by his initial inability fully to enter into the shooting story and his retreat to the second cooking sequence. Aggressive concerns, however, fleetingly appeared in this apparently nonaggressive narrative: the discovery of the eggbeater stimulated the thought that "someone's shirt" could get caught in it. Throughout the hour, Bobby followed a pattern of introducing a potential danger and then developing an immediate solution (the eggbeater could be oiled; dangerous poisonous snakes could be tricked and killed, and so on). When he was unable to find reliable solutions, he became dysfluent or simply brought those sequences to an abrupt end.

Bobby introduced this second narrative both linguistically and through the activity of demarcating the story space by constructing a wall. In this mode Bobby emphasized the friendly, cooperative dyad together against aggressive intrusion and attack. His and the analyst's aggression was justified as the reasonable response of good men to outside badness. Bobby's frequent references to comparative sizes and quantities and the need for equal distribution of armaments may have served his need for reassurance that the analyst would remain an ally. Although Bobby at first emphasized the equality between himself and the analyst, as the play continued he began to express the wish to be more powerful than the analyst. In the manifest story narrative goodness and badness were absolute and clearly differentiated: the robbers were trying to steal Bobby's money and so he was good to fight them off. The latent image in the story, however, was of Bobby as robber—the money he brought to the play session was really his father's, and Bobby stole both the doctor's kit and the lion's teeth. One might speculate that Bobby wished to steal the power and potency of the big men but was afraid of their dangerous retaliation should they discover these secret wishes. The specificity of his fears was presented in the shooting play: he would be wounded, his body pierced; he would be killed.

Bobby's discomfort in recognizing his own badness was given its most vivid presentation when he imagined he had encountered a piece of "doo-doo" during the cooking play: he became visibly anxious and then was able to continue the play only by excluding the invited guests. But it was during the shooting play when aggression and danger were clearly and elaborately represented as coming from outside the dyad that Bobby was most directly engaged with the analyst, conveying pleasure in their companionship.

He utilized multiple transformations of the properties and functions of objects, rather than of characters, in the service of maintaining a balance between his wish for aggressive prowess and his wish for safety. He relied on his imaginative transformations to maintain a feeling of safety for himself in his particular role and let it be known that he wanted to be the most powerful only after he had forged a companionable, equitable alliance with the adult.

Bobby's concepts of good and bad were highly stable but required a good deal of justification for his increasingly elaborate attacks; and so the attacking robbers also became more ferocious and dangerous. As he finally let loose with a volley of gunfire, Bobby appeared to reach the bounds of his clear delineation between his identification with the good guys and his repudiation of the bad robbers, and he stopped shooting abruptly, announcing, "That's enough shooting for today."

Eddy

Eddy's interest in bodies and bodily transformations was a central theme. His concerns about his own body and its integrity were presented in the context of his recognition of, and confusion about, anatomical differences between the sexes, experiences of toileting, and theories about birth and babies. From the beginning of his second session, Eddy invited the analyst into the play on his own terms—instructing the analyst what to do and responding only to those queries that added to the elaboration of *his* story. After he made some squiggle drawings in which he repeatedly listed body parts, Eddy drew a lion, explaining, "Lions roar and eat people." In a reference to toy "transformers," he distinguished between "robot" lions and "real" lions. In the process of drawing, he noticed a broken toy giraffe and suggested that a lion had broken its neck. Eddy wanted to repair the giraffe and earnestly offered, "Mommy could fix it with her new tape."

As Eddy turned his attention to building a tall robot with blocks, he instructed the analyst to draw a robot. In this sequence he illustrated a crucial concern: who would be the powerful attacker and who would be the victim of bodily damage. As he piled the blocks higher, he alternated between his description of the robot eating the lion, the lion eating the robot, and the robot becoming the lion. He glanced at the analyst's drawing and arrived at a compromise: "*You* draw a lion robot!" As he put the final block onto his creation, the structure swayed and Eddy was momentarily frightened. He protected his face with his hands, shaking and arching his body away from the robot. When the robot did not fall, Eddy regained his composure and admired his creation. With some bravado he commanded the analyst to "put *my* name on *this* robot!"

Eddy elaborated on this theme of transformations, bodily damage, and anatomical differences in the next sequence as he explored the contents of the dollhouse. Spotting a small toilet among the furniture, he interspersed comments about pieces of furniture he described as broken with questions about the toy toilet and statements about "poo." He returned to attacking the robot with an airplane while stating that robots "poo and pee." Suddenly, as an aside, Eddy asked, "How do girls pee?" When the analyst did not respond to his question, Eddy introduced "two ladies doing poo and a boy doing poo." The boy was then put into a drawer, and Eddy again turned his attention to the "broken" pieces of dollhouse furniture.

Eddy's discomfort at the perils of being small and vulnerable—as opposed to being big and powerful—was elaborated further when he introduced a baby into the play. This baby doll climbed into the big robot. When the robot began to think about "broken arms, legs, and feet," Eddy quickly dismantled the block structure and asserted, "I'm not the robot!" He then fixed the broken parts and constructed a new and improved robot that was not only taller but had guns "to shoot bad guys." When the analyst persisted in questioning Eddy about the identity of the bad guys, his queries were at first ignored and then the gun-toting robot was entirely abandoned. Quite suddenly, Eddy announced that his father had bought him a transformer and moments later instructed the analyst to build a mother and a father robot. After only one had been completed Eddy dubbed it the "bad robot" and attacked it with a jet plane. He backed away as the "bad robot" tumbled down and quickly returned to talking about the different sizes of the dollhouse furniture.

Eddy's retreat from attacking and crashing was, however, short-lived. Perhaps now confident about his safety with the analyst, Eddy engaged him physically for the first time. After assigning hand puppets, Eddy had his duck bite the analyst's doctor puppet and then, with much laughter, reversed the roles. The doctor was easily transformed into a daddy who hit a boy puppet, who in turn beat up the daddy. A pig and mother puppet repeated the same sequence of reversals as the analyst continued to carry out Eddy's enthusiastic instructions. The fighting became increasingly exciting as a boy hit a girl puppet; the original duck bit the pig's nose; and the boy returned to repeatedly banging the girl puppet while Eddy jubilantly announced, "Little boy is now big!" As if to insist on his power regardless of size, Eddy introduced a baby puppet who not only smashed the daddy but then wildly jumped onto the mommy puppet and hit her. With glee, he stated that the mommy was scared. Throughout this sequence Eddy did not allow any of the analyst's questions about the puppet's motivation to interrupt the pleasurable exchange of hitting, biting, and jumping.

Just prior to the end of this second session, Eddy shifted away from the puppets to pumping gas, first into cars and then into the dollhouse. As the analyst signaled the end of the session, Eddy again built a "high-up" robot. Just before leaving the room, he presented a complete identification with invincible power as he pointed to the robot and said, "Now I'm inside."

Analytic Perspectives. The theme of the body—its integrity and power—was central to Eddy's narrative. Although his body was in perpetual danger, Eddy consistently warded off potential injury by constructing figures that were both bigger than life and capable of reparative or compensatory transformations. Relying on the elaborate displacements of robots, drawings, and puppets, Eddy was free to represent the dangerous as well as the exciting aspects of aggressive actions. The latter was best illustrated in his story of the hitting mother and father and the boy baby who wanted to be powerful enough to intrude on this exciting activity. Although Eddy gave specific representation in play to his wish to be powerful, the fear of the powerful retaliatory attacker was also apparent. Both occurred continuously in his play as if realization of the wish inevitably entailed a dangerous consequence.

In addition to simply ending play sequences in which aggressive acts might lead to injury, Eddy relied heavily on turning passive into active and identifying with the aggressor. In one sequence he built a robot that became invulnerable to the lion's attack by becoming powerful enough to devour the lion. Perhaps in response to his identification with the now endangered lion, Eddy executed another play transformation by combining the two characters. He introduced a lion robot who did not wish to eat anyone. When a fight between characters *was* enacted, Eddy often assumed the role of the healing doctor or fixer who could repair any damage incurred.

It was during the play sequence of the gun-toting robot fighting off bad guys that Eddy made his only reference to his father. This reference in which Eddy linked his father and the transformers suggested that the latent conflict for Eddy involved his wish to usurp his father's power and his fear he might be punished as "the bad guy."

In his play, Eddy was able to represent the various themes associated with aggressive urges in the context of exercising tremendous control over the attributes of his constructions and their transformations as well as over the activities of the analyst. Throughout the session Eddy responded to the analyst's clarifying questions either by ignoring them entirely or by contradicting any of the analyst's observations of the action (for example, analyst: "What is the mouse doing?" Eddy: "Talk"; analyst: "What is the mouse saying?" Eddy: "No talk, just eating"). Sometimes this response suggested that Eddy felt the analyst was trying to control him by his questions. At other times, his reversal of the "facts" of the play seemed to reflect his ease in transforming the roles and properties of the characters within the story. In addition, by making use of the analyst as a functional prop and directing his activities in the play, Eddy could turn to him as a safe ally. By neutralizing the potentially dangerous powers of this adult, Eddy achieved some freedom in presenting the locus of aggressivity as continually shifting, thereby becoming able to explore the more destructive aspects of aggression.

Although Eddy's play was dominated by his wish for power, his fear of retaliation and damage to his body, and his pleasure in the excitement associated with aggressivity, he was able to sustain his play and his affectionate relationship to the analyst by placing the danger and badness outside himself. References to the father as the vanquished bad guy—during sequences involving the robot constructions and puppet fights—suggested Eddy's specific wish to usurp father's power and his fear that he would in turn be punished for his own aggressive, bad guy attacks.

Although Eddy was anxious at moments, his imaginative play remained coherent throughout the hour. Although the central themes were sustained over the course of the session, his preoccupation with changes in the shape, form, and function of bodies seemed to stimulate some of the rapid shifts in his story line. Transformations, for Eddy, were presented for the purpose of expressing his own wishes for increased power, and rapid bodily changes were used to reestablish safety in the face of potential retribution for aggressive acts. In addition, transformations allowed Eddy the opportunity to represent and master the anxiety associated with his questions about anatomical differences between boys and girls, children and adults.

Eddy seemed very clear in his notions about good and bad and struggled with his expectation of swift retaliation for his aggressivity. Relying entirely on robots, lions, and puppets to express his attacking wishes, Eddy always branded this cast of characters as "bad" and required that they be punished. His adherence to displacement and to a pattern of harsh response toward the aggressors in play seemed to reflect the conditions under which he felt aggressivity was "acceptable"; exciting urges for aggressive action could be portrayed as long as they were repudiated with equal vigor. In turn, Eddy was able to give expression to aggressive wishes both directly and through harsh punishments while maintaining a firm sense of right and wrong, good and bad.

While Eddy directly ascribed the wish to be powerful to characters within his narratives, in a less dramatic way he exerted his power directly by relegating the analyst to the predominantly passive role of onlooker. Eddy used transformations of the body to express his wish to be big and powerful, the destroyer, not the destroyed, as well as to ward off his fear that permanent injury would be the consequence of these wishes. In addition, bodily transformations provided a vehicle for representing his awareness of anatomical differences and his associated anxiety. Although one could describe his rapid shifts in play between "broken, damaged, little, vulnerable" and "whole, repaired, big, powerful" as unstable, Eddy's use of these shifts formed a consistent pattern that could be summarized as "It's okay to be the powerful attacker as long as you're punished for it and as long as any damage that results from either attack or punishment can be repaired instantly."

Jim

Jim entered the session carrying a transformer toy that could change from a robot to a plane. He said the toy was damaged and demonstrated its transformations, pointing out that the plane's wing was broken and stating emphatically that he preferred the toy as an intact robot. As he flew the plane around the room he repeatedly asked the analyst which transformation he liked best, simultaneously pointing out its deficiencies. He remained preoccupied with the transformations and with the analyst's opinion about which figure was the "best" for the first five minutes of the session, ignoring his mother's presence and subsequent departure from the room. After many crash landings of the plane, Jim made clear his identification with its power and vulnerability as he crash-landed himself on the floor. This was followed by an aside as to where he should put his jacket and where "the guy" (referring at once to the transformer and himself) should sit. When the analyst suggested the chair as a place for the jacket and for sitting, Jim sat on the table instead, grinning at the analyst as if waiting for a response. After a few moments, he got up, and flung his jacket onto the table.

This "naughtiness" was followed by multiple plane crashes and Jim's rediscovery of the eggbeater used in the previous session to attack the analyst. In this episode Jim seemed to struggle with his urge to engage in exciting attacks on the analyst and his fear of retaliation. At first Jim explained that he was keeping the eggbeater away from the bad guy robot so that he would not crash. But when the analyst queried whether the robot ever got hurt, Jim anxiously grinned and again went at the analyst's face with the eggbeater. When the analyst backed away and put his hand up to stop the attack, Jim talked about "that guy" who wanted to be bad. His confusion and defensive reversals of attacker and victim were dramatically represented as he used the robot to attack the analyst's face and announced, "I'll stop ya!" He explained that the robot wanted to attack the analyst because the analyst wanted to attack him. And why did the analyst wish to attack? "Because he was attacking you." He alternated between describing the analyst as the "biggest bad guy" and imprisoning the evil robot to "keep him out of mischief."

Jim abruptly moved to another part of the room, grabbed some puppets and again attacked the analyst. With increasing intensity he bounced each of the puppets on the analyst's shoulder because "it's fun." He then punished the attacking boy puppet, however, by putting him in "the trapper" and dousing him with hot and cold water. Announcing the end of the boy's punishment, Jim moved further away from the analyst and anxiously clutched at his genitals. Continuing his frenzied movements about the room, Jim went to a stack of cardboard building blocks. As he attempted to lift the entire stack, the blocks fell on top of him; with much dramatic vocalization and excitement, Jim threw himself to the floor. Again, he made a direct attack and tried to dump blocks on the analyst's head. In an apparent effort to ward off retaliation from the analyst, Jim referred to the robot/bad guy as needing to hide from the analyst. Following three episodes of hiding the attacking robot, Jim excitedly built a "secret" hideout with the blocks, lay down in the middle of it in plain view of the analyst, and invited him to look for him. When the analyst finally "found" him, Jim looked confused about whether he had really hidden himself. His repeated question, "Did you really see me?" suggested his difficulty at this moment in determining the difference between "pretend" and "real."

Jim's precarious balance between being the powerful attacker or the victim vulnerable to injury was again demonstrated as he crashed his body onto the secret hideout and then immediately upended the nearby table while commenting on this feat of strength to the analyst. He then lifted a folding chair on top of his head, announcing, "I can even lift *this* up!" When the analyst commented on his wish to show him how strong he was, Jim's frenzied activity subsided briefly. He sat in the folding chair and clutched his genitals just before suggesting that he put the chair on top of the analyst's head. After moving toward the adult with the folded chair, Jim let the chair fall on top of his tumbling body and asked excitedly, "What fell on me?" This was repeated two more times until he returned the chair to its place up against the wall. His involvement in both the excitement of crashing and the fear of damage was apparent as he carefully leaned the folding chair against a rubber doorstop so "it won't hurt the wall."

Jim continued to play with the possibility of danger and injury with repeated attacks on the analyst's body. While briefly using the evil robot as an agent, Jim then went for a cardboard block and with a smile lifted it high over his head before dropping it on the analyst's. As Jim grabbed the block, the analyst leaned toward Jim with an irritated, puzzled expression. Jim stared back briefly before getting another block for a second attack. When the analyst said, "I don't really like having blocks dropped on my head," Jim moved away and again took up the "evil" transformer, flying it toward the adult's head while intently watching the analyst's face for a reaction. On the second flyby, he again crashed himself to the floor, grabbing a toy giraffe which he used as a baseball bat. As he swung the bat, Jim expressed his wish for competency and power *and* his feelings of inadequacy and vulnerability by first stating that he always hit the baseball and then that he could never hit it. Jim articulated his explanation for his lack of success by having the toy animal say that he was missing his body and feet: "They were chopped off." Here, the associations between Jim's aggressive wishes, his fear of retaliation in the form of bodily injury, and his worries about being incompetent and vulnerable were especially clear. Apparently in compensation for its bodily deficits, the toy giraffe bashed blocks onto the bad boy robot, squashing him under the blocks to "keep him from being bad." To the robot's angry question about why he was being squashed, the animal replied, "To keep you out of mischief!"

Jim again took hold of the "broken" giraffe and began kicking wildly at the blocks. He boisterously proclaimed that he was a good kicker in spite of various body parts being "chopped off." After bending the animal's legs and assuring himself that these could not be chopped off, he threw it into the dungeon for kicking and being bad. The psychological distance Jim achieved in these fleeting displacements was very limited, and in this instance he followed the bad giraffe by throwing himself between the analyst's arms and legs, announcing, "I'm in pungeon!" Giggling and anxious, Jim rolled out of the "pungeon" and writhed on the floor. The analyst commented that all of the exciting mischief made for worries about being bad and punished. He wondered if the giraffe had had its head chopped off for being bad. Jim responded with an enthusiastic, "Yeah!" and immediately displayed his strength by again upending the table. Jim then maneuvered close to the analyst, fingering the buttons on the analyst's jacket. When the end of the session was announced, Jim abandoned this more subdued and affectionate bid for contact and engaged in a frenzied cleanup of the room. As he left, Jim made a last comment about the need to repair the damaged giraffe and then went out without his jacket.

Analytic Perspectives. This session contained eight consecutive play sequences that presented in play Jim's notion that he is bad because of his wish to be powerful and destructive and his fear that the expression of the wish inevitably will bring retaliatory injury and punishment. He identified himself with the robot plane that did not work right and with the broken toy giraffe, identifications that suggest he experienced his aggressive urges as profoundly dangerous and destructive. He was not able to preserve the integrity of his body but was continually threatened from within and without by his aggressivity. He vividly presented the frighteningly destructive and annihilating aspects of aggressivity in which the whole body and the whole person can be destroyed or irreparably damaged. No reparation appeared possible, only punishment in kind.

Jim's play suggested his wish to have the analyst recognize him as the best and most powerful and his associated fear that the analyst would damage him because of his wishes. Jim seemed unable to sustain a consistent location for the source of his aggressivity; whether it was in him and was his justifiable response to the analyst's dangerousness or it was the analyst who was the source were possibilities that continually shifted. Jim was not able to sustain any trusting alliance with the analyst, instead using him as an object for his own projections. His reliance on projection, a defense employed probably in the service of managing the anxiety aroused by his aggression, interfered with his ability to ally himself with the analyst and probably contributed to his inability to locate and sustain a source for the aggressive actions and intentions. In using the analyst to represent his own aggressive fantasies, Jim experienced himself as continually in danger of destruction and/or punishment. Shifts between characters, attributes, and roles were both dramatic and frenzied; though strongly demarcated, none held up for long or seemed to bind his anxiety sufficiently. Frequent switching of roles and attributes of various characters dominated Jim's narrative and was most often apparent in the context of themes of aggressivity, "good and bad," and punishment. These changes were especially confusing because Jim used pronouns inconsistently when he assigned roles to various characters in the play. Jim's rapidly shifting pronominal use and unclear referents increased the analyst's difficulty in following the narrative accompanying his play. For example, in the play sequence involving a giraffe, he stated, in succession: "I'm gonna kick her if I had a head. See, he's a bad kicker and she's a bad hitter [referring to the giraffe]. But they [legs] were chopped off I gather, I gather. So he gets to bend his leg because she's not supposed to be chopped off, right?"

Although Jim seemed to have specific ideas of his own, he showed little interest in or awareness of the listener's perspective, failing to provide enough information to enable the adult to follow his script of the play. The constant projection onto the analyst of the locus of aggression placed Jim in a psychologically intolerable position to which he responded by repeatedly relocating the aggression in himself. Perhaps some of the shifts could be understood as a wish to protect simultaneously himself and the analyst, by presenting himself as alone in the playroom, both the attacker and the object of attack, both powerful and impotent, both invulnerable and damaged. Jim rarely used language to talk about the aggressive acts he portrayed and instead relied heavily on accompanying noises to dramatize them.

Anxiety was Jim's dominant affect, at moments giving way to reveal his excitement and pleasure in his fantasies of being the aggressive destroyer.

Jim most often referred to the changing and fragmenting parts of toys, fantasy figures, and his own body. This apparent ease of transformation in his play constructions increased the level of anxiety associated with aggressivity. Bodily damage and loss of body parts were the expected consequences of his own attacking behavior. The anxiety accompanying aggressive actions was additionally intensified by his seeming inability clearly to differentiate between himself and others as either the source or the intended victim of his wish to attack. Although he attempted to reassure himself by relying on his notion of the body as transformable (in the ease of its repair), Jim's anxiety seemed instead to be heightened. This was presented in his many scenes of dismemberment and destruction.

In this respect, Jim displayed a level of moral uncertainty that threatened the stability of his ego organization: he was unable to delineate between his own goodness or badness and anyone else's. In turn his presentations in play were equally unstable and confused.

In contrast to Bobby's and Eddy's solutions, Jim's were characterized by inconsistency and instability. The attacker became the attacked; the source of badness shifted rapidly from inside the self to outside; and bodies and objects were threatened continually with complete destruction. Jim's one stable pattern was that he always experienced power as catastrophically destructive and that its expression must be met with swift and equally catastrophic punishment.

Aggressivity in the Mind of the Oedipal Boy

These boys appeared to struggle with central dilemmas concerning destructive aggression. The dilemmas reflected both the wish to be powerful and invulnerable and the fear that to be powerful and invulnerable might put one in jeopardy. For each boy the capacity to suspend disbelief, to try on a variety of possibilities through the transformations of play, and the availability of reality as an escape created a psychological domain in which different aspects of aggression could be explored. For these boys play became the central vehicle through which to represent the dilemmas generated by aggressive wishes and to try out solutions. Play made it possible for each boy to represent his various views about the expression and regulation of aggression in a continual dialogue within the self.

The language skills of the three boys seemed to reflect their capacity for, and ways of, relating to the analyst in the research settings. Bobby, for example, was most intent on keeping the analyst involved in his play. His statements were usually intelligible, and numerous revisions or clarifications of utterances suggested his intent to keep the analyst informed at all times. Eddy's speech was also clear, but he used shorter, directive statements, had fewer revisions or clarifying comments, and contradicted or ignored the analyst's comments. These characteristics reflected his different style of involvement with and use of the analyst as a prop and object of control in the play. Jim's frequently unintelligible and chaotic language matched his equally fragmented play. Dysfluencies in Jim's speech, in contrast to Bobby's, did not facilitate his subsequent language formulations or appear to be related to an intent to maximize clarity of communication with the analyst.

Although all three boys were concerned with destruction and bodily damage, Bobby and Eddy were better able to employ language to change the story line and attributes of character in order to forestall potential dangers. Language did not adequately serve Jim in similar efforts; direct action of attacking and being attacked was far more prominent in his session.

These three boys struggled with three dilemmas concerning their aggressive wishes. Each boy employed notions about the "flexibility" of the body. Not only could one body part be substituted for another as needed, but body parts could be damaged and instantly fixed. But the "benefits" of such body flexibility at times seemed to be outweighed by a substantial "risk"— if the body was so easily transformed, perhaps it could be too easily damaged.

The second dilemma had to do with "morality," or goodness versus badness, especially the question of where badness should be located. If badness was kept too firmly outside the child, he might then feel in danger of attack from the bad guys, but if the child located the badness inside himself, the environment might then be seen as potentially retaliatory. The boys' presentation of things as good or bad was variable with regard to both the location and the intensity of moral judgment. The relative stability of these concepts allowed for a greater degree of flexibility in the representation and assignment of aggressive actions in play. When the notion of who was good and bad became more blurred and inconsistent, aggressive urges seemed to be experienced as more frightening. Without the clear delineation of good versus bad, the child may be unable to maintain a necessary distinction between the source of aggression and the dangerous consequences of its expression.

Finally, each boy struggled with his wish for "power" and his fear of retaliation for actions intended to win or demonstrate powerfulness. The questions of who has power and what it is to be used for were reflected in each boy's play. The dilemma here seemed to be that if the child presented himself as having all the power, then he feared the adult's retaliation; but if the child attributed all the power to the adult, then the child felt too vulnerable.

Perhaps one of the more striking features in these boys' presentations of aggressivity was the apparent absence of guilt either in the inhibition of activities or as a source of subsequent anxiety. Close scrutiny of these research hours helps clarify the status of the superego while the child is still in the midst of the oedipal phase and lends credence to the psychoanalytic concept that internalization of moral aims and imperatives occurs as the result of negotiating the oedipal phase and not before. The boys in this study were able to recognize the differences between right and wrong and good and bad, but moral judgments concerning their own aggressivity continued to be determined by an external set of rules and fears of retaliation. Psychoanalytic views of the postoedipal structuralization of the superego (A. Freud, 1965; Sandler, 1960; Kennedy and Yorke, 1982) and developmental psychologists' conceptualizations of stages of moral development (Kohlberg, 1973; Rest, 1983; Leslie, 1987) are consistent in suggesting that it is not until well into latency that children begin to rely on internal and internalized rules and expectations as an *independent* source of behavior and good or bad feelings about the self. The prominence and pleasure seen in the representation of destructive urges—as in the boys discussed—may be possible only prior to the consolidation of this subjective and autonomous sense of morality. Although they know the difference between right and wrong, the experience of prohibitions and potential dangers as *external* may, in fact, allow oedipal children to give rich expression to aggressivity as long as the perceived consequences are suspended or controlled in imaginative play.

The boys in this study presented a view of their bodies as being easily transformable. The belief that body parts could be readily lost and/or changed not only served as a powerful source of the boys' fears of castration and damage, but also fueled magical solutions concerning easy reparation of bodily injuries. There was substantial variation in the degree to which the children's play employed a notion of bodily transformations for its restitutive or reparative advantages, as opposed to its stimulation of fear of damage.

These boys demonstrated characteristic and stable patterns in their attempts at resolving these three dilemmas as well as characteristic relationships among the three dilemmas. All three boys seemed to equate power with notions of destructive and attacking activities, and all judged such destructive attacks as dangerous to the integrity of the body. It was not just that they wished to be the best, the most potent, and the most skilled— and to be admired for these characteristics; rather, it was as if they experienced their power *through* the destruction of the other. It appeared that it was the wish to attack the body of the other that made them so concerned with the integrity of their own body. All three boys presented their attacks as justifiable self-defense. And all three suggested via their affect that exercising the capacity to attack and destroy was pleasurable in its own right, even if morally "bad."

Aggressivity was richly presented in the play of these three oedipal-aged boys. Indeed, it was probably the most consistent and boldly choreographed story line. If one had only the script and surface descriptions, one might imagine that they were aggressive bullies and tyrants in their daily lives. Yet all were children whose teachers and families considered them to be "within normal limits"; during their sessions as well as in their school and home lives, they displayed a capacity for concern and empathy.

When caught up in their presentations of aggressivity, each boy was capable, within a range, of suspending disbelief and generating for himself and the analyst a pretended reality in which attack and destruction were enacted with a sense of conviction. For Bobby and Eddy, the use of displacements and of checks and balances on aggressive presentations seemed to be more available than for Jim, who was more immediately threatening and threatened and less able to move between pretending and doing.

Theoretically, the touchstone of the oedipal phase is triadic relationships—internal mental structures in which the child represents himself in relation to his parents. In the archetypal situation, the boy internally views himself in a rivalrous relation with his father, toward whom he expresses hostile and competitive behavior and from whom he anticipates retaliation. The boy represents himself in an affectionate relation with his mother toward whom he expresses tender and longing feelings and from whom he wishes exclusive love. In a previous report (Cohen et al., 1987), we described ways in which such phenomena were observed in the play activities of children in this study. Our present focus, however, is not on the triadic phenomenon but on the presentation of aggressivity. From this perspective, it is of interest that even in the oedipal phase, a good deal of the displays of aggressivity retains preoedipal configurations in which the child becomes the ally of the father-analyst against an external danger or threat. Thus, some of the aggressivity within the play of these children may seem more phallic than oedipal, having to do with the display of potency. In addition, although the alliance with the adult male may defend against the dangers that would arise from the full expression of rivalry, it may also reflect precursors of the boy's more complete identification with his father that will be the heir of the Oedipus complex.

The dominance and vividness of the play lines of aggressivity seemed heightened because they were presented in relative isolation from other themes associated with the oedipal phase. It was as if, in their play, the boys had embarked on telling the story of the inner experience of aggressivity in all its variations, and that the other complementary oedipal themes became overshadowed or lost. We believe that this presentation of aggressivity in isolation—and in bold relief—is a major characteristic of the oedipal-aged boy. Indeed, it is found at the beginning of Sophocles' dramatization of the Oedipus myth when the young Oedipus attacks and kills his father at the crossroads for failing to yield to him. Oedipus' destructive, unbalanced rage occurs in the drama as an offstage event. For these boys in the oedipal phase such characteristics occupied center stage.

The dominance, vividness, conviction, and isolation of aggressive presentations were marked out as being *within play* by the conventions of play and by the relationship between the child and the analyst.

The children entered into the aggressive dramatizations by indicating both verbally and behaviorally that they knew it was play and by recognizing the presence of the analyst ("Let's use . . ." or "Let's pretend . . ."). In a complementary fashion, they terminated the display of aggressivity by clear verbal or behavioral markers of transition. Jim moved closest to actually attacking the analyst; however, he used the conventions of play to permit real attacks that exceeded the bounds of pretend. Although these bounds could be recalled for him and he could pretend to be playing, he was more like those children who enter treatment because of their disruptive behavior and who bring actual attacking behavior, rather than imagined attacks, into the treatment situation.

For the oedipal boys of this study, the murder and shooting in the play were strongly experienced while simultaneously being highly contained. The most powerful container of aggressivity was the recognition by the child that he was playing in the presence of, and quite often with, another person whose feelings he monitored and whom he brought along in the unfolding drama. We believe that such containment by internalized objects is a hallmark of the achievement of oedipal-phase regulation of aggressive presentations in the inner life of children.

Aggressivity defines one of the story lines within the full configuration of the Oedipus complex. Previously, we have described the child's presentations in play of aspects of oedipal love and curiosity, particularly primal scene fantasies (Cohen et al., 1987). There are deep, underlying structures of experience relating to size, bodily integrity, goodness and evil, danger and safety, love and hate, life and death, which appear to find their expression in the various story lines of the oedipal drama. These additional dimensions of the Oedipus complex include the variety of ways in which children relate to their parents as individuals and as a couple, their attempts to create an increasingly useful and accurate picture of adult relationships and their place among them, their worries and desires, and their picture of their own bodies and the bodies of others.

The overarching developmental task of the oedipal phase is to bring together these multiple story lines in a preliminary integration and structuralization that can be characterized as a theory of mind. The play of the oedipal child involves hypothesis testing about how the mind works. How, why, and whom do we love and hate? How do we regulate the expression of these primary affects? What does it mean to hate someone you also love? Does hate destroy? This early oedipal theory of mind is reworked again and again in the course of a lifetime. From the perspective of this study, we can see how the child's play itself creates such integrations, thereby moving development forward. The play of the oedipal child can be seen as thought experiments in which derivatives of unconscious fantasies are given representation along with the accompanying powerful affects. By portraying in play the wish for power, the wish to destroy, fears of retaliation, fantasies about the body and gender, and by trying out different combinations or relations between these affects and fantasies, the oedipal boy begins to understand how his mind works and how the minds of others work.

The study of children's play in a clinical setting gives us an opportunity to explore the relationship between the child's implicit theory of his mind and our theory of the oedipal mind.

Bashing, attacking, killing, hurting, and other destructive activities presented in the play of oedipal-phase children should not be understood simply as a response to frustration or as a gauge of their capacity to control impulses. Rather, these dramatizations and activities reflect the children's attempt to portray in play their dilemma negotiating the valence between loving and destructive feelings in the context of object relationships, mastery of the environment, and development of a self. A crucial dilemma of the oedipal phase is created by children's newly acquired capacity to recognize themselves as an active agent of aggressive wishes. That is, their urges to dominate, hurt, and vanquish are directed at those figures they love most intensely. It is their response to these urges that generates conflict and their attempts at resolution.

Oedipal children struggle to find a balance between aggressive urges and the moral imperatives they develop in order to protect those they love. In addition, they must negotiate the balance between the pleasure associated with power and the potentially dangerous consequences associated with possible retaliation. Their use in play of language, displacement, the analyst, and the setting for representing aggressivity offers a view of the degree of comfort, security, and self-reliance they have achieved in these negotiations.

The study of the play of oedipal children reveals central characteristics of the oedipal mind. The capacity to suspend disbelief and the ability to generate large narrative structures allow them to explore aspects of their own mind and, as they confront the core oedipal questions, to develop an integrated theory of how their mind works.

References

Cohen, D. J.; Marans, S.; Dahl, K.; Marans, W.; Cohen, P.; and Lewis, M. (1987). Discussions with oedipal children. *Psychoanal. Study Child*, 42:59–83.

Freud, A. (1965). *Normality and Pathology in Childhood*. New York: Int. Univ. Press.

Kennedy, H., and Yorke, C. (1982). Steps from outer to inner conflict viewed as superego precursors. *Psychoanal. Study Child*, 37:221–228.

Kohlberg, L. (1973). Continuities in childhood and adult moral development revisited. In *Life-span Developmental Psychology*, ed. P. B. Baltes and S. W. Shaie. New York: Academic Press.

Leslie, A. (1987). Pretense and representation: The origins of "theory of mind." *Psychol. Rev.*, 94:412–426.

Rest, J. (1983). Morality. In *Handbook of Child Psychology*, vol. 3, ed. P. Mussen. New York: Wiley.

Sandler, J. (1960). On the concept of superego. *Psychoanal. Study Child*, 15:128–162.

19

Play: "Time to Murder and Create"

Steven L. Ablon, M.D.

In *Little Gidding* T. S. Eliot writes about "a time to murder and create." Throughout the history of humankind we have struggled to understand the vicissitudes of birth and death. These struggles and explorations are knitted into the fabric of the ongoing details of our lives and are powerfully captured in art, literature, and science. Early in childhood we begin to puzzle over murder (death, destruction, injury) and creation (birth, sex).

In analysis, a child's play often highlights how play can serve as a vehicle to struggle with, integrate, and master concerns about death, destruction, and injury. These compelling concerns are intimately connected to painful feelings of powerlessness and anxiety. Efforts by the child in analysis to master these issues involve the elaboration of themes. Often the play has a repetitive aspect suggestive of trauma and efforts at mastery. As in a dream or a nightmare (Mack, 1974), there is a kind of desperate creativity. Many authors have explored the relationships between play, creativity, and artistic and scientific achievement. In this chapter I will describe how a period of play in the analysis of a seven-year-old boy facilitated his struggles with painful affects, especially powerlessness, anger, and destructiveness. At the same time I will suggest that play facilitates an inborn tendency toward progressive development that is powerfully augmented in the analytic process. As Winnicott said, "Heredity, in the main, is the individual's inherent tendency to grow, to integrate, to relate to objects, to mature" (1965, p. 137). I agree with Winnicott that "the theory assumes a genetic tendency in the individual towards emotional development as towards physical growth; it assumes a continuity from the time of birth (or just before) onwards; it assumes a gradual growth of ego-organization and strength, and the individual's gradual acceptance of the personal instinctual life, and of responsibility for its real and imagined consequences" (1965, p. 116).

In a broad sense creativity can be thought of as involving the production of something new or different from its original components. Although the tendency to link creativity with producing has a seemingly anal component, this does not imply an exclusively anal focus. Rather I think it emphasizes the importance of the body throughout the life span, especially in early development. As a result, many of our most compelling metaphors involve the body. In this sense, to create is connected not only with producing but also with giving birth to, envisaging, acquiring insight, sensing, and so on. In addition, the infant's and young child's organizing and shaping of their relationship to the world, animate and inanimate, are profoundly creative efforts.

It is commonly recognized that play is an important aspect of creativity. Whether the play entails action or is entirely mental, central to it is a freedom of recombination that leads to something new. The play involves a trying out of actions, roles, ideas, and fantasies; it is characterized by a reversibility, multiple possible combinations, and further departures from newly discovered organization. In play and creativity, affect is central and has many functions, the provision of motivation among them. At the same time, organization, integration, and mastery of affect are facilitated by the creative aspects of play. There are many extremely painful affects to be experienced, borne, and put in perspective. Murderousness, rage, destructiveness, and the related helplessness are instances of these powerful affects. The creative potential of play helps children and indeed all of us maintain affective vigor and progressive development.

Sam's Analysis

Sam was six years old when his parents first consulted me. They were worried because Sam was having frequent temper tantrums. He was very resistant to being asked to get dressed or come to meals. Sam would refuse, yelling and becoming highly agitated. His parents said it was very difficult to discipline him or set limits. When they restricted his television or took toys away, Sam yelled, "Who cares?" and became more desperate. When his parents made him sit on the screened porch until he was calmer, Sam would yell piteously. Recently he began to climb off the porch onto a large oak tree. He could not climb down the tree and was often found perched precariously on the branches. When forbidden to do this and told how dangerous it was, Sam insisted that nothing could hurt him.

I learned from his parents that Sam was tense and active as a baby. They adored him but were puzzled and frustrated by his irritability, his irregular sleeping patterns, and his difficulty with breast-feeding. Sam rarely seemed serene or placid, and his parents responded by feeling uncertain and anxious. Sam was in the middle of battles about toilet training when at age two and a half his brother Eddie was born. Sam's angry outbursts began after Eddie's birth. A few months later, because of the father's work, the family moved, leaving Sam's mother feeling dislocated, isolated, burdened, and depressed. In addition, Sam's father developed asthma, which included both mild and severe episodes. The father was stoical about his illness and the subject was rarely discussed, although episodes of wheezing necessitating the use of an inhaler were not infrequent. At age three and a half Sam rather abruptly became toilet trained. He did well in kindergarten where he had a number of friends, although he tended to be verbally but not physically bossy.

Sam was a large, somewhat pudgy boy with curly red hair and a lively sparkle in his eyes. He related easily and enthusiastically. At first he wanted his mother to join him in my office but after several sessions said she could stay in the waiting room. I shall focus on a three-month period after about one year of analysis, but shall first provide a brief overview of Sam's play in the first year in order to set the stage.

Initially, Sam was eager to play board games, inventing his own versions. It became clear that his winning and being a great winner were very important. Sam often reported to his mother his prowess as a winner, and we came to understand this in relation to his competition with his brother and his fears about his father's vulnerability. We also explored how in his version of chess the queen was strong and dangerous and had to protect the king who, like his father, sometimes seemed weak and vulnerable. I sensed that exploring the dangerousness of the queen would come later. After several months the feelings became more intense in our relationship. Sam elaborated how helpless and weak I was and how he could beat me, kill and bomb me, in various games. Sam explained that it was crucial that I not retaliate, not learn from him, and not do these things to him.

When it seemed safe that I would not retaliate, we began to learn about Raycor, a big, brown, furry monster, even bigger than a house, who lived in a pit. Many guys fell into Raycor's pit where they were squashed, punched, stabbed, and killed. This was played by Sam with great intensity and sound effects. As the play developed, Raycor bit and ate the bad guys and took all their money. Sam emphasized that bad guys were bad guys and good guys were good guys—and that they never changed. As the play developed further, both good and bad guys were thrown into Raycor's "sticky, stinking, yucky hole." Sam, wondering which holes in the body were the deepest, decided that the mouth was. He found a hole in the radiator cover and played at who got stuck in it and who could come out. Guys were trapped and became desperate and scary; Sam wondered whether somehow the trapped dead guys could get out.

At the same time Sam was making and acquiring huge amounts of paper money and littering the office with it. He seemed to be consuming money and excreting it all over the room. During this time, Sam explained that the hole was hungry and that a chess piece, the bishop, could eat the hungry hole and that only the bishop could go into the hole, front, back, and middle, with a stick and get people out. Thus Sam explored his voraciousness, his fear of feeling powerless, and his related exploding rage and destructiveness. The bishop and his stick were related to Sam's sexual excitement and fears that were part of these fantasies. During this play Sam often held onto the front of his pants.

As the play unfolded near the end of the first year of analysis, Sam began to ask questions about me. He wondered if I had children. He told me his brother, Eddie, was four now and that Sam had been three when he was born. Sam said, "I love my brother. I have to. No, I hate him and love him. For now I like him. I liked having my mommy and daddy only for me, but I like Eddie." Sam's associations to trying to climb on my roof and to climbing the oak tree helped us explore how he felt severely punished for hating Eddie and wanting his mommy and daddy to himself. Subsequently Sam played a game of war, saying he loved war and would kill me, chop my head off. In the battles, fighters would bite, eat, and swallow each other. Sam became increasingly murderous and destructive. He broke my pencils, stabbed my blotter, spilled water in the wastebasket, knocked over chairs, ripped leaves off my plants, and broke paper clips, calling them Eddie. Sam said, "Eddie's at the bottom of the pit. I'll fix him, I'll kill him." Then he yelled that he was good and I was "bad, weird, the enemy," and he would cut me, chop me to bits, and drop me in the hole. Sam wanted to climb out of my office window. He told me Eddie had finished school for the summer but he, Sam, had another month left. I talked with him about how Eddie got to stay home with his mother and how then Sam felt full of killing, biting, chopping feelings—just as when Eddie was born and he was punished.

At this point Sam, over a three-month period, turned with a kind of desperate creativity to a different form of play. This period seemed to offer a particular perspective on Sam's use of play to explore, organize, and master his overwhelming sense of powerlessness, rage, fear, and destructiveness. He now created and explored the characteristics of a series of creatures he constructed out of paper with a stapler, scissors, tape, and crayons. These objects seemed to embody the affects with which Sam struggled. The scissors cut, bit, and ate. The stapler bit, stabbed, held together. The tape held, stuck, hung, protruded, and connected. The paper contained, survived, was transformed, and reborn. The crayons intensified detail, uniqueness, and feeling. First Sam cut out paper men and I was instructed to do the same. His men were outnumbered but came out of planes and their guns destroyed all of mine (fig. 1). As my men lay dead and dying, he stomped on them. Some men who did not have guns helped in the fight by stinking really badly and killing in that way. Sam used a lot of supplies and left torn paper littered over the floor. This developed into Sam making an alien with "big laser eyes and lots of teeth" (fig. 2) who could be killed only by thirty shots plus twenty shots under water. Sam tore off the heads of my men, tore off "his eyes, his nose, his mouth, and all of him." More vicious were "biters, an army of them that nothing can survive (fig. 3). Some can bite the air also." Sam held his penis during these attacks. He told me, "We aren't enemies; our people are enemies." He developed a machine that could put his people back together, and in the whole world only he had this machine and I would never have it. My men had their tongues ripped off and died because of it. Sam's men had a tongue that went in and out (fig. 4). When it was broken, Sam could fix it. Once touched by his tongue, which could be made longer and longer, my men were crushed. When Sam needed a part for his men, he ripped it off one of mine. He often did not share the scissors or stapler. When struggling with my feelings about being enslaved and destroyed, I commented on his ordering me to do things. Sam said, "You can do it; it's not so bad. I don't ask you a lot." I believe he was reminding me of the primary maternal preoccupation (Winnicott, 1965, pp. 37–55, 83–92) and the need for me to survive his destructive attacks on me and my supplies.

Despite the destruction and aggression expressed in pounding the staples into the paper, Sam's constructions showed a careful attention to detail and craftsmanship. Occasionally he explained how and why something was designed, saying that every detail was important. Sam created a new, many-legged, many-teethed monster (figs. 5–6) who made men bleed by ripping them apart and pulling their eyes out in a few seconds. As this play was elaborated and continued over several weeks, Sam became calmer. He made a biting dragon that needed an eye (fig. 7) and an alligator with a powerful spiked tail (fig. 8). These tore apart creatures I was instructed to make, such as clams and buffaloes. After constructing a man with a red and black biting mouth (fig. 9), Sam made a black hole that sucked men in and tore off their arms and legs and the tops of their heads. He explained with enjoyment but considerable trepidation that you could escape the black hole by having something cut off or by going to another planet where you would be all alone forever. There was also a moon that could freeze you and a sun that burned you up as it sucked you into its mouth. "Nothing can survive its

Figure 1

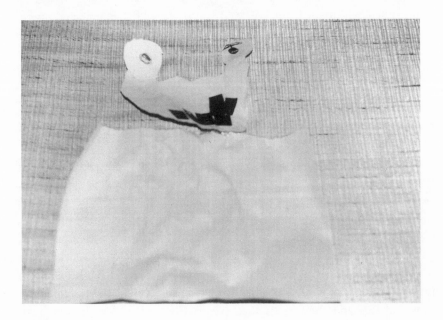

Figure 2

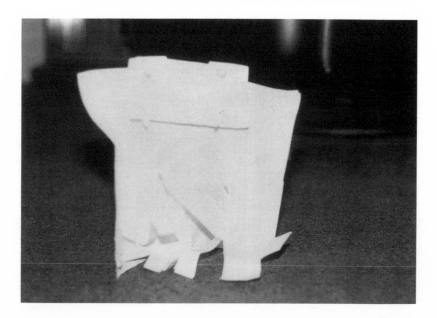

Figure 3

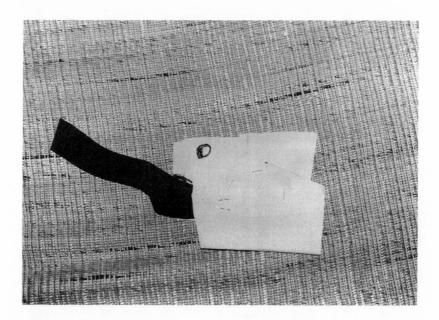

Figure 4

Figure 5

Figure 6

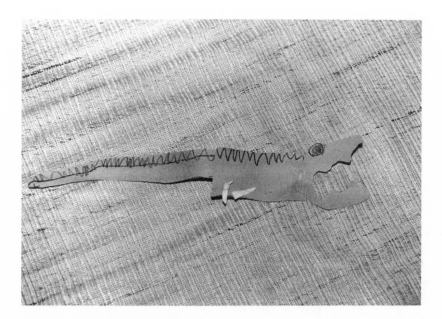

Figure 7

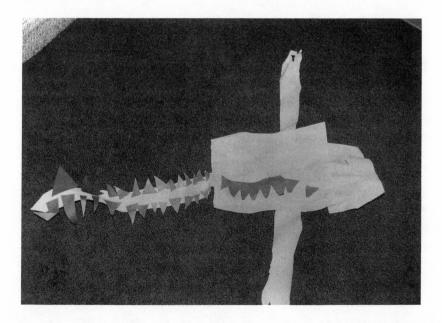

Figure 8

Figure 9

fires." Then Sam told me that the scissors were very hungry. For weeks I was instructed to make sandwiches, ice-cream cones with forty-eight scoops, cakes with a million candles, whole and sliced watermelon, and hamburgers. These were torn to shreds by the scissors, which afterward became 112 percent less hungry. When Sam did not come to analysis for a day, the scissors grew hungrier and "could eat for a million years and still be hungry." Sam said, "I'm not eating or tearing; it's the scissor who hasn't eaten for a year when he was younger. Now he is seven. He didn't eat because he didn't want to. He didn't have a mommy. He would have eaten her up in a second, so he couldn't have a mommy."

Although there are many possible meanings to Sam's play, he was adamant about not hearing my ideas. Perhaps this was related to his mother's tendency to explain things to him and his guarding the creative "central still and silent spot of the patient's ego-organization" (Winnicott, 1965, p. 189). In any case, staying close to his experience as expressed in the play at the moment reminded me of Heraclitus' statement that you cannot cross the same stream twice. It seemed that the play as created and developed by Sam with its many symbols, metaphors, and affects was richer than my theories and musings. In Sam's construction of affectively powerful symbols and metaphors, the play created structure and integrative experience. As

Nietzsche advised, "I tell you, you must have chaos in you, if you would give birth to a dancing star." I sensed this in Sam when he told me that it turned out that the hungry scissors and he had the same birthday. Sam wanted a birthday cake for the hungry scissors—chocolate and vanilla. After this, these constructions ended.

For the next year and a half Sam continued to elaborate these issues. For a while this took the form of a mad scientist who had a bad and destructive slave. The mad scientist eventually made the slave good, and they went on an adventure to secure great amounts of money. Subsequently Sam explored the experience of a "pooper" (paratrooper) who because he flew sideways and was bad got twenty-five cents instead of a trillion dollars, was covered with mud, taped up like a mummy, and kept in jail for twenty-four hours a day for twenty years. Sam continued this work by inventing rules for an elaborate game. At first he cheated and mercilessly and cruelly defeated me time after time. This gave Sam another arena to struggle with—his help-lessness, weakness, destruction, cruelty, humiliation—how bad players can become good players, how if you lose you can win next time, and how impossibly high requirements to be a most valuable player can become modified. In addition, Sam increasingly was able to express his attachment and affection for me. He spoke sadly about how hard it was when there were interruptions and we had to wait until we would be together again. At the same time the struggles that brought Sam to analysis had largely resolved. His development was progressing well, and he seemed to be a competent, energetic, happy boy.

Discussion

In his play in analysis Sam struggled with his murderousness and rivalry toward his brother and with his hunger, rage, and love for his depressed mother and ailing father. Sam's struggles as expressed in his play were woven into a rich fabric of experiences and feelings of murder and creation. In 1912 Hug-Hellmuth wrote, "No event among the abundant phenomena of human life is insignificant for the child. In particular the beginning and end of life, the entrance and exit of individuals, are inexhaustible sources of his 'whys' and 'wherefores.' Once he is aware of the eternal riddle of life, he pursues it as the goal of all investigation, playful and serious. For in *life and death* he sees *love and hate, cruelty and pity* joined to each other" (p. 499).

Although the technical approaches in child-analytic work of Anna Freud and Melanie Klein varied considerably, they both appreciated the powerful affects observed in children's play in analysis. Anna Freud emphasized the importance of mastering the interplay of sex and aggression: "There is no doubt that our clinical task is rendered more difficult by the fact that neither libido nor aggression are ever observable singly, i.e., in pure culture; except in the most pathological instances, they are always fused and for the purpose of study their respective actions have to be disentangled. But this, I believe, is true for biology as well as for psychology: sexual mastery cannot be achieved without the appropriate admixture of aggression; aggression cannot be integrated into normal life without an admixture of libido; equally, on the higher plane, death cannot be attained except via the vicissitudes of life" (1972, p. 175).

This was powerfully expressed and integrated in Sam's play, as was the fear of annihilation, love, hatred, anxiety, guilt, and grief, as highlighted by Klein: "An intrinsic element of a deep and full personality is wealth of phantasy life and the capacity for experiencing emotions freely. These characteristics, I think, presuppose that the infantile depressive position has been worked through, that is to say, that the whole gamut of love and hatred, anxiety, grief and guilt in relation to primary objects has been experienced again and again. This emotional development is bound up with the nature of defences. Failure in working through the depressive position is inextricably linked with a predominance of defences which entail a stifling of emotions and of phantasy life, and hinder insight" (1950, p. 46).

In his play Sam was able to bring symbolic expression to his affects, conflicts, fears, wishes and fantasies. There was an increasing freedom in his affective and fantasy life both in his play in analysis and in his life. Stone underscores how "aggression arises in the drive to master actual or threatened traumatic helplessness" (1976, p. 220). This was explored in Sam's play where we elaborated the terrible helplessness of creatures facing Raycor and the biting, tearing, burning constructions, the sun and the moon, and how one could be safe only by being these powerful destructive forces.

Sam's constructions, his biters, alligators, dragons, involved a high level of activity. As Winnicott wrote, "To control what is outside one has to do things not simply to think or to wish, and *doing things takes time*. Playing is *doing*" (1968, p. 592). Vygotsky (1978) expands on this by emphasizing how action and activity require an adaptation to reality. The materials Sam used, the staples, scissors, and tape, have their limitations, even though they are chosen among many objects and can be put to many uses. Scissors basically must be used in cutting, crayons in coloring. The combination of repetition and gradual expansion of aspects of Sam's constructions is also reminiscent of Greenacre's views about play and the establishment of a sense of reality. Greenacre observed, "Still another source of repetitive tendencies is to be considered, although little attention has generally been paid to it in this connection, viz., the necessity for repetition of experience in establishing the sense of reality. While this is obviously important in infancy, it enters into life situations in later life as well" (1959, p. 65).

In addition, as Susan Isaacs points out:

> There is a wealth of evidence to show that phantasies are active in the mind long before language has developed, and that even in the adult they continue to operate alongside and independently of words. Meanings, like feelings, are far older than speech. . . . Words are a means of *referring* to experience, actual or phantasized, but are not identical with it, not a substitute for it. Words may evoke feelings and images and actions, and point to situations; they do so by virtue of being signs of experience, not of being themselves the main material of experience. . . . It has sometimes been suggested that unconscious phantasies such as that of "tearing to bits" would not arise in the child's mind before he had gained the conscious knowledge that tearing a person to bits would mean killing them. Such a view does not meet the case. It overlooks the fact that such knowledge is *inherent* in bodily impulses as a vehicle of instinct, in the excitation of the organ, i.e., in this case, the mouth. (1948, pp. 84–86)

Isaacs also quotes Samuel Butler's charming way of putting it: "When the lady drank to the gentleman only with her eyes, and he pledged with his, was there no conversation because there was neither noun nor verb?" (p. 84). Play affords Sam the opportunity to experience his destructive feelings, fears and fantasies, and bodily sensations that sometimes precede but more often go beyond our verbal experiences. This viewpoint is concisely stated by Melanie Klein: "Thus, not only does symbolism come to be the foundation of all phantasy and sublimation but, more than that, upon it is built up the subject's relation to the outside world and to reality in general" (1930, p. 238).

As Sam began his constructions and I thought about my role, I was reminded of a comment by Marion Milner: "Perhaps, in ordinary life, it is good teachers who are most aware of these moments, from outside, since it is their job to provide the conditions under which they can occur, so to stage-manage the situation that imagination catches fire and a whole subject or skill lights up with significance" (1952, p. 88). I watched Sam's growth and mastery as he struggled with his nearly overwhelming feelings of anxiety, destructiveness, murder, love, hunger, and guilt. I felt confirmed in my sense that play embodies an innate human potential with great possibilities for mastering painful affects and facilitating progressive development. Winnicott seemed of the same mind: "In other words, it is play that is the *universal*, and which belongs to health; playing facilitates growth and therefore health; playing leads into group-relationships; playing can be a form of communication in psychotherapy; and, lastly, psychoanalysis has been developed as a highly specialized form of playing in the service of communication" (1968, p. 593).

When an analysis goes well, there is a unique play possible in which the analyst tries to appreciate the symbolic affective communication of the child and attempts to communicate this appreciation with tact and sensitivity in symbolic terms and, when accessible, in verbal terms. The analyst's work requires different adaptations, as was the case with Sam where sometimes I was the stage manager and other times I was, as Winnicott wrote, "repudiated, reaccepted, and perceived objectively. This complex process is highly dependent on there being a mother or mother-figure prepared to participate and to give back what is handed out" (1968, p. 596). In this process Winnicott helpfully warns about the uses of interpretation. "Interpretation outside the ripeness of the material is indoctrination and produces compliance. . . . A corollary is that resistance arises out of interpretation given outside the area of the overlap of the patient's and the analyst's playing. Interpretation when the patient has no capacity to play is simply not useful, or causes confusion. When there is mutual playing, then interpretation according to accepted psychoanalytic principles can carry the therapeutic work forward. *This playing has to be spontaneous and not compliant or acquiescent*" (p. 597).

As we study how Sam used play to master destructive feelings and fantasies, it is important to note how play in analysis can facilitate mastery and development. Play facilitates the elaboration of symbolism and metaphor, which in turn provides a kind of scaffolding for structuralization, integration, and organization of affectively charged experience. The child analyst, by having an interest in and appreciation of the child's efforts to play, catalyzes an innate developmental thrust in the child to play out anxious, painful, and compelling experiences, fantasies, and feelings. The analyst uses verbal and nonverbal means to communicate to the child the willingness to follow the child's communications and experience and to not persist in disrupting and redirecting the explorations out of the analyst's own conflicts and overwhelming affects. In time this often includes a shared understanding of defense, conflict, the past, and transference. In Sam's analysis an understanding of aspects of the past as reexperienced and reenacted still lay ahead. For him the therapeutic action of play in analysis involved the use of symbolism in relating inner and outer reality and in exploring and surviving murderousness. In *Playing and Reality* Winnicott wrote, "When symbolism is employed the infant is already clearly distinguishing between fantasy and fact, between inner objects and external objects, between primary creativity and perception" (1971, p. 6). Play in this sense is a process and "the task of reality acceptance is never completed. . . . no human being is free from the strain of relating inner and outer reality, and . . . relief from this strain is provided by an intermediate area of experience" (p. 13).

The issue of being able to exist and feel real is linked by Winnicott to the transitional object and the ability of the transitional object to survive the child's destructiveness. The relationships among destructiveness, survival, love, reality, and progressive development are described in a powerful way by Margery Williams in *The Velveteen Rabbit*:

"What is REAL?" asked the Rabbit one day, when they were lying side by side near the nursery fender, before Nana came to tidy the room. "Does it mean having things that buzz inside you and a stick-out handle?"

"Real isn't how you are made," said the Skin Horse. "It's a thing that happens to you. When a child loves you for a long, long time, not just to play with, but REALLY loves you, then you become Real."

"Does it hurt?" asked the Rabbit.

"Sometimes," said the Skin Horse, for he was always truthful. "When you are Real you don't mind being hurt."

"Does it happen all at once, like being wound up," he asked, "or bit by bit?"

"It doesn't happen all at once," said the Skin Horse. "You become. It takes a long time. That's why it doesn't often happen to people who break easily, or have sharp edges, or who have to be carefully kept. Generally, by the time you are Real, most of your hair has been loved off, and your eyes drop out and you get loose in the joints and very shabby. But these things don't matter at all, because once you are Real you can't be ugly, except to people who don't understand." (1981, pp. 14–16)

In his construction of biters, tearers, burners, and freezers, Sam in displacement was able to destroy me, his brother, his depressed mother, and his vulnerable father; despite the piles of ripped paper we survived. In the transference he was able to be starved and so hungry he ate his mother up, and she returned in the next analytic hour to be devoured again. During these constructions and destructions I was interested in what Sam was doing and pleased with what he was creating for himself. Winnicott's hypothesis about the genetic roots of this seem plausible: "The favourable circumstances necessary at this stage are these: that the mother should continue to be alive and available, available physically and available in the sense of not being preoccupied with something else. The object-mother has to be found to survive the instinct-driven episodes, which have now acquired the full force of fantasies of oral sadism and other results of fusion. Also, the environment-mother has a special function, which is to continue to be herself, to be empathic towards her infant, to be there to receive the spontaneous gesture, and to be pleased" (1965, p. 76).

Out of the hate, destructiveness, ruthlessness, there emerged reparation, concern, repair, and a sense of Sam's contribution to me. Perhaps this began with the constructions that Sam had me keep in his box in the office and later evolved in games in which he at first mercilessly defeated me but gradually allowed me to win and was interested in what it was like for me constantly to lose and be destroyed. In addition, gradually for Sam there was an increasing sadness about the scissors that were so hungry that they could not have a mother and about not always winning games that were viciously fought. As Winnicott wrote, "Here being depressed is an achievement, and implies a high degree of personal integration, and an acceptance of responsibility for all the destructiveness that is bound up with living, with the instinctual life, and with anger at frustration" (1965, p. 176). The related issues of overcoming fears of annihilation and separation are well expressed by the Skin Horse: "'The Boy's Uncle made me Real,' he said. 'That was a great many years ago; but once you are Real you can't become unreal again. It lasts for always'" (Williams, 1981, p. 16).

Although Sam's constructions marked a period in his analysis that is easily identified as creative, this only highlights the intimate ongoing connection between play in child analysis and creativity. Greenacre struggled with the same sense of continuum and underlying creativity in play. "I use the term creativity in a somewhat different sense . . . to mean the capacity for or activity of making something new, original or inventive, no matter in what field. It is not merely the making of a product, even a good product, but of one which has the characteristic of originality. No absolute dividing line between creativity and productivity can be made" (1959, p. 62). In this sense play in the analytic setting is a creative effort similar to that in music, art, and literature. Freud spoke to this point as well: "Might we not say that every child at play behaves like a creative writer, in that he creates a world of his own, or, rather, re-arranges the things of his world in a new way which pleases him? It would be wrong to think he does not take that world seriously; on the contrary, he takes his play very seriously and he expends large amounts of emotion on it" (1908, pp. 143–144). Sam's play in analysis lends support to the aphorism that art creates nature. Sam's play was his art, and this relationship fueled the creation of his nature on a wider and freer path of progressive development. This is something that artists have often pointed out. Thomas Mann wrote, "The truth is, that every piece of work is a realization, fragmentary but complete in itself, of our individuality; and this kind of realization is the sole and painful way we have of getting the particular experience—no wonder, then, that the process is attended by surprises!" (1930, p. 41).

As I have argued earlier, for the creative possibilities of play to be facilitated, the analyst does best to reach for a freedom and openness in his or her own person. Bion put it well: "To the analytic observer, the material must appear as a number of discrete particles, unrelated and incoherent. The coherence that these facts have in a patient's mind is not relevant to the analyst's problem. His problem—I describe it in stages—is to ignore that coherence so that he is confronted by the incoherence and experiences incomprehension of what is presented to him. . . . this state must endure until a new comprehension emerges" (1980, p. 15).

Creative forces in play powerfully facilitate the emergence of new comprehensions, which are most crucial in the affective realms and involve symbols other than words. Play provides these symbols in terms of the process of acting on materials, objects, sounds, space, and time. This action, in Sam's case, involved paper, scissors, staples, and crayons. Sometimes there is a ritualized or repetitive quality to the play. Although this impedes a freedom and fluidity that are valuable aspects of creative play, stylized play also communicates the nature of anxieties, conflicts, painful affects which, as they are elaborated and understood, allow the play to develop additional freedom and richness. At first Sam's play involved board games and was more repetitive and confined. These games communicated his anxieties about competition, weakness, vulnerability, murderousness, destruction, and retaliation. Sam's increasing ability to use symbols to elaborate, communicate, organize, and integrate these affects enhanced the creative thrust of his play. Greater freedom in combinatory play led to a greater richness in what might be called his art of rearrangement. Sam utilized this in his constructions to create and integrate both his omnipotent destructive rage and the experience of intolerable helplessness. Play's creative potential made possible a time for Sam to murder and to create.

References

Bion, W. R. (1980). *Bion in New York and Sao Paulo*. Perthshire: Cluni Press.

Freud, A. (1972). Comments on aggression. *The Writings of Anna Freud*, 8:151–175.

Freud, S. (1908). Creative writers and day-dreaming. *S.E.*, 19:141–153.

Greenacre, P. (1959). Play in relation to creative imagination. *Psychoanal. Study Child*, 14:61–80.

Hug-Hellmuth, H. (1912). The child's concept of death. *Psychoanal. Q.*, 34:499–516, 1965.

Isaacs, S. (1948). The nature and function of fantasy. *Int. J. Psychoanal.*, 29:73–97.

Klein, M. (1930). The importance of symbol-formation in the development of the ego. In *Contributions to Psycho-Analysis, 1921–1945*. London: Hogarth Press, 1948, pp. 236–253.

———. (1950). On the criteria for the termination of a psycho-analysis. In *Envy and Gratitude and Other Works, 1946–1963*. New York: Free Press, 1984, pp. 43–47.

Mack, J. E. (1974). *Nightmares in Human Conflict*. Boston: Houghton Mifflin.

Mann, T. (1930). *A Sketch of My Life*. Darmstadt: Harrison.

Milner, M. (1952). The role of illusion in symbol formation. In *The Suppressed Madness of Sane Men*. London: Tavistock, pp. 83–113.

Stone, L. (1971). Reflections on the psychoanalytic concept of aggression. *Psychoanal. Q.*, 40:195–244.

Vygotsky, L. S. (1978). *Mind in Society*. Cambridge, Mass.: Harvard Univ. Press.

Williams, M. (1981). *The Velveteen Rabbit*. Philadelphia: Running Press.

Winnicott, D. W. (1965). *The Maturational Processes and the Facilitating Environment*. New York: Int. Univ. Press.

———. (1968). Playing: Its theoretical status in the clinical situation. *Int. J. Psychoanal.*, 49:591–598.

———. (1971). *Playing and Reality*. New York: Basic Books.

Contributors

Steven L. Ablon, M.D., is training and supervising analyst at the Boston Psychoanalytic Society and Institute and assistant professor of psychiatry at Massachusetts General Hospital, Harvard Medical School.

Samuel Abrams, M.D., is clinical professor of psychiatry at the New York University Medical Center, New York, and training and supervisory analyst at the Psychoanalytic Institute, New York University Medical Center.

Delia Battin, M.S.W., is training and supervising analyst on the faculty of the New York Freudian Society and training and supervisory psychoanalyst at the Western New England Institute for Psychoanalysis.

Martin S. Bergmann, M.D., is clinical professor of psychology in the New York University postdoctoral program and training and supervisory psychoanalyst at the New York Freudian Society.

Donald J. Cohen, M.D., is Irving B. Harris Professor of Child Psychiatry, Pediatrics and Psychology; director, Child Study Center, Yale University School of Medicine; and training and supervisory analyst at the Western New England Institute for Psychoanalysis.

Matthew Cohen, M.Phil., is a graduate student in the Department of Anthropology at Yale University.

Phyllis M. Cohen, Ed.D., is associate clinical professor of child development at the Child Study Center, Yale University School of Medicine.

Alice B. Colonna, M.A., is a lecturer at the Child Study Center, Yale University School of Medicine.

E. Kirsten Dahl, Ph.D., is associate professor of child psychoanalysis at the Child Study Center, Yale University School of Medicine.

James M. Herzog, M.D., is senior scholar in child psychiatry at the Children's Hospital Medical Center and psychoanalytic scholar in residence at the Beth Israel Hospital, Boston.

Robert A. King, M.D., is assistant professor of child psychiatry at the Child Study Center, Yale University School of Medicine.

Laurie Levinson, Ph.D., is on the faculty of the Psychoanalytic Institute at New

York University Medical Center and the faculty of the New York Freudian Society.

Eugene J. Mahon, M.D., is on the faculty of the Columbia Psychoanalytic Center for Training and Research and assistant clinical professor of psychiatry at the Columbia College of Physicians and Surgeons, New York.

Steven Marans, M.S.W., is Harris Assistant Professor of Child Psychoanalysis at the Child Study Center, Yale University School of Medicine.

Wendy Marans, M.Sc., is associate research scientist at the Child Study Center, Yale University School of Medicine.

Linda C. Mayes, M.D., is the Arnold Gesell Associate Professor of Child Development at the Child Study Center, Yale University School of Medicine.

Peter B. Neubauer, M.D., is clinical professor of psychiatry at the Psychoanalytic Institute, New York University, and chairman emeritus of child psychoanalysis at the Columbia University Psychoanalytic Center.

Mortimer Ostow, M.D., is emeritus professor of pastoral psychiatry at the Jewish Theological Seminary of America; attending psychiatrist at Montefiore Medical Center in New York; and president of the Psychoanalytic Research and Development Fund, Inc.

Samuel Ritvo, M.D., is clinical professor of psychiatry at the Yale University Child Study Center and training and supervising analyst at the Western New England Institute for Psychoanalysis.

Albert J. Solnit, M.D., is Sterling Professor Emeritus, Pediatrics and Psychiatry, and senior research scientist at the Child Study Center, Yale University School of Medicine; commissioner for the Department of Mental Health, State of Connecticut; and training and supervising analyst at the Western New England Institute for Psychoanalysis.

Index